W9-AIT-566

BLACK&DECKER®

THE COMPLETE GUIDE TO
BUILDING DECKS

A Step-by-Step Manual for
Building Basic and Customized Decks

CREATIVE
PUBLISHING
international

CHANHASSEN, MINNESOTA

www.creativepub.com

Contents

Copyright © 2001
Creative Publishing international, Inc.
18705 Lake Drive East
Chanhassen, Minnesota 55317
1-800-328-3895
www.creativepub.com
All rights reserved

Printed in U.S.A. by Quebecor World
10 9 8 7

President/CEO: Michael Eleftheriou
Vice President/Publisher: Linda Ball
Vice President/Retail Sales & Marketing: Kevin Haas

Executive Editor: Bryan Trandem
Creative Director: Tim Himsel
Managing Editor: Michelle Skudlarek
Editorial Director: Jerri Farris

For revised edition:
Editor: Thomas G. Lemmer
Project Manager: Julie Caruso
Production Artists: Lynne Beckedahl, Kari Johnston
Assisting Art Director: Kevin Walton
Technical Production Editor: Keith Thompson
Photographer: Tate Carlson
Scene Shop Carpenter: Dan Widerski

THE COMPLETE GUIDE TO BUILDING DECKS
Created by: The Editors of Creative Publishing international, Inc.,
in cooperation with Black & Decker. Black & Decker® is a trademark
of The Black & Decker Corporation and is used under license.

Library of Congress
Cataloging-in-Publication Data

The complete guide to building decks : a
step-by-step manual for building basic and
advanced decks.
   p. cm.
Includes index.
ISBN 0-86573-427-5 (pbk.)
   1. Decks (Architecture, Domestic)--Design
and construction--Amateurs' manuals.
I. Creative Publishing international.
TH4970 .C645 2001
690'.893--dc21
                    00-065931

Cover photo of redwood deck courtesty of California
Redwood Association

Portions of *The Complete Guide to Building Decks*
are taken from *Portfolio of Unique Deck Ideas*
and the Black & Decker® books *Building Decks*, *Advanced Deck Building* and *Great Decks & Furnishings*. Other books in the Black & Decker® Home
Improvement Library™ include:

*New Everyday Home Repairs, Carpentry: Tools •
Shelves • Walls • Doors, Basic Wiring & Electrical
Repairs, Workshop Tips & Techniques, Advanced
Home Wiring, Carpentry: Remodeling, Landscape
Design & Construction, Bathroom Remodeling,
Built-In Projects for the Home, Refinishing &
Finishing Wood, Exterior Home Repairs & Improvements, Home Masonry Repairs & Projects,
Building Porches & Patios, Flooring Projects &
Techniques, Advanced Home Plumbing, Remodeling Kitchens, Stonework & Masonry Projects,
Finishing Basements & Attics, Sheds, Gazebos &
Outbuildings, Customizing Your Home, Building &
Finishing Walls & Ceilings, The Complete Photo
Guide to Home Repair, The Complete Photo
Guide to Home Improvement, The Complete
Photo Guide to Outdoor Home Improvement, The
Complete Guide to Home Plumbing, The Complete Guide to Home Wiring, The Complete Guide
to Painting & Decorating, The Complete Guide to
Creative Landscapes, The Complete Guide to
Home Masonry, The Complete Guide to Home
Carpentry, The Complete Guide to Home Storage,
The Complete Guide to Windows & Doors, The
Complete Guide to Bathrooms.*

Introduction

This updated edition of the best-selling deck building manual, *The Complete Guide to Building Decks,* is filled with everything necessary to help you design, plan, and build a cost effective deck that will provide years of enjoyment.

In addition to the material found in the previous edition, this revised and updated version features the most current construction methods and techniques, redesigned favorites as well as additional step-by-step projects, and information regarding the recent trends in alternative decking materials, such as plastic/wood composites and PVC vinyl.

The first section of the book illustrates how to evaluate your home and your activities to determine what kind of deck will suit your specific needs. A portfolio of beautiful photographs demonstrating some of the many styles, functions, and accessories is provided to help generate ideas and inspire your creativity.

The next section, Deck Basics, defines and discusses in detail the materials and tools necessary for deck projects. Everything from the location and function of structural components, to options in decking patterns, stairs, and railings is covered. Essential information about lumber, concrete, and other necessary hardware and materials is provided. A guide to the hand and power tools required in deck construction is also included, along with those tools that can be found at rental centers.

The Design & Planning section explains how to design the best deck for your home and how to properly plan the project. The section also demonstrates the best methods for creating precise, easy-to-follow plans that allow you to obtain a building permit. Information on working with your local building officials and codes is also included.

The section on Basic Deck Building Techniques shows how to lay out and install the deck you have designed on paper. Step-by-step instructions are provided, illustrating how to build each component of a basic deck: ledgers, footings, posts, beams, joists, decking, stairs, and railings. The specific tools and materials required for each of these techniques are listed. This section also contains methods for finishing your deck to protect it against moisture, as well as maintenance and repair techniques for keeping your deck structurally sound and looking new.

The Advanced Deck Building Techniques section moves beyond simple construction to show you how to create more complex deck structures and solve problems that may arise on building sites. Step-by-step instructions demonstrated in this section include working on steep slopes, creating multiple levels, constructing unusual angles and curves, and creating complex stairways and railing designs. Make sure you are familiar with basic deck building techniques before using these methods.

The last two sections of *The Complete Guide to Building Decks* contain building plans for eight frequently built deck designs and four common deck furnishing projects. Each plan provides a materials list and building details that can easily be modified to meet your specific site measurements and local building codes. All that is left is to obtain a building permit before you begin construction. Information about the tools, materials, and techniques necessary to build from any one of these plans is discussed in previous sections of this book.

These thorough instructions and helpful tips make this revised edition of *The Complete Guide to Building Decks* a comprehensive manual that will help you build a beautiful, long-lasting deck as quickly, easily, and economically as possible.

Redwood deck photo courtesy of California Redwood Association

Designing a Great Deck

A deck is one of the most useful home improvements you can make. It adds beauty and value to your home and offers a way to expand your living area into the outdoors.

Plan your deck with your house site and the surrounding landscaping in mind. There are many factors to consider in planning the shape, size, and location of a deck. A great deck design makes the best possible use of available outdoor space while meshing gracefully with the beauty and functionality of your home.

Instead of settling for a flat, simple surface, design your deck to incorporate a large tree, boulders, shrubs, a pond, or a landscaped slope. It will become the focal point for your yard. Decks provide solutions for almost every house and lot configuration—from wraparound decks that take advantage of small yards by using the space surrounding the house to detached decks that can be located anywhere in the yard to create a private sanctuary away from the busy household and the rest of the world.

Study the photographs on the following pages to see how other homeowners planned and built according to their unique circumstances. As you look at these and other decks in books, magazines, and your neighborhood, think of how these ideas might lead to solutions for your needs.

An island deck is an appealing way to fill an outlying area of the yard and make it more functional. This multi-level island deck creates many comfortable, private spaces for entertaining large groups or just enjoying an evening outdoors.

A multilevel deck uses stairs connecting each level to conquer a slope that otherwise would get little use.

An elevated deck creates two functional areas: a large living space above and a carport and storage area beneath. A secluded spot and a spectacular view make use of a rooftop deck in the unique tower structure.

A magnificent view is an important consideration in this two-level deck plan. Patio doors allow access to one of the levels from most rooms in the house. The lower level provides a nice shaded option on sunny days.

This low-profile deck takes advantage of the natural alcove created by the shape of the house. The relatively small deck appears larger because of the two levels, which also make the space more visually appealing. The arbor creates a greater sense of privacy while providing some shade from direct sunlight.

A deck can make an attractive transition between the indoor and outdoor spaces of your home. Curves, angles, and distinctive railing patterns and materials incorporated into the deck design help create visual interest. An arbor supports climbing plants, provides some privacy and relief from the sun, and can help visually tie the overall deck design together.

Decks also offer better use of areas close to the house or caught in the corners of L- or U-shaped structures. This is particularly true for small and narrow yards. A low-profile deck or a multilevel deck will expand and improve the usefulness of these spaces. Built-in benches and planters also increase the feeling of spaciousness.

Separate activity areas can be distinguished by the use of different decking patterns. And multilevel doesn't mean only those levels separated by stairways on a high deck or in a landscape with steep slopes. A low-profile deck or long rectangular space will be more interesting if it is built with distinct platforms layered with only one or two steps between each level.

(above) **This low-profile deck** makes good use of the limited space available. The separate levels define access points and activity areas, while the built-in benches help outline the edges of the deck and provide additional seating areas.

(right) **Entrances tucked around corners** or hidden from view make ideal candidates for low-profile decks. This deck gives the home a more open, inviting entrance and creates a cozy perch to enjoy a warm evening.

Composite decking materials give a deck an interesting and distinctive look. Composites are practical choices because they require very little maintenance and will never crack, split, rot, or rust.
(left) Fiberglass decking gives your deck a beautiful finish and is among the easiest products to install.
(below) Durable plastic/wood composites are available in colors that complement any wood tone.
(bottom) PVC vinyl and plastics create elegant and unique looking decks that will last a lifetime.

Photo courtesy of Pultronex Corporation / E-Z Deck

Photo courtesy of Timber Tech

Photo courtesy of EON Outdoor Systems, Inc.

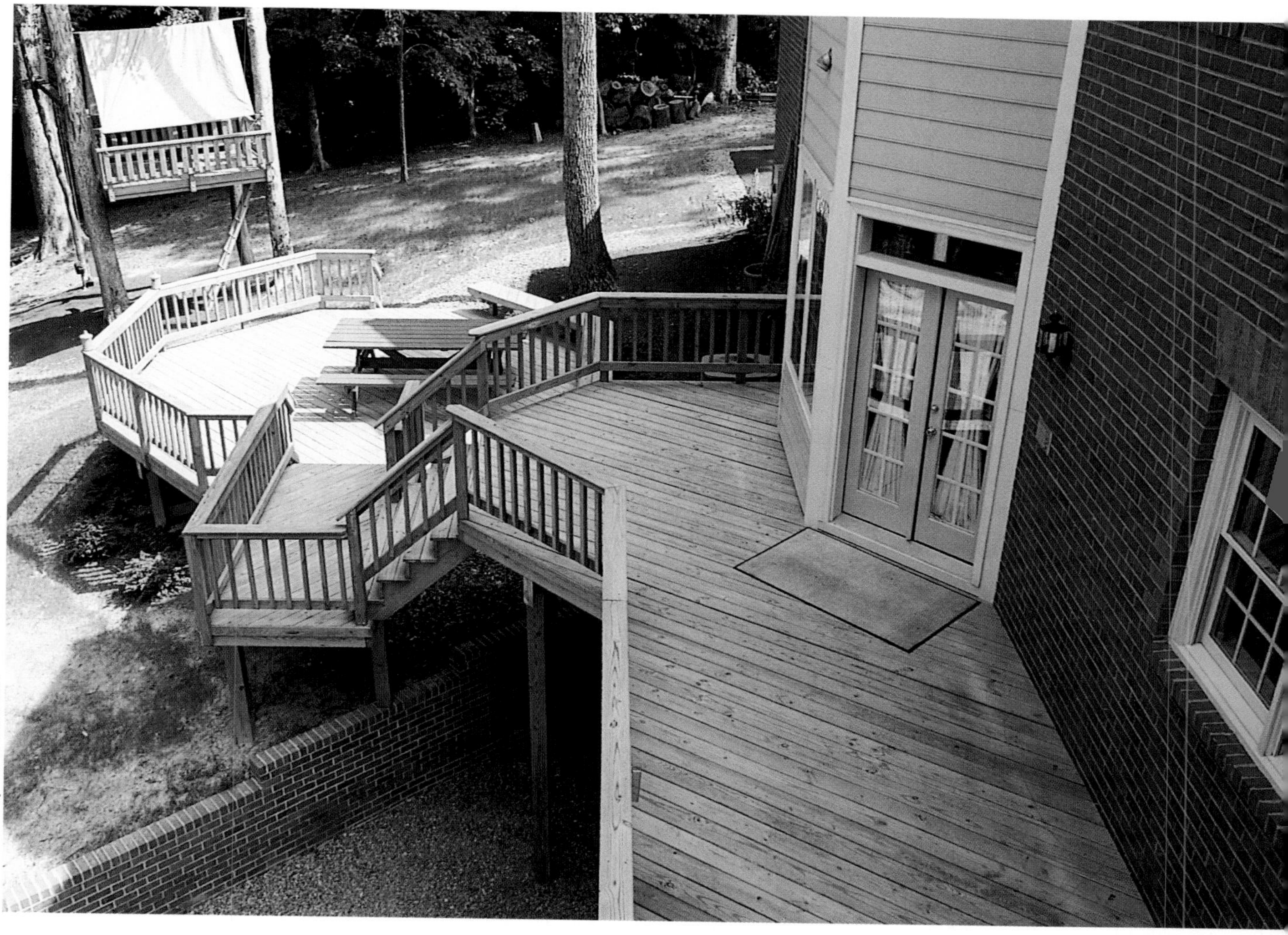

Photo courtesy of Archadeck

(above) **A multilevel deck** snakes around this house from the second story to the ground level, creating usable outdoor living space both above and below the deck.

(right) **This wraparound deck** offers a number of activity areas. The rich color of the finished redwood and the hand-grip railing design are distinctive treatments.

Redwood deck photo courtesy of California Redwood Association

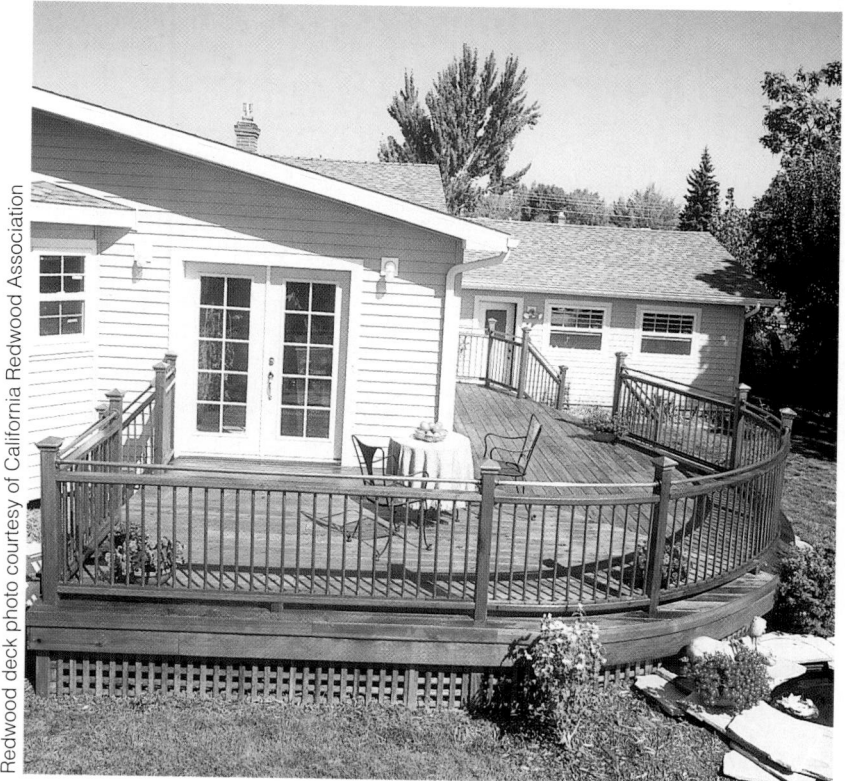

(top left) **Multiple levels can be used** to mask the height of a pool or spa and separate activity areas. An arbor dressed with hanging plants creates an attractive sunblock.

(top right) **A raised deck accessed from the second story** of the house also creates a sheltered sitting area on the patio below. The upper level basks in the sun throughout the day, while the lower level rests in shady comfort.

(left) **The design of this low-profile deck** creates a graceful transition from the house to the lawn. This simple deck is very pleasing because it matches the house design and provides a perfect place from which to enjoy the tranquil setting.

This rustic wraparound deck complements the house style with rich tones and a modest design. Multiple activity areas are created in the available space, allowing the deck to blend into the surrounding environment.

If the available space is limited but includes a rooftop capable of supporting a deck, incorporate this creative solution into your plans. These unique spaces expand living areas upward and offer vantage points unnoticed before.

Rooftop areas such as those over a garage or carport offer excellent opportunities to provide additional outdoor living space in a cramped environment. Most rooftop decks use lightweight materials, such as vinyl or acrylics, to decrease the additional weight placed on the roof. Check with your local building inspector to see if your roof is suited to making use of this innovative idea.

The rooftop of a garage may be an ideal deck location for homes with challenging terrain or limited space. This redwood deck capitalizes on the space and view from the top of the garage.

Redwood deck photo courtesy of California Redwood Association

A multilevel rooftop deck takes advantage of every available space for this house with a very limited yard. Several separate activity areas are established. The upper deck is accessed from the master bedroom suite.

Photo courtesy of Western Wood Products Association

The roof of a glass-enclosed hot tub area is also the floor of the second-story deck. While it does require professional installation, this design shows the opportunities that creative use of space can provide.

Photo courtesy of Lindal Cedar Homes, Inc.; Seattle, WA

Multilevel decks are your best option when you want to maximize the usable outdoor space or deal with significant slopes. They can be used to tackle almost any uneven or unmanageable terrain you may encounter. These decks create vertical living space in small yards. They also provide an easy way to access different areas of multilevel houses.

Multilevel deck designs often include a number of levels that are linked by steps or stairways. A ground-level patio can be incorporated into the design, perhaps sheltered under a second-story deck level. Multilevel decks effectively break an outdoor area into separate activity areas, providing a way for family members to enjoy several activities at once.

This multistory house built into a sloping yard benefits from a multilevel deck. A series of low-profile deck platforms connected by stairways follows the contour of the slope and creates multiple access points for the house. Notice that the rooftop deck over the four-season porch provides an outdoor seating area for the upper level of the house.

Photos this page courtesy of Milt Charno & Associates, Inc.

The uneven terrain of this yard is conquered by combining deck styles. Multiple levels are connected with short, wide steps that progress to an island-style area that offers plenty of activity space and easy access to the yard.

(right) **Instead of one long, steep stairway,** shorter stairways linked by small open landings scale this slope. Descending from the top level of the house, users have the option of continuing downward or turning off onto other levels.

Photo courtesy of Milt Charno & Associates, Inc.

Photo courtesy of Archadeck

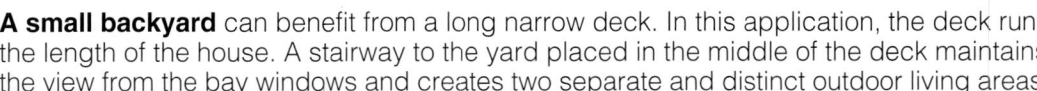

A small backyard can benefit from a long narrow deck. In this application, the deck runs the length of the house. A stairway to the yard placed in the middle of the deck maintains the view from the bay windows and creates two separate and distinct outdoor living areas.

Photo courtesy of Milt Charno & Associates, Inc.; George Lyons photographer

A multilevel deck is centered around a retaining wall filled with colorful plantings. The deck also makes maximum use of the L- and U-shaped spaces created by the house design. Breaking the deck into multiple levels creates diverse activity areas within the delightful landscape. The gradual slope of the stairways allows the deck to flow along the contour of the yard.

Deck
Basics

Parts of a Deck

Structural parts of a deck include posts, beams, ledgers, and joists. They support and distribute the weight of the deck. For economy and durability, use pressure-treated lumber for these parts (and most building codes require it). The other parts of a deck include the decking, facing, railings, and stairway. Use redwood or cedar for these visible parts.

Ledgers anchor an attached deck to a house. Ledgers support one end of all joists.

Concrete footings with post anchors support the weight of the deck and hold the deck posts in place. They are made by pouring concrete into tube forms. Local climates and building codes determine depth of footings. **Post anchors** should be made of galvanized steel to resist corrosion.

Posts transfer the weight of the deck to the footings. They are attached to the post anchors with galvanized nails.

Beams provide the main structural support for the deck. A beam is usually made from a pair of 2 × 8s or 2 × 10s fastened to the deck posts.

Joists support the decking. For an attached deck, the joists are fastened at one end to the **ledger,** and at the other end to the **header joist.** The **outside joists** can be covered with redwood or cedar **facing** boards for appearance.

Decking is the main feature of any deck. The decking boards are attached to the joists with galvanized screws or nails.

Railing parts include **railing posts** and **balusters** attached to the header and outside joists, a horizontal **rail,** and a **cap.** Building codes may require railings on decks 24" or more above ground level.

A stairway is made from a pair of **stringers** fastened to the side of the deck, and a series of **treads** attached to the stringers with metal cleats.

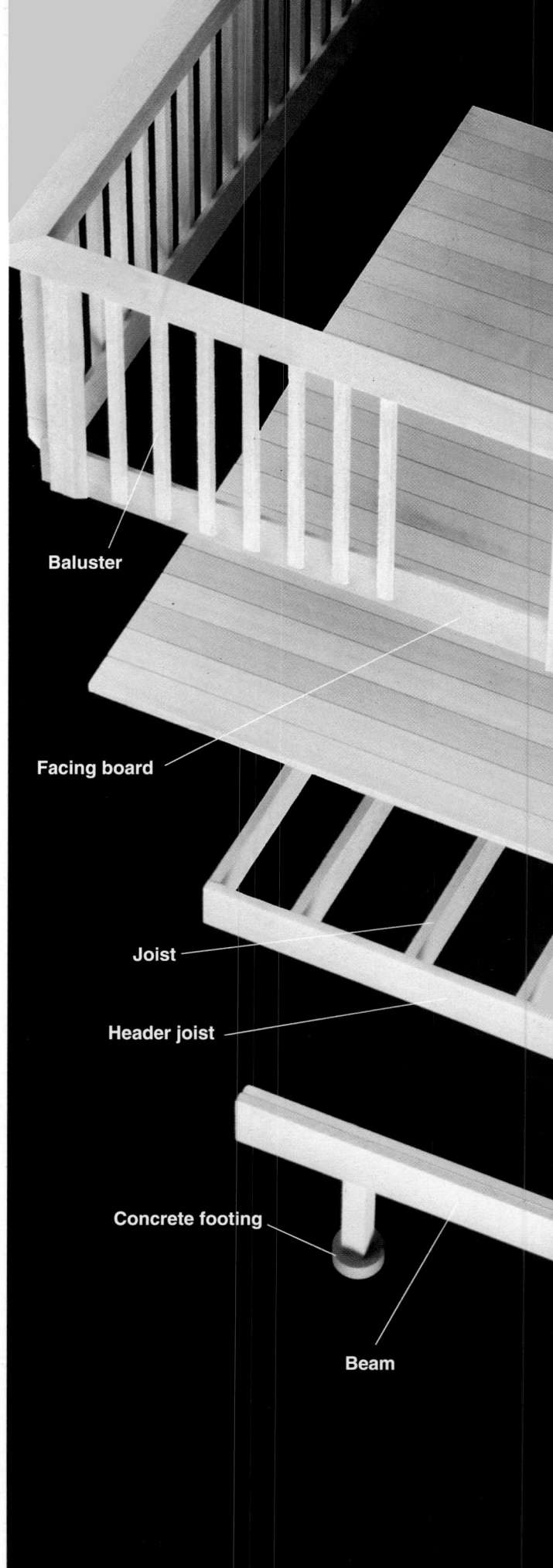

Baluster

Facing board

Joist

Header joist

Concrete footing

Beam

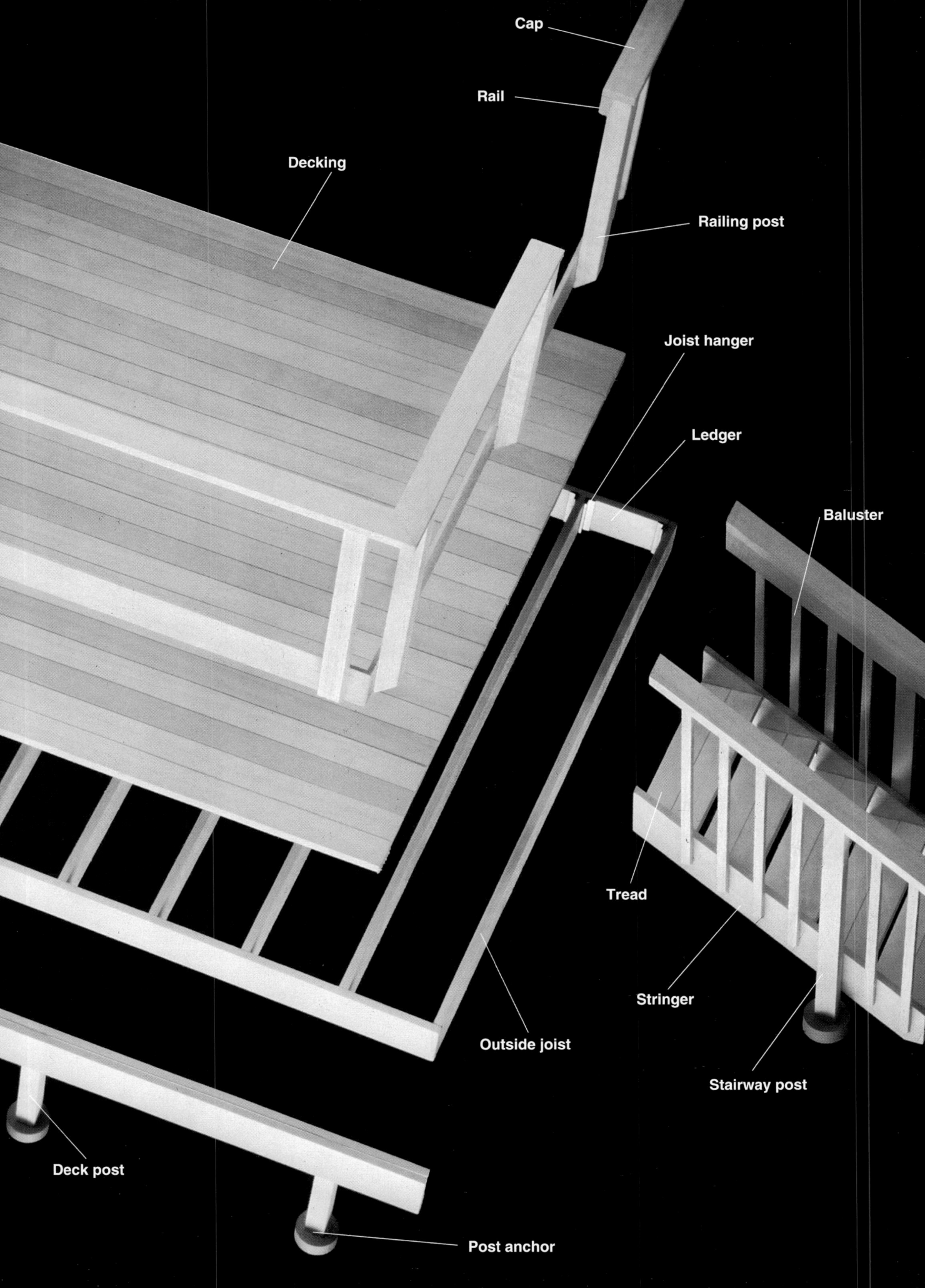

Decking Patterns

Decking is an important element of a deck, and can be installed using a variety of board sizes and design patterns. The decking pattern deter-mines the spacing and layout of the joists. For example, a normal, straight decking pattern requires joists that are spaced 16" on-center.

Diagonal pattern adds visual interest to a deck. Diagonal patterns require joists that are spaced closer together than for straight patterns.

Parquet pattern requires double joists and blocking to provide a support-ing surface for attaching the butted ends of decking boards.

A diagonal decking pattern requires that the joist spacing be 12" on-center. Parquet patterns and some other designs may require extra support, like double joists or extra blocking. For sturdy, flat decking, use 2 × 4 or 2 × 6 lumber. Thinner lumber is more likely to twist or cup.

Framed opening for a tree requires extra blocking between joists. Short joists are attached to blocking with joist hangers.

Border pattern gives an elegant, finished look to a deck. Install trim joists to support the border decking.

Stairways

Platform steps feature wide treads. Each step is built on a framework of posts and joists.

Build the stairway with lumber that matches the rest of the deck. If possible, stair treads should use the same board pattern as the surface decking. On decks more than 24" high, local codes may require stairway handrails.

Stairway Styles

Open steps have metal cleats that hold the treads between the stringers. The treads on this stairway are built with 2 × 6s to match the surface decking.

Boxed steps, built with notched stringers and solid risers, give a finished look to a deck stairway. Pre-drill ends of treads to prevent splitting.

Long stairways sometimes require landings. A landing is a small platform to which both flights of stairs are attached. See pages 150 to 159.

Railings

Railings usually are required by building code on any deck that is more than 24" high. Select a railing design that fits the style of your home.

For example, on a low, ranch-style house, choose a deck railing with wide, horizontal rails. On a Tudor-style home with a steep roof, choose a railing with closely spaced, vertical balusters. See pages 188 to 201 for information on how to build other railing styles, including a curved railing.

Some areas may require an easily gripped hand rail for stairways (pages 196 to 197). Check with your local building inspector.

Preshaped products let you easily build decorative deck railings. Railing products include shaped handrails, balusters, and posts.

Railing Styles

Vertical balusters with posts and rails are a good choice for houses with strong vertical lines. A vertical baluster railing like the one shown above is a good choice where children will be present.

Horizontal railings are often used on low, ranch-style homes. Horizontal railings are made of vertical posts, two or more wide horizontal rails, and a railing cap.

Lattice panels add a decorative touch to a deck. They also provide extra privacy.

Lumber

When constructing a deck, select a wood that is not prone to rot or insect attack. Three types are recommended: heart cedar, heart redwood and pressure-treated lumber.

The heartwood of cedar and redwood is highly resistant to decay; the sapwood is not, and must be treated with a preservative when used for outdoor structures.

Because cedar and redwood are somewhat expensive, many deck builders use these woods only on the visible parts of decks and use less expensive pressure-treated lumber, with its telltale green tint, on less visible parts. The preservatives in pressure-treated wood provide a high resistance to decay. You must, however, wear eye protection, a particle mask and gloves, and cover your skin when working with pressure-treated lumber.

Many deck builders seal the ends of all boards, even if they are pressure-treated, to ensure that the end grain doesn't rot.

When selecting wood for your deck, inspect the lumber for warping and twisting. Also inspect the end grain. Lumber with a vertical grain will cup less as it ages.

Store lumber a few inches off the ground and use blocks between each row to ensure air flow. Keep the wood covered with a waterproof tarp.

NOTE: The materials lists for the plans in this book include a waste allowance of 10 to 15%.

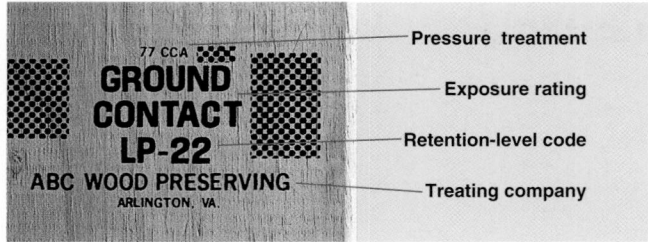

Pressure-treated lumber stamps list the type of preservative and the chemical retention level, as well as the exposure rating and the name and location of the treating company.

Cedar grade stamps list the mill number, moisture content, species, lumber grade and membership association. Western red cedar (WRC) or incense cedar (INC) for decks should be heartwood (HEART) with a maximum moisture content of 15% (MC15).

LUMBER CONTROVERSY UPDATE

For homeowners sensitive to the environment, choosing lumber for a deck can be difficult. On the one hand, pressure-treated lumber uses chemicals that are potentially harmful, requiring that you take common-sense precautions when handling it. Many homeowners are nervous about handling this material, though studies show that pressure-treated lumber is safe when handled according to simple EPA guidelines.

It can be argued, in fact, that using pressure-treated lumber actually protects existing forests. Because pressure-treated lumber used in a deck typically resists rot for at least as long as it takes to grow replacement lumber, some experts assert that its use actually reduces the harvest of new trees. With cedar and redwood sources dwindling, using pressure-treated pine can be seen as an environmentally sound choice.

If you live in an arid climate, you can bypass the controversy. Because wood can't rot if its moisture content is less than 20%, decks built in the Southwest and other very dry climates can safely be built from untreated pine lumber. It's always a good idea, though, to use pressure-treated lumber for deck posts.

Another option is to use wood/polymer composites. These composite materials are made of recycled plastics and waste wood, and are used for decking and other nonstructural components.

Inspect lumber for flaws. Sight along each board to check for warping and twisting. Return any boards with serious flaws. Check for loose knots. Boards used for structural parts should have only small knots that are tight and ingrown.

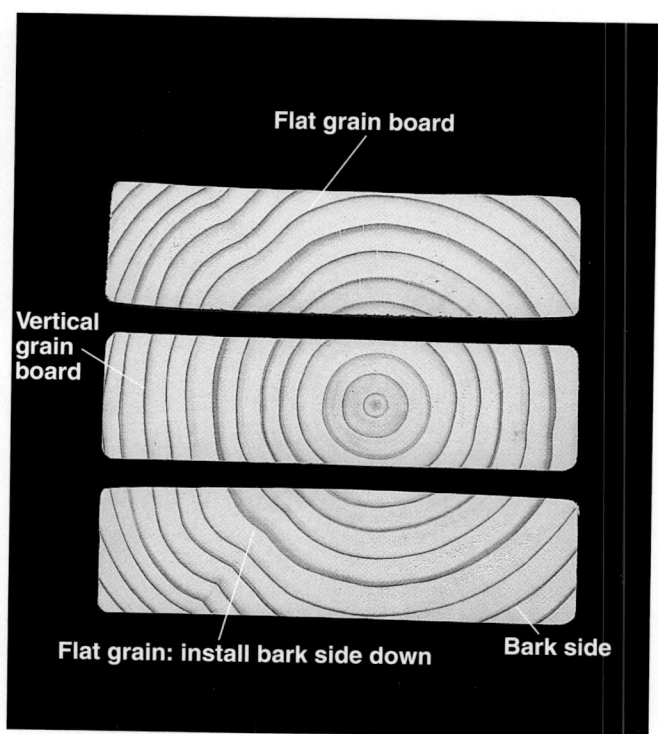

Check end grain of decking boards. Boards with flat grain tend to "cup," and can trap standing water if not installed properly. Recent research indicates that flat grain boards cup toward the bark side (not away from it, as was previously thought in the industry), and should be installed so the bark side faces down.

Store lumber so that it stays dry and warp-free. Use supports to keep the wood stack a few inches off the ground. Use spacer blocks to support each row of lumber, and to allow air circulation between boards. Cover the lumber stack with heavy plastic or a waterproof tarp.

Seal cut edges of all lumber, including pressure-treated wood, by brushing on clear liquid sealer-preservative. Chemicals used in pressure treatment do not always penetrate completely. Sealer-preservative protects all types of wood from rot.

Hardware & Fasteners

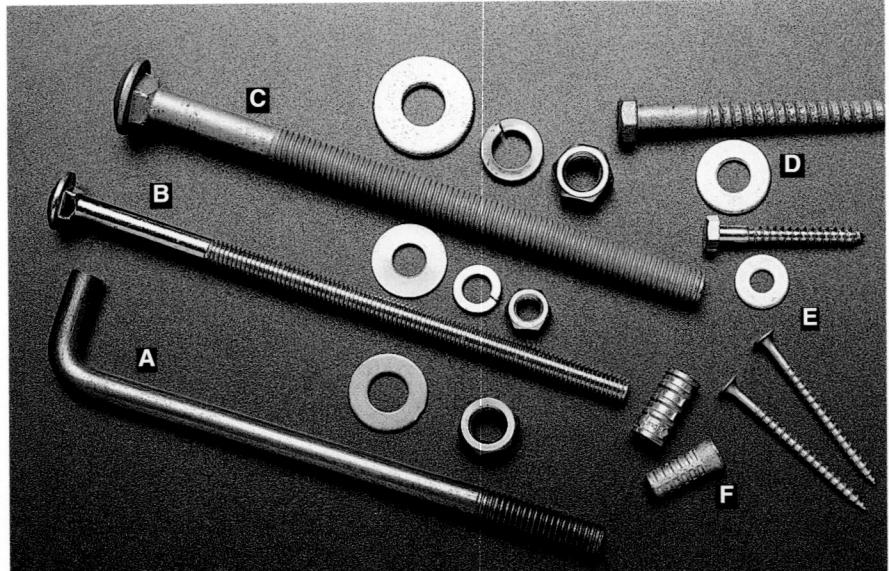

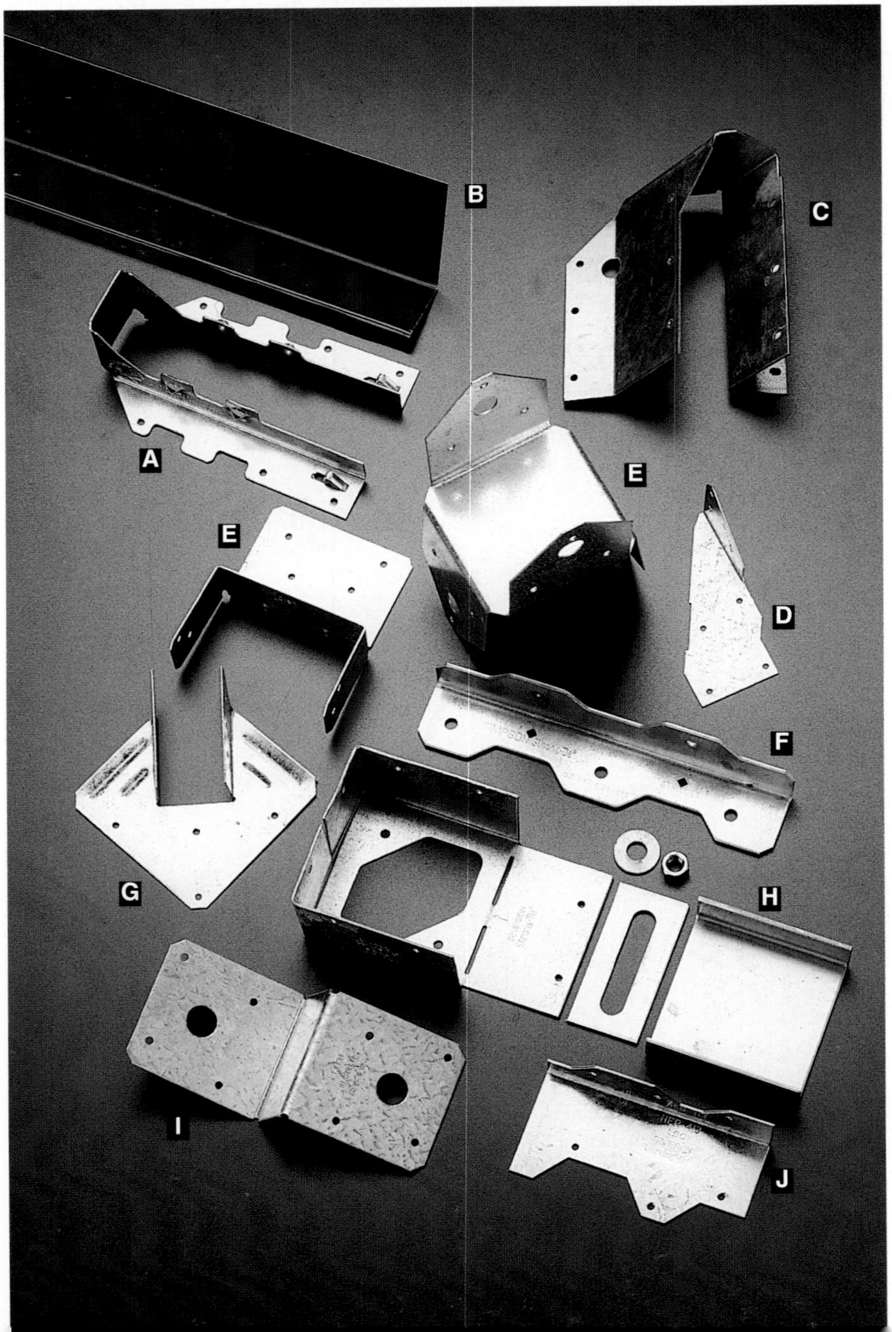

Build your deck with galvanized lumber connectors, nails, and screws. Galvanized metal products resist rust and will not stain treated wood. Use stainless steel screws if you are installing cedar or redwood decking—galvanized screws may react with natural chemicals in the wood to produce some staining.

Seal heads of counterbored screws with silicone caulk to prevent water damage.

Metal lumber connectors are used to create strong joints with wood framing members. Post anchors, post-beam caps, joist hangers, cleats, and brackets are available at lumberyards and home improvement centers.

(Top photo) Deck fasteners include: J-bolt with nut and washer (A), carriage bolts with washers and nuts (B, C), galvanized lag screws and washers (D), corrosion-resistant deck screw (E), masonry anchor (F).

(Bottom photo) Metal connectors used in deck building include: joist hanger (A), flashing (B), angled joist hanger (C), rafter tie (D), post-beam caps (E), stair cleat (F), H-fit joist ties (G), post anchor with washer and pedestal (H), joist tie (I), angle bracket (J).

Joist ties strengthen and support beams fastened to posts in sandwich beam constuction.

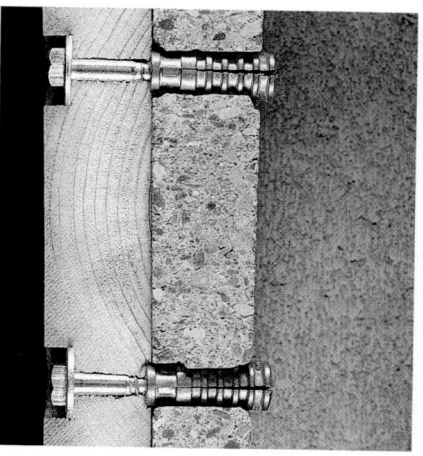

Masonry anchors with lag screws hold the ledger to stone, brick, or concrete blocks.

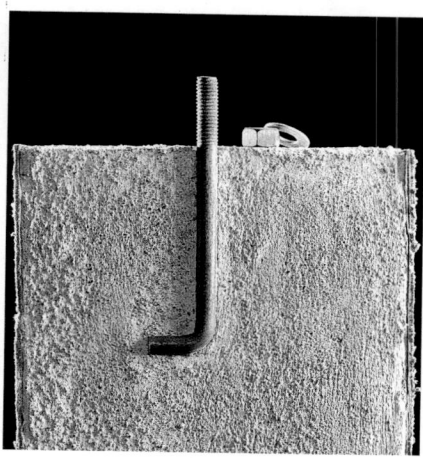

J-bolts with nuts and washers hold the post anchors to the concrete footings.

Post anchors hold deck posts in place, and raise the base of the posts to help prevent water from entering end grain of wood.

Angle brackets help reinforce header and outside joists. Angle brackets are also used to attach stair stringers to the deck.

Joist hangers are used to attach joists to the ledger and header joist. Double hanger is used when decking pattern requires a double-width joist.

Angled joist hangers are used to frame decks that have unusual angles or decking patterns.

Stair cleats support the treads of deck steps. Cleats are attached to stair stringers with ¼" x 1¼" galvanized lag screws.

Post-beam caps secure beams on top of posts.

Concrete

Use concrete to make solid footings that will support the weight of the deck (see page 40). Concrete for footings is made from a mixture of portland cement, sand, and coarse gravel (¼" to 1½" in diameter). These materials can be purchased separately and mixed at home, or you can buy bags containing the premixed dry ingredients. For larger amounts, buy ready-mixed concrete in trailer loads.

For most deck projects, mixing your own concrete is easy and inexpensive. Mix concrete in a wheelbarrow or with a power mixer, available at rental centers.

The estimation charts on the opposite page give approximate volumes of concrete. You may have a small amount of concrete left over after pouring post footings.

Mix concrete ingredients in a wheelbarrow. Use a ratio of 1 part portland cement (A), 2 parts sand (B), and 3 parts coarse gravel (C). Or, use the cubic-foot volumes shown in the chart (page opposite).

Amount of Concrete Needed (cubic feet)

Number of 8" Diameter Footings	Depth of Footings (feet)			
	1	2	3	4
2	¾	1½	2¼	3
3	1	2¼	3½	4½
4	1½	3	4½	6
5	2	3¾	5¾	7½

Amount of Concrete Needed (cubic feet)	Dry Ingredients for Self-mix			60-lb. bags of premixed dry concrete
	94-lb. bags of portland cement	Cubic feet of sand	Cubic feet of gravel	
1	⅙	⅓	½	2
2	⅓	⅔	1	4
3	½	1½	3	6
4	¾	1¾	3½	8
5	1	2¼	4½	10
10	2	4½	9	20

Buying & Mixing Concrete

Buy premixed bags of dry concrete for small jobs. A 60-lb. bag creates about ½ of a cubic foot of concrete. A 90-lb. bag creates about ⅔ of a cubic foot.

Rent a power cement mixer to blend large amounts of cement, gravel, sand, and water quickly.

Buy ready-mixed concrete for larger jobs. Trailer loads are available at rental centers, and are sold by the cubic yard. One cubic yard equals 27 cubic feet.

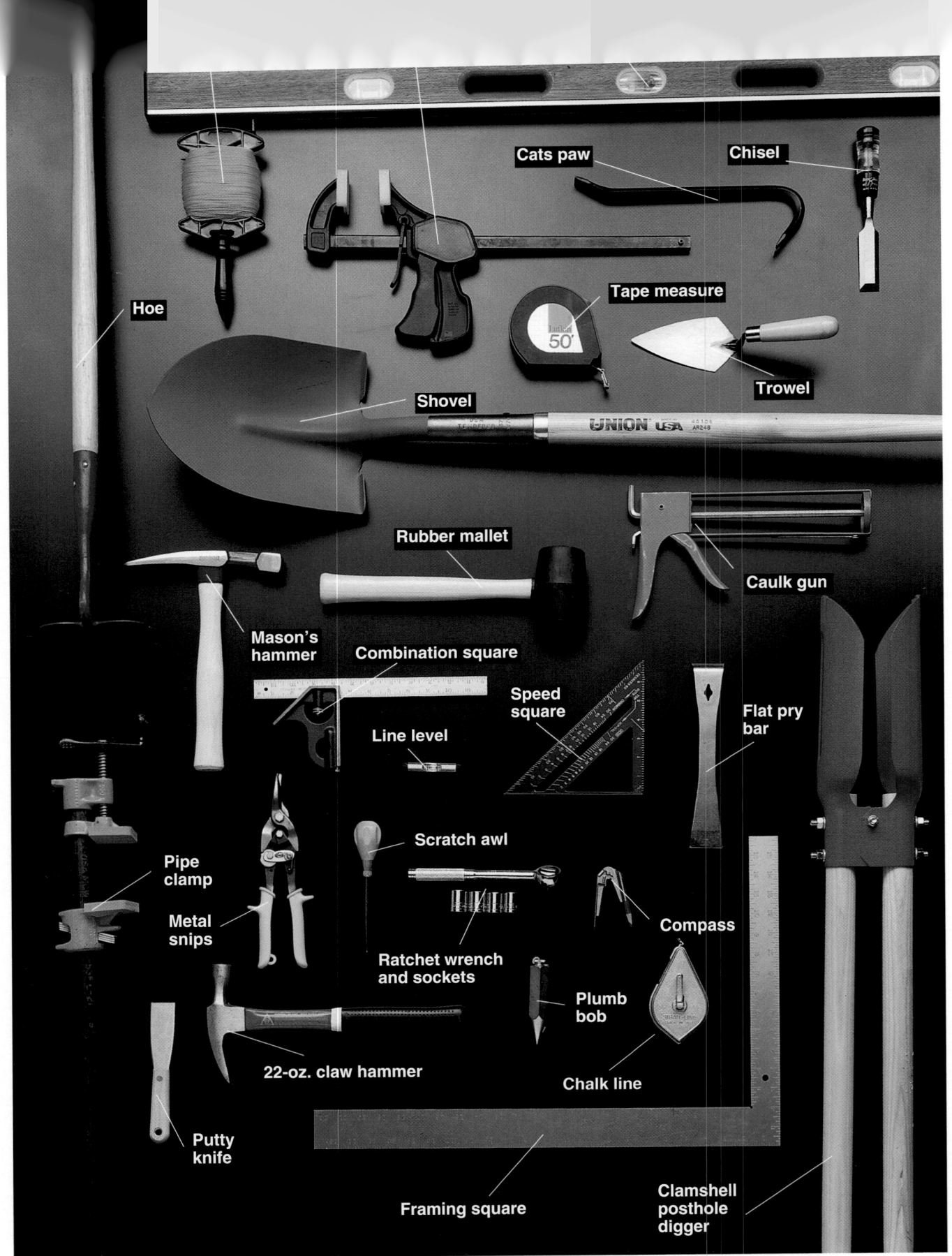

Hand tools for deck building should have heavy-duty construction. Metal tools should be made from high-carbon steel with smoothly finished surfaces. Buy quality hand tools that are well balanced and have tight, comfortably molded handles. There is no substitute for quality.

Tool Basics

With a set of basic hand and power tools, you can complete any of the deck projects shown in this book. You may already own many of the tools needed. If you buy new tools, invest in quality, heavy-duty products that will provide long service.

Some specialty tools, like power miter saws or reciprocating saws, are available at tool rental centers. Or, they can be purchased at home improvement stores.

Always wear eye protection when using tools. Always wear a particle mask and work gloves when sawing or handling pressure-treated lumber, to avoid excessive contact with the chemicals in the wood.

Tools for finishing and maintaining a deck include: rubber gloves (A), shop vacuum (B), 14-gauge extension cord (C), pressure sprayer (D), hydraulic jack and handle (E), eye protection (F), scrub brush (G), paint brush (H), particle mask (I), and orbital sander (J).

Power tools include: power miter saw (A), 14.4-volt cordless trim saw with a 5⅜"-blade (B), reciprocating saw with 6" and 8" blades (C), ⅜" drill and bits (D), jig saw (E), and ½" hammer drill and bits (F).

Design & Planning

A building permit is granted after an official from the building inspections department has reviewed and approved your deck plans. Consulting a building official early in the planning process can help ensure that the approval process is a smooth one.

Planning Your Project

When building a deck, the importance of planning cannot be overemphasized. Poor planning almost always leads to frustration and disappointment; good planning helps ensure that your new deck will be an attractive, functional space that adds value to your home.

Careful planning helps guarantee that your deck will meet your needs—both aesthetically and functionally. Good planning also makes for a trouble-free construction process. Review the appropriate building techniques to be sure you understand how to build your design.

Begin the planning process by gathering ideas about how you will use your deck and what it will

look like. Then check with your local building office to determine what building code requirements that deck must meet. Use this information and develop your initial idea into detailed plan drawings that will guide construction. Finally, return to the building official; he will review your plans and grant you a permit to begin work.

Keep in mind that adjusting the size of a deck section a few inches may significantly change the amount and cost of lumber you need or the waste. For example, shortening the width of a deck level from 10'6" to 10'3" means 10'-long lumber can be used for 10'-long joists rather than cutting 12'-long lumber down to 10'3".

Where to Find Deck Ideas

Purchased deck plans, sales literature, and home improvement magazines are good sources of ideas. Deck plans are widely available, but you may need to revise them extensively to make them work for your building site. Sales literature from lumber suppliers and hardware manufacturers often features photos and plan drawings of elaborate decks, which you can use to develop your own design.

A great source of creative inspiration for your deck planning are books that contain color photographs of deck and landscape design, such as these titles from the *Portfolio of Ideas* series.

Personal scouting is perhaps the best source of ideas. Whenever you go out for a drive or walk, keep an eye open for unique, attractive decks. Carry a camera to photograph construction details—after getting the consent of the property owner.

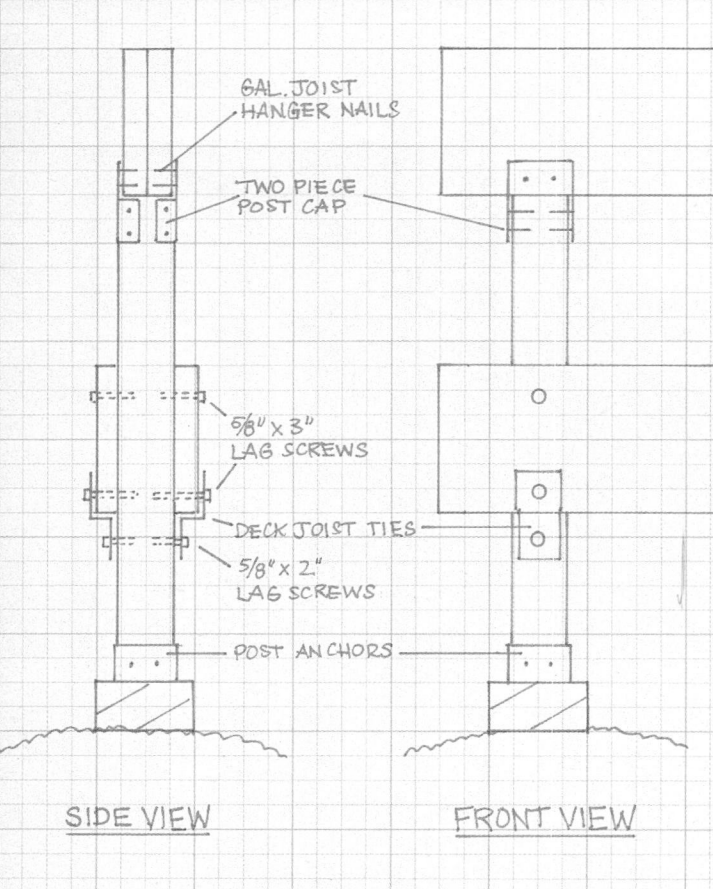

Labels on the illustration:
- GAL. JOIST HANGER NAILS
- TWO PIECE POST CAP
- 5/8" x 3" LAG SCREWS
- DECK JOIST TIES
- 5/8" x 2" LAG SCREWS
- POST ANCHORS

SIDE VIEW   FRONT VIEW

Draw detailed illustrations of the joinery methods you plan to use on all structural members of your deck. Your building official will want to see details on post-footing connections, post-beam joints, beam-joist joints, and ledger connections.

Working with Building Officials

In most regions, you must have your plans reviewed and approved by a building official if your deck is attached to a permanent structure or if it is more than 30" high. The building official makes sure that your planned deck meets building code requirements for safe construction.

These pages show some of the most common code requirements for decks. But before you design your project, check with the building inspection division of your city office, since code regulations can vary from area to area. A valuable source of planning information, the building official may provide you with a free information sheet outlining the relevant requirements.

Once you have completed plans for your deck, return to the building inspections office and have the official review them. If your plans meet code, you will be issued a building permit, usually for a small fee. Regulations may require that a field inspector review the deck at specified stages in the building process. If so, make sure to comply with the review schedule.

Plan-approval Checklist

When the building official reviews your deck plans, he or she will look for the following details. Make sure your plan drawings include this information when you visit the building inspection office to apply for a building permit.

- Overall size of the deck.
- Position of the deck relative to buildings and property lines. The deck must be set back at least 5 ft. from neighboring property.
- Location of all beams and posts.
- Size and on-center (OC) spacing of joists.
- Thickness of decking boards.
- Height of deck above the ground.
- Detailed drawings of joinery methods for all structural members of the deck.
- Type of soil that will support the concrete post footings: sand, gravel, or clay.
- Species of wood you will be using.
- Types of metal connectors and other hardware you plan to use when constructing your deck.

Footing diameter and depth is determined by your building official, based on the estimated load of the deck and on the composition of your soil. In regions with cold winters, footings must extend below the frost line. Minimum diameter for concrete footings is 8".

Tips for Working with Building Officials

Metal flashings must be used to prevent moisture from penetrating between the ledger and the wall.

Beams may overhang posts by no more than 1 ft. Some local building regulations require that, wherever possible, beams should rest on top of posts, secured with metal post-beam caps.

Engineered beams, such as a laminated wood product or steel girder, should be used on decks with very long joist spans, where standard dimension lumber is not adequate for the load.

Railings are required for any deck more than 24" above the ground; railings must be at least 36" in height, and the bottom rail must be positioned so there is no more than 6" of open space below it. Vertical balusters can have no more than 4" between them.

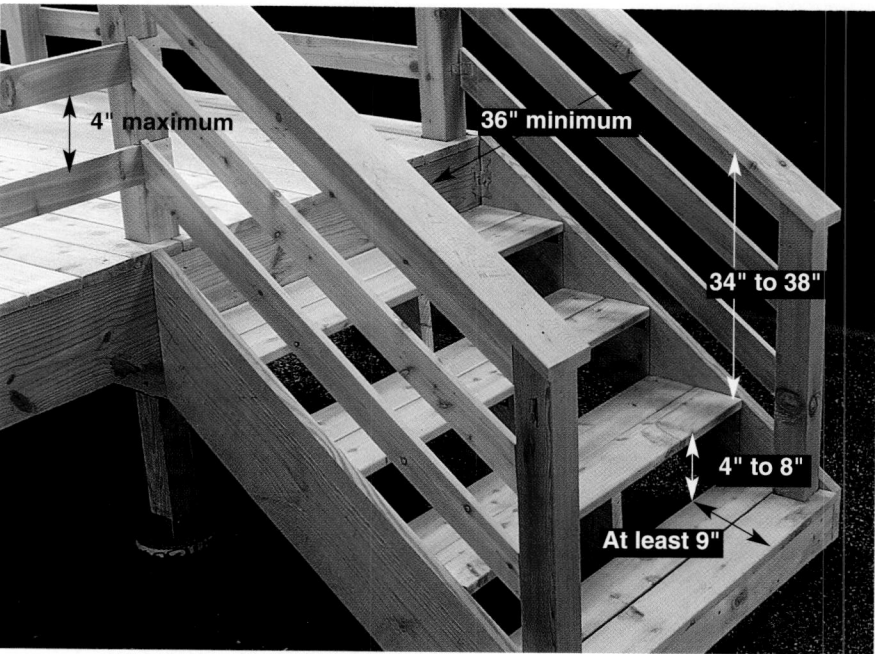

Stairs must be at least 36" wide. Vertical step risers must be between 4" and 8", and treads must have a horizontal run of at least 9". A single staircase can have no more than 12 steps; for longer runs, two staircases are required, separated by a landing. Stair railings should be 34" to 38" above the noses of the step treads, and there should be no more than 6" of space between the bottom rail and the steps. The space between the rails or balusters should be no more than 4".

Determining Lumber Size

A deck has seven major structural parts: the ledger, decking, joists, one or more beams, posts, stairway stringers, and stairway treads. To create a working design plan and choose the correct lumber size, you must know the span limits of each part of the deck. The ledger is attached directly to the house and does not have a span limit.

A span limit is the safe distance a board can cross without support from underneath. The maximum safe span depends on the size and wood species of the board. For example, 2 × 6 southern pine joists spaced 16" on-center can safely span 9'9", while 2 × 10 joists can span 16'1".

Begin planning by first choosing size and pattern for the decking. Use the tables on the opposite page. Then determine the size and layout of the joists and beams, using the information and span tables on pages 44 to 45. In general, a deck designed with larger-size lumber, like 2 × 12 joists and beams, requires fewer pieces, because the boards have a large span limit. Next, compute the correct size for posts, using the table on the opposite page. Finally, choose the stair and railing lumber that fits your plan, again using the tables on the opposite page.

Use the design plans to make a complete list of the quantities of each lumber size your deck requires. Add 10% to compensate for lumber flaws and construction errors. Full-service lumberyards have a fine lumber selection, but prices may be higher than those at home improvement centers. The quality of lumber at home centers can vary, so inspect the wood and hand-pick the pieces you want or add a larger percentage to compensate for lumber flaws. Both lumberyards and home centers will deliver lumber for a small fee and you can usually return unused, uncut lumber if you keep your receipts.

Dimension & Span Limit Tables for Deck Lumber

Nominal vs. Actual Lumber Dimensions: When planning a deck, remember that the actual size of lumber is smaller than the nominal size by which lumber is sold. Use the actual dimensions when drawing a deck design plan.

Nominal	Actual
1 × 4	¾" × 3¾"
1 × 6	¾" × 5¾"
2 × 4	1½" × 3½"
2 × 6	1½" × 5½"
2 × 8	1½" × 7¼"
2 × 10	1½" × 9¼"
2 × 12	1½" × 11¼"
4 × 4	3½" × 3½"
6 × 6	5½" × 5½"

Recommended Decking Span Between Joists: Decking boards can be made from a variety of lumber sizes. For a basic deck use 2 × 4 or 2 × 6 lumber with joists spaced 16" apart.

Decking Boards	Recommended Span
1 × 4 or 1 × 6, laid straight	16"
1 × 4 or 1 × 6, laid diagonal	12"
2 × 4 or 2 × 6, laid straight	16"
2 × 4 or 2 × 6, laid diagonal	12"
2 × 4, laid on edge	24"

Recommended Post Size: Choose post size by finding the load area for the deck. To find the load area, multiply the distance between beams by the distance between posts. For example, on a deck that has one beam spaced 10 feet from the ledger, with posts spaced 7 feet apart, the load area is 70. If this deck is less than 6 feet high, the recommended post size is 4 × 4.

	Load Area				
	Multiply distance between beams (feet) by the distance between posts (feet).				
Deck Height	48	72	96	120	144
Up to 6 ft.	4 × 4	4 × 4	6 × 6	6 × 6	6 × 6
More than 6 ft.	6 × 6	6 × 6	6 × 6	6 × 6	6 × 6

Minimum Stair Stringer Sizes: Size of stair stringers depends on the span of the stairway. For example, if the bottom of the stairway lies 7 feet from the deck, build the stringers from 2 × 12s. Stringers should be spaced no more than 36" apart. Use of a center stringer is recommended for stairways with more than three steps.

Span of Stairway	Stringer Size
Up to 6 ft.	2 × 10
More than 6 ft.	2 × 12

Recommended Railing Sizes: Size of posts, rails, and caps depends on the spacing of the railing posts. For example, if railing posts are spaced 6 feet apart, use 4 × 4 posts and 2 × 6 rails and caps.

Space Between Railing Posts	Post Size	Cap Size	Rail Size
2 ft. to 3 ft.	2 × 4	2 × 4	2 × 4
3 ft. to 4 ft.	4 × 4	2 × 4	2 × 4
4 ft. to 6 ft.	4 × 4	2 × 6	2 × 6

Understanding Loads

The supporting structural members of a deck—the posts, beams, and joists—must be sturdy enough to easily support the heaviest anticipated load on the deck. They must not only carry the substantial weight of the surface decking and railings, but also the weight of people, deck furnishings, and, in some climates, snow.

The charts and diagrams shown here will help you plan a deck so the size and spacing of the structural members are sufficient to support the load, assuming normal use. These recommendations are followed in most regions, but you should still check with your local building official for regulations that are unique to your area. In cases where the deck will support a hot tub or pool, you must consult your local building inspections office for load guidelines.

When choosing lumber for the structural members of your deck, select the diagram below that best matches your deck design, then follow the advice for applying the charts on the opposite page. Since different species of wood have different strengths, make sure to use the entries that match the type of lumber sold by your building center. When selecting the size for concrete footings, make sure to consider the composition of your soil; dense soils require footings with a larger diameter.

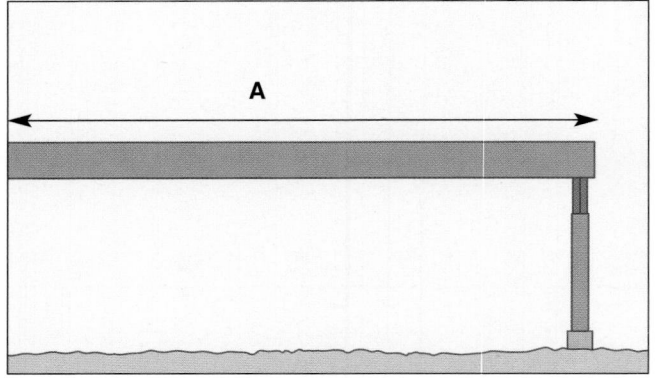

Post-and-beam or notched-post deck: Using Chart 1, determine the proper size for your joists, based on the on-center (OC) spacing between joists and the overall length, or span, of the joists (A). For example, if you will be using southern pine joists to span a 12-ft. distance, you can use 2 × 8 lumber spaced no more than 16" apart, or 2 × 10 lumber spaced no more than 24" apart. Once you have determined allowable joist sizes, use Chart 2 to determine an appropriate beam size, post spacing, and footing size for your deck.

Cantilevered deck: Use the distance from the ledger to the beam (A) to determine minimum joist size, and use A + (2 × B) when choosing beam and footing sizes. For example, if your deck measures 9 ft. from ledger to beam, with an additional 3-ft. cantilevered overhang, use 9 ft. to choose a joist size from Chart 1 (2 × 6 southern pine joists spaced 16" apart, or 2 × 8 joists spaced 24" apart). Then, use A + (2 × B), or 15 ft., to find an appropriate beam size, post spacing, and footing size from Chart 2. NOTE: If your deck cantilevers more than 18" beyond the support beam, add 1" to the recommended diameter for footings.

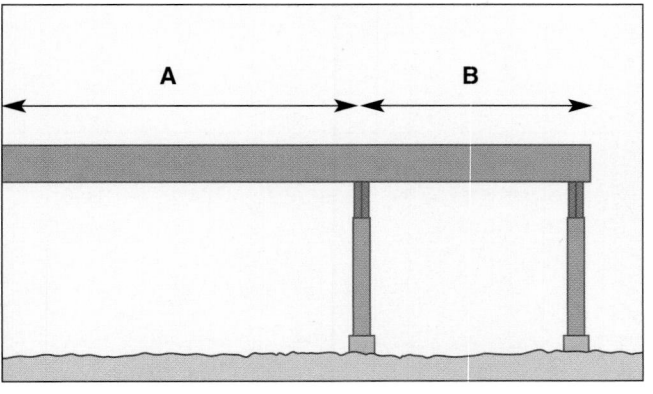

Multiple-beam deck: Use distance A or B, whichever is larger, when determining joist size from Chart 1. For example, if your deck measures 8 ft. to beam #1 and another 4 ft. to beam #2, you can use 2 × 6 southern pine joists. Referring to Chart 2, use the total distance A + B to determine the size of beam #1, the spacing for the posts, and the size of the footings. Use joist length B to determine the size of beam #2, the post spacing, and footing size. For example, with an overall span of 12 ft. (8 ft. to the first beam, 4 ft. to the second), beam #1 could be made from two southern pine 2 × 8s; beam #2, from two 2 × 6s.

Chart 1

Size	Southern Pine			Ponderosa Pine			Western Cedar		
	12" OC	16" OC	24" OC	12" OC	16" OC	24" OC	12" OC	16" OC	24" OC
2 × 6	10 ft. 9"	9 ft. 9"	8 ft. 6"	9 ft. 2"	8 ft. 4"	7 ft. 0"	9 ft. 2"	8 ft. 4"	7 ft. 3"
2 × 8	14 ft. 2"	12 ft. 10"	11 ft. 0"	12 ft. 1"	10 ft. 10"	8 ft. 10"	12 ft. 1"	11 ft. 0"	9 ft. 2"
2 × 10	18 ft. 0"	16 ft. 1"	13 ft. 5"	15 ft. 4"	13 ft. 3"	10 ft. 10"	15 ft. 5"	13 ft. 9"	11 ft. 3"
2 × 12	21 ft. 9"	19 ft. 0"	15 ft. 4"	17 ft. 9"	15 ft. 5"	12 ft. 7"	18 ft. 5"	16 ft. 0"	13 ft. 0"

Chart 2

Footing cells show three values in the order: Clay Sand Gravel.

Joist Length		Post Spacing 4'	5'	6'	7'	8'	9'	10'	11'	12'
6'	Southern Pine Beam	1–2×6	1–2×6	1–2×6	2–2×6	2–2×6	2–2×6	2–2×8	2–2×8	2–2×10
	Ponderosa Pine Beam	1–2×6	1–2×6	1–2×8	2–2×8	2–2×6	2–2×8	2–2×10	2–2×10	2–2×12
	Corner Footing	6 5 4	7 6 5	7 6 5	8 7 6	9 7 6	9 7 6	10 8 7	10 8 7	10 9 7
	Intermediate Footing	9 8 7	10 8 7	10 9 7	11 9 8	12 10 9	13 10 9	14 11 10	14 12 10	15 12 10
7'	Southern Pine Beam	1–2×6	1–2×6	1–2×6	2–2×6	2–2×6	2–2×8	2–2×8	2–2×10	2–2×10
	Ponderosa Pine Beam	1–2×6	1–2×6	1–2×8	2–2×6	2–2×8	2–2×10	2–2×10	2–2×10	2–2×12
	Corner Footing	7 5 5	7 6 5	8 7 6	9 7 6	9 8 7	10 8 7	10 8 7	11 9 8	11 9 8
	Intermediate Footing	9 8 7	10 8 7	11 9 8	12 10 9	13 11 9	14 11 10	15 12 10	15 13 11	16 13 11
8'	Southern Pine Beam	1–2×6	1–2×6	2–2×6	2–2×6	2–2×8	2–2×8	2–2×8	2–2×10	2–2×10
	Ponderosa Pine Beam	1–2×6	2–2×6	2–2×8	2–2×8	2–2×8	2–2×10	2–2×10	2–2×10	3–2×10
	Corner Footing	7 6 5	8 6 6	9 7 6	9 8 7	10 8 7	10 8 7	11 9 8	11 9 8	12 10 9
	Intermediate Footing	10 8 7	11 9 8	12 10 9	13 11 9	14 11 10	15 12 10	16 13 11	16 13 12	17 14 12
9'	Southern Pine Beam	1–2×6	1–2×6	2–2×6	2–2×6	2–2×8	2–2×8	2–2×8	2–2×10	2–2×10
	Ponderosa Pine Beam	1–2×6	2–2×6	2–2×8	2–2×8	2–2×8	2–2×10	2–2×10	2–2×10	3–2×10
	Corner Footing	7 6 5	8 7 6	9 7 6	10 8 7	10 9 7	11 9 8	12 10 8	12 10 9	13 10 9
	Intermediate Footing	10 9 7	12 10 8	13 10 9	14 11 10	15 12 10	16 13 11	17 14 12	17 14 12	18 15 13
10'	Southern Pine Beam	1–2×6	1–2×6	2–2×6	2–2×6	2–2×8	2–2×8	2–2×10	2–2×12	2–2×12
	Ponderosa Pine Beam	1–2×6	1–2×6	2–2×8	2–2×8	2–2×10	2–2×10	2–2×12	3–2×10	3–2×12
	Corner Footing	8 6 6	9 7 6	10 8 7	10 8 7	11 9 8	12 10 8	12 10 9	13 11 9	14 11 10
	Intermediate Footing	11 9 8	12 10 9	14 11 10	15 12 10	16 13 11	17 14 12	17 14 12	18 15 13	19 16 14
11'	Southern Pine Beam	1–2×6	2–2×6	2–2×6	2–2×8	2–2×8	2–2×10	2–2×10	2–2×12	2–2×12
	Ponderosa Pine Beam	2–2×6	2–2×6	2–2×8	2–2×8	2–2×10	2–2×12	2–2×12	3–2×10	3–2×12
	Corner Footing	8 7 6	9 7 6	10 8 7	11 9 8	12 9 8	12 10 9	13 11 9	14 11 10	14 12 10
	Intermediate Footing	12 9 8	13 11 9	14 12 10	15 12 10	16 13 11	17 14 12	17 14 12	18 15 13	19 16 14
12'	Southern Pine Beam	1–2×6	2–2×6	2–2×6	2–2×8	2–2×8	2–2×10	2–2×10	2–2×12	2–2×12
	Ponderosa Pine Beam	2–2×6	2–2×6	2–2×8	2–2×10	2–2×10	2–2×12	2–2×10	2–2×12	3–2×10
	Corner Footing	9 7 6	10 8 7	10 9 7	11 9 8	12 10 8	13 10 9	14 11 10	14 12 10	15 12 10
	Intermediate Footing	12 10 9	14 11 10	15 12 10	16 13 11	17 14 12	18 15 13	19 16 14	20 16 14	21 17 15
13'	Southern Pine Beam	1–2×6	2–2×6	2–2×6	2–2×8	2–2×8	2–2×10	2–2×10	2–2×12	3–2×10
	Ponderosa Pine Beam	2–2×6	2–2×6	2–2×8	2–2×8	2–2×12	2–2×12	2–2×12	3–2×12	3–2×12
	Corner Footing	9 7 6	10 8 7	11 9 8	12 10 8	13 10 9	13 11 9	14 12 10	15 12 10	15 13 11
	Intermediate Footing	13 10 9	14 12 10	15 13 11	17 14 12	18 15 13	19 15 13	20 16 14	21 17 15	22 18 15
14'	Southern Pine Beam	1–2×6	2–2×6	2–2×6	2–2×8	2–2×10	2–2×10	2–2×12	3–2×10	3–2×12
	Ponderosa Pine Beam	2–2×6	2–2×8	2–2×8	2–2×10	2–2×12	3–2×10	3–2×12	3–2×12	Eng Bm
	Corner Footing	9 8 7	10 8 7	11 9 8	12 10 9	13 11 9	14 11 10	15 12 10	15 13 11	16 13 11
	Intermediate Footing	13 11 9	15 12 10	16 13 11	17 14 12	18 15 13	20 16 14	21 17 15	22 18 15	23 18 16
15'	Southern Pine Beam	2–2×6	2–2×6	2–2×6	2–2×8	2–2×10	2–2×10	2–2×12	3–2×10	3–2×12
	Ponderosa Pine Beam	2–2×6	2–2×8	2–2×8	2–2×10	3–2×10	3–2×12	3–2×12	3–2×12	Eng Bm
	Corner Footing	10 8 7	11 9 8	12 10 8	13 10 9	14 11 10	14 12 10	15 12 11	16 13 11	17 14 12
	Intermediate Footing	14 11 10	15 12 11	17 14 12	18 15 13	19 16 14	20 17 14	21 17 15	22 18 16	23 19 17

KEY (example):

10	8	7
14	11	10

KEY: Clay Sand Gravel

Developing Your Deck Plan

Once you have a rough idea of what you want your deck to look like, you'll need to develop the concept into a workable plan. Especially for complicated, elaborate decks, it is crucial that you have detailed plan drawings to help organize and direct your work. Good plans also make it possible to create an accurate materials list. In addition, your building inspector will insist on seeing plan drawings before granting you a work permit.

One surefire method is to hire a landscape designer to develop a detailed deck blueprint, but this process is often expensive and is less rewarding than creating your own design. With careful, thoughtful work, you can develop a plan tailored exactly to your needs, and save money in the process.

Computer software makes the deck design process simpler. These programs range from relatively inexpensive but full-featured software designed for the do-it-yourself consumer (above), to specialized CAD software used mostly by design professionals. Some consumer software programs include a "library" of stock deck designs that you can revise to suit your needs.

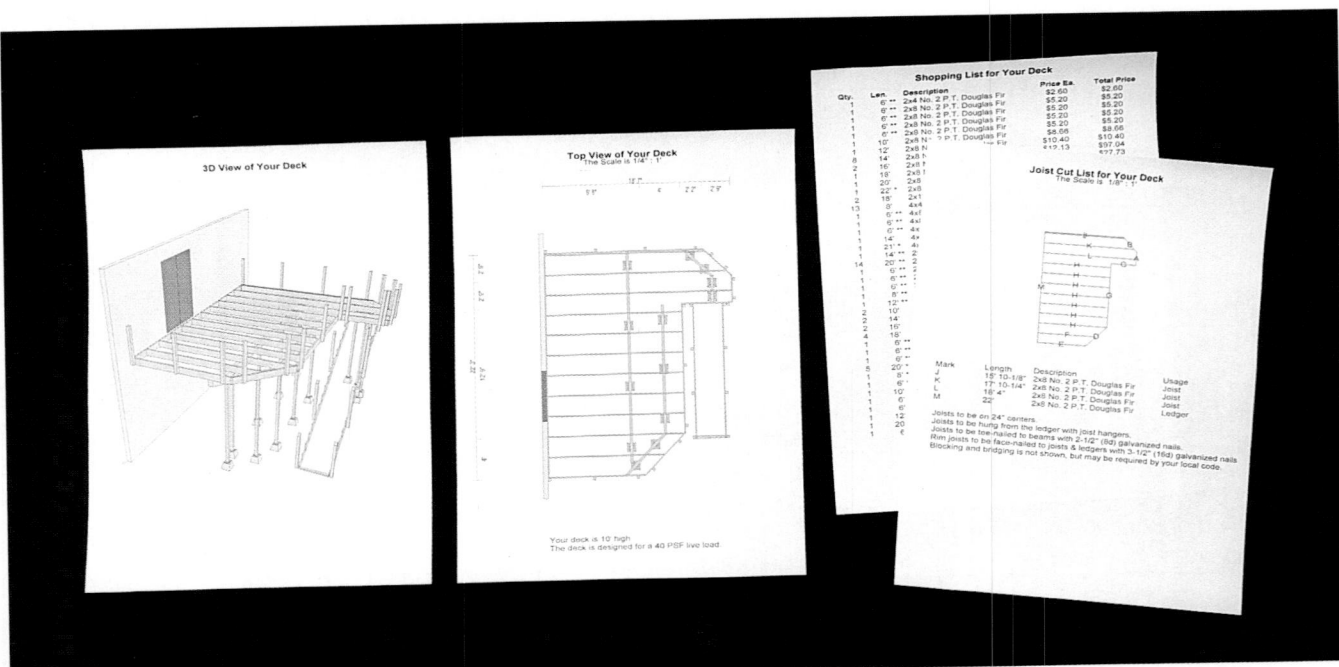

Computer printouts generated by deck-design software provide three-dimensional views of finished deck designs (left), detailed structural drawings (center), and a complete list of the materials needed (right). Some design programs can even print out contracts and forms, such as building permit applications.

Tips for Developing a Deck Plan

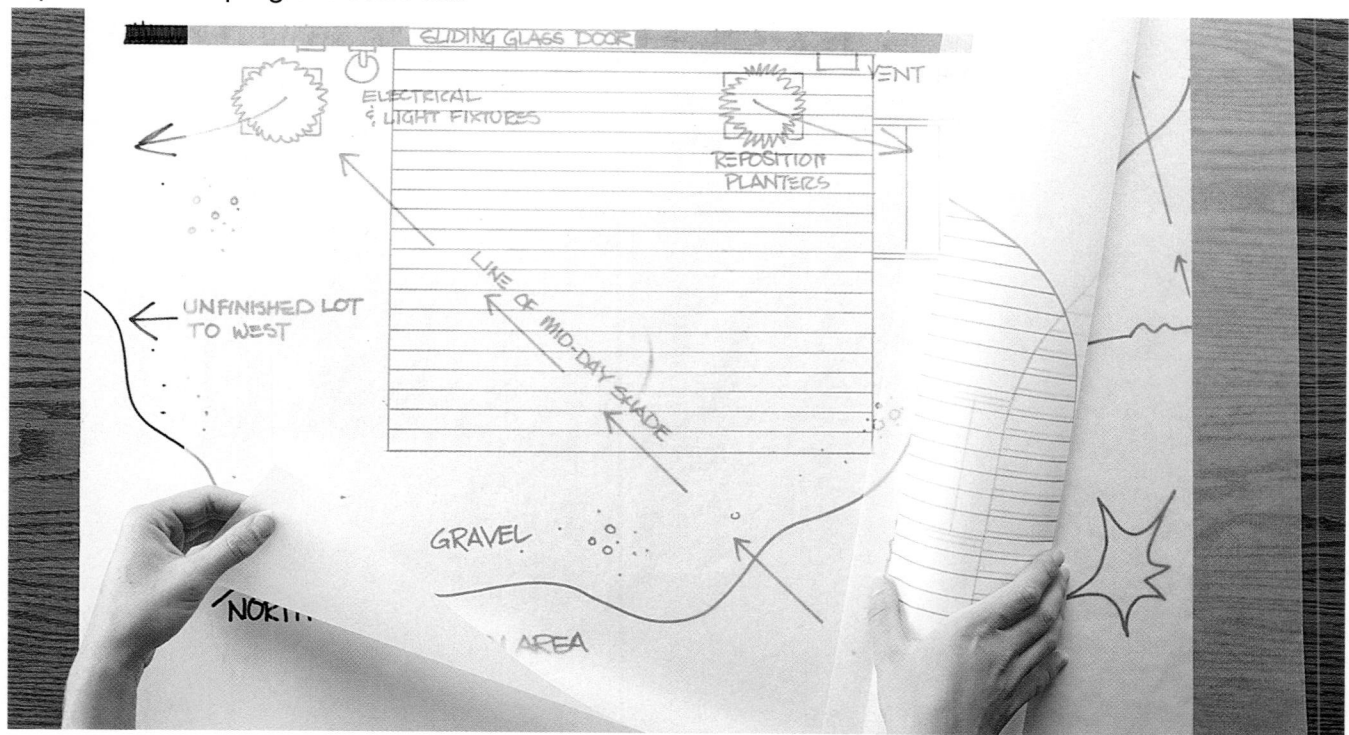

Use tracing paper to sketch different deck layouts. Then, test your ideas by overlaying the deck sketches onto a drawing of your building site. Make sure to consider sun patterns and the locations of existing landscape features when developing a deck plan.

Adapt an existing deck plan, either borrowed from a book (like those on page 204 to 289) or magazine, or purchased in blueprint form. Tracing paper, pens, and measuring tools are all you need to revise an existing deck plan.

Use drafting tools and graph paper if you are creating a deck plan from scratch. Use a generous scale, such as 1" equals 1 ft., that allows you to illustrate the deck in fine detail. Remember to create both overhead plan drawings and side elevation drawings of your project.

Make a map of the features of your house and yard. Include any features that might affect how you build and use your deck, like sun and shade patterns, trees, and other landscaping details. For accurate measurements, use long tape measure and hold it level and perpendicular to the house.

Creating Site Drawings

Create site drawings of a building area before designing a deck. Show all details that may affect how you build and use the deck.

Building a deck requires two types of site drawings. A **plan view** shows the building site as viewed from directly overhead. An **elevation** shows the vertical details of the site as it is viewed from the side or front.

As you create site drawings, consider how the features of house and yard influence the deck design. Remember that the building site is affected by weather, time of day, and seasonal changes. For example, if your deck will be used mainly for summertime evening meals, look at the sun, shade, and wind patterns on the site during this time of day.

Everything You Need

Tools: pencil or marker, eraser, 50-ft. tape measure, ruler, compass, line level.

Materials: large sheets of paper.

Supplies: mason's string.

How to Create Plan-view Site Drawings

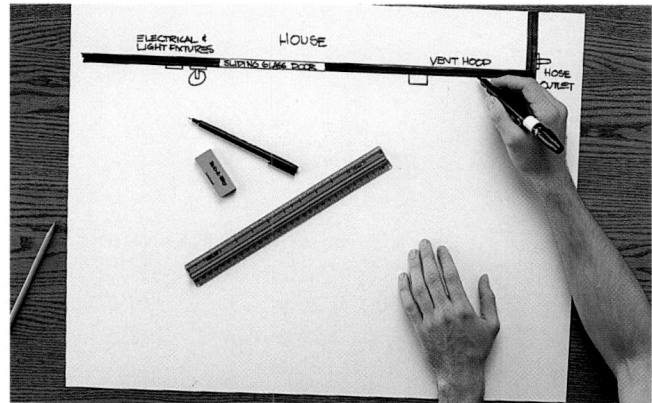

1 Sketch position of house and yard on a large sheet of paper, using a scale of 1" equals 1 foot. Show position of doors, windows, and outdoor utilities, like garden hose spigots, or light fixtures.

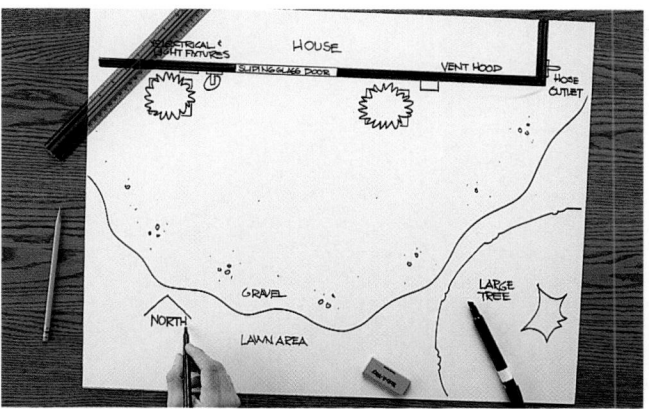

2 Add a symbol to the site drawing to indicate north. Mark the location of trees, gardening beds or planters, and any other landscaping features. Show any overhead or underground utility lines.

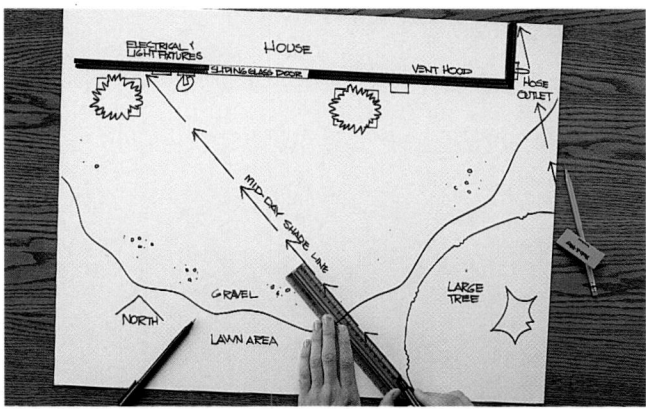

3 Observe the deck site during the time of day when the deck will be used most often. Outline shade and sun patterns on the site drawing.

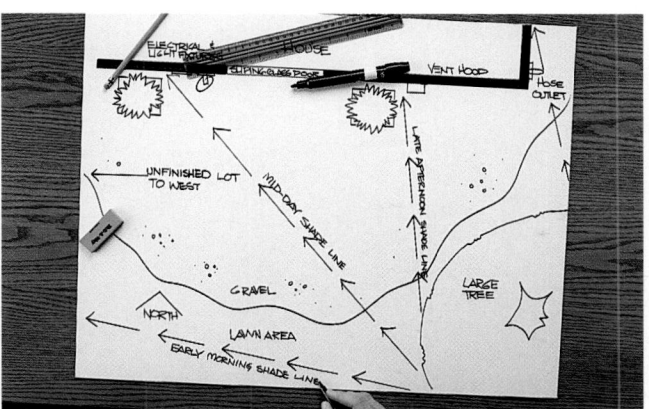

4 Show how the site changes throughout the day. Outline shade and sun patterns at different times, and quality of nearby view. Note changes in winds, traffic noise, and neighborhood activity.

How to Create Elevation Site Drawings

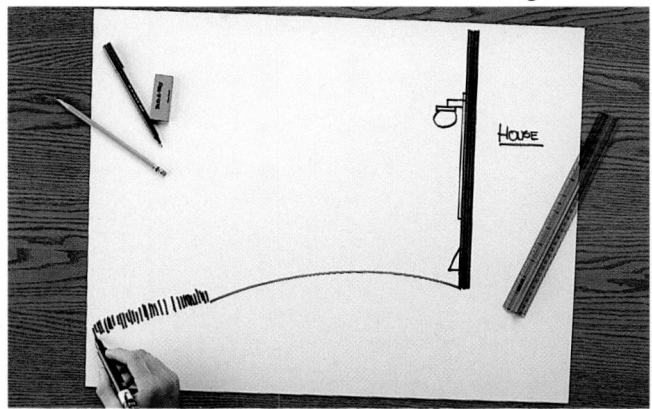

1 Create a side-view elevation map of your site, showing the slope of the ground and the position of the house. For accuracy, stretch level mason's strings from the house, and use the strings for reference to determine slope of ground.

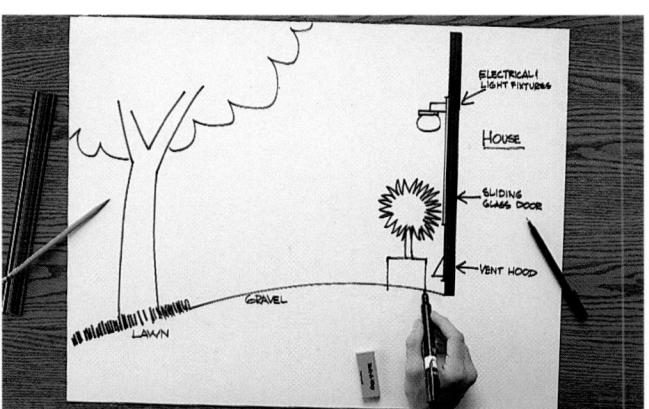

2 Add any other features that will affect how you build and use the deck, like the height of tree branches or telephone wires, shrubs, flowerbeds, or other landscaping details.

Drawing Design Plans

Design plans help you estimate lumber and hardware needs, and provide the measurements needed to lay out the deck and cut the lumber. If a work permit is required by local codes, you must have design plans.

You will need two types of design drawings for a deck project. A **plan view** shows the parts of the deck as they are viewed from directly overhead. An **elevation** shows the deck parts as viewed from the side or front.

To avoid confusion, do not try to show all parts of the deck in a single plan view. First, draw one plan that shows the outline of the deck and the pattern of the decking boards. Then make another plan that shows the underlying ledger, joists, beams, and posts.

Everything You Need

Tools: pencil or marker, eraser, ruler.

Materials: site drawing, large sheets of paper, sheets of tissue paper.

How to Draw Design Drawings

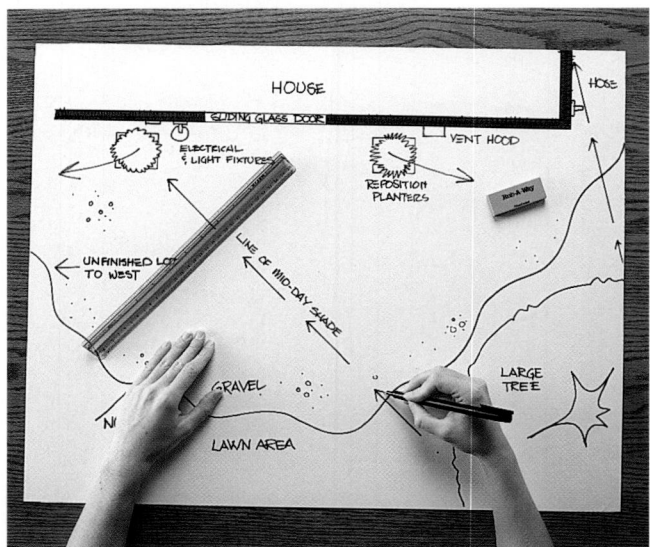

1 Use the scaled site drawings (pages 48 to 49) to help establish the size and shape of the deck.

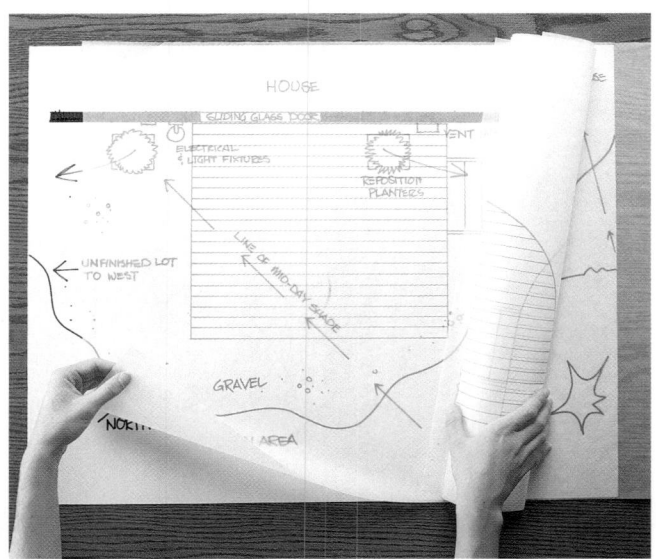

2 Lay a sheet of tissue paper over the site drawing and tape in position. Experiment with deck ideas by sketching different designs on separate sheets of tissue paper.

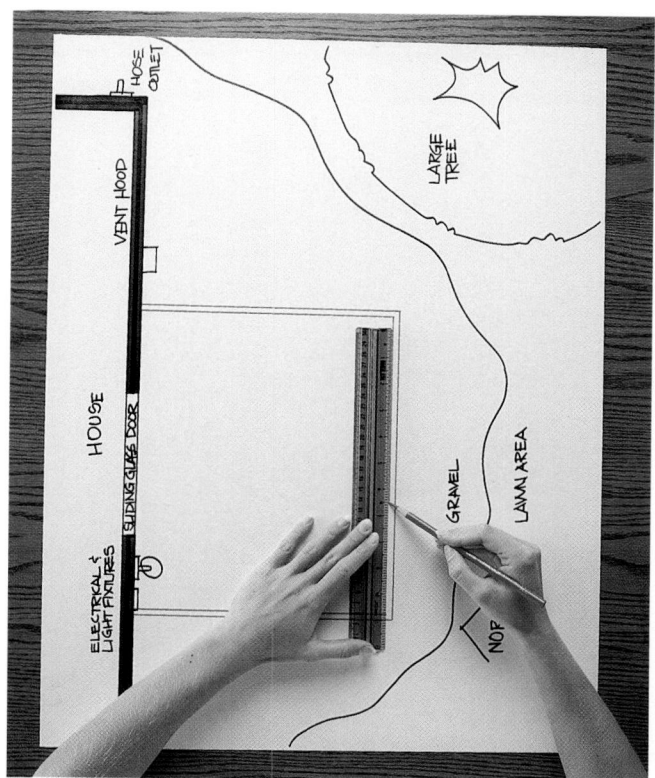

3 Make copies of the scaled site drawing. Use a ruler and sharp pencil to draw the outline of the deck on one copy of the scaled site drawing.

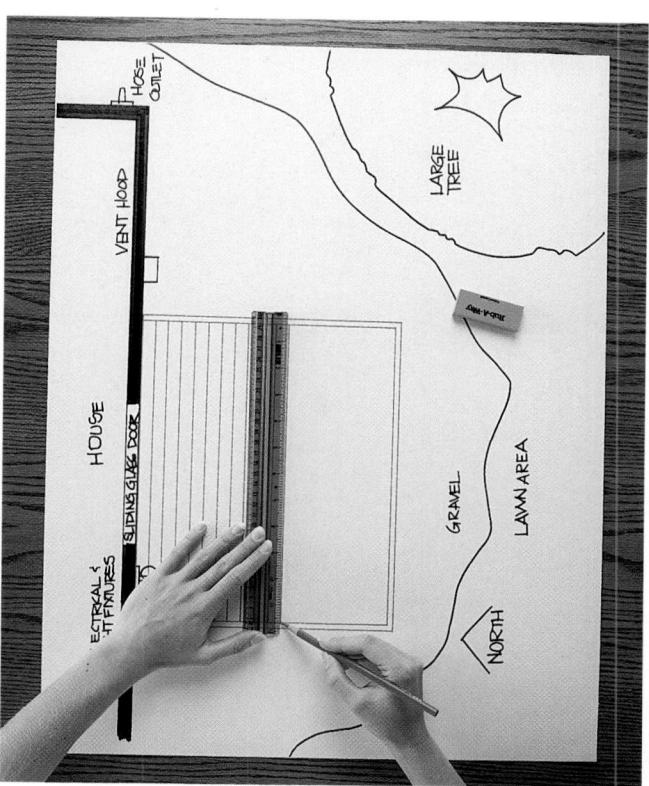

4 Draw in the decking pattern over the outline. Indicate the size and type of lumber and hardware to be used. Save this plan for reference.

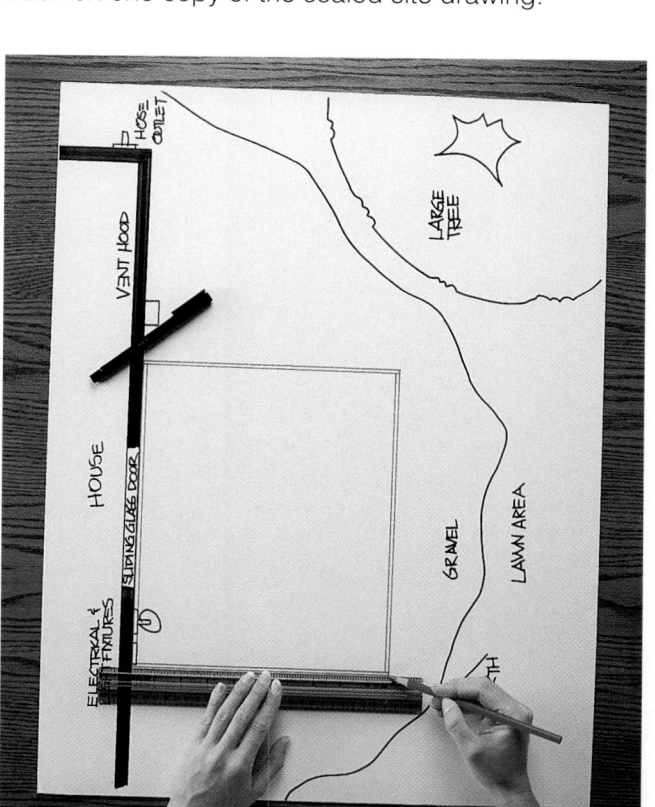

5 On a second copy of the scaled site drawing, draw another outline of the deck. Draw in the ledger, the outside joists, and the header joist.

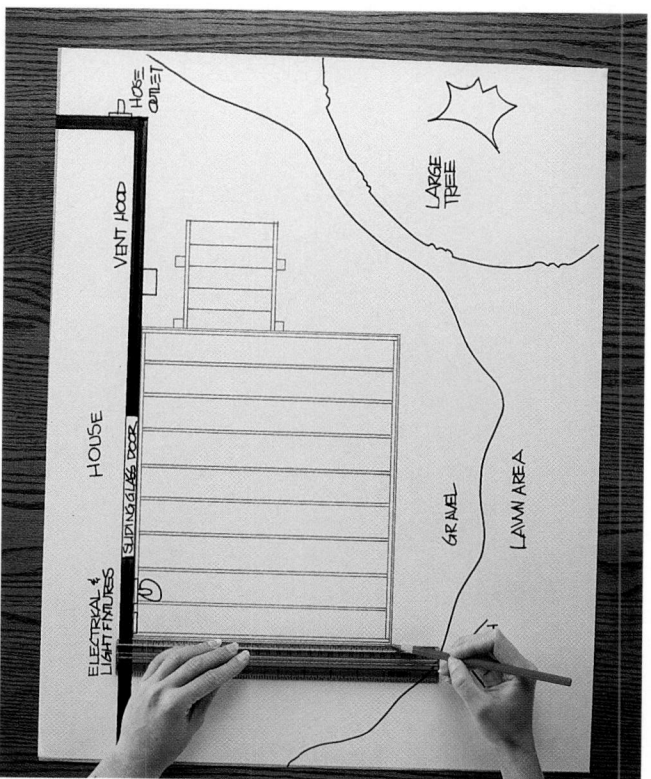

6 Draw the inner joists, and any blocking. Show any facing boards that will be used. Show the stairway stringers, treads, and posts.

(continued next page)

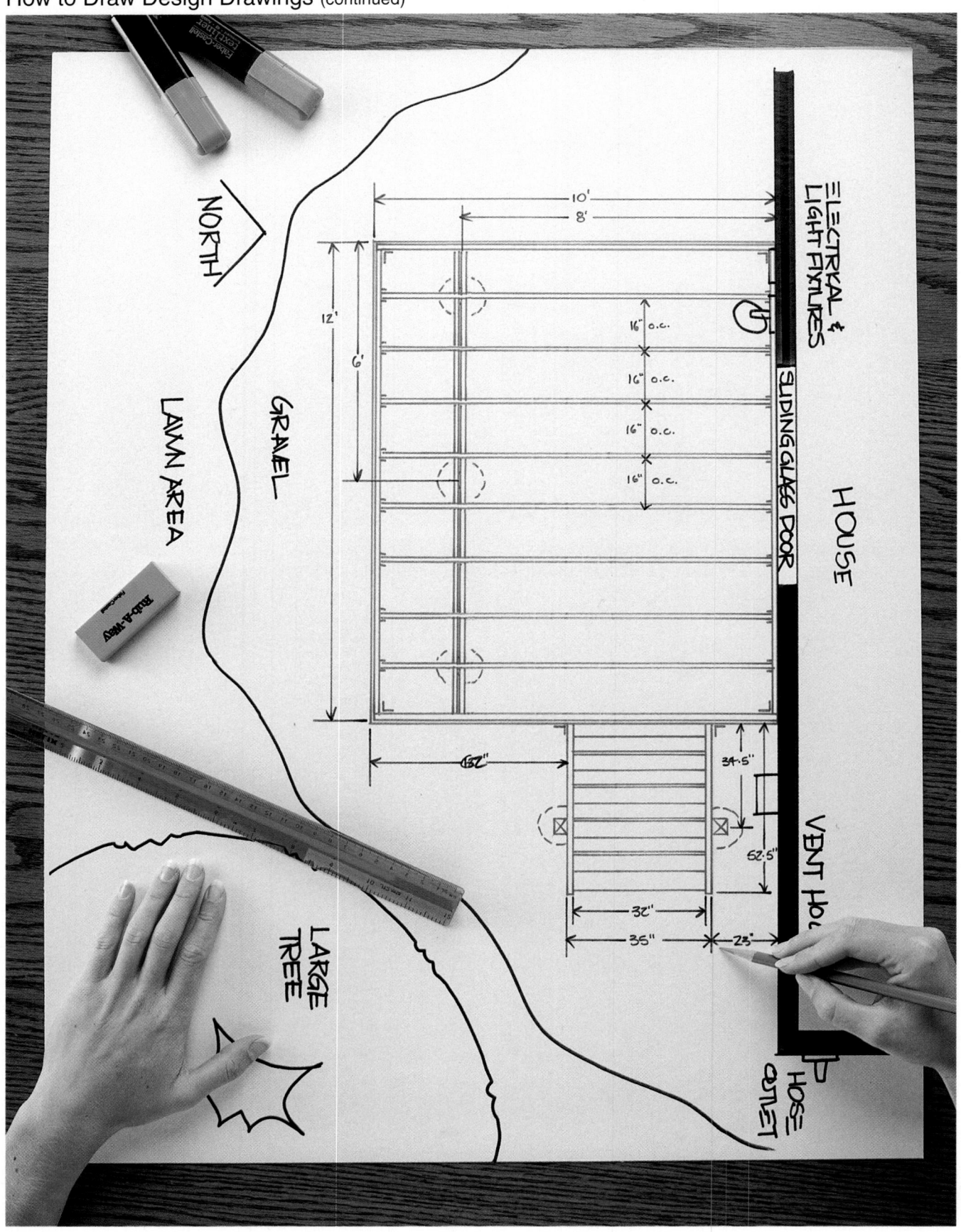

7 Draw in the deck beam and posts, and show the location of the concrete footings. List all deck dimensions on the plan. Save this drawing for reference when ordering lumber and hardware.

How to Draw Design Elevations

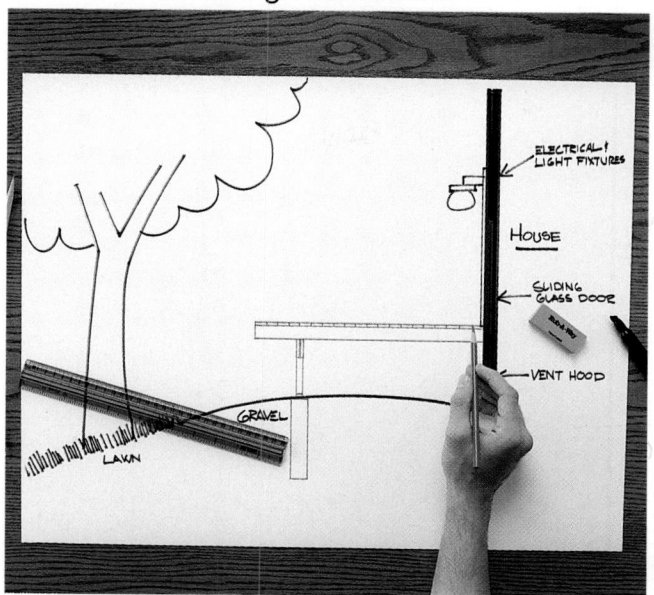

1 Draw in the basic deck platform on the site elevation drawing (page 51). Draw in the beam and the posts.

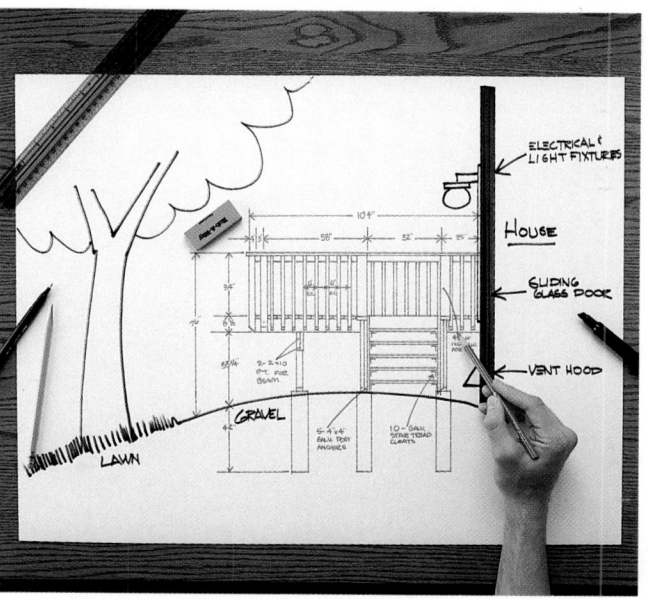

2 Add the stairway to the elevation drawing, then draw in the railing posts, balusters, rails and caps. List all dimensions on the drawing, and indicate size, type, and quantities of lumber and hardware needed. Save this drawing for reference.

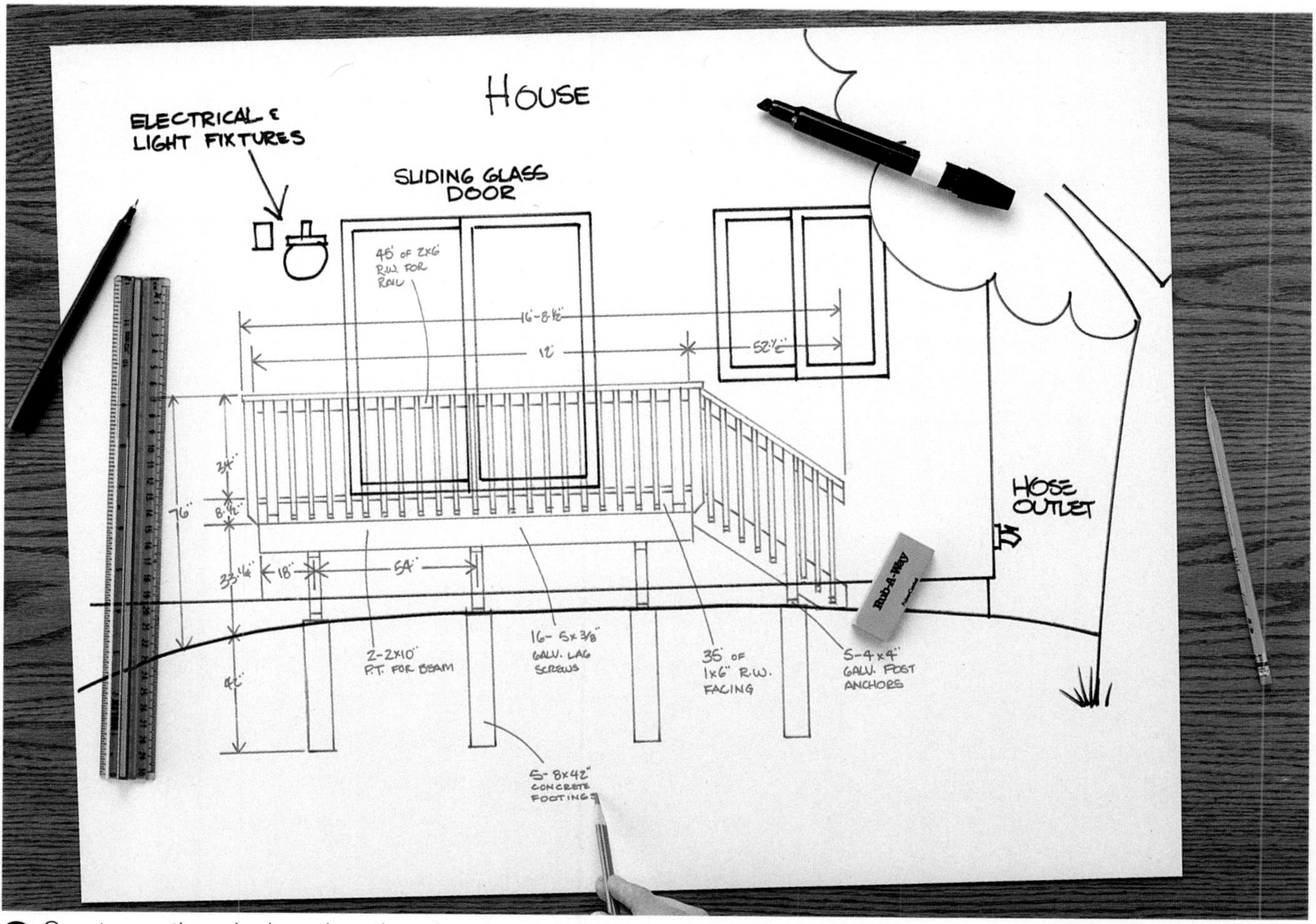

3 Create another design elevation showing the deck as viewed from the front. Include all deck dimensions, and indicate the size and type of lumber and hardware to be used. Save this drawing for reference.

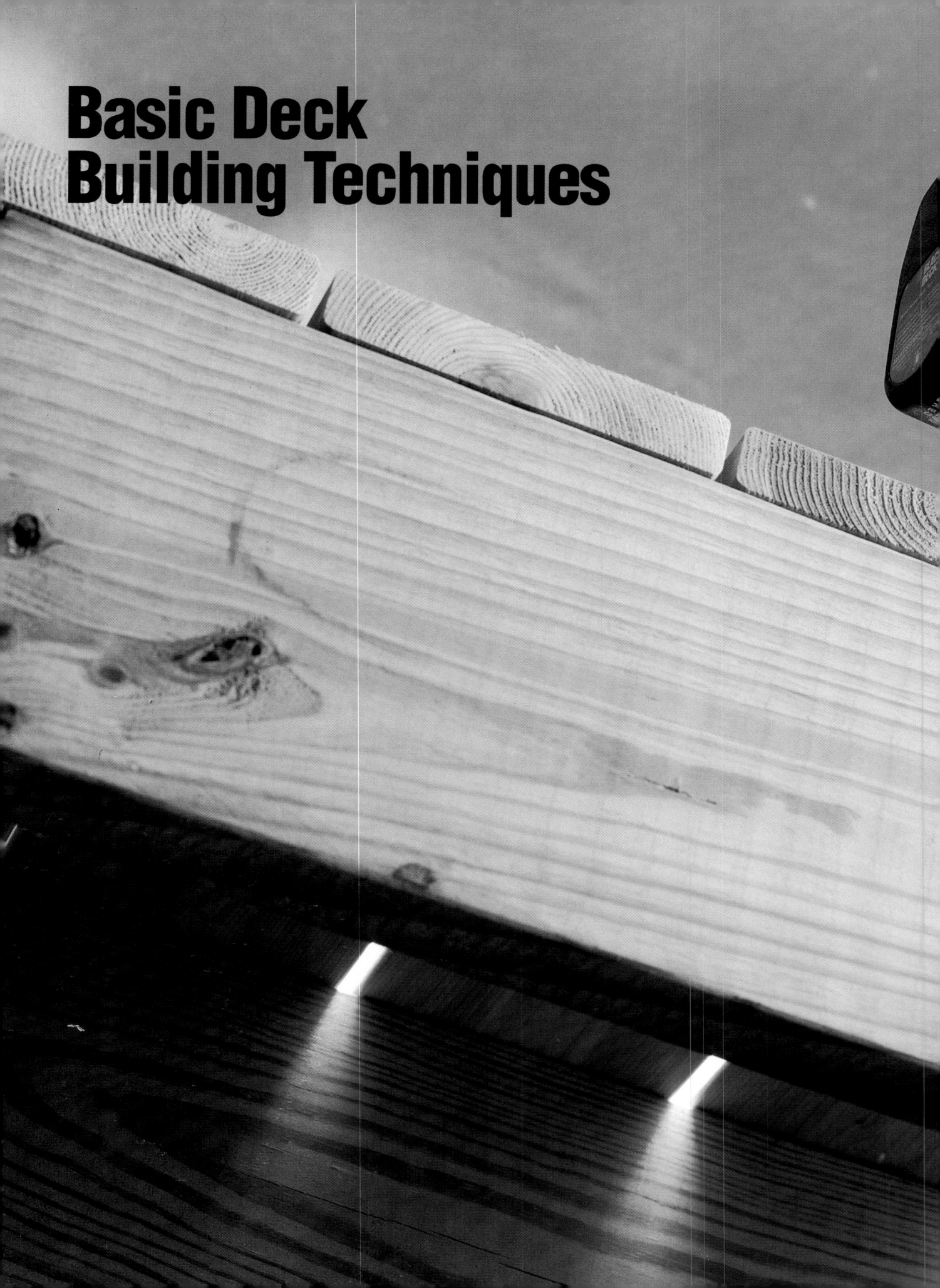

Basic Deck Building Techniques

Building Decks: A Step-by-Step Overview

Review the design plan (pages 50 to 53) and the directions on pages 58 to 115 before beginning deck construction. Build the deck in several stages, and gather tools and materials for each stage before beginning. Arrange to have a helper for the more difficult stages.

Check with local utilities for the location of underground electrical, telephone, or water lines. Apply for a building permit, where required, and make sure a building inspector has approved the deck design before beginning work.

The time it takes to build a deck depends on the size and complexity of the design. A rectangular deck, about 10 ft. × 14 ft., can be completed in two or three weekends.

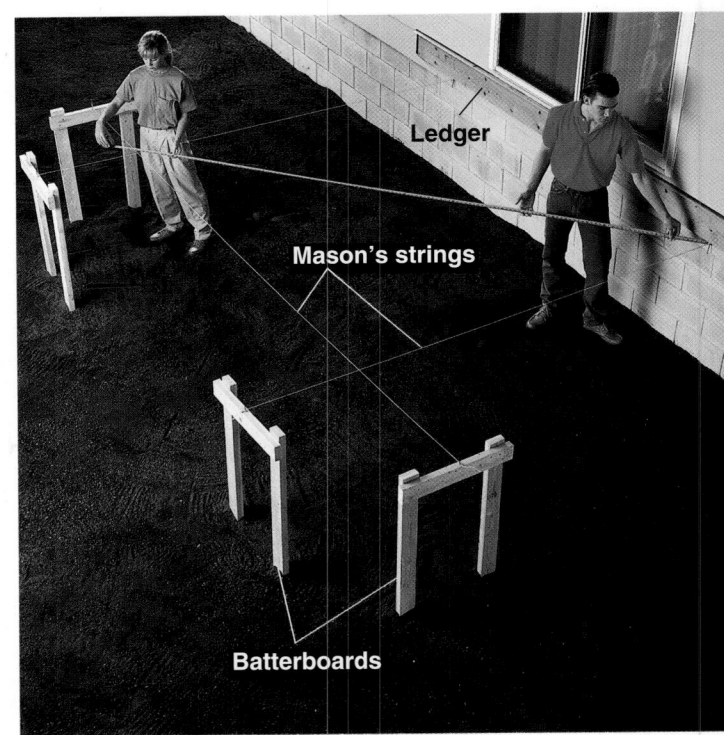

1 Install a ledger to anchor the deck to the house and to serve as reference for laying out footings (pages 58 to 63). Use batterboards and mason's strings to locate footings, and check for square by measuring diagonals (pages 64 to 69).

2 Pour concrete post footings (pages 70 to 73), and install metal post anchors (pages 75 to 76). Set and brace the posts, attach them to the post anchors, and mark posts to show where beam will be attached (pages 76 to 79).

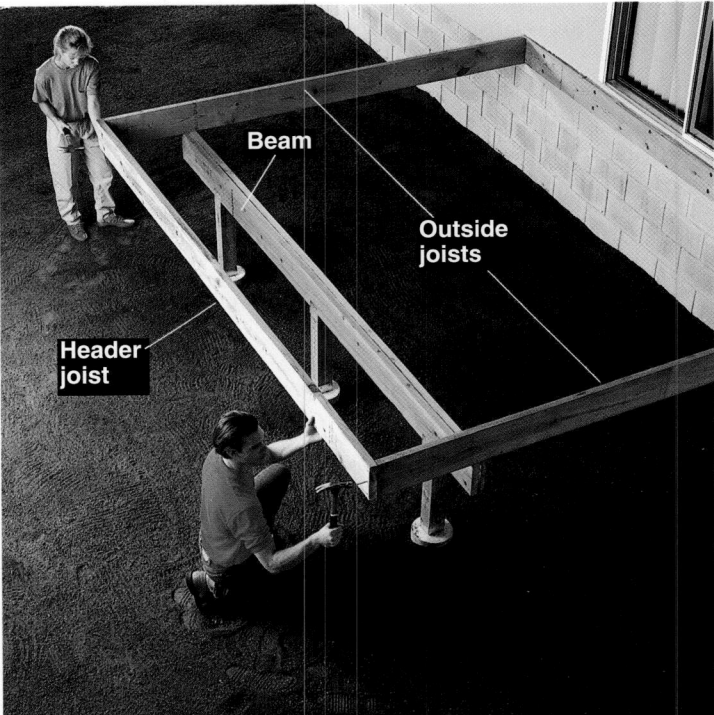

3 Fasten the beam to the posts (pages 80 to 85). Install the outside joists and header joist, using galvanized nails (pages 86 to 87).

4 Install metal joist hangers on the ledger and header joist, then hang the remaining joists (pages 88 to 91). Most decking patterns require joists that are spaced 16" on center.

5 Lay decking boards, and trim them with a circular saw (pages 92 to 95). If desired for appearance, cover pressure-treated header and outside joists with redwood or cedar facing boards (page 95).

6 Build deck stairs (pages 102 to 107). Stairs provide access to the deck and establish traffic patterns.

7 Install a railing around the deck and stairway (pages 108 to 115). A railing adds a decorative touch and may be required on any deck that is more than 24" above the ground.

Installing a Ledger

The first step in building an attached deck is to fasten the ledger to the house. The ledger anchors the deck and establishes a reference point for building the deck square and level. The ledger also supports one end of all the deck joists, so it must be attached securely to the framing members of the house.

Install the ledger so that the surface of the decking boards will be 1" below the indoor floor level. This height difference prevents rainwater or melted snow from seeping into the house.

Everything You Need

Tools: pencil, level, circular saw with carbide blade, chisel, hammer, metal snips, caulk gun, drill and bits (¼" twist, 1" spade, ⅜" and ⅝" masonry), ratchet wrench, awl, rubber mallet.

Materials: pressure-treated lumber, galvanized flashing, 8d galvanized common nails, silicone caulk, ⅜" × 4" lag screws and 1" washers, lead masonry anchors for ⅜" lag screws (for brick walls).

Supplies: 2 × 4s for braces.

Ledger (shown in cross section) is made from pressure-treated lumber. Lap siding is cut away to expose sheathing and to provide a flat surface for attaching the ledger. Galvanized flashing tucked under siding prevents moisture damage to wood. Countersunk ⅜" × 4" lag screws hold ledger to header joist inside house.

How to Attach a Ledger to Lap Siding

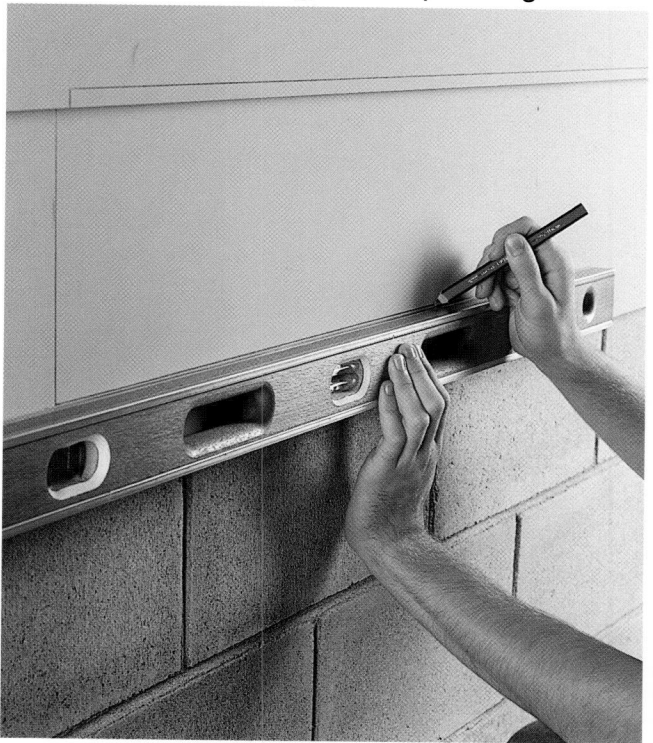

1 Draw an outline showing where the deck will fit against the house, using a level as a guide. Include the thickness of the outside joists and any decorative facing boards that will be installed.

2 Cut out siding along outline, using a circular saw. Set blade depth to same thickness as siding, so that blade does not cut into sheathing.

3 Use a chisel to finish the cutout where circular saw blade does not reach. Hold the chisel with the bevel-side in.

4 Measure and cut ledger from pressure-treated lumber. Remember that ledger will be shorter than overall length of cutout.

(continued next page)

How to Attach a Ledger to Lap Siding (continued)

5 Cut galvanized flashing to length of cutout, using metal snips. Slide flashing up under siding.

6 Center the ledger in the cutout, underneath the flashing. Brace in position, and tack ledger into place with 8d galvanized nails. Apply a thick bead of silicone caulk to crack between siding and flashing.

7 Drill pairs of ¼" pilot holes spaced every 2 feet, through the ledger and sheathing and into the header joist.

8 Counterbore each pilot hole to ½" depth, using a 1" spade bit.

9 Attach ledger to wall with ⅜" × 4" lag screws and washers, using a ratchet wrench.

10 Seal lag screw heads with silicone caulk. Seal the crack between the wall and the sides and bottom of the ledger.

How to Attach a Ledger to Masonry

1 Measure and cut ledger. Ledger will be shorter than overall length of outline. Drill pairs of ¼" pilot holes every 2 feet in ledger. Counterbore each pilot hole to ½" depth, using a 1" spade bit.

2 Draw a outline of the deck on the wall, using a level as a guide. Center ledger in outline on wall, and brace in position. Mark the pilot hole locations on wall, using an awl or nail. Remove ledger.

(continued next page)

How to Attach a Ledger to Masonry (continued)

3 Drill anchor holes 3" deep into masonry, using a ⅝" masonry bit.

4 Drive lead masonry anchors for ⅜" lag screws into drilled holes, using a rubber mallet.

5 Attach ledger to wall with ⅜" × 4" lag screws and washers, using a ratchet wrench. Tighten screws firmly, but do not overtighten.

6 Seal the cracks between the wall and ledger with silicone caulk. Also seal the lag screw heads.

How to Attach a Ledger to Stucco

1 Draw outline of deck on wall, using a level as a guide. Measure and cut ledger, and drill pilot holes (page 61, step 1). Brace ledger against wall, and mark hole locations, using a nail or awl.

2 Remove ledger. Drill pilot holes through stucco layer of wall, using a ⅜" masonry bit.

3 Extend each pilot hole through the sheathing and into the header joist, using a ¼" bit. Reposition ledger and brace in place.

4 Attach ledger to wall with ⅜" × 4" lag screws and washers, using a ratchet wrench. Seal the lag screw heads and the cracks between the wall and ledger with silicone caulk.

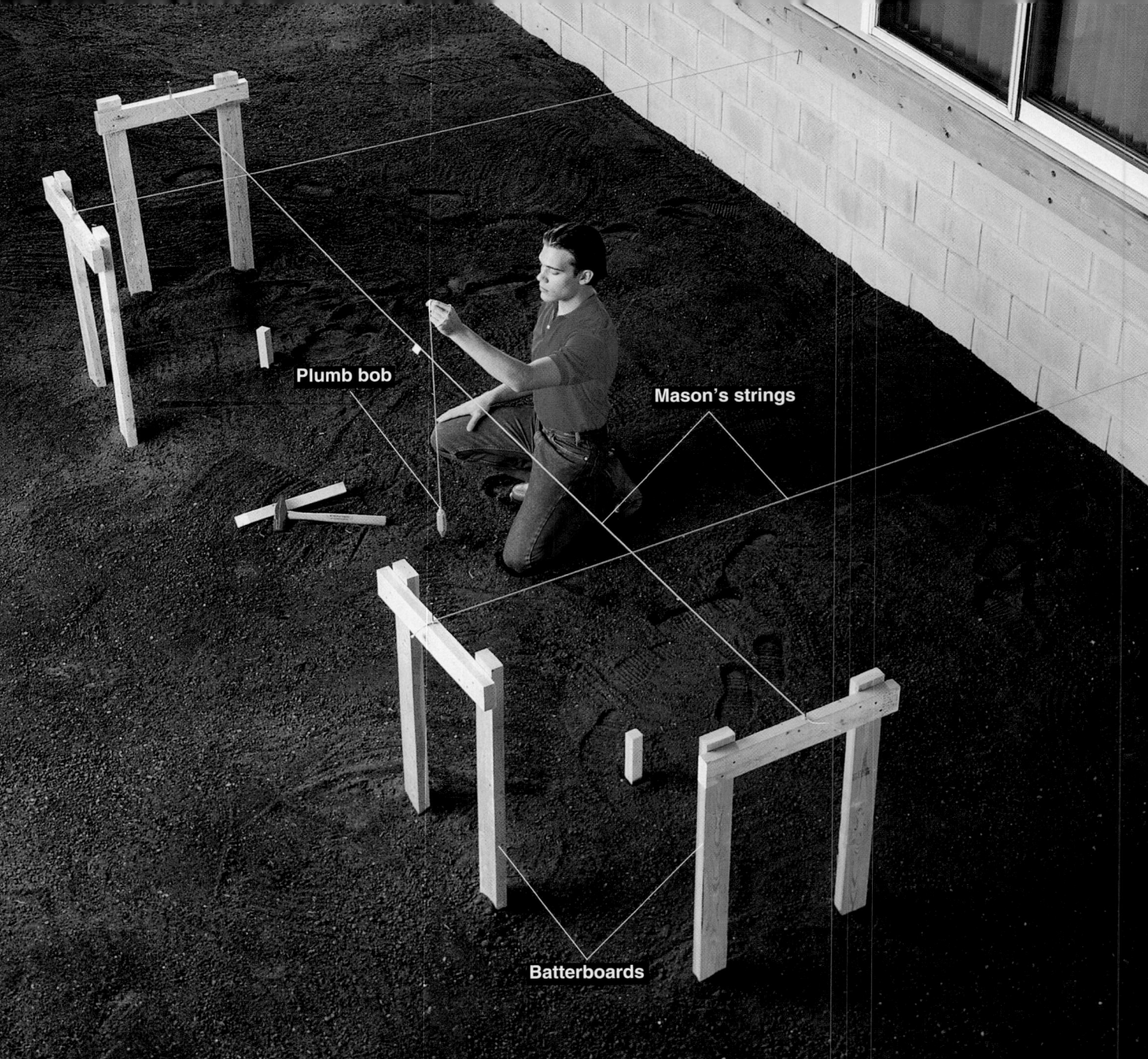

Plumb bob

Mason's strings

Batterboards

Mason's strings stretched between ledger and batterboards are used to position footings for deck posts. Use a plumb bob and stakes to mark the ground at the exact centerpoints of footings.

Locating Post Footings

Establish the exact locations of all concrete footings by stretching mason's strings across the site. Use the ledger board as a starting point. These perpendicular layout strings will be used to locate holes for concrete footings, and to position metal post anchors on the finished footings. Anchor the layout strings with temporary 2 × 4 supports, often called batterboards.

Everything You Need

Tools: tape measure, felt-tipped pen, circular saw, screwgun, framing square, masonry hammer, claw hammer, line level, plumb bob.

Supplies: 2 × 4s, 10d nails, 2½" wallboard screws, mason's strings, masking tape.

How to Locate Post Footings

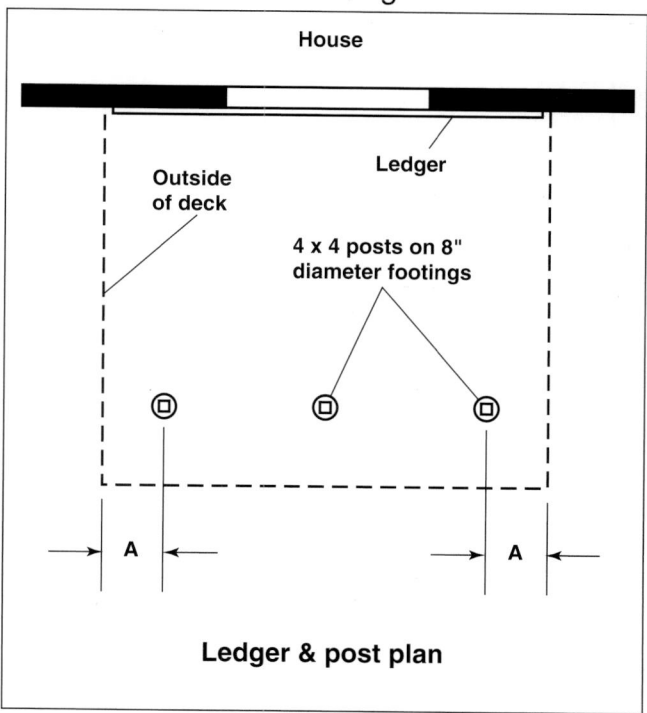

House

Ledger

Outside of deck

4 x 4 posts on 8" diameter footings

A

A

Ledger & post plan

1 Use the design plan (page 52) to find distance (A). Measure from the side of the deck to the center of each outside post. Use the elevation drawings (page 53) to find the height of each deck post.

2 Cut 2 × 4 stakes for batterboards, each about 8" longer than post height. Trim one end of each stake to a point, using a circular saw. Cut 2 × 4 crosspieces, each about 2 feet long.

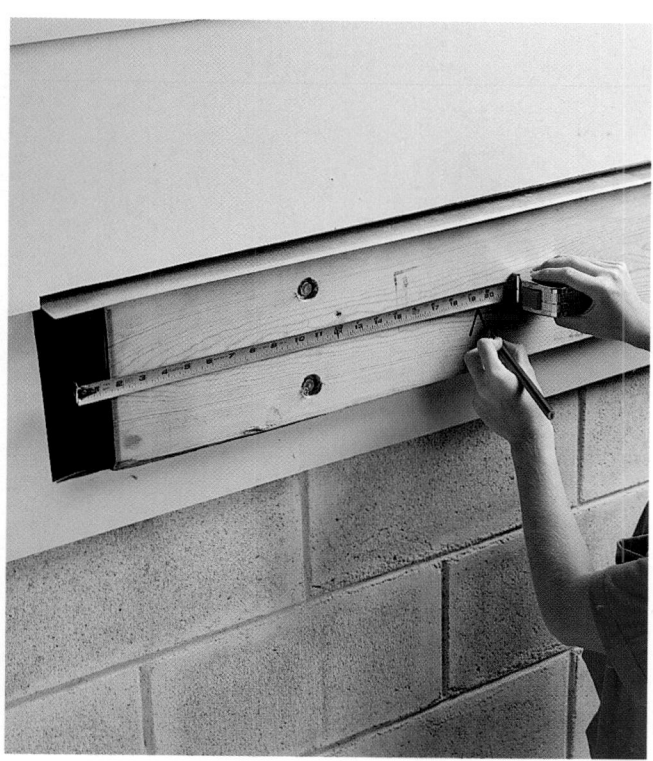

3 Assemble batterboards by attaching crosspieces to stakes with 2½" wallboard screws. Crosspieces should be about 2" below tops of stakes.

4 Transfer measurement A (step 1) to ledger, and mark reference points at each end of ledger. String lines will be stretched from these points on ledger. When measuring, remember to allow for outside joists and facing that will be butted to the ends of the ledger.

(continued next page)

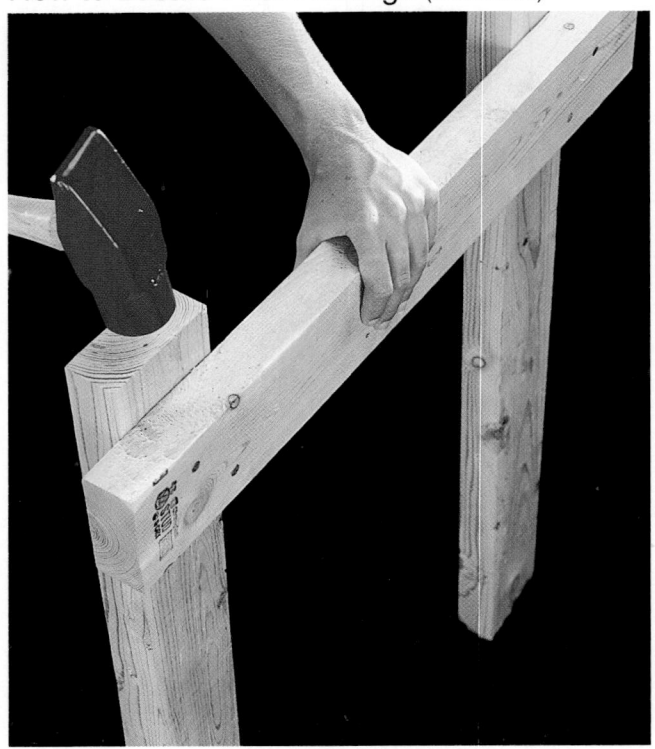

5 Drive a batterboard 6" into the ground, about 2 feet past the post location. Crosspiece of batterboard should be parallel to the ledger.

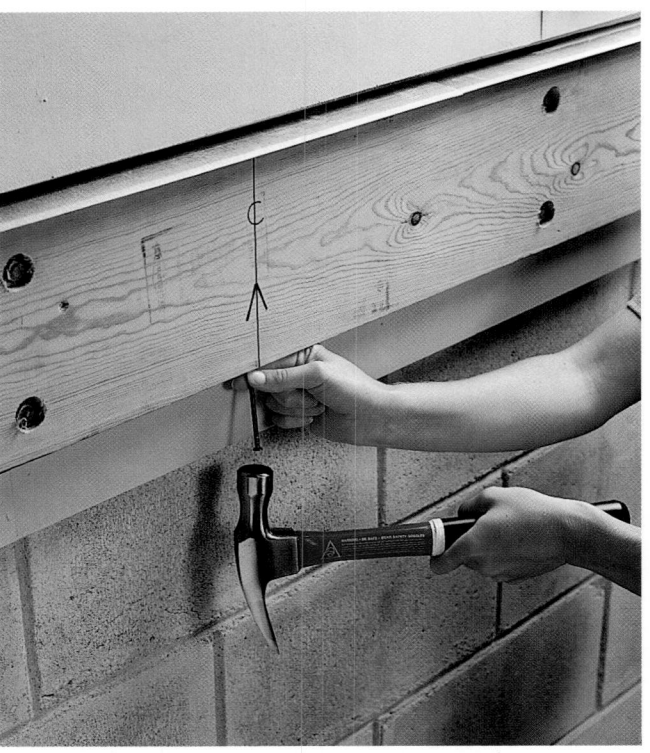

6 Drive a 10d nail into bottom of ledger at reference point (step 4). Attach a mason's string to nail.

7 Extend the mason's string so that it is taut and perpendicular to the ledger. Use a framing square as a guide. Secure the string temporarily by wrapping it several times around the batterboard.

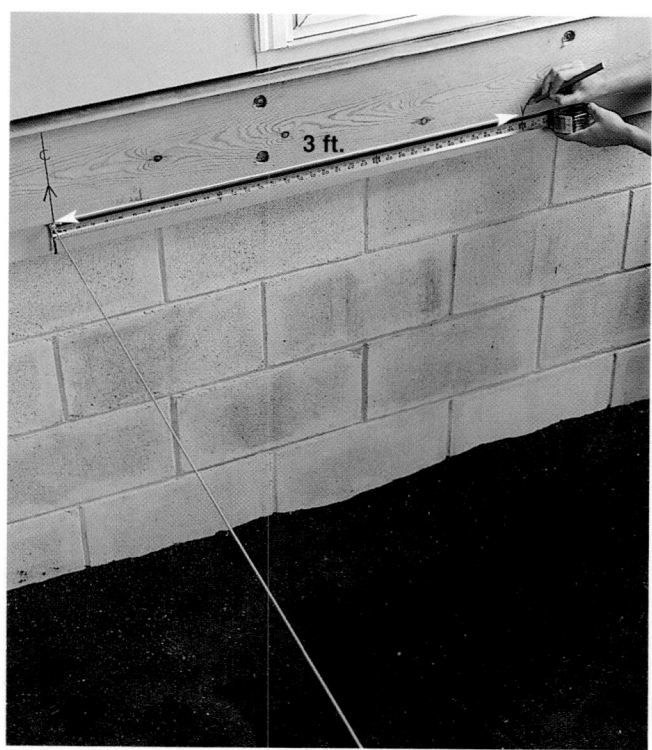

8 Check the mason's string for square using "3-4-5 carpenter's triangle." First, measure along the ledger 3 feet from the mason's string and mark a point, using a felt-tipped pen.

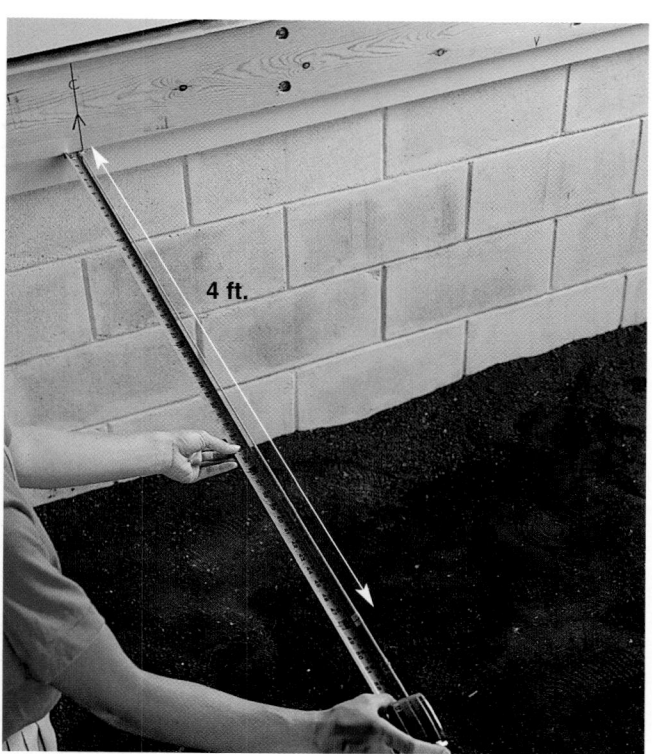

9 Measure mason's string 4 feet from edge of ledger, and mark with masking tape.

10 Measure distance between marks. If string is perpendicular to ledger, the distance will be exactly 5 feet. If necessary, move string left or right on batterboard until distance between marks is 5 feet.

11 Drive a 10d nail into top of batterboard at string location. Leave about 2" of nail exposed. Tie string to nail.

(continued next page)

How to Locate Post Footings (continued)

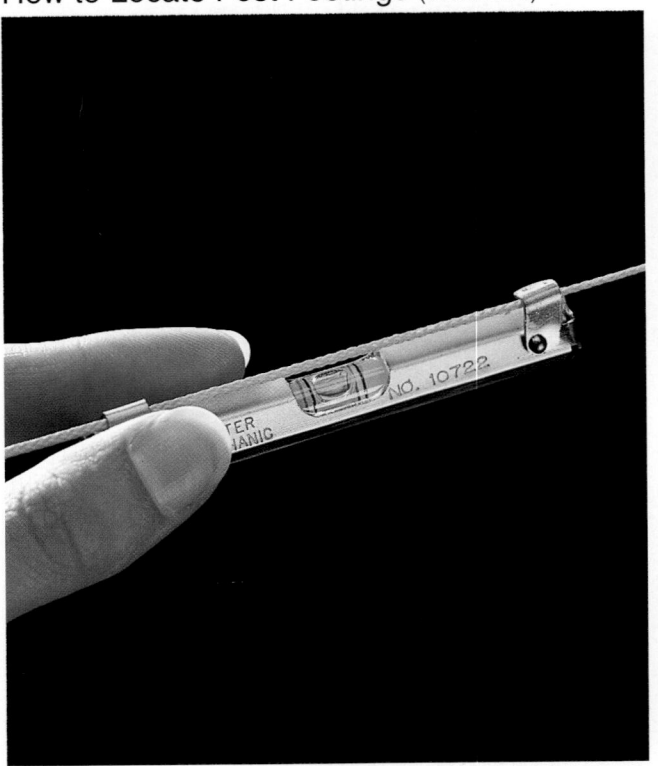

12 Hang a line level on the mason's string. Raise or lower string until it is level. Locate other outside post footing, repeating steps 5 to 12.

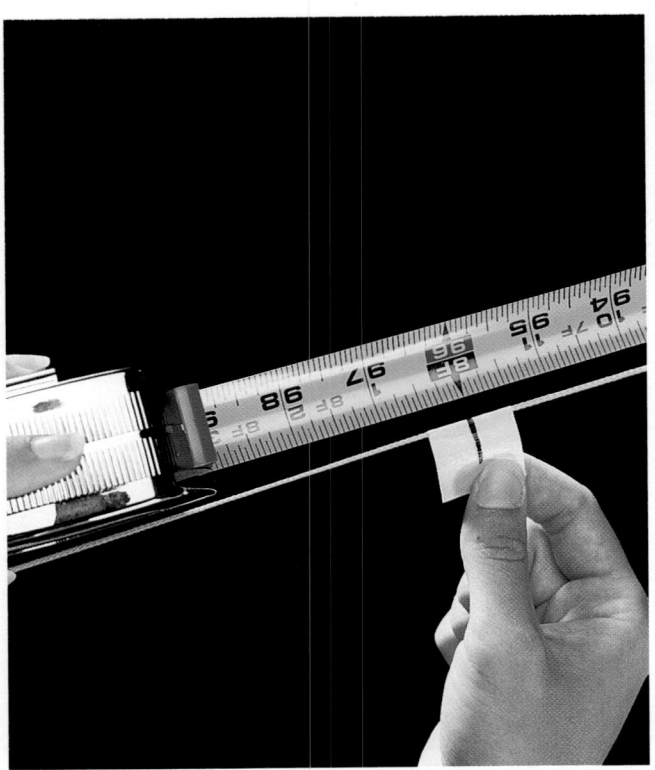

13 Measure along mason's strings from ledger to find centerpoint of posts. Mark centerpoints on stings, using masking tape.

14 Drive additional batterboards into ground, about 2 feet outside mason's strings and lined up with post centerpoint marks (step 13).

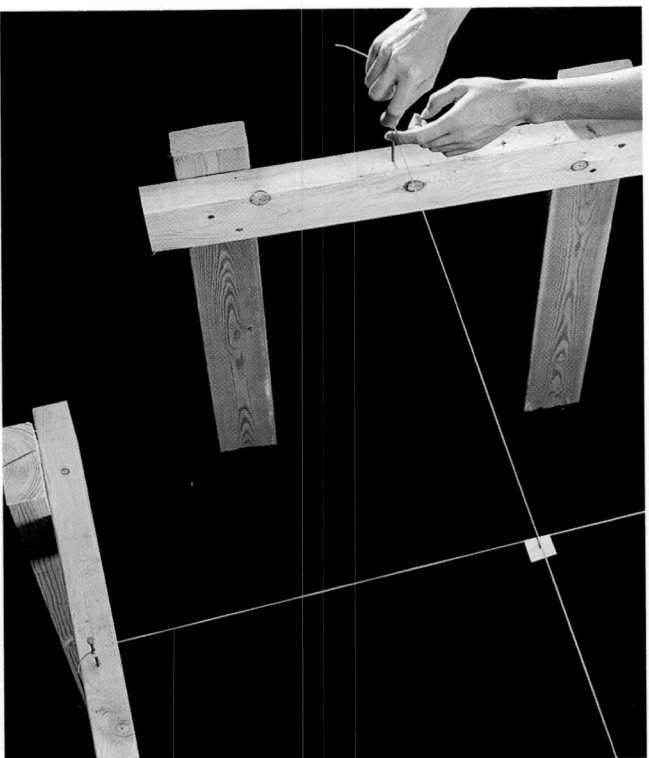

15 Align a third cross string with the centerpoint marks on the first strings. Drive 10d nails in new batterboards, and tie off cross string on nails. Cross string should be close to, but not touching, the first strings.

16 Check strings for square by measuring distances A-B and C-D. Measure diagonals A-D and B-C from edge of ledger to opposite corners. If strings are square, measurement A-B will be same as C-D, and diagonal A-D will be same as B-C. If necessary, adjust strings on batterboards until square.

17 Measure along the cross string and mark center-points of any posts that will be installed between the outside posts.

18 Use a plumb bob to mark post centerpoints on the ground, directly under the marks on the mason's strings. Drive a stake into ground at each point. Remove mason's strings before digging footings.

Digging & Pouring Footings

Concrete footings hold deck posts in place and support the weight of the deck. Check local codes to determine the size and depth of footings required for your area. In cold climates, footings must be deeper than the soil frost line.

To help protect posts from water damage, each footing should be poured so that it is 2" above ground level. Tube-shaped forms let you extend the footings above ground level.

It is easy and inexpensive to mix your own concrete by combining portland cement, sand, gravel, and water. See pages 32 to 33 for more information on buying and mixing concrete.

Before digging, consult local utilities for location of any underground electrical, telephone, or water lines that might interfere with footings.

Everything You Need

Tools: power auger or clamshell posthole digger, tape measure, pruning saw, shovel, reciprocating saw or handsaw, torpedo level, hoe, trowel, shovel, old toothbrush, plumb bob, utility knife.

Materials: 8" concrete tube forms, portland cement, sand, gravel, J-bolts.

Supplies: wheelbarrow, scrap 2 × 4.

Power augers quickly dig holes for post footings. They are available at rental centers. Some models can be operated by one person, while others require two people.

How to Dig & Pour Post Footings

1 Dig holes for post footings with a clamshell digger or power auger, centering the holes on the layout stakes. For holes deeper than 35", use a power auger.

2 Measure hole depth. Local building codes specify depth of footings. Cut away tree roots, if necessary, using a pruning saw.

3 Pour 2" to 3" of loose gravel in the bottom of each footing hole. Gravel will provide drainage under concrete footings.

4 Add 2" to hole depth so that footings will be above ground level. Cut concrete tube forms to length, using a reciprocating saw or handsaw. Make sure cut is straight.

5 Insert tubes into footing holes, leaving about 2" of tube above ground level. Use a level to make sure tops of tubes are level. Pack soil around tubes to hold them in place.

(continued next page)

6 Mix dry ingredients for concrete in a wheelbarrow, using a hoe.

7 Form a hollow in center of dry concrete mixture. Slowly pour a small amount of water into hollow, and blend in dry mixture with a hoe.

8 Add more water gradually, mixing thoroughly until concrete is firm enough to hold its shape when sliced with a trowel.

9 Pour concrete slowly into tube form, guiding concrete from wheelbarrow with a shovel. Use a long stick to tamp the concrete, filling any air gaps in the footing.

10 Level the concrete by pulling a 2 × 4 across the top of the tube form, using a sawing motion. Add concrete to any low spots. Retie the mason's strings on the batterboards, and recheck measurements.

11 Insert a J-bolt at an angle into the wet concrete at center of the footing.

12 Lower the J-bolt slowly into the concrete, wiggling it slightly to eliminate any air gaps.

13 Set the J-bolt so ¾" to 1" is exposed above concrete. Brush away any wet concrete on bolt threads with an old toothbrush.

14 Use a plumb bob to make sure the J-bolt is positioned exactly at center of post location.

15 Use a torpedo level to make sure the J-bolt is plumb. If necessary, adjust the bolt and repack concrete. Let concrete cure, then cut away exposed portion of tube with a utility knife.

Setting Posts

Posts support the deck beams and transfer the weight of the deck to the concrete footings. For maximum strength, the posts must be plumb.

To prevent rot or insect damage, use pressure-treated lumber for posts, and make sure the factory-treated end faces down.

Use metal post anchors to attach the posts to the concrete footings. Post anchors have drainage holes and pedestals that raise the ends of the wood posts above the concrete footings.

Everything You Need

Tools: pencil, framing square, ratchet wrench, tape measure, power miter saw or circular saw, hammer, screwgun, level, combination square.

Materials: metal post anchors, nuts for J-bolts, lumber for posts, 6d galvanized common nails, 2" wallboard screws.

Supplies: long, straight 2 × 4; 1 × 4s; pointed 2 × 2 stakes.

How to Attach Post Anchors

1 Mark the top of each footing as a reference line for installing post anchors. Lay a long, straight 2 × 4 flat across two or three concrete footings, parallel to the ledger, with one edge tight against the J-bolts.

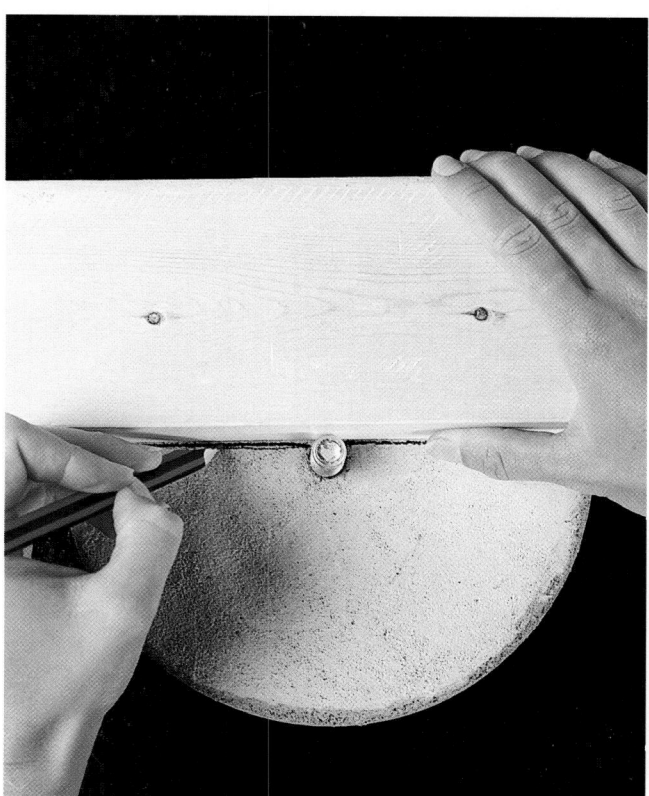

2 Draw a reference line across each concrete footing, using a edge of the 2 × 4 as a guide. Remove the 2 × 4.

3 Place a metal post anchor on each concrete footing, and center it over the J-bolt.

(continued next page)

How to Attach Post Anchors (continued)

4 Use a framing square to make sure the post anchor is positioned square to the reference line drawn on the footing.

5 Thread a nut over each J-bolt, and tighten it securely with a ratchet wrench.

How to Set Posts

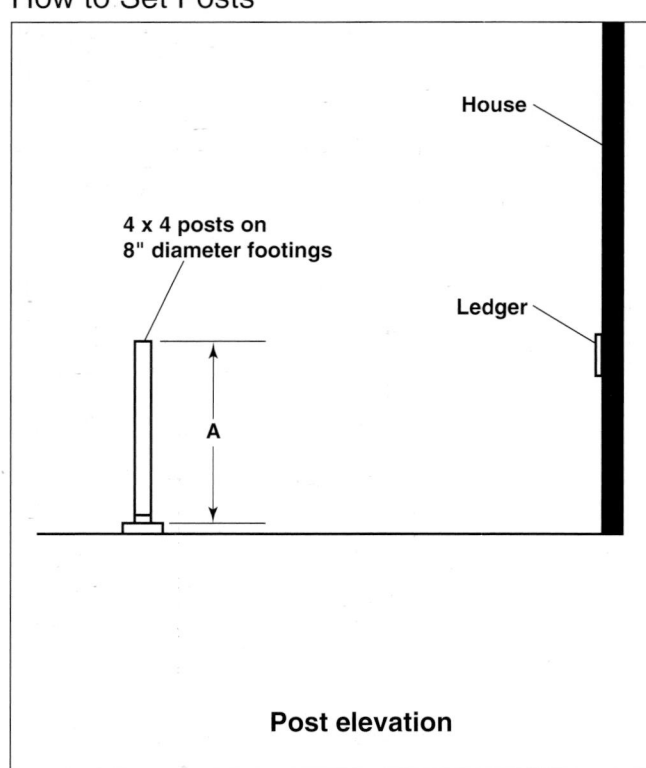

House

4 x 4 posts on
8" diameter footings

Ledger

A

Post elevation

1 Use the elevation drawing from the design plan (page 53) to find the length of each post (A). Add 6" for a cutting margin.

2 Cut posts with power miter saw or circular saw. Make sure factory-treated ends of posts are square. If necessary, square them by trimming with a power miter saw or circular saw, and then paint the cut edges with sealer/preservative.

3 Place the metal pedestal into the anchor, then set the post on top of the pedestal. Tack the post to the anchor with a single 10d or 16d joist hanger nail.

4 Brace post with a 1 × 4. Place the 1 × 4 flat across post, so that it crosses the post at a 45° angle about halfway up.

5 Attach the brace to the post temporarily with a single 2" wallboard screw.

6 Drive a pointed 2 × 2 stake into the ground next to the end of the brace.

(continued next page)

7 Use a level to make sure the post is plumb. Adjust the post, if necessary.

8 Attach the brace to the stake with two 2" wallboard screws.

9 Plumb and brace the post on the side perpendicular to the first brace.

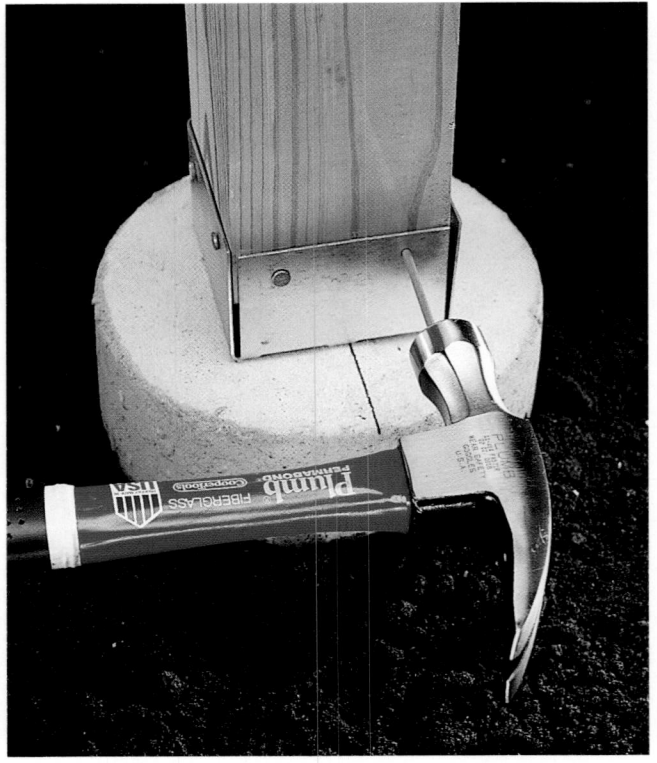

10 Attach the post to the post anchor with 10d or 16d joist hanger nails.

11 Position a straight 2 × 4 with one end on the ledger and the other end across the face of the post. Level the 2 × 4, then lower its post end ¼" for every 3 ft. between the ledger and the post (for water runoff). Draw a line on the post along the bottom of the 2 × 4. This line indicates the top of the joists.

12 From the line shown in step 11, measure down and mark the posts a distance equal to the width of the joists.

13 Use a square to draw a line completely around the post. This line indicates the top of the beam. From this line, repeat steps 12 and 13 to determine the bottom of the beam.

Installing a Beam

Use metal post-beam caps to secure deck beams to post tops. Post-beam caps ensure strong post to beam joints, and are required by many local building codes.

Everything You Need

Tools: tape measure, pencil, circular saw, paint brush, combination square, screwgun, drill, ⅜" auger bit, 1" spade bit, ratchet wrench, caulk gun, reciprocating saw or handsaw.

Materials: pressure-treated lumber, clear sealer-preservative, 2½" galvanized deck screws, 10d joist hanger nails, ⅜" × 8" carriage bolts with washers and nuts, ⅜" × 2" lag screws, silicone caulk.

Deck beams attach to the posts to help support the weight of the joists and decking. Installation methods depend on the deck design and local codes, so check with a building inspector to determine what is acceptable in your area.

In a saddle beam deck, the beam is attached directly on top of the posts. Metal fasteners, called post-beam caps, are used to align and strengthen the beam-to-post connection. The advantage is that the post bears the weight of the deck.

A notched-post deck requires 6 × 6 posts notched at the post top to accommodate the full size of the beam. The deck's weight is transferred to the posts, as in a post-and-beam deck.

A sandwich beam has two beam members that are sandwiched around posts. Because this method has less strength than a saddle beam design, local codes may restrict its use, or may require that the beam members be reinforced with joist ties (step 2, page 146).

How to Prepare a Beam for Installation

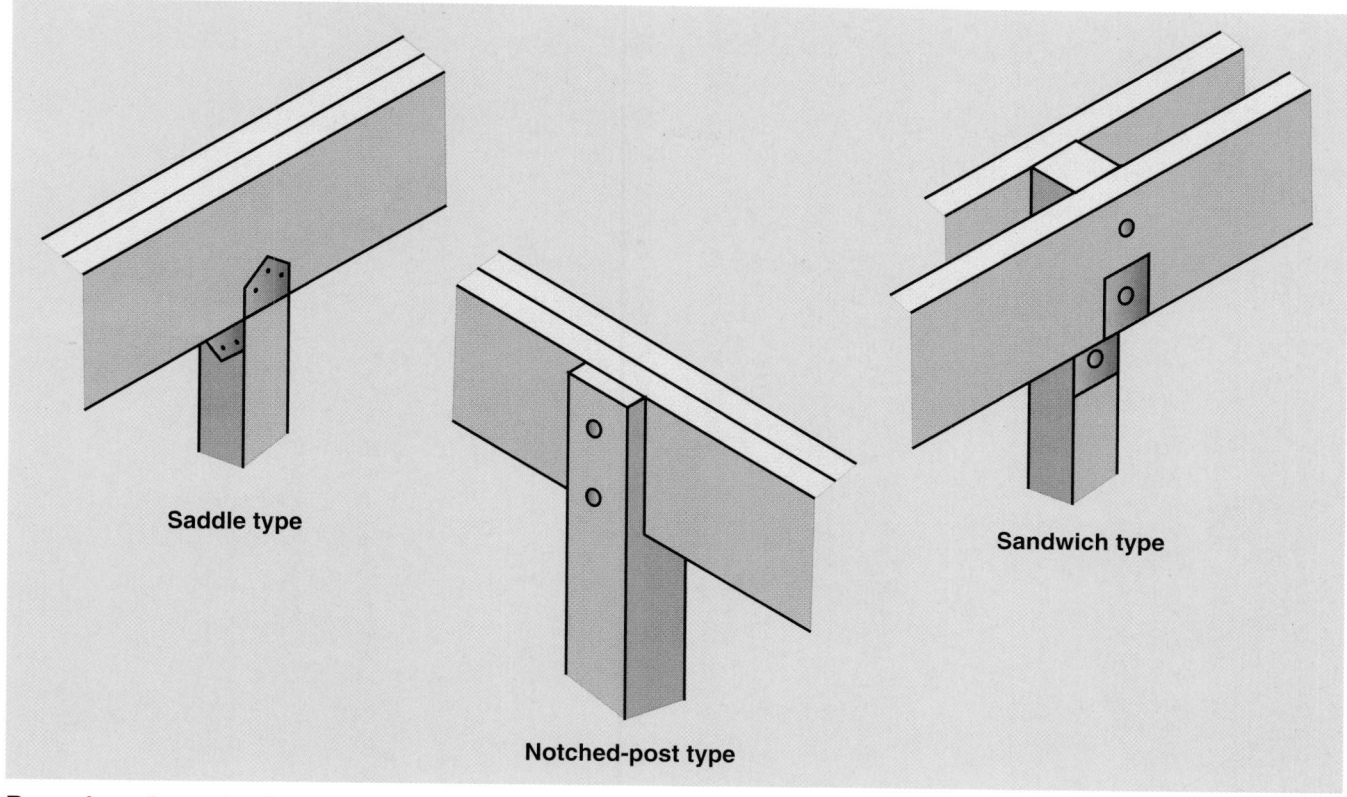

Saddle type

Notched-post type

Sandwich type

Beam length can be found in the deck design plan (page 52). Three methods of beam installation are shown above. Check with a building inspector in your area to determine which method is acceptable.

1 Measure and mark two straight pressure-treated boards to length. Cut boards with a circular saw. Seal cut ends with clear sealer-preservative.

2 Hold beam boards together. Measure and mark the post locations on the tops and sides of boards, using a combination square as a guide.

81

How to Install a Beam for a Saddle Beam Deck

1 Cut each post at the line indicating the bottom of the beam (page 79), using a reciprocating saw.

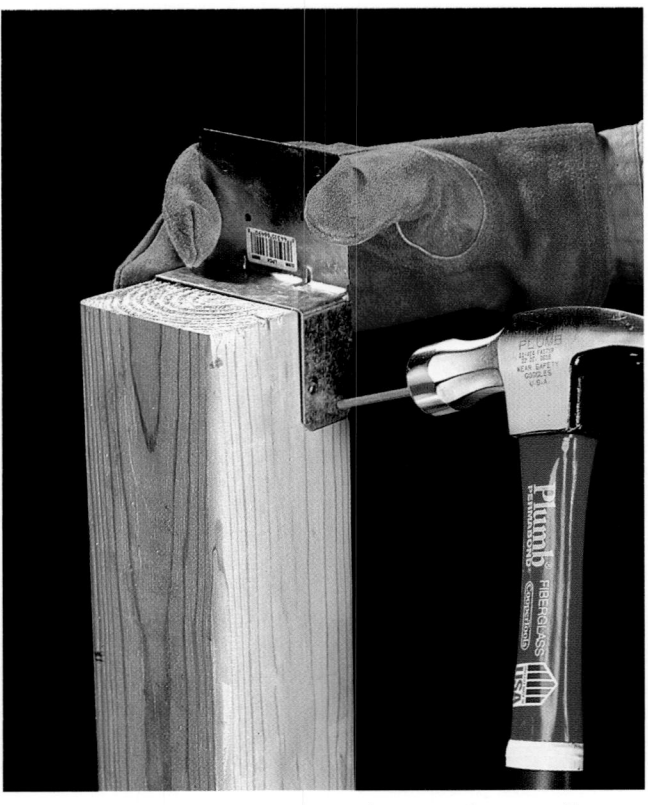

2 Attach post-beam caps to the top of posts. Fasten on opposite sides, using 10d joist hanger nails.

3 With someone's help, lift the beam into the post-beam caps. Make sure the crown side is up. Align the post location marks with the post-beam caps.

4 Fasten the post-beam cap to the beam on both sides, using 10d joist hanger nails

How to Install a Beam for a Notched-Post Deck

1 Remove 6 × 6 posts from post anchors and cut to finished height. Measure and mark a 3" × 7½" notch at the top of each post. Trace the lines on all sides, using a framing square.

2 Use a circular saw to rough-cut the notches, then a reciprocating saw or hand saw to finish. Reattach posts to the post anchors (pages 76-78), with the notch-side facing away from the deck.

3 With someone's help, lift beam (crown side up) into the notches. Align beam and clamp to posts. Counterbore two ½"-deep holes, using a 1" spade bit, then drill ⅜" pilot holes through the beam and post, using a ⅜" auger bit.

4 Insert carriage bolts to each pilot hole. Add a washer and nut to the counterbore-side of each, and tighten using a ratchet. Seal both ends with silicone caulk.

How to Install a Beam for a Sandwich Beam Deck

1 With the crown side up, place one beam member against the inner side of posts. Align post location marks on beam member with beam height marks on posts. Tack in position with 2½" deck screws. Repeat for second beam member on the outer side of posts.

2 On the inner beam member, counterbore two holes ½" deep, using 1" spade bit.

3 At the center of the counterbore holes, drill ⅜" pilot holes through the entire beam-post-beam assembly, using a ⅜" auger bit.

4 Thread a ⅜" × 8" carriage bolt through each pilot hole, with a washer and nut on the inner side with the counterbore. Tighten with a rachet wrench until the nut is snug and recessed in the counterbore hole.

5 Seal around the nuts in the counterbore holes with silicone caulk.

6 Cut tops of posts flush with top edge of beam, using a reciprocating saw or handsaw. Seal cut ends of posts with clear sealer-preservative. Reinforce beam members with joist ties (step 3, page 146).

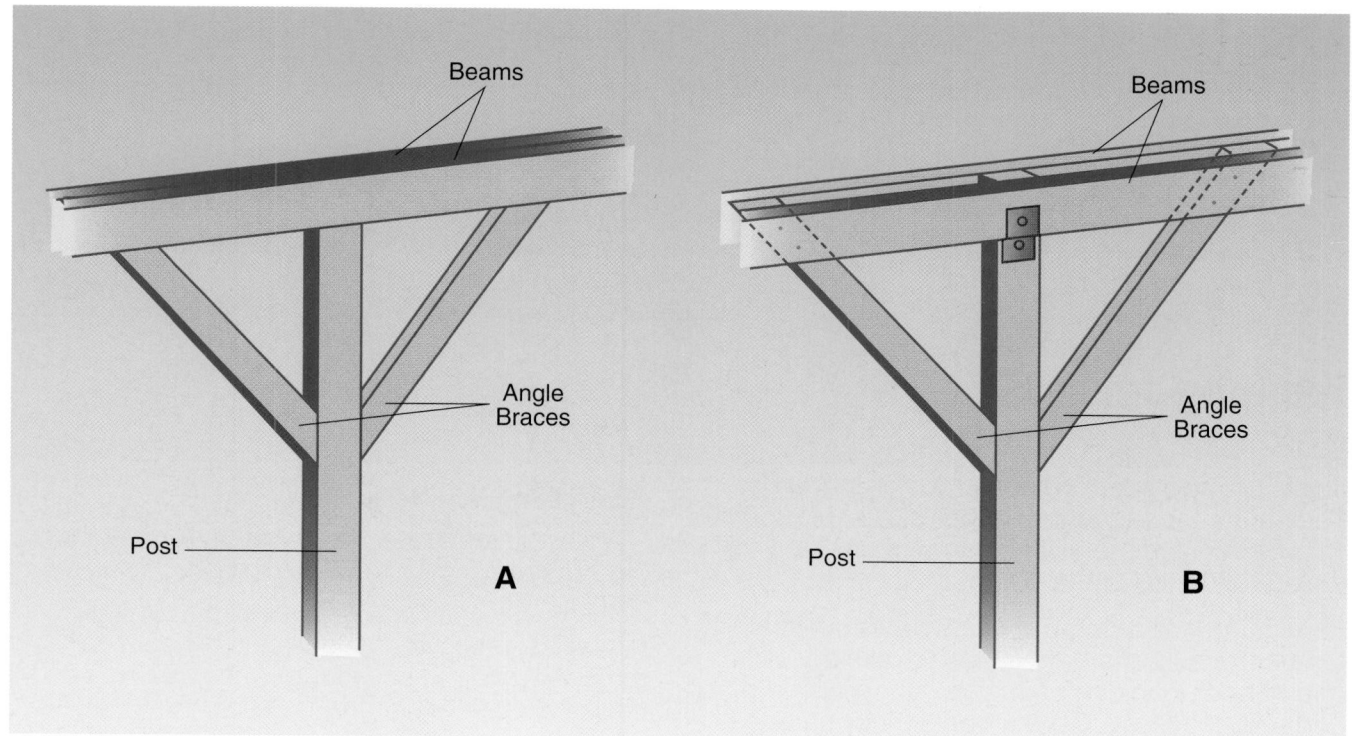

Reinforce elevated decks with beveled 4 × 4 Y-braces. For a solid beam (A), attach with lag screws to the sides of the post and the bottom of the beam. On a sandwich beam (B), use carriage bolts to mount the braces in between the two beam members.

Hanging Joists

Joists provide support for the decking boards. They are attached to the ledger and header joist with galvanized metal joist hangers, and are nailed to the top of the beam.

For strength and durability, use pressure-treated lumber for all joists. The exposed outside joists and header joist can be faced with redwood or cedar boards for a more attractive appearance (page 95).

Everything You Need

Tools: tape measure, pencil, hammer, combination square, circular saw, paintbrush, drill, twist bits (1/16", 1/4"), 1" spade bit.

Materials: pressure-treated lumber, clear sealer-preservative, 10d and 16d galvanized common nails, 10d joist hanger nails, joist angle brackets, galvanized metal joist hangers, 3/8" × 4" lag screws and 1" washers.

How to Hang Joists

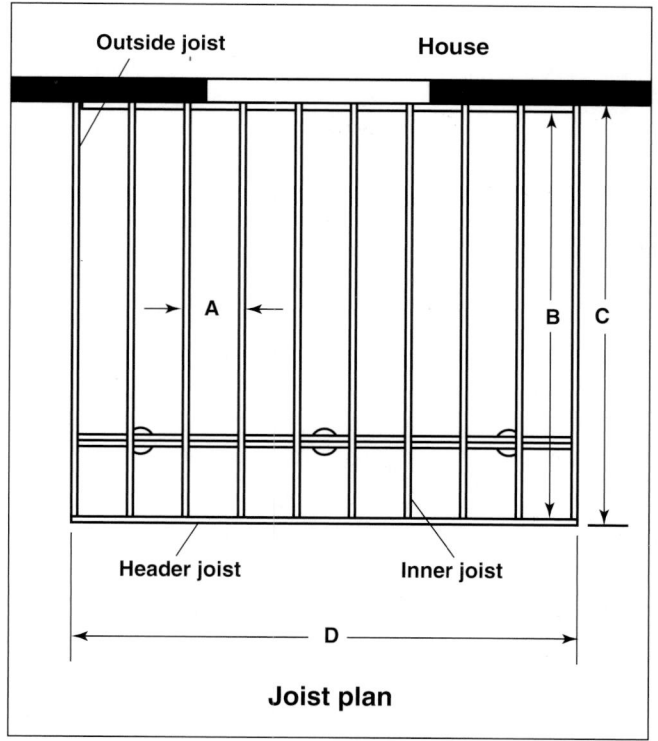

Joist plan

1 Use the design plan (page 52) to find the spacing (A) between joists, and the length of inner joists (B), outside joists (C), and header joist (D). Measure and mark lumber for outside joists, using a combination square as a guide. Cut joists with a circular saw. Seal cut ends with clear sealer-preservative.

2 Drill three ⅟₁₆" pilot holes, spaced about 3" apart, through one end of each outside joist.

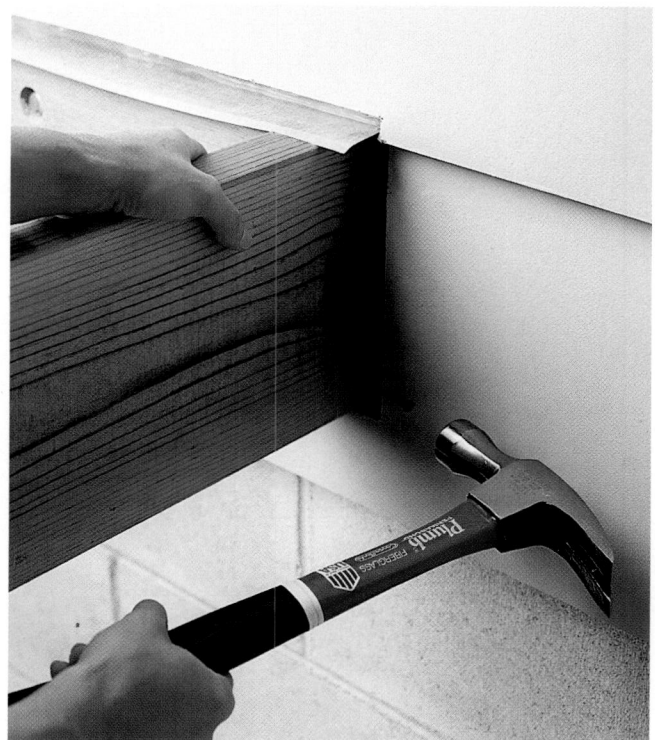

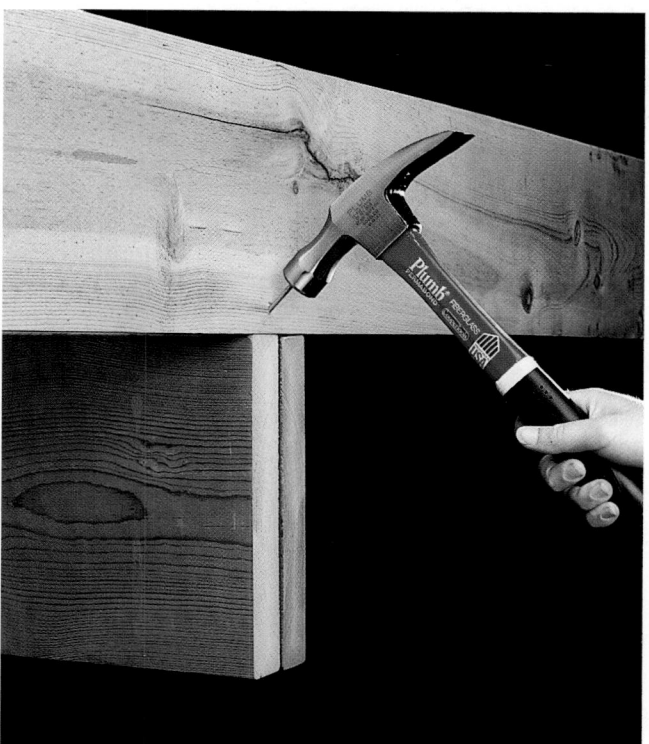

3 Fasten the outside joists in position at ends of ledger with 16d galvanized common nails driven into the ledger.

4 Attach the outside joists to the top of the beam by toenailing them with 10d galvanized common nails.

(continued next page)

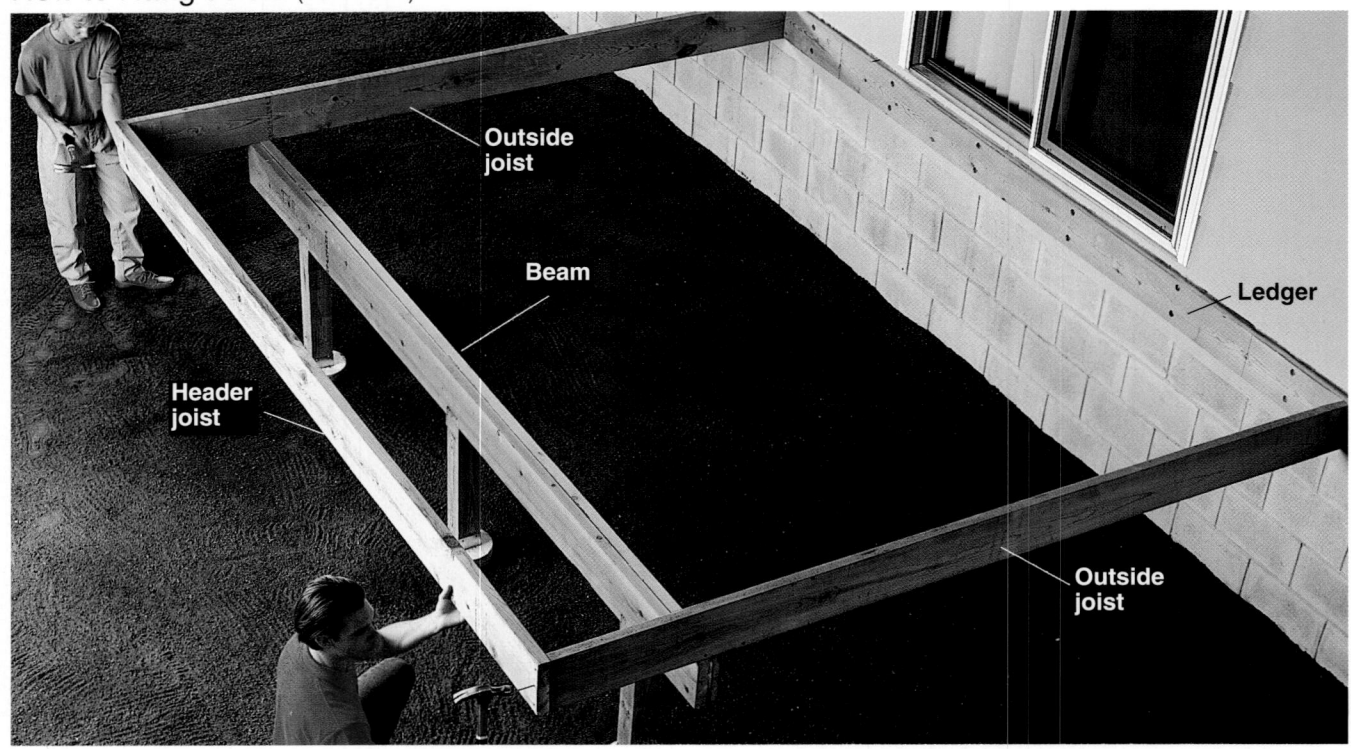

5 Measure and cut header joist. Seal cut ends with clear sealer-preservative. Drill 1/16" pilot holes at each end of header joist. Attach header to ends of outside joists with 16d galvanized common nails.

6 Strengthen each inside corner of the deck frame with an angle bracket. Attach the brackets with 10d joist hanger nails

7 Measure along ledger from edge of outside joist, and mark where joists will be attached to ledger.

8 Draw the outline of each joist on the ledger, using a combination square as a guide.

9 Measure along the beam from outside joist, and mark where joists will cross the beam. Draw the outlines across top of both beam boards.

10 Measure along the header joist from the outside joist, and mark where joists will be attached to header joist. Draw the outlines on the inside of the header, using a combination square as a guide.

11 Attach joist hangers to the ledger and to the header joist. Position each hanger so that one of the flanges is against the joist outline. Nail flanges to framing member with 10d galvanized common nails.

(continued next page)

12 Cut a scrap board to use as a spacer. Hold spacer inside each joist hanger, then close the hanger around the spacer.

13 Nail the remaining side flange to the framing member with 10d joist hanger nails. Remove spacer.

14 Measure and mark lumber for joists, using a combination square as a guide. Cut joists with a circular saw.

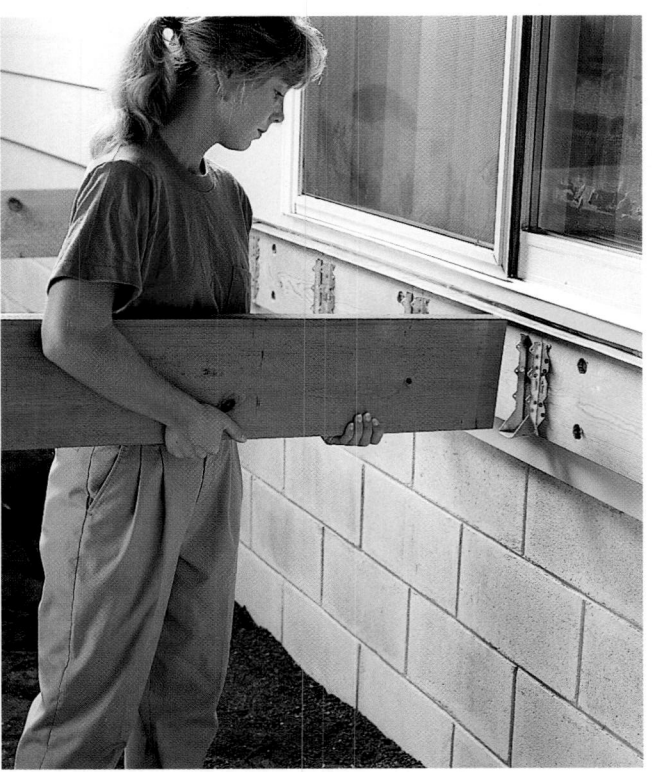

15 Seal cut ends with clear sealer-preservative. Place joists in hangers with crowned side up.

16 Attach the ledger joist hangers to the joists with 10d joist hanger nails. Drive nails into both sides of each joist.

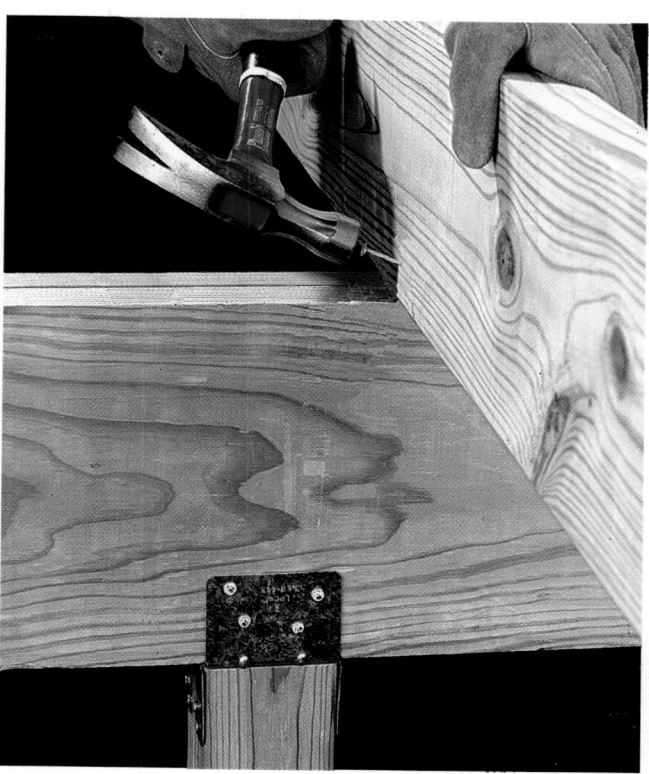

17 Align the joists with the outlines drawn on the top of the beam. Anchor the joists to the beam by toenailing from both sides with 10d galvanized nails.

Alternate method: Fasten joists to beams using H-fit joist ties for strength and durability.

18 Attach the joists to the header joist hangers with 10d joist hanger nails. Drive nails into both sides of each joist.

Laying Decking

Buy decking boards that are long enough to span the width of the deck, if possible. If boards must be butted end-to-end, make sure to stagger the joints so they do not overlap from row to row. Predrill the ends of boards to prevent screws or nails from splitting the wood.

Install decking so that there is a ⅛" gap between boards to provide drainage. Boards naturally "cup" as they age (page 29). Lay boards with the bark side facing down, so that the cupped surface cannot hold standing water.

Everything You Need

Tools: tape measure, circular saw, screwgun, hammer, drill, ⅛" twist bit, pry bar, chalk line, jig saw or handsaw.

Materials: decking boards, 2½" corrosion-resistant deck screws, galvanized common nails (8d, 10d), redwood or cedar facing boards.

How to Lay Decking

1 Position the first row of decking flush against the house. First decking board should be perfectly straight, and should be precut to proper length. Attach the first decking board by driving a pair of 2½" corrosion-resistant deck screws into each joist.

2 Position remaining decking boards so that ends overhang outside joists. Space boards about ⅛" apart. Attach boards to each joist with a pair of 2½" deck screws driven into each joist.

Alternate method: Attach decking boards with 10d galvanized common nails. Angle the nails toward each other to improve holding power.

(continued next page)

3 If boards are bowed, use a pry bar to lever them into position while fastening.

4 Drill ⅛" pilot holes in ends of boards before attaching them to outside joists. Pilot holes prevent screws from splitting decking boards at ends.

5 After every few rows of decking are installed, measure from edge of the decking board to edge of header joist. If measurements show that the last board will not fit flush against the edge of the deck, adjust board spacing.

6 Adjust board spacing by changing the gaps between boards by a small amount over three or four rows of boards, Very small spacing changes will not be obvious to the eye.

7 Use a chalk line to mark the edge of decking flush with the outside of deck. Cut off decking, using a circular saw. Set saw blade ⅛" deeper than thickness of decking so that saw will not cut side of deck. At areas where circular saw cannot reach, finish cutoff with a jig saw or handsaw.

8 For a more attractive appearance, face the deck with redwood or cedar facing boards. Miter-cut corners, and attach boards with deck screws or 8d galvanized nails.

Alternate facing technique: Attach facing boards so that edges of decking overhang facing.

Decking Materials: Alternatives to Wood

Composite materials

PVC vinyl

Fiberglass reinforced plastic (FRP)

A variety of alternative decking materials on the market offer lower-maintenance alternatives to wood. Although these materials may initially be more expensive than wood, they often carry lifetime warranties and can be cheaper than wood over the long run.

Composite materials blend together wood fibers and recycled plastics to create a rigid product that, unlike wood, will not rot, splinter, warp, or crack. Painting or staining is unnecessary. Like wood, these deck boards can be cut to size, using a circular saw with a large tooth blade.

PVC vinyl and plastic decking materials are shipped in kits that contain everything necessary to install the decking other than the deck screws. The kits are pre-ordered to size, usually in multiples of the combined width of a deck board and the fasteners. The drawback of PVC vinyl decking is that it expands and contracts with freeze/thaw cycles.

Fiberglass reinforced plastic (FRP) decking will last a lifetime. Manufacturers claim that the material is three times as strong as wood and not affected by heat, sunlight, or severe weather. The decking is pre-ordered to size but if necessary, it can be cut using a circular saw with diamond-tip blade or masonry blade.

Aluminum decking systems are considerably more expensive than other wood alternatives and are not widely available, but they offer sturdy, lightweight, and waterproof outdoor flooring. Simple decking designs are very easy to install, although more elaborate designs and floor patterns can be quite difficult.

Most of these products are specifically designed with the do-it-yourselfer in mind. Though the installation methods and fastening systems vary from manufacturer to manufacturer, most are designed to accommodate standard building dimensions, such as 16" joist spacing.

Prior to placing an order for any material, check with your local building department. Some areas may require a permit or have restrictions against certain materials. Also remember: these are general installation instructions. Always follow the installation methods recommended by the manufacturer of the product you select.

Photo courtesy of MasterMark Plastics

Plastic/wood composites are available in colors that complement any wood tone. The decking is installed with screws driven through the top of the deck boards into the joists, in the same way as standard lumber.

Photo courtesy of Timbertech

Other plastic/wood composites use a tongue-and-groove system for fastening deck boards to the joists. This blind-screw method leaves no holes in the deck floor.

Photo courtesy of EON Outdoor Systems, Inc.

PVC vinyl and plastic deck materials also use a blind-screw method. A T-clip system simplifies installation and creates a uniform decking pattern.

Photo courtesy of Pultronex Corporation / EZ Deck

Fiberglass decking is installed with retaining clips, so each deck board snaps easily into place. The result is a sturdy structure that will last a lifetime.

How to Lay Composite Decking

1 Lay composite decking as you would wood decking (pages 93-95). Position with the factory crown up so water will run off, and space rows ⅛" to ¼" apart for drainage.

2 Pre-drill pilot holes at ¾ the diameter of the fasteners, but do not countersink. Composite materials allow fasteners to set themselves. Use spiral shank nails, hot-dipped galvanized ceramic coated screws, or stainless steel nails or deck screws.

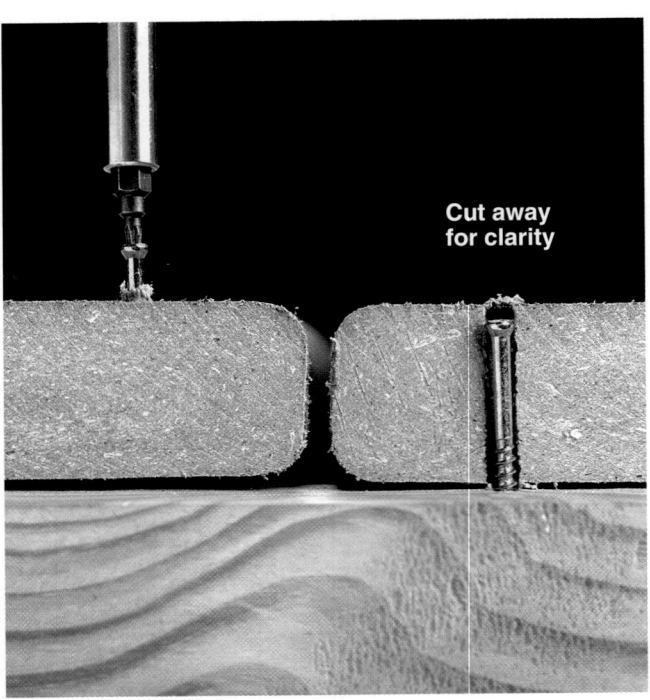

Cut away for clarity

Alternate method: Attach composite decking with self-tapping composite screws. These specially designed screws require no pilot holes. If the decking "mushrooms" over the screw head, use a hammer to tap back in place.

3 Lay remaining decking. For boards 16-ft. or shorter, leave a gap at deck ends and any butt joints, ¹⁄₁₆" for every 20°F difference between the temperature at the time of installation and the expected high temperature for the year.

How to Install Tongue-and-Groove Decking

1 Position starter strip at far end of deck. Make sure it is straight and properly aligned. Attach with 2½" galvanized deck screws driven into the lower runner found under the lip of the starter strip.

2 Fit tongue of a deck board into groove of starter strip. There will be approximately a ¼" gap between the deck board and the starter strip. Fasten the deck board to the joists with 2½" galvanized deck screws, working from the middle out to the sides of the deck.

3 Continue to add decking. To lay deck boards end-to-end, leave a ⅛" gap between them, and make sure any butt joints are centered over a joist.

4 Place final deck board and attach with 2½" galvanized deck screws driven through top of the deck board into the joist. If necessary, rip final board to size, then support the board with a length of 1 × 1 and attach both to the joist. Attach facing boards to conceal exposed ends (page 95).

How to Lay Decking with a T-clip System

1 Insert 2" galvanized deck screws into T-clips. Loosely attach one T-clip to the ledger at each joist location.

2 Position a deck board tight against the T-clips. Loosely attach T-clips against bottom lip on front side of deck board, just tight enough to keep the board in place. Fully tighten T-clips at back of board, against the house.

3 Push another deck board tightly against the front T-clips, attach T-clips at front of the new board, then fully tighten the previous set of T-clips. Add another deck board and repeat the process, to the end of the deck.

4 Cover exposed deck board ends. Miter-cut corners of the facing and drill pilot holes ¾ the diameter of the screws. Attach with 3" galvanized deck screws.

How to Install a Fiberglass Decking System

1 Place a length of retaining clips on top of the first joist. Center it on the joist and fasten with 2" galvanized deck screws. Attach lengths of retaining clips to the subsequent joists, so that the clips are perfectly aligned with the first length of clips, creating straight rows.

2 Place the open face of a decking board perpendicular to the joists, resting on top of a row of clips. Apply firm pressure to the top of the deck board until the decking snaps into place over the retaining clips. Work along the row, snapping the deck board in place. Attach the remaining deck boards in place, snapping each onto a row of retaining clips.

3 Cut the over-hanging ends of the decking boards flush with the outside joists, using a circular saw with a fresh carbide-tipped blade or a masonry cut-off disc.

4 Use 2" galvanized deck screws to attach the prefabricated facing, covering the exposed hollow ends and creating a decorative trim. Cover the screw heads with the screw caps.

Building Stairs

Building deck stairs requires four calculations.

Number of steps depends on the vertical drop of the deck. The vertical drop is the distance from the surface of the deck to the ground.

Rise is the vertical space between treads. Building codes require that the rise measurement be about 7".

Run is the depth of the treads. A convenient way to build deck stairs is to use a pair of 2 × 6s for each tread.

Span is figured by multiplying the run by the number of treads. The span lets you locate the end of the stairway, and position support posts.

Everything You Need

Tools: tape measure, pencil, framing square, level, plumb bob, clamshell posthole digger, wheelbarrow, hoe, circular saw, hammer, drill, ⅛" twist bit, 1" spade bit, ratchet wrench, caulk gun.

Materials: sand, portland cement, gravel, J-bolts, metal post anchors, 2 × 12 lumber, metal cleats, ¼" × 1¼" lag screws, joist angle brackets, 10d joist hanger nails, ⅜" × 4" lag screws and 1" washers, 2 × 6 lumber, 16d galvanized common nails, silicone caulk.

Supplies: long, straight 2 × 4; pointed stakes; masking tape.

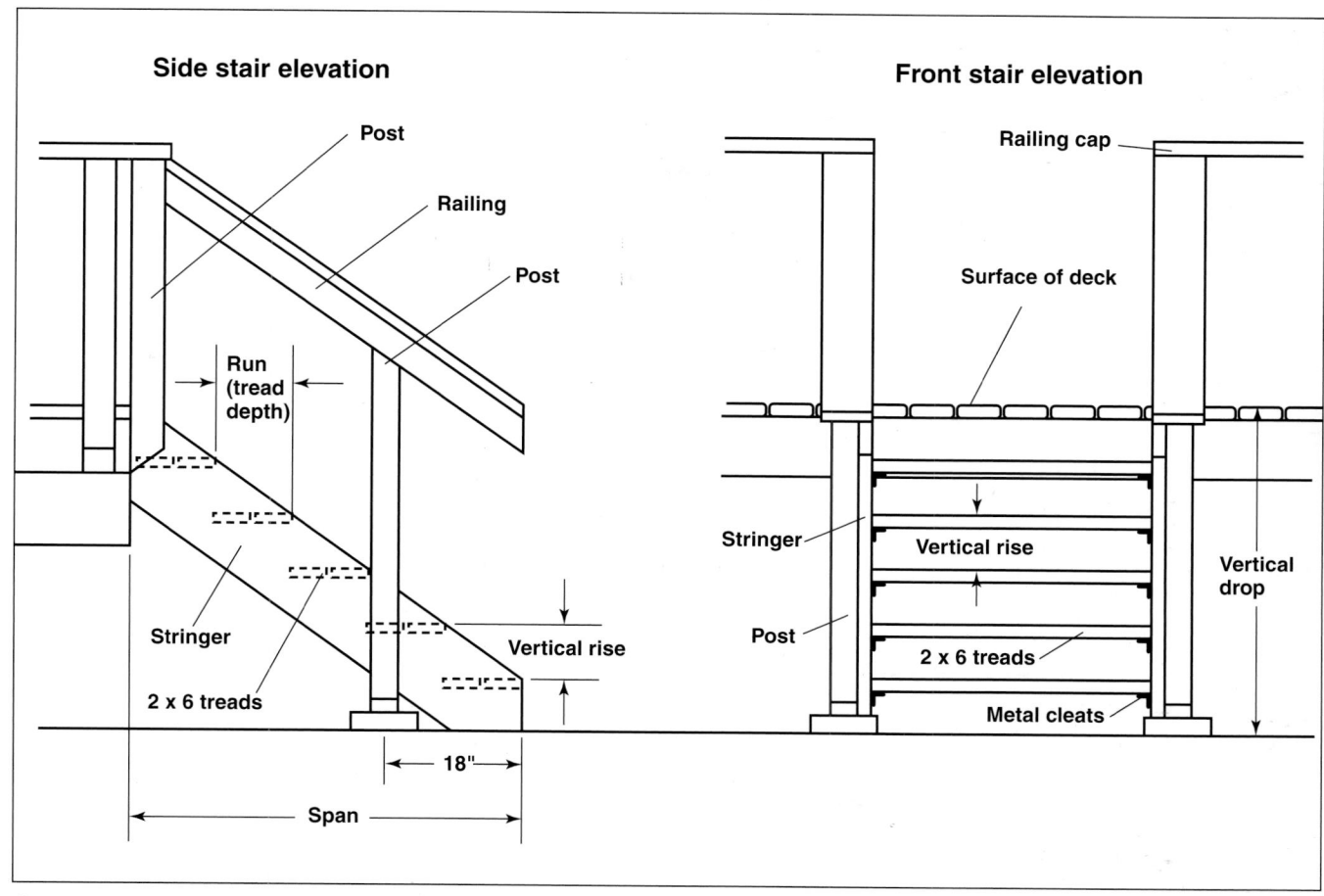

Side stair elevation

Post

Railing

Post

Run (tread depth)

Stringer

2 x 6 treads

Vertical rise

18"

Span

Front stair elevation

Railing cap

Surface of deck

Stringer

Vertical rise

Post

2 x 6 treads

Metal cleats

Vertical drop

A common deck stairway is made from two 2 × 12 stringers, and a series of 2 × 6 treads attached with metal cleats. Posts set 18" back from the end of the stairway help to anchor the stringers and the railings. Calculations needed to build stairs include the number of steps, the rise of each step, the run of each step, and the stairway span.

How to Find Measurements for Stairway Layout

			Sample Measurements (39" High Deck)	
1. Find the number of steps: Measure vertical drop from deck surface to ground. Divide by 7. Round off to nearest whole number.	Vertical drop:			39"
	÷ 7 =			5.57"
	Number of steps:	=		= 6
2. Find step rise: Divide the vertical drop by the number of steps.	Vertical drop:			39"
	Number of steps:	÷		÷ 6
	Rise:	=		= 6.5"
3. Find step run: Typical treads made from two 2 × 6s have a run of 11¼". If your design is different, find run by measuring depth of tread, including any space between boards.	Run:			11¼"
4. Find stairway span: Multiply the run by the number of treads. (Number of treads is always one less than number of steps.)	Run:			11¼"
	Number of treads:	×		× 5
	Span:	=		= 56¼"

How to Build Deck Stairs

1 Use the stairway elevation drawings (page 103) to find measurements for stair stringers and posts. Use a pencil and framing square to outline where stair stringers will be attached to the side of the deck.

2 Locate the post footings so they are 18" back from the end of stairway span. Lay a straight 2 × 4 on the deck so that it is level and square to side of deck. Use a plumb bob to mark the ground at centerpoints of footings.

3 Dig holes and pour footings for posts (pages 70 to 73). Attach metal post anchors to footings and install 4 × 4 posts (pages 74 to 79).

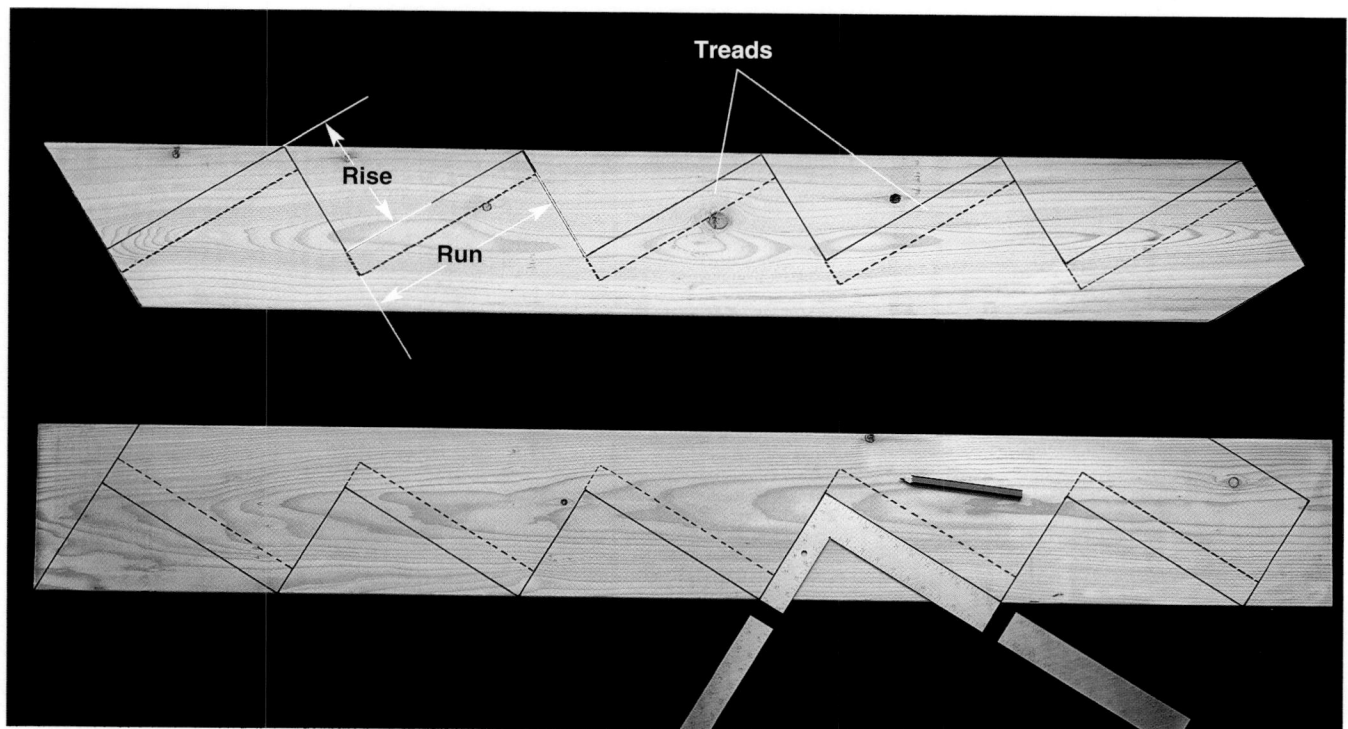

Treads

Rise

Run

4 Lay out stair stringers. Use tape to mark the rise measurement on one leg of a framing square, and the run measurement on the other leg. Beginning at one end of stringer, position the square with tape marks flush to edge of board, and outline the rise and run for each step. Then draw in the tread outline against the bottom of each run line. Use a circular saw to trim ends of stringers as shown.

5 Attach metal tread cleats flush with bottom of each tread outline, using ¼" × 1¼" lag screws. Drill ⅛" pilot holes to prevent the screws from splitting the wood.

6 Attach angle brackets to upper ends of stringers, using 10d joist hanger nails. Brackets should be flush with cut ends of stringers.

(continued next page)

7 Position the stair stringers against side of deck, over the stringer outlines. Align top point of stringer flush with the surface of the deck. Attach stringers by nailing the angle brackets to the deck with 10d joist hanger nails.

8 Drill two ¼" pilot holes through each stringer and into each adjacent post. Counterbore each hole to depth of ½", using a 1" spade bit. Attach stringers to posts with ⅜" × 4" lag screws and washers, using a ratchet wrench. Seal screw heads with silicone caulk.

9 Measure width of stair treads. Cut two 2 × 6s for each tread, using a circular saw.

10 For each step, position the front 2 × 6 on the tread cleat, so that the front edge is flush with the tread outline on the stringers.

11 Drill ⅛" pilot holes, then attach the front 2 × 6s to the cleats with ¼" × 1¼" lag screws.

12 Position the rear 2 × 6s on the cleats, allowing a small space between boards. Use a 16d nail as a spacing guide. Drill ⅛" pilot holes, and attach 2 × 6s to cleats with ¼" × 1¼" lag screws.

Stair Variations

Notched stringers precut from pressure-treated wood are available at building centers. Edges of cutout areas should be coated with sealer-preservative to prevent rot.

Installing a Deck Railing

Railings must be sturdy, and firmly attached to the framing members of the deck. Never attach railing posts to the surface decking. Check local building codes for guidelines regarding railing construction. Most codes require that railings be at least 36" above decking. Vertical balusters should be spaced no more than 4" apart. In some areas, a grippable handrail for any stairway over four treads may be required. Check with your local building inspector for the building codes in your area.

Everything You Need

Tools: tape measure, pencil, power miter saw, drill, twist bits (⅛", ¼"), 1" spade bit, combination square, awl, ratchet wrench, caulk gun, level, reciprocating saw or circular saw, jig saw with wood-cutting blade.

Materials: railing lumber (4 × 4s, 2 × 6s, 2 × 4s, 2 × 2s), clear sealer-preservative, ⅜" × 4 lag screws and 1" washers, silicone caulk, 2½" corrosion-resistant deck screws, 10d galvanized common nails.

How to Install a Deck Railing

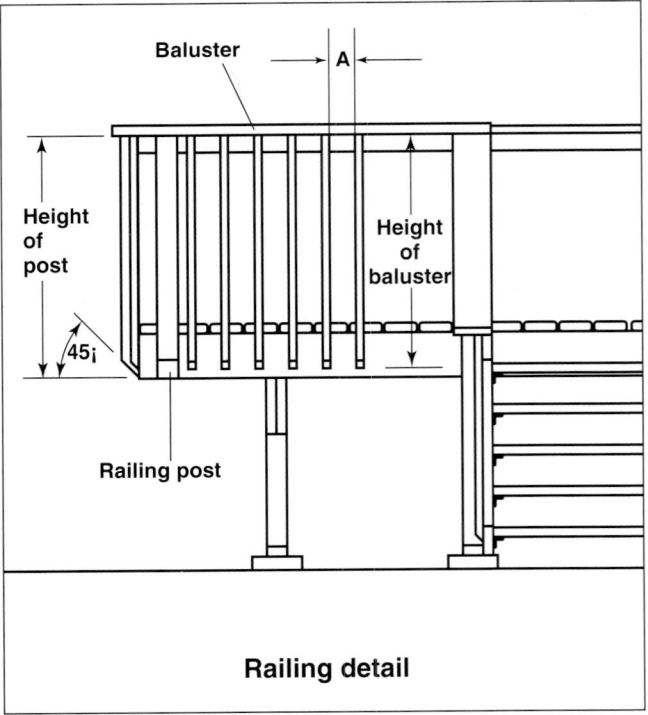

Railing detail

1 Refer to the deck design plan (pages 52 to 53) for spacing (A) and length of railing posts and balusters. Posts should be spaced no more than 6 feet apart.

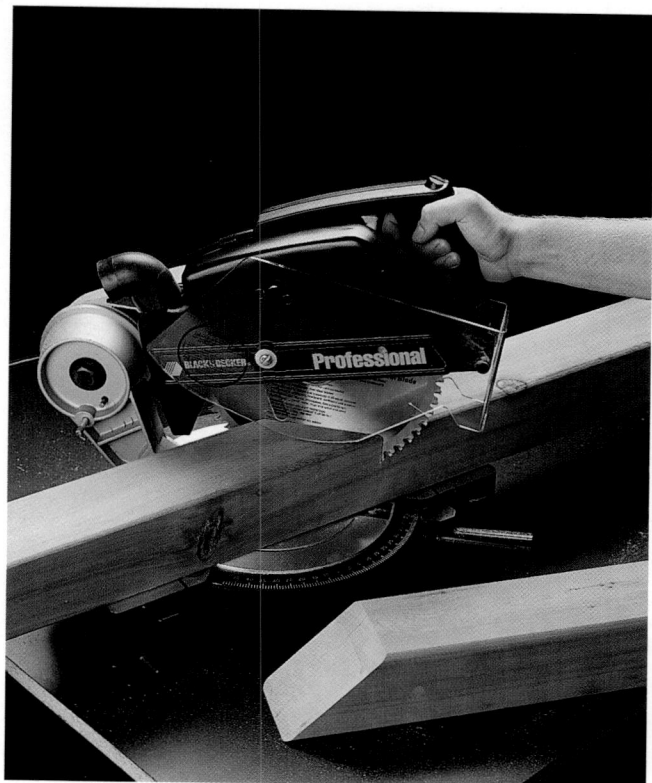

2 Measure and cut 4 × 4 posts, using a power miter saw or circular saw. Cut off tops of the posts square, and cut the bottoms at 45° angle. Seal cut ends of lumber with clear sealer-preservative.

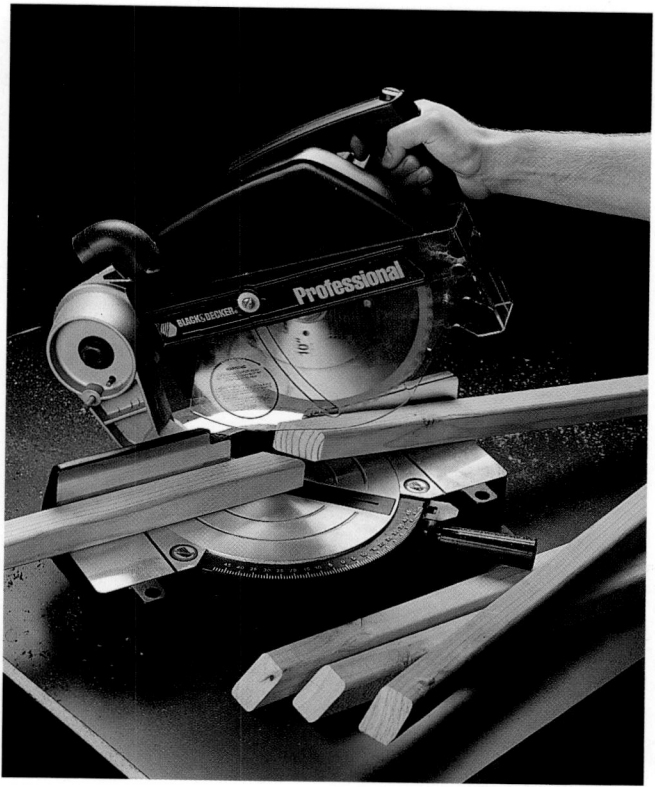

3 Measure and cut balusters for main deck, using a power miter saw or circular saw. Cut off tops of the balusters square, and cut bottoms at 45° angle. Seal cut ends of lumber with clear sealer-preservative.

4 Drill two ¼" pilot holes through bottom end of each post, spaced 2" apart. Counterbore each pilot hole to ½" depth, using a 1" spade bit.

5 Drill two ⅛" pilot holes near bottom end of each baluster, spaced 4" apart. Drill two ⅛" pilot holes at top of each baluster, spaced 1½" apart.

(continued next page)

6 Measure and mark position of posts around the outside of the deck, using a combination square as a guide. Plan to install a post on outside edge of each stair stringer.

7 Position each post with beveled end flush with bottom of deck. Plumb post with a level. Insert a screwdriver or nail into pilot holes and mark side of deck.

8 Remove post and drill ¼" pilot holes into side of deck.

9 Attach railing posts to side of deck with ⅜" × 4" lag screws and washers, using a ratchet wrench. Seal screw heads with silicone caulk.

10 Measure and cut 2 × 4 side rails. Position rails with edges flush to tops of posts, and attach to posts with 2½" corrosion-resistant deck screws.

11 Join 2 × 4s for long rails by cutting ends at 45° angles. Drill $\frac{1}{16}$" pilot holes to prevent nails from splitting end grain, and attach rails with 10d galvanized nails. (Screws may split mitered ends.)

12 Attach ends of rails to stairway posts, flush with edges of posts, as shown. Drill $\frac{1}{8}$" pilot holes, and attach rails with 2½" deck screws.

13 At stairway, measure from surface of decking to the top of the upper stairway post (A).

14 Transfer measurement A to lower stairway post, measuring from the edge of the stair stringer.

(continued next page)

How to Install a Deck Railing (continued)

Rail parallel to stringer

15 Position 2 × 4 rail against inside of stairway posts. Align rail with top rear corner of top post, and with the pencil mark on the lower post. Have a helper attach rail temporarily with 2½" deck screws.

Deck rail   **Stair rail**

16 Mark the outline of the post and the deck rail on the back side of the stairway rail.

17 Mark the outline of the stairway rail on the lower stairway post.

18 Use a level to mark a plumb cutoff line at the bottom end of the stairway rail. Remove the rail.

19 Extend the pencil lines across both sides of the stairway post, using a combination square as a guide.

20 Cut off lower stairway post along diagonal cutoff line, using a reciprocating saw or circular saw.

21 Use a jig saw to cut the stairway rail along the marked outlines.

22 Position the stairway rail flush against top edge of posts. Drill ⅛" pilot holes, then attach rail to posts with 2½" deck screws.

(continued next page)

23 Use a spacer block to ensure equal spacing between balusters. Beginning next to a plumb railing post, position each baluster tight against spacer block, with top of baluster flush to top of rail. Attach each baluster with 2½" deck screws.

24 For stairway, position baluster against stringer and rail, and adjust for plumb. Draw diagonal cutoff line on top of baluster, using top of stair rail as a guide. Cut baluster on marked line, using power miter saw. Seal ends with clear sealer-preservative.

25 Beginning next to upper stairway post, position each baluster tight against spacer block, with top flush to top of stair rail. Attach baluster with 2½" deck screws.

26 Position 2 × 6 cap so edge is flush with inside edge of rail. Drill ⅛" pilot holes, and attach cap to rail with 2½" deck screws driven every 12". Also drive screws into each post and into every third baluster. For long caps, bevel ends at 45°. Drill ¹⁄₁₆" pilot holes, and attach at post using 10d nails.

27 At corners, miter ends of railing cap at 45°. Drill ⅛" pilot holes, and attach cap to post with 2½" deck screws.

28 At top of stairs, cut cap so that it is flush with stairway rail. Drill ⅛" pilot holes and attach cap with 2½" deck screws. NOTE: Some areas may require a gripable hand rail (pages 196 to 197). Check your local building codes.

29 Measure and cut cap for stairway rail. Mark outline of post on side of cap, and bevel-cut the ends of the cap.

30 Position cap over the stairway rail and balusters so that edge of cap is flush with inside edge of rail. Drill ⅛" pilot holes, and attach cap to rail with 2½" deck screws driven every 12". Also drive screws through cap into stair post and into every third baluster.

Open space below a deck can be covered with a *skirt* to improve the appearance of the deck. A 2 × 4 framework built between the bottom of the deck and the ground supports the skirting materials. Common choices for skirting materials include lap siding (above) and lattice panels (page 119).

Finishing the Underside of a Deck

When finishing the underside of a deck, you have two broad choices: give the space a functional use, or hide it with a decorative screen. The option you choose depends largely on the site. If your deck is fairly tall and the ground beneath it is flat, you can turn the space into a functional patio or storage area. But if the area beneath the deck is narrow or steeply sloped, your best option is to make the skirt area more attractive by screening it with landscape plants or wood panels, or by blanketing the soil with a ground cover, such as decorative gravel.

To inhibit weed growth on bare ground under a deck, cover the earth with a layer of landscape fabric before finishing the area.

Everything You Need

Tools: pencil, plumb bob, hammer, drill, level, circular saw with carbide blade, maul.

Materials: pressure treated lumber, lattice panels, landscape fabric, corrosion-resistant deck screws (1½", 3"), ½" rebar, galvanized metal plates.

Options for Finishing the Underside of a Deck

A sheltered, shady patio covered with decking boards or brick pavers can be installed if the ground under the deck is flat. In this example, the expansive area under a large overhead deck is transformed into usable space by laying a ground-level deck platform with built-in benches.

Storage space can be created by walling-in the skirt area with siding materials and installing an access door. This space is ideal for storing yard-care tools and materials, gardening supplies, or children's outdoor toys.

Enclosed porch can be created by laying a waterproof material over the decking surface, finishing the floor area under the deck, then building finished walls around the skirt area, complete with doors and windows. In this example, the area under a small balcony deck has been transformed into a weathertight entry porch.

Ground covers, such as bark chips, gravel, or shrubs, ease the visual transition between the deck and surrounding landscape. Before laying bark or gravel, cover the ground with landscape fabric to inhibit the growth of weeds. For the deck shown above, bark chips and shrubs complement the wood used in the deck and house.

How to Build a Skirt Frame on Uneven Ground

Stud height

1 Cut 2 × 4 sole plates to follow the slope of the ground. Position them directly below the inside edge of the outside deck joist, using a plumb bob as a guide. Lay out stud locations on the outside joist, spaced every 2 ft., and use the plumb bob to mark corresponding locations on the sole plate. Studs will extend from the sole plate to a point about 4" up from the bottom edge of the joists.

2 Mark bevel angles for the bottoms of the studs by holding each stud in a plumb position, with the top against the inside face of the rim joist and the bottom against the inside edge of the sole plate. Scribe a cutting line on the stud, following the edge of the sole plate. Measure the angle with a speed square (page 177), then set the blade of your circular saw to match.

3 Cut studs to length (step 1), then attach the studs to the sole plates with 3" deck screws driven through the bottoms of the sole plates. Attach 1 × 4 braces across the studs near the top to maintain the proper spacing.

4 Position the frame against the inside face of the rim joist. To reduce the likelihood of rot, use temporary 2 × 4 spacers to elevate the frame slightly off the ground. Check for plumb, then attach the frame to the rim joist with 3" deck screws.

5 Secure sole plate joints with galvanized metal plates attached with deck screws.

6 Check to make sure the frame is plumb, then drill ½"-diameter holes through the sole plate between each pair of studs. Drive 1-ft.-long lengths of ½"-diameter steel rebar through the holes and into the ground.

7 Remove the scrap 2 × 4 blocks under the sole plate, then cut skirting materials to fit over the frame. (We used ⅜"-thick cedar lattice panels.) Attach the materials to the frame with 1½" deck screws. Joints between the panels should be aligned over a frame stud.

Finishing a New Deck

Finish a deck with clear sealer-preservative or staining sealer. Sealer-preservatives protect wood from water and rot, and are often used on cedar or redwood because they preserve the original color of the wood. If you want the wood to look weathered, wait several months before applying sealer-preservative.

Staining sealers, sometimes called toners, are often applied to pressure-treated lumber to give it the look of redwood or cedar. Staining sealers are available in a variety of colors.

For best protection, use finishing products with an alkyd base. Apply fresh finish each year.

Everything You Need

Tools: orbital sander, sandpaper, shop vacuum, pressure sprayer, eye protection, paint brush.

Materials: clear sealer-preservative or staining sealer.

Use an orbital sander to smooth out any rough areas before applying finish to decking boards, railings, or stair treads.

How to Finish a Redwood or Cedar Deck

1 Test wood surface by sprinkling water on it. If wood absorbs water quickly, it is ready to be sealed. If wood does not absorb water, let it dry for several weeks before sealing.

2 Sand rough areas and vacuum deck. Apply clear sealer to all wood surfaces, using a pressure sprayer. If possible, apply sealer to underside of decking and to joist, beams, and posts.

3 Use a paint brush to work sealer into cracks and narrow areas that could trap water.

How to Finish a Pressure-treated Deck

1 Sand rough areas and vacuum the deck. Apply a staining sealer (toner) to all deck wood, using a pressure sprayer.

2 Use a paint brush to smooth out drips and runs. Porous wood may require a second coat of staining sealer for even coverage.

Inspect hidden areas regularly for signs of rotted or damaged wood. Apply a fresh coat of finish yearly.

Maintaining a Deck

Inspect your deck once each year. Replace loose or rusting hardware or fasteners, and apply fresh finish to prevent water damage.

Look carefully for areas that show signs of damage. Replace or reinforce damaged wood as soon as possible (pages 124 to 127).

Restore an older, weathered deck to the original wood color with a deck-brightening solution. Brighteners are available at any home improvement store.

Everything You Need

Tools: flashlight, awl or screwdriver, screwgun, putty knife, scrub brush, rubber gloves, eye protection, pressure sprayer.

Materials: 2½" corrosion-resistant deck screws, deck brightener.

Tips for Maintaining an Older Deck

Use an awl or screwdriver to check deck for soft, rotted wood. Replace or reinforce damaged wood (pages 124 to 127).

Clean debris from cracks between decking boards with a putty knife. Debris traps moisture, and can cause wood to rot.

Drive new fasteners to secure loose decking to joists. If using the old nail or screw holes, new fasteners should be slightly longer than the originals.

How to Renew a Deck

1 Mix deck-brightening solution as directed by manufacturer. Apply solution with pressure sprayer. Let solution set for 10 minutes.

2 Scrub deck thoroughly with a stiff scrub brush. Wear rubber gloves and eye protection.

3 Rinse deck with clear water. If necessary, apply a second coat of brightener to extremely dirty or stained areas. Rinse and let dry. Apply a fresh coat of sealer or stain (pages 120 to 121).

Repairing a Deck

Replace or reinforce damaged deck wood as soon as possible. Wood rot can spread and weaken solid wood.

After replacing or reinforcing the rotted wood, clean the entire deck and apply a fresh coat of clear sealer-preservative or staining sealer. Apply a fresh coat of finish each year to prevent future water damage.

Everything You Need

Tools: cat's paw or flat pry bar, screwgun, awl or screwdriver, hammer, chisel, eye protection, pressure-sprayer, circular saw, scrub brush, paint brush, hydraulic jack, drill or hammer drill, ⅝" masonry bit, level, ratchet wrench.

Materials: sealer-preservative or staining sealer, galvanized nails (6d, 10d), deck lumber, baking soda, corrosion-resistant deck screws, ⅝" masonry anchor, ⅜" lag screw.

Supplies: rubber gloves, bucket, concrete block, scrap plywood.

How to Repair Damaged Decking & Joists

1 Remove nails or screws from the damaged decking board, using a cat's paw or screwgun. Remove the damaged board.

2 Inspect the underlying joists for signs of rotted wood. Joists with discolored, soft areas should be repaired and reinforced.

3 Use a hammer and chisel to remove any rotted portions of joist.

4 Apply a thick coat of sealer-preservative to damaged joist. Let dry, then apply a second coat of sealer. Cut a reinforcing joist (sister joist) from pressure-treated lumber.

5 Treat all sides of sister joist with clear sealer-preservative, and let dry. Position sister joist tightly against the damaged joist, and attach with 10d nails driven every 2 feet.

6 Attach sister joist to ledger and header joist by toenailing with 10d nails. Cut replacement decking boards from matching lumber, using a circular saw.

7 If the existing decking is gray, "weather" the new decking by scrubbing with a solution made from 1 cup baking soda and 1 gallon warm water. Rinse and let dry.

(continued next page)

How to Repair Damaged Decking & Joists (continued)

8 Apply a coat of sealer-preservative or staining sealer to all sides of the new decking boards.

9 Position the new decking and attach to joists with galvanized deck screws or nails. Make sure space between boards matches that of existing decking.

How to Replace a Post on an Older Deck

1 Build a support, using plywood scraps, a concrete block, and a hydraulic jack. Place 1½" layer of plywood between head of jack and beam. Apply just enough pressure to lift the beam slightly.

Anchor pad

2 Remove the nails or lag screws holding the damaged post to the anchor pad and to the beam. Remove the damaged post and the wood anchor pad on the concrete pier.

3 Drill a hole in the middle of the concrete pier, using a hammer drill and a ⅝" masonry bit. Insert ⅝" masonry anchor into hole.

4 Position galvanized post anchor on pier block, and thread a ⅜" lag screw with washer through the hole in the anchor and into the masonry anchor. Tighten the screw with a ratchet wrench.

5 Cut new post from pressure-treated lumber, and treat cut ends with sealer-preservative. Position post and make sure it is plumb.

6 Attach the bottom of the post to the post anchor, using 10d or 16d joist hanger nails. Attach the post to the beam by redriving the lag screws, using a ratchet wrench. Release the pressure on the jack and remove the support.

Advanced Techniques

Advanced Deck Features

On the following pages you will see illustrations of several decks, each containing several advanced features that are usually found only on elaborate decks designed and built by professionals.

Incorporating these features into a deck you design and build yourself is not as difficult as you might imagine. First, you'll need a good understanding of basic deck-building skills, as demonstrated in the previous chapter.

Once you are confident of your basic skills, you will need to learn a few special construction methods. These techniques are highlighted on the following few pages. The remainder of this chapter presents step-by-step instructions for these construction methods.

Hot tubs installed on a deck must have extra beams and closely spaced joists to support the extra weight. See pages 184 to 187.

Stairway railings must be installed on any stairway with more than two steps, and should have grippable handrails. See pages 196 to 197.

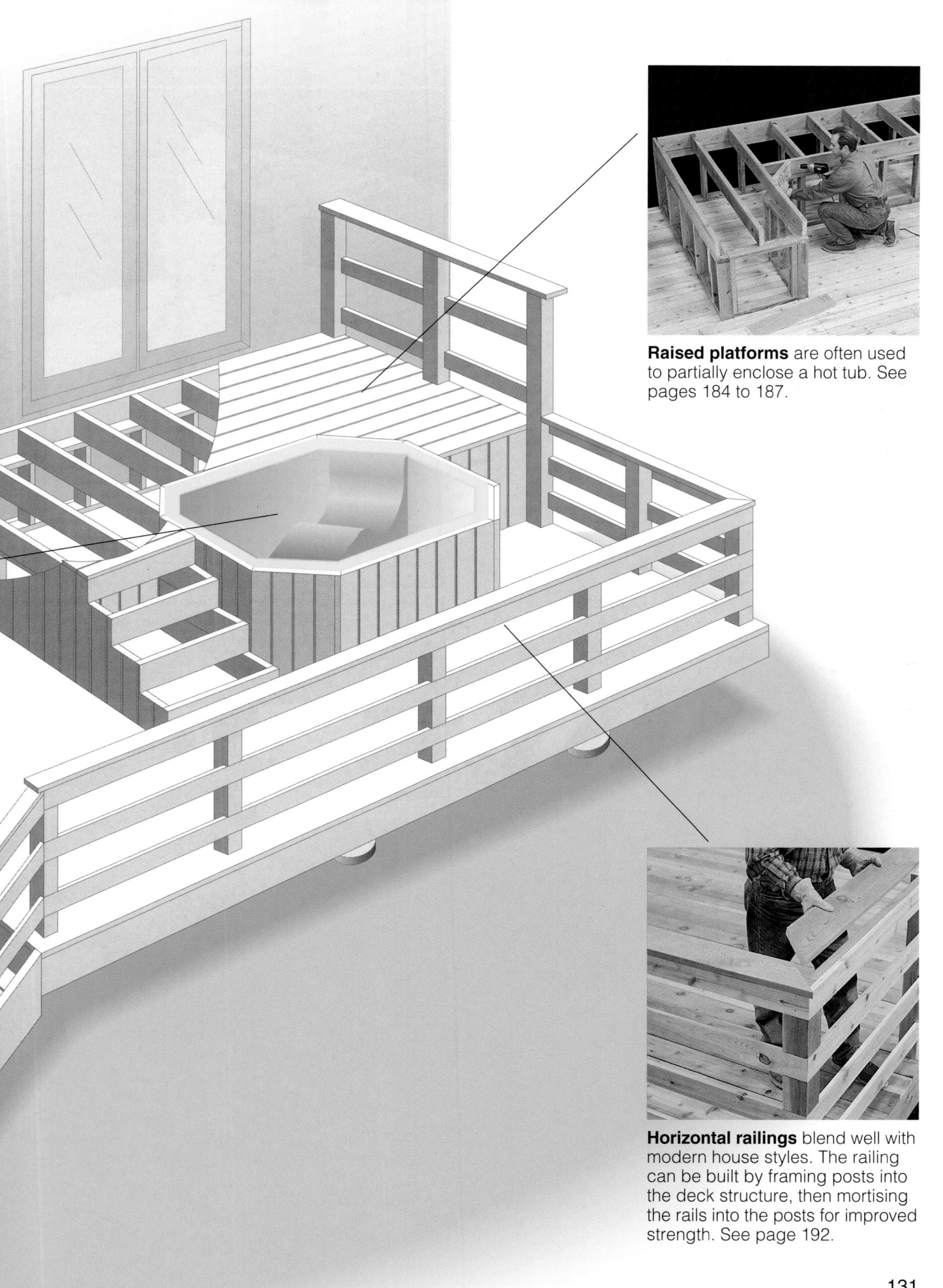

Raised platforms are often used to partially enclose a hot tub. See pages 184 to 187.

Horizontal railings blend well with modern house styles. The railing can be built by framing posts into the deck structure, then mortising the rails into the posts for improved strength. See page 192.

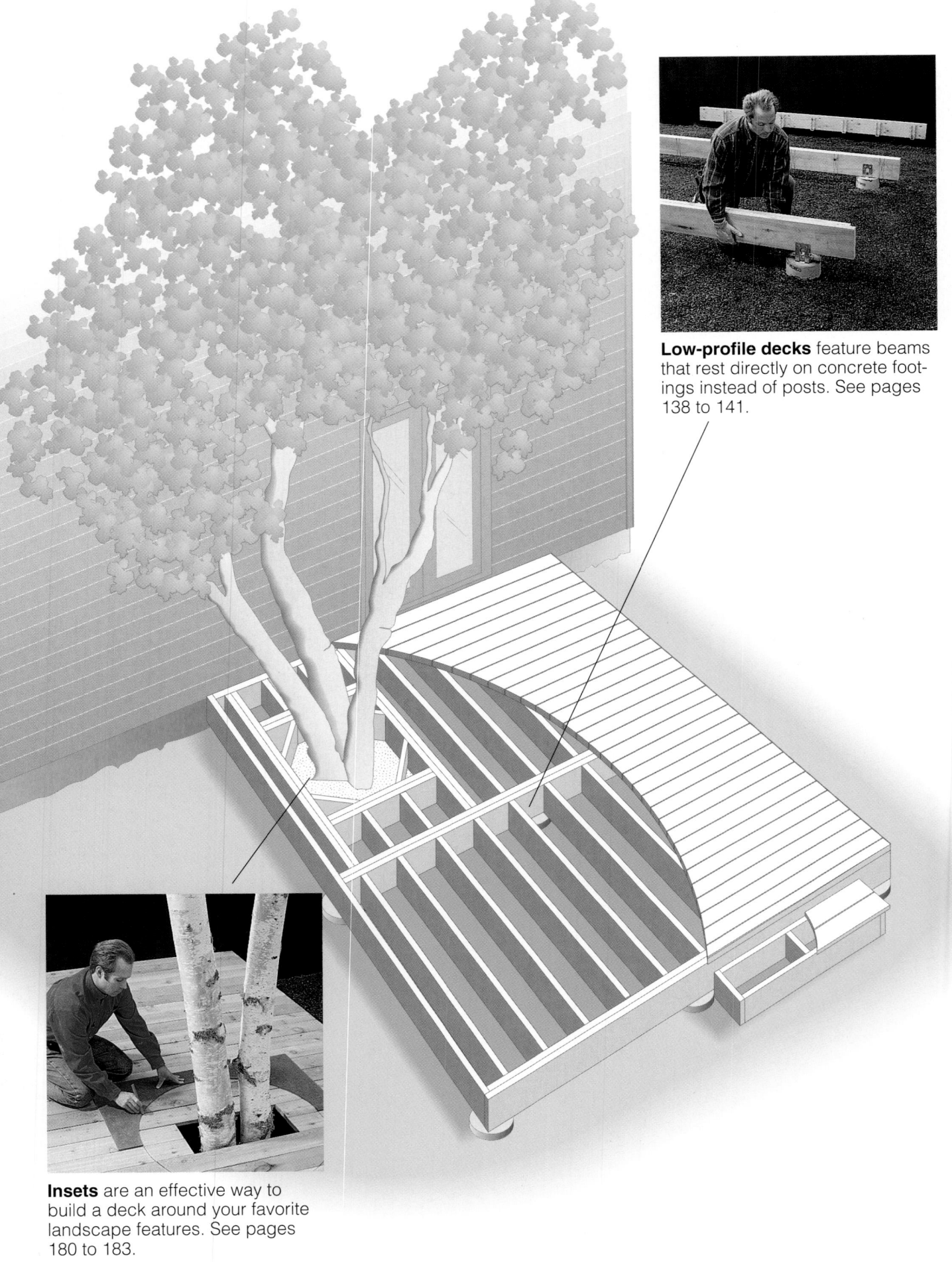

Low-profile decks feature beams that rest directly on concrete footings instead of posts. See pages 138 to 141.

Insets are an effective way to build a deck around your favorite landscape features. See pages 180 to 183.

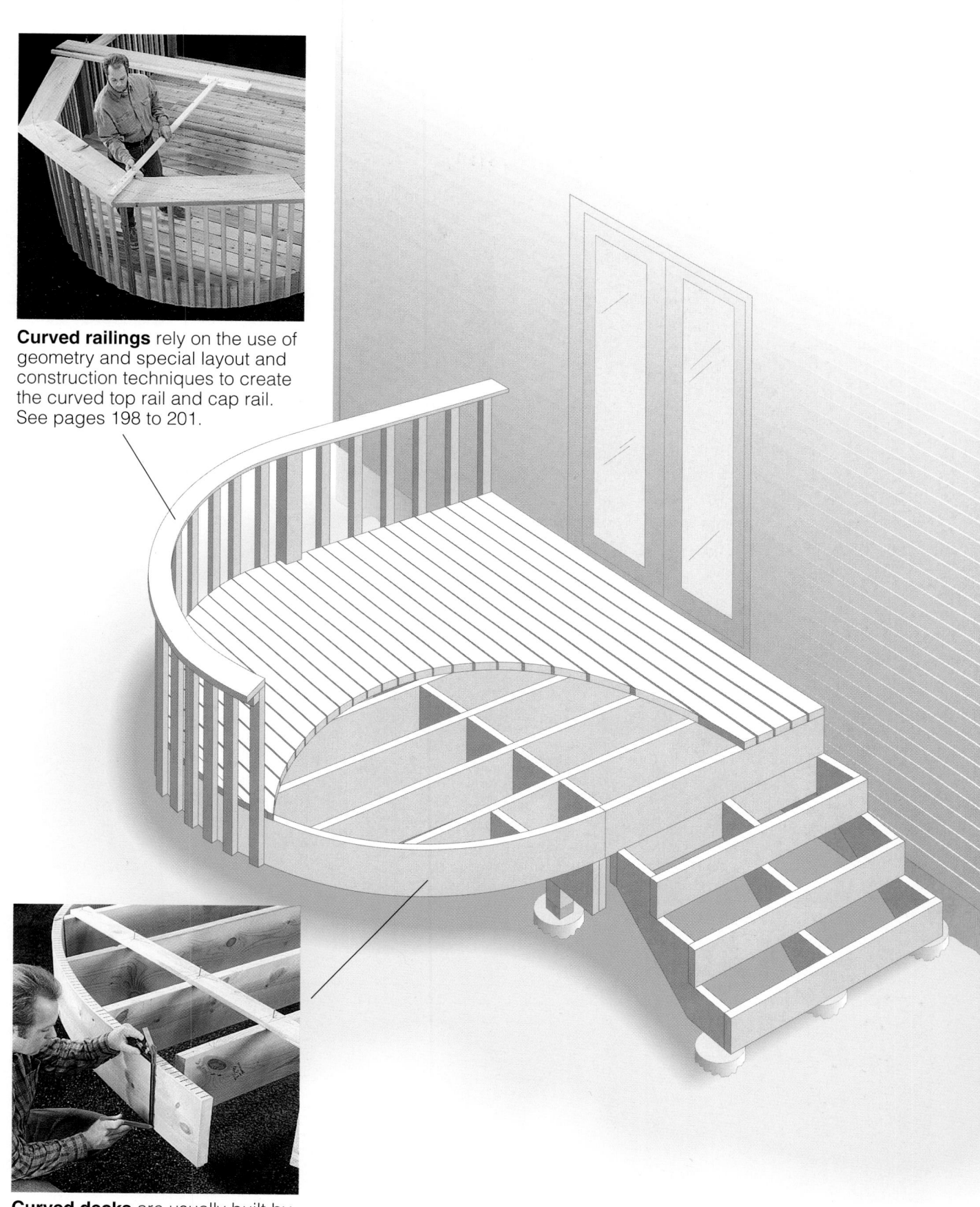

Curved railings rely on the use of geometry and special layout and construction techniques to create the curved top rail and cap rail. See pages 198 to 201.

Curved decks are usually built by cutting joists to a circular outline, then attaching a curved rim joist. See pages 174 to 179.

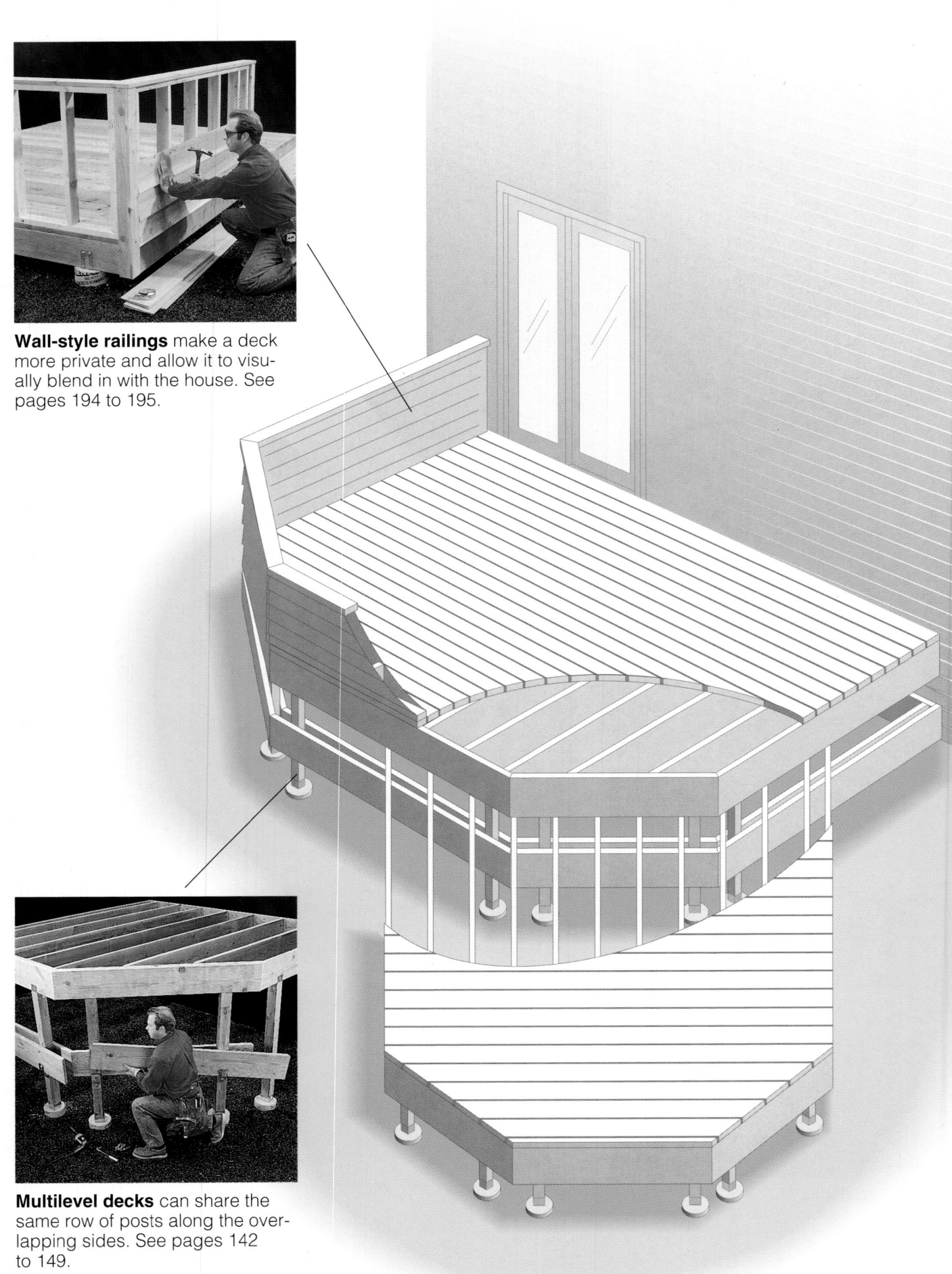

Wall-style railings make a deck more private and allow it to visually blend in with the house. See pages 194 to 195.

Multilevel decks can share the same row of posts along the overlapping sides. See pages 142 to 149.

Vertical railings use balusters attached to rails that are mortised into the posts, providing greater strength and a more finished appearance. See pages 190 to 192.

Decorative treatments like lattice panels can conceal the area below a deck. See pages 116 to 119.

Landings are required whenever a deck stairway has 12 or more steps. See pages 150 to 159.

Deck layout traditionally is done with batterboards and strings, but some situations require other layout methods. For angled decks, the board template method (left) described on pages 170 to 171 is easier than batterboards. For a very high deck or one built on a steep slope (right), the layout is often done by constructing the outer framework first, then elevating it with a temporary wall to find the exact location for footings and posts (pages 160 to 165).

Advanced Construction Tips

The step-by-step overview shown on pages 56 to 57 outlines the basic steps of deck construction, but more complicated decks require special materials and techniques, like those shown here. If you're building an angled deck, for instance, it is easier to do the basic on-site layout using a board template rather than strings and batterboards. And for a deck with many angles, a speed square is very helpful for marking and cutting lumber.

Whenever possible, build your deck so the beams rest on top of the posts—an arrangement that is stronger than attaching beam timbers to the sides of posts with lag screws.

Post cross-bracing helps stabilize a deck platform, and may be required for raised four-post decks and for stairway landings. For best results, install braces diagonally between support posts.

Cross blocks

Cross blocks between joists help stabilize decks that have very long joist spans. Cross braces are also recommended when constructing a curved deck.

Post-beam caps allow you to rest beams on top of posts. Some local codes require that, wherever possible, beams rest on top of posts, attached with post-beam caps. Two types of post-beam caps are widely available: a single piece cap (left) for use when the beam is the same width as the posts, and an adjustable two-piece cap (right) that can be used when the beam and the posts are different widths.

Post anchors elevate the bottoms of posts above footings, helping prevent rot. The post rests on a metal pedestal that fits over a J-bolt embedded in the footing. Once the post is set in place, a nut is screwed onto the J-bolt, the metal flange is bent up against the post, and the post anchor is secured to the post with nails.

How to Build a Beam Using Dimensional Lumber

1 Cut the timbers to size. Sight along the boards to check for crowning, then position the timbers so any crowns are facing the same direction. Nail the timbers together at the ends, using galvanized 16d nails.

2 Turn the beam on edge, and where the timbers are not flush, toenail the higher board down into the lower one so the edges are forced into alignment. If necessary, use clamps to draw the boards into position. Facenail the timbers together, using rows of 16d nails spaced about 16" apart.

3 Attach post-beam caps to the outside posts, but leave the caps loose on inside posts. Position the beam in the caps, with the crowned edge up. Check for gaps at the inside posts, and shim under the post-beam caps, if necessary. Secure the beam to the caps and posts with 10d joist hanger nails.

Beams for a low-profile deck often rest directly on concrete footings, with no posts. Because low-profile decks may require 2 × 8 or 2 × 6 joists, an intermediate beam may be required to provide adequate support for these narrower joists. At each end of the last beam, the outside timber must be 1½" longer than the inside timber, creating a recess where the end of the rim joist will fit.

Building Low-profile Decks

Building a deck that sits very close to the ground generally is easier than constructing a very high deck, but low-profile situations do require some design modifications. If the deck is extremely low (8" to 12" high), it is best to rest the beams directly on the concrete footings, since posts are not practical. The joists usually are hung on the faces of the beams rather than resting on top of the beams; cantilever designs are rarely used. Since the ledger is mounted so low on the house, it may need to be anchored to the foundation wall rather than to the rim joist (right).

A deck that is more than 12" above the ground should have at least one step, either box-frame style, or suspended from the deck.

Masonry sleeves are used to attach a ledger to a masonry foundation. Drill 3"-deep guide holes for the sleeves, using a ⅝" masonry bit, then drive sleeves for ⅜"-diameter lag screws into the holes. Position the ledger, then attach it with lag screws driven through the ledgers and into the masonry sleeves.

Support Options

Direct-bearing hardware is used to secure beams when the deck is very low to the ground. Carefully set the footing forms so the tops are at the planned height, then pour concrete and set the hardware into the wet concrete. Use layout strings to ensure that the hardware is aligned correctly.

Posts and post-beam caps can be used if the full deck height is more than 18". Posts less than 9" tall are prone to splitting.

Step Options

Box-frame steps are simple platforms constructed from dimensional lumber and covered with decking boards. Box-frame steps are best suited to mild climates where there is little chance the step will be heaved by frost. See page 141.

Suspended steps are hung from the underside of the deck. The steps are constructed with joists attached to the lower portions of the deck joists. Suspended steps are a good option in cold-weather climates, where box-frame steps would be susceptible to frost heave. However, this method cannot be used if the step joists run perpendicular to the deck joists. See page 141.

How to Build a Low-profile Deck

1 Install the ledger, then lay out and dig footings. If beams will rest directly on footings, use tube forms. Raise the tubes to the proper height and check them for plumb as you pour the concrete. Smooth off the surfaces of the footings, and insert direct-bearing hardware while the concrete is still wet, using layout strings to ensure that the hardware is aligned correctly.

2 Construct beams (page 137), then set the beams into the direct-bearing hardware. Drill pilot holes and use 3½" lag bolts to secure the beam to the hardware. Mark joist locations on the faces of the beams, then install joist hangers.

3 Cut and install all joists, attaching them with joist-hanger nails. Complete your deck, using standard deck-building techniques. Install a box-frame or suspended step, if desired (page opposite).

How to Build a Box-frame Step

1 Construct a rectangular frame for the step, using dimension lumber (2 × 6 lumber is standard), joining the pieces with deck screws. The step must be at least 36" wide and 9" deep. Cut cross blocks and install them inside the frame, spaced every 16".

2 Dig a flat-bottomed trench where the step will rest, about 4" deep. Fill the trench with compactible gravel, and pack with a tamper. Set the step in position, then measure and attach deck boards to form the tread of the step.

How to Build a Suspended Step

1 Screw 2 × 4 furring strips against one side of the deck joists where the step joists will be installed. These strips provide an offset so the step joists will not conflict with the joist hangers attached to the beam. Use a reciprocating saw to make 1½"-wide notches in the rim joist adjacent to the furring strips. NOTE: To maintain adequate structural strength, notches in the joists should be no more than 1½" deep.

2 Measure and cut step joists, allowing about 3 ft. of nailing surface inside the deck frame, and 9" or more of exposed tread. Make sure the step joists are level with one another, then attach them to the deck joists, using deck screws. Cut and attach deck boards to the tread area of the step.

Constructing Multilevel Decks

A multilevel deck has obvious advantages, but many do-it-yourselfers are wary of building such a deck, feeling that it is too complex. In reality, however, a multilevel deck is nothing more than two or more adjacent deck platforms set at different heights. You can build a multilevel deck with the same simple construction techniques used to build a standard deck—with one exception: For efficiency, multilevel decks usually are designed so the platforms share a single support beam on the side where they meet. For this reason, it is essential that the shared posts and beams be sturdy enough to carry the load of both platforms.

Except for the shared beam, the separate platforms on a multilevel deck are independent and can use different construction methods. For example, the upper level might use a post and beam design with decking boards installed perpendicular to the joists, while the lower level might use a curved cantilever design with decking laid at an angle. If your time and budget are limited, you can build your deck in phases, completing one platform at a time, at your convenience.

Remember to include railings (pages 188 to 201) and stairs (pages 150 to 159) where needed. Any deck platform more than 30" above the ground—or above a lower deck platform—requires a railing.

Different support methods can be used in the same multilevel deck. In the deck shown here, the top platform is supported by a beam resting on top of posts, while the lower platform is supported by 2 × 12 beam timbers sandwiched around the posts. The opposite side of the lower platform might use yet another support method, such as a set-back beam supporting cantilevered joists.

Design Options

The shared beam method has one beam supporting both platforms where they overlap. The upper platform rests directly on the beam, while the lower hangs from the face of the beam. This method is an economical choice, since only one beam is required, and it is well suited for relatively flat building sites where the deck levels are close together. See pages 144 to 145.

The shared post method has two beams supported by the same row of posts. The top platform is supported by a beam resting on top of the posts, while the beam for the lower platform is built from 2 × 12 timbers sandwiched around the posts. This method often is used when there is a considerable drop between levels. It also is a good choice if you want to complete your deck in phases, delaying construction of the lower platform until a later date. See pages 146 to 147.

The support-wall method features a top platform supported by a stud wall that rests on the lower platform, directly over the beam and posts. Unlike the methods listed above, the support-wall method requires that the lower deck platform be built first. This method is a good choice when you want to use decorative wall materials, such as cedar siding, to cover the gap between the two platforms. The support-wall method also works well if you want to complete your deck in phases, delaying construction of the upper level. See pages 148 to 149.

How to Use the Shared Beam Method

Joist location

Final cut-off

Beam location

1 After laying out and installing the ledger and all posts and footings, mark the posts to indicate where the beam will rest. Use a straight 2 × 4 and level to establish a point that is level with the top of the ledger, then measure down a distance equal to the height of the joists plus the height of the beam. Cut off the posts at this point, using a reciprocating saw.

2 Position a post-beam cap on each post. Construct a beam from 2 × 10 or 2 × 12 dimension lumber (page 137), then position the beam in the post-beam caps. If the beam is crowned, install it so the crowned side is up; if there is a gap between the middle cap and the beam, shim under the gap. Secure the post-beam caps to the posts and beam with galvanized deck screws.

3 Lay out joist locations for the upper platform on the ledger and on the top of the beam, then use a carpenter's square to transfer joist marks for the lower platform onto the face of the beam. Attach joist hangers at the joist layout lines on the ledger.

4 Measure, cut, and install joists for the upper platform, leaving a 1½" setback to allow for the thickness of the rim joist. At the beam, secure the joists by toenailing with 16d galvanized nails.

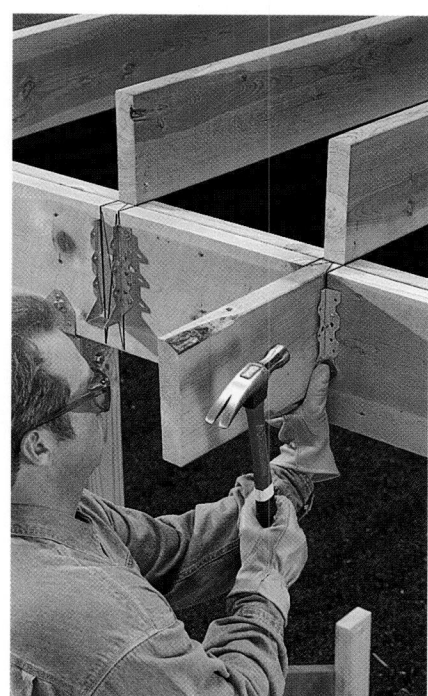

5 Attach joist hangers for the lower platform along the face of the beam, using a scrap piece of lumber as a spacer. Cut and install the joists for the lower platform.

6 Cut rim joists for both the upper and lower platforms, and attach them to the ends of the joists by endnailing with 16d nails. Complete the deck, using standard deck-building techniques.

How to Use the Shared Post Method

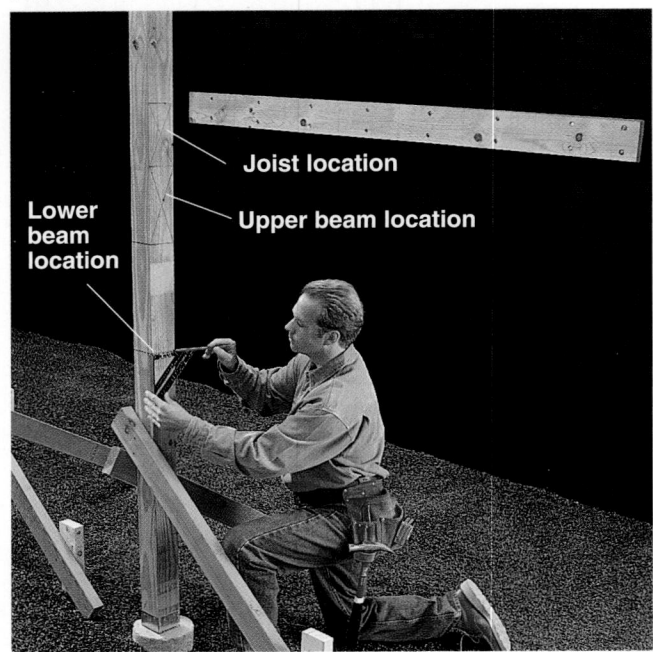

Lower beam location

Joist location

Upper beam location

1 After laying out the deck and installing the ledger and all footings and posts, mark the posts to indicate where both beams will rest. Begin by finding a point level with the top edge of the ledger (page 144), then measure down and mark cutting lines where the bottom of the top beam will rest. For the lower beam, measure down and mark a point on the posts where the top edge of the beam will be positioned.

2 Use a reciprocating saw to cut off the posts at the lines marking the bottom edge of the top beam. Construct the top beam and install it, using post-beam caps (page 137).

3 Align bearing surfaces of joist ties with the line indicating the bottom of the lower beam on each post. Drill pilot holes and attach with ⅜ × 3" lag screws. Install beam members and drive lag screws through the joist ties, beams, and into posts. Also drive lag screws 1½" from the top edge of each beam to secure to posts.

4 Lay out and mark the joist locations on the ledger and on the top edges of both the upper and lower beam, using a carpenter's square as a guide.

5 Cut and install the joists for the lower platform, toenailing them to the beams with 16d galvanized nails. Cut rim joists for the lower platform and endnail them to the ends of the joists. Cut and install the joists and rim joist for the upper platform.

6 Attach nailing blocks to the sides of the posts where necessary to provide surfaces for attaching decking boards. Complete the deck, using standard deck-building techniques.

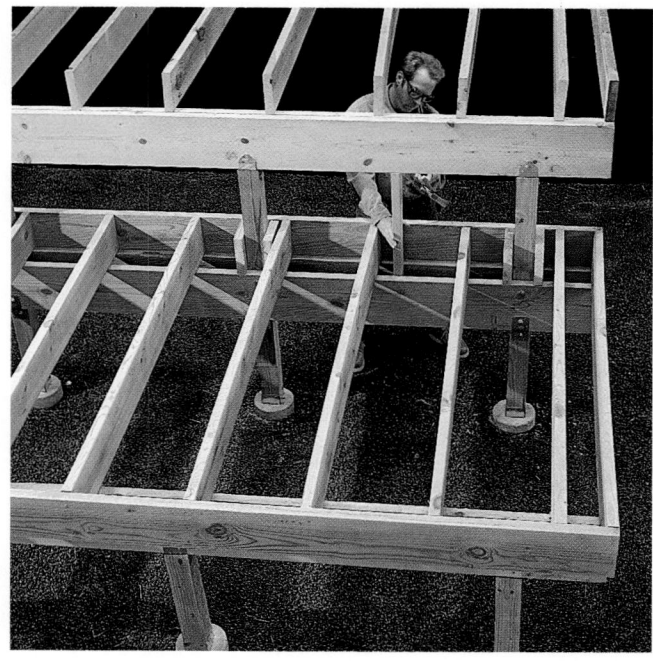

Framing option: If you plan to finish the gap between the upper and lower platform with a decorative wall treatment (pages 194 to 195), install nailing strips between the platforms to provide surfaces for attaching siding materials. Nailing strips and posts should be spaced so the intervals are no more than 16".

How to Use the Support-wall Method

1 Lay out and install the ledger and all posts and footings, then frame the lower platform, using standard deck-building techniques.

2 Use a straight 2 × 4 and level to establish a reference point level with the bottom of the ledger, then find the total height for the support wall by measuring the vertical distance to the top of the lower platform. Cut the wall studs 3" less than this total height, to allow for the thickness of the top and bottom plates.

3 Cut 2 × 4 top and bottom plates to cover the full width of the upper platform, then lay out the stud locations on the plates, 16" on center. Cut studs to length, then assemble the support wall by endnailing the plates to the studs, using galvanized 16d nails.

4 Set a long "sway" brace diagonally across the stud wall, and nail it near one corner only. Square the wall by measuring the diagonals and adjusting until both diagonal measurements are the same. When the wall is square, nail the brace at the other corner, and to each stud. Cut off the ends of the brace flush with the plates.

5 Raise the support wall into position, aligning it with the edge of the beam and the end of the deck. Nail the sole plate to the beam with 16d galvanized nails driven on both sides of each stud.

6 Adjust the wall so it is plumb, then brace it in position by nailing a 1 × 4 across the end stud and outside joist.

7 Lay out joist locations for the upper platform, and install joist hangers on the ledger. Cut joists so they are 1½" shorter than the distance from the ledger to the front edge of the wall. Install the joists by toenailing them to the top plate with 16d nails. Remove the braces.

8 Measure and cut a rim joist, and attach it to the ends of the joists by endnailing with 16d nails. Also toenail the rim joist to the top plate of the support wall. Complete the deck, using standard deck-building techniques. To cover the support wall with siding, see pages 194 to 195.

Building Stairways with Landings

Designing and building a stairway with a landing can be one of the most challenging elements of a deck project. Precision is crucial, since building codes have very exact standards for stairway construction. To ensure that the steps for both the top and bottom staircases have the same vertical rise and tread depth, the landing must be set at the right position and height.

Even for professional builders, designing a stairway layout is a process of trial and revision. Begin by creating a preliminary layout that fits your situation, but as you plan and diagram the project, be prepared to revise the layout to satisfy code requirements and the demands of your building site. Measure your site carefully, and work out all the details on paper before you begin any work. Accuracy and meticulous planning will help ensure that your steps are level and uniform in size.

Remember that any stairway with more than three steps requires a railing (pages 196 to 197).

Building a stairway with a landing is a six-stage project:

- Creating a preliminary layout (page 154)
- Creating a final layout (page 155)
- Building a stairway landing (pages 155 to 156)
- Laying out stringers (page 157)
- Building the lower staircase (page 158)
- Building the upper staircase (page 159)

A landing functions essentially as a large step that interrupts a tall stairway. For the builder, the landing provides a convenient spot from which to change the direction of the stairway. For the homeowner, the landing provides a spot to catch your breath momentarily while climbing.

Stairway Design Options

Straight layout with no landing may be unavoidable if space on the building site is limited. In this example, the straight stairway layout provides a direct, quick path from a balcony deck to a ground-level platform deck below.

Straight layout with landing is relatively easy to plan and build, but requires more yard space than other stairway designs.

L-shaped layout is used when the building site requires that the stairway change directions.

U-shaped layout is a good choice when space is limited. In the situation shown above, a U-shaped stairway is the most efficient way to connect deck platforms separated by a long vertical rise.

Anatomy of a Stair with Landing

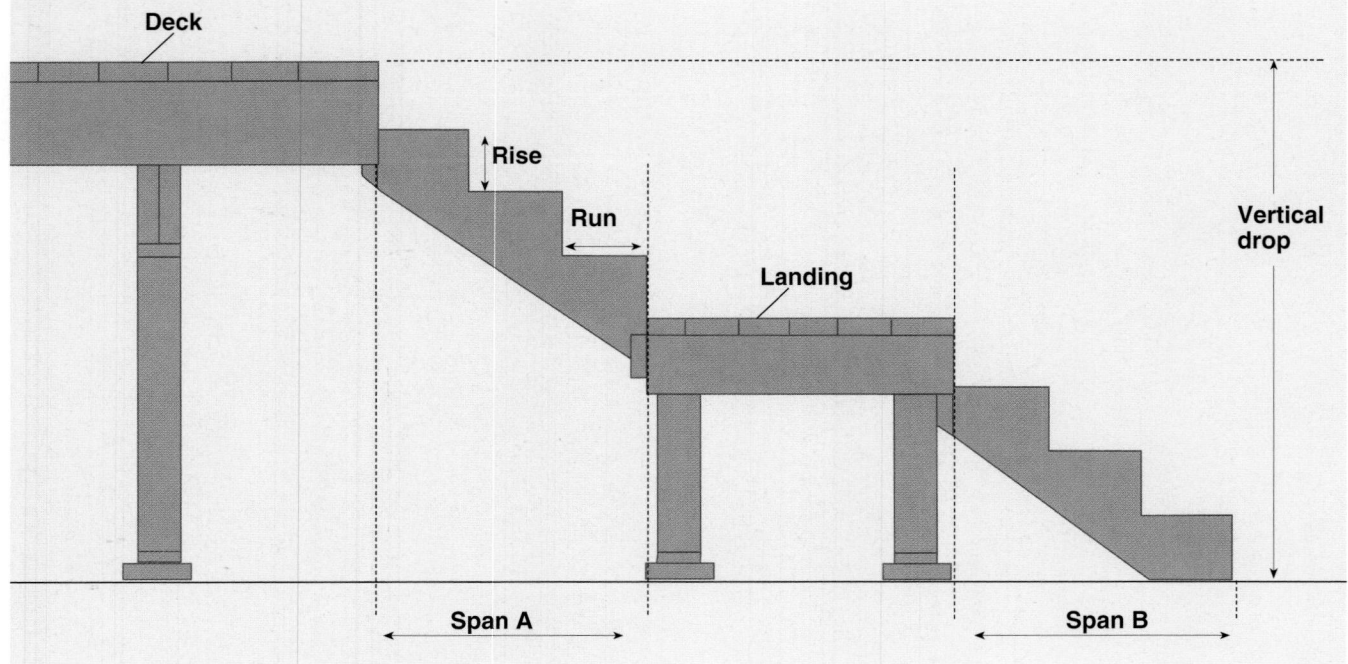

Deck

Rise

Run

Vertical drop

Landing

Span A

Span B

Stairway Basics

The goal of any stairway is to allow people to move easily and safely from one level to another. When designing a deck stairway, the builder must consider the **vertical drop**—the vertical distance from the surface of the deck to the ending point; and the **span**—the horizontal distance from the starting point to the end of the stairway.

During the planning stage, the vertical drop is divided into a series of equal-size steps, called **rises**. Similarly, the horizontal span is divided into a series of equal-size **runs.** On a stairway with a landing, there are two span measurements to consider: the distance from the deck to the edge of the landing, and from the landing to the end point on the ground. In general, the combined horizontal span of the staircases, not counting the landing, should be 40% to 60% more than the total vertical drop.

For safety and comfort, the components of a stairway must be built according to clearly prescribed guidelines, as listed at right.

The challenge when planning a stairway is adjusting the preliminary layout and the step dimensions as needed to ensure that the stairway fits the building site and is comfortable to use.

Rises must be no less than 4" and no more than 8" high.

Runs, the horizontal depth of each step, must be at least 9". The number of runs in a staircase is always one less than the number of rises.

Combined sum of the step rise and run should be about 18" to 20". Steps built to this guideline are the most comfortable to use.

Variation between the largest and smallest rise or run measurement can be no more than ⅜".

Stair width must be at least 36", so two people can comfortably pass one another on the stairway.

Stringers should be spaced no more than 36" apart. For added support, a center stringer is recommended for any staircase with more than three steps.

Landings serve as oversized steps; their height must be set as precisely as the risers for the other steps in the stairway. Landings should be at least 36" square, or as wide as the staircase itself. U-shaped stairways should have oversized landings, at least 1 ft. wider than the combined width of the two staircases. Landings very often require reinforcement with diagonal cross braces between the support posts.

Concrete footings should support all stringers resting on the ground.

Construction Details for Stairways

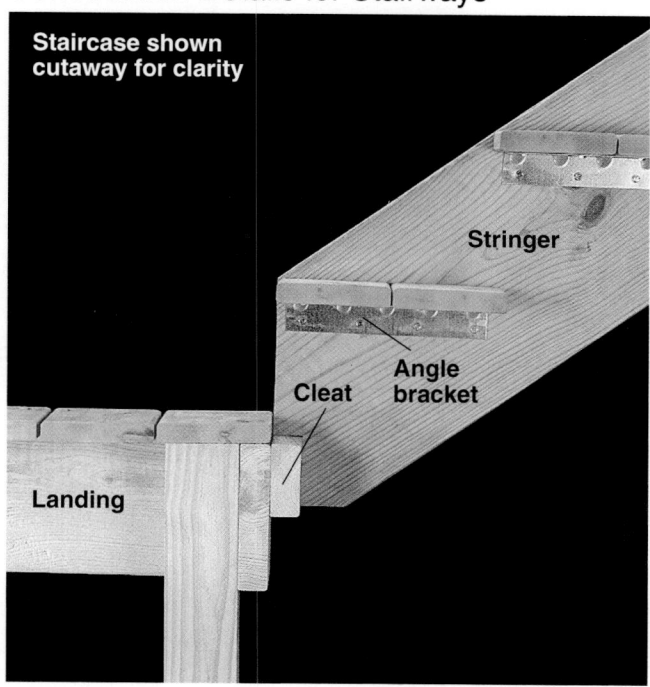

Stringers for the top staircase rest on a 2 × 4 cleat attached to the side of the landing. The stringers are notched to fit around the cleat. On the outside stringers, metal cleats support the treads.

Steps may be boxed in the riser boards, and may have treads that overhang the front edge of the step for a more finished look. Treads should overhang the riser boards by no more than 1".

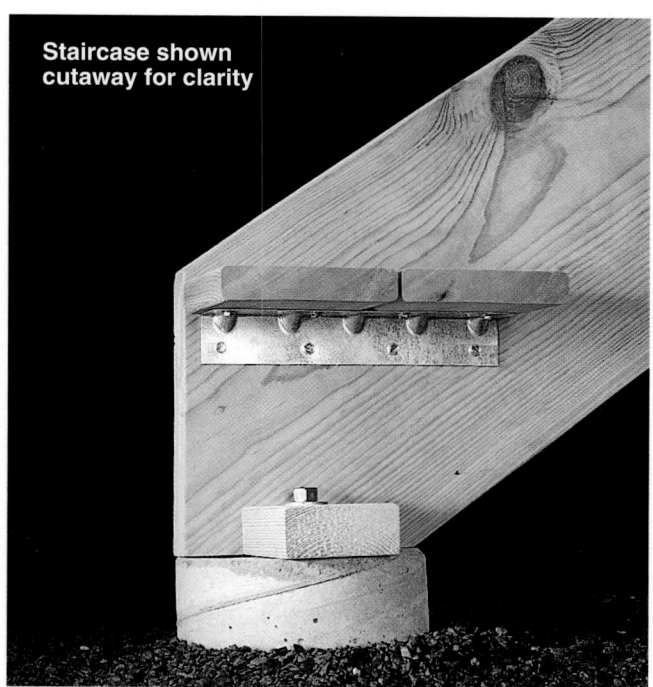

Concrete footings support the stringers for the lower staircase. J-bolts are inserted into the footings while the concrete is still wet. After the footings dry, wooden cleats are attached to the bolt to create surfaces for anchoring the stringers. After the staircase is positioned, the stringers are nailed or screwed to the cleats.

Center stringers are recommended for any staircase that has more than 3 steps or is more than 36" wide. Center stringers are supported by a 2 × 6 nailer attached to the bottom of the rim joist with metal straps. The bottom edge of the nailer is beveled to match the angle of the stringers. The center stringer is attached by driving deck screws through the back of the nailer and into the stringer.

How to Create a Preliminary Layout

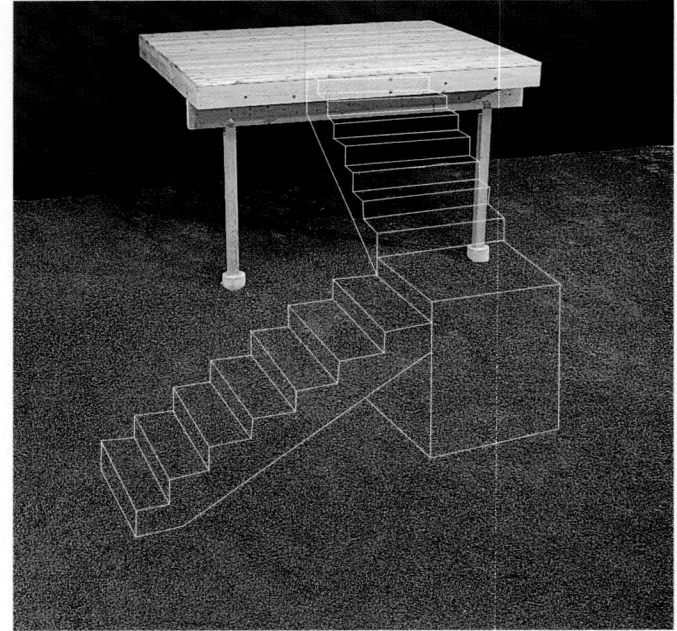

1 Evaluate your building site and try to visualize which stairway design best fits your needs (page 151). When creating a preliminary layout, it is generally best to position the landing so the upper and lower staircases will be of equal length. Select a general design idea.

2 Establish a rough starting point for the stairway on the deck, and an ending point on the ground that conforms with your design. Mark the starting point on the rim joist, and mark the ending point with two stakes, spaced to equal the planned width of your stairway. This is a rough layout only; later calculations will give you the precise measurements.

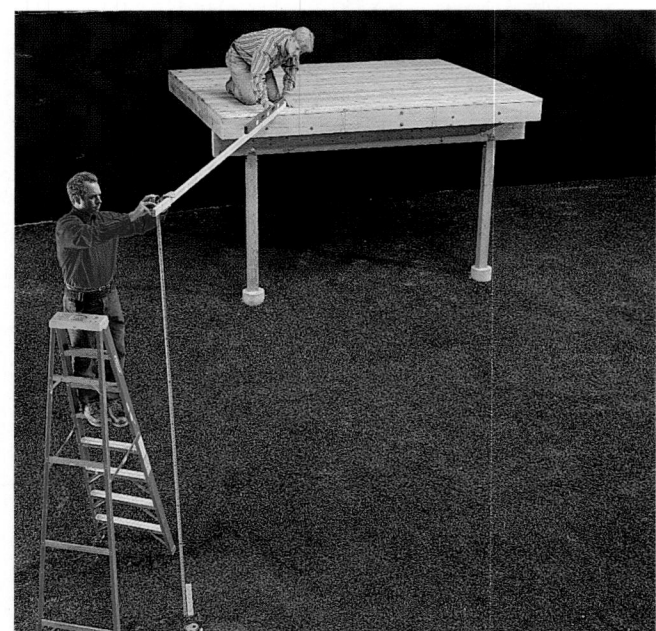

3 To determine the vertical drop of the stairway, extend a straight 2 × 4 from the starting point on the deck to a spot level with the deck directly over the ending point on the ground. Measure the distance to the ground; this measurement is the total vertical drop. NOTE: If the ending point is more than 10 ft. from the starting point, use a mason's string and line level to establish a reference point from which to measure.

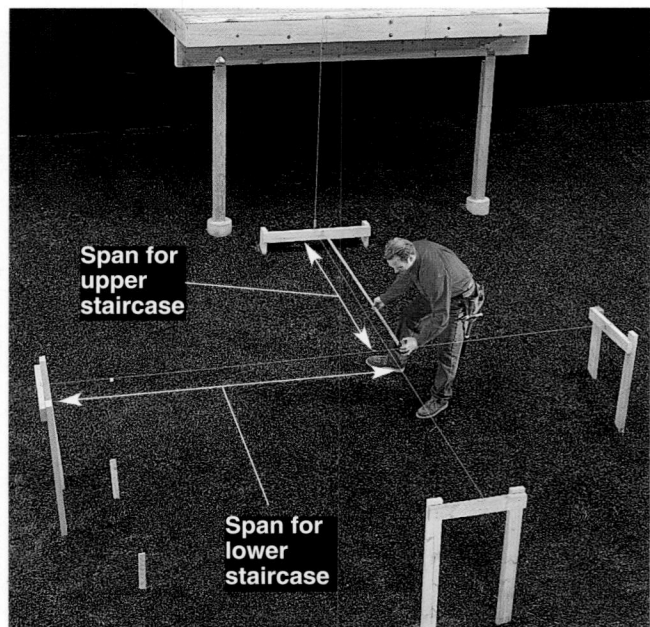

4 Measure the horizontal span for each staircase. First, use batterboards to establish level layout strings representing the edges of the staircases. Find the span for the upper staircase by measuring from a point directly below the edge of the deck out to the edge of the landing. Measure the span for the lower staircase from the landing to the endpoint.

How to Create a Final Layout—an Example

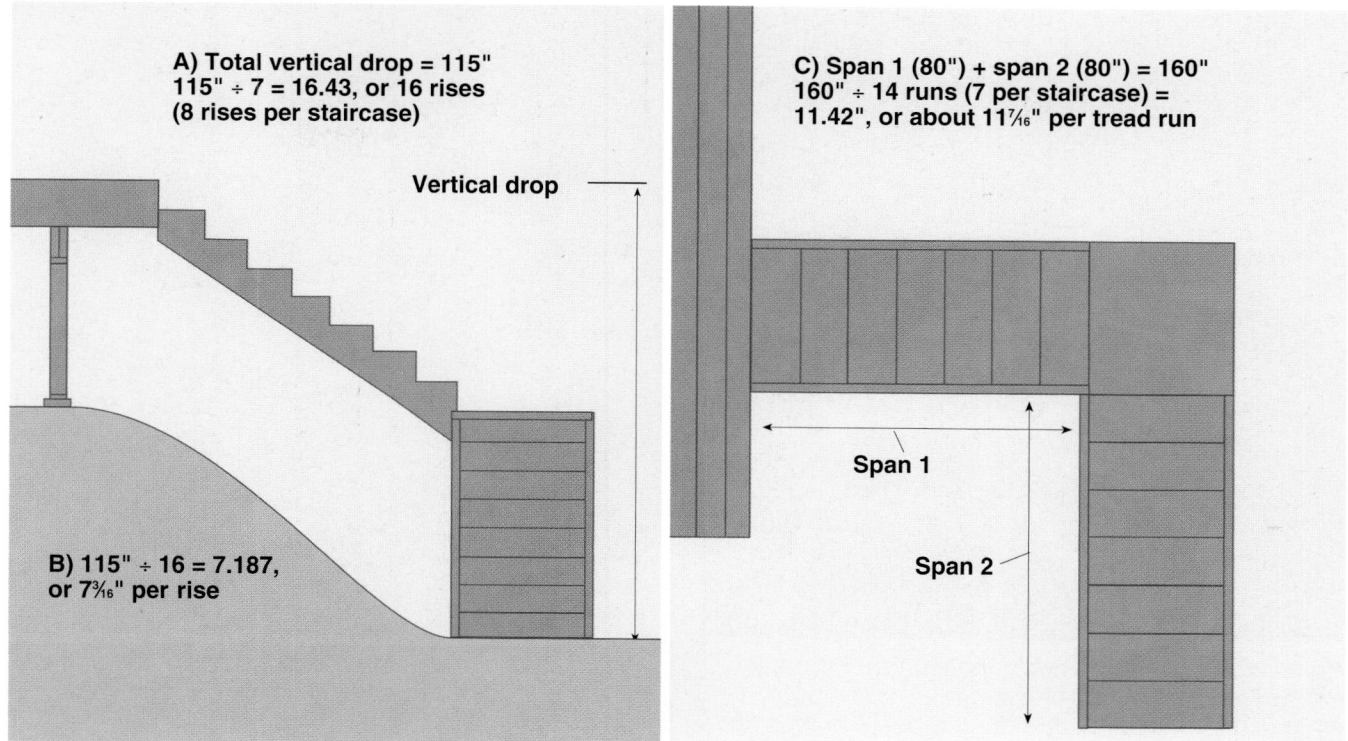

A) Total vertical drop = 115"
115" ÷ 7 = 16.43, or 16 rises
(8 rises per staircase)

Vertical drop

B) 115" ÷ 16 = 7.187,
or 7³⁄₁₆" per rise

C) Span 1 (80") + span 2 (80") = 160"
160" ÷ 14 runs (7 per staircase) =
11.42", or about 11⁷⁄₁₆" per tread run

Span 1

Span 2

1 Find the total number of step rises you will need by dividing the vertical drop by 7, rounding off fractions. (A, example above). Next, determine the exact height for each step rise by dividing the vertical drop by the number of rises (B).

2 Find the horizontal run for each step by adding the spans of both staircases (not including the landing), then dividing by the number of runs (C). Remember that the number of runs in a staircase is always one less than the number of rises.

3 If the layout does not conform with the guidelines on page 152, adjust the stairway starting point, ending point, or landing, then recalculate the measurements. After finding all dimensions, return to your building site and adjust the layout according to your final plan.

How to Build a Stairway Landing

1 Begin construction by building the landing. On a flat surface, build the landing frame from 2 × 6 lumber. Join the corners with 3" deck screws, then check for square by measuring diagonals. Adjust the frame until the diagonals are equal, then tack braces across the corners to hold the frame square.

2 Using your plan drawing, find the exact position of the landing on the ground, then set the frame in position and adjust it for level. Drive stakes to mark locations for the landing posts, using a plumb bob as a guide. Install the footings and posts for the landing.

(continued next page)

How to Build a Stairway Landing (continued)

3 From the top of the deck, measure down a distance equal to the vertical drop for the upper staircase. Attach a 2 × 4 reference board across the deck posts at this height. Position a straightedge on the reference board and against the landing posts so it is level, and mark the posts at this height. Measure down a distance equal to the thickness of the decking boards, and mark reference lines to indicate where the top of the landing frame will rest.

4 Attach the landing frame to the posts at the reference lines. Make sure the landing is level, then secure it with joist ties attached to the posts with ⅝" × 3" lag screws. Cut off the posts flush with the top of the landing frame, using a reciprocating saw.

5 Remove the diagonal braces from the top of the landing frame, then cut and install joists. (For a diagonal decking pattern, space the joists every 12".) Attach the decking boards, and trim them to the edge of the frame.

6 For extra support and to help prevent sway, create permanent cross braces by attaching 2 × 4 boards diagonally from the bottoms of the posts to the inside of the landing frame. Brace at least two sides of the landing. Remove the temporary braces and stakes holding the posts.

Tips for Laying Out Stairway Stringers

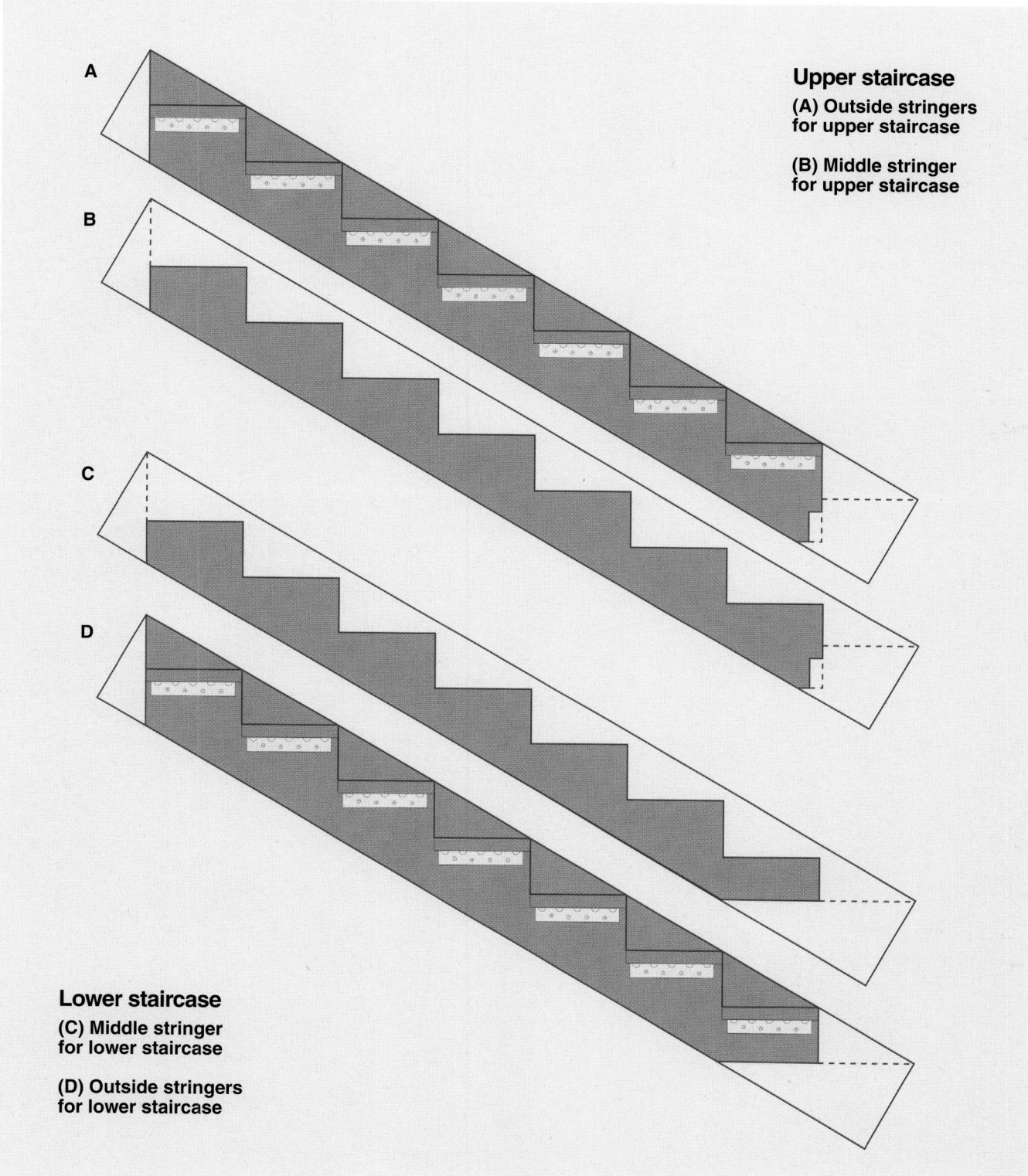

Upper staircase

(A) Outside stringers for upper staircase

(B) Middle stringer for upper staircase

Lower staircase

(C) Middle stringer for lower staircase

(D) Outside stringers for lower staircase

Lay out stringers on 2 × 12 lumber using a carpenter's square. Trim off the waste sections with a circular saw, finishing the notched cuts with a handsaw—in the illustrations above, the waste sections are left unshaded. In standard deck construction, the outside stringers are fitted with metal tread supports that are attached to the inside faces of the stringers. The middle stringer in each flight of stairs is notched to create surfaces that support the stair treads—when cut, these surfaces must align with the tops of the metal tread supports. For the upper staircase stringers, notches are cut at the bottom, front edges to fit over a 2 × 4 cleat that is attached to the landing (see page 153). The top of each notch should lie below the nose of the bottom tread by a distance equal to one rise plus the thickness of a decking board.

How to Build the Lower Staircase

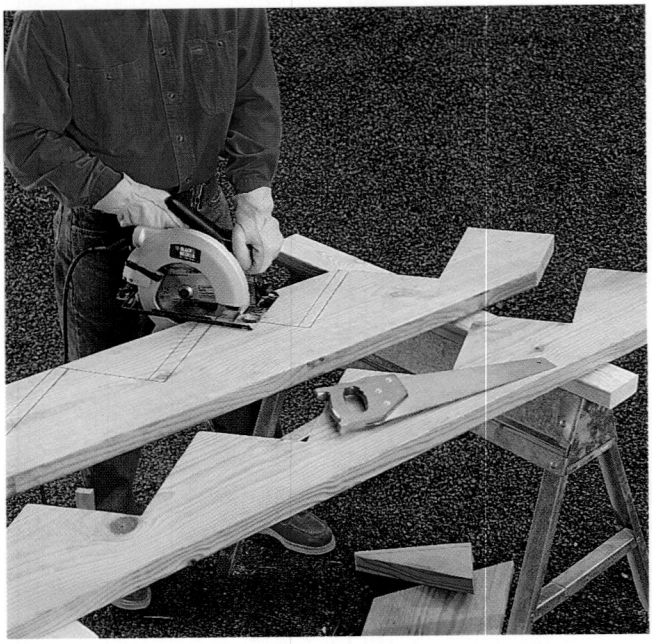

1 Lay out and cut all stringers for both the upper and lower staircases (page 157). For the center stringers only, cut notches where the treads will rest. Start the notches with a circular saw, then finish the cuts with a handsaw. Measure and cut all tread boards.

2 Use ¾"-long lag screws to attach angle brackets to the stringers where the treads will rest, then turn the stringers upside down and attach the treads with lag screws. Gap between tread boards should be no more than ⅜".

3 Dig and pour a concrete footing to support each stringer. Make sure the footings are level and are the proper height to the landing. Install a metal J-bolt in each footing while the concrete is wet, positioning the bolts so they will be offset about 2" from the stringers. After the concrete dries, cut 2 × 4 footing cleats, drill holes in them, and attach them to the J-bolts with nuts (see construction details, page 153).

4 Attach a 2 × 6 nailer to the landing to support the center stringer (page 153), then set the staircase in place, making sure the outside stringers are flush with the top of the decking. Use corner brackets and joist-hanger nails to anchor the stringers to the rim joist and nailer. Attach the bottoms of the stringers by nailing them to the footing cleats.

How to Build the Upper Staircase

1 Measure and cut a 2 × 4 cleat to match the width of the upper staircase, including the stringers. Use lag screws to attach the cleat to the rim joist on the landing, flush with the tops of the joists. Notch the bottoms of all stringers to fit around the cleat (page 153), and attach angle brackets on the stringers to support the treads.

2 To support the center stringer at the top of the staircase, measure and cut a 2 × 6 nailer equal to the width of the staircase. Attach the nailer to the rim joist with metal straps and screws.

3 Position the stringers so they rest on the landing cleat. Make sure the stringers are level and properly spaced, then toenail the bottoms of the stringers into the cleat, using galvanized 16d nails. At the top of the staircase, use angle brackets to attach the outside stringers to the rim joist and the middle stringer to the nailer.

4 Measure, cut, and position tread boards over the angle brackets, then attach them from below, using ¾"-long lag screws. The gap between tread boards should be no more than ⅜". After completing the stairway, install railings (pages 196 to 197).

Building Decks on Steep Slopes

Constructing a deck on a steep slope can be a complicated job if you use standard deck-building techniques. Establishing a layout for posts and footings is difficult on steeply pitched terrain, and construction can be demanding when one end of the deck is far above your head.

Professional deck contractors adapt to steep slope situations by using a temporary post-and-beam support structure, and by slightly altering the construction sequence. Rather than beginning with post-footing layout, experienced builders begin by constructing the outer frame and raising it onto a temporary support structure. Once the elevated frame is in position, the locations of the permanent posts and footings can be determined.

In most instances, you will need helpers when building a deck on a steep slope. To raise and position the deck frame on temporary supports, for example, you will need the help of three or four other people.

On some building sites, a deck may be at a considerable height above the ground. Always exercise caution when working at heights on a ladder or scaffold (page opposite).

The directions on the following pages show the construction of a deck featuring a corner-post design, but the technique can easily be adapted to cantilevered decks.

Positioning and measuring posts on a steep slope is much easier if the deck frame is already in position, resting on temporary supports.

Safety Tips for Building Decks on Slopes

Stepladders should be used in the open position only if the ground is level. On uneven ground you can use a closed stepladder by building a support ledger from 2 × 6 scraps (inset) and clamping it to a post. Lean the closed ladder against the ledger, and level the base of the ladder, if necessary (below). Never climb onto the top step of the ladder.

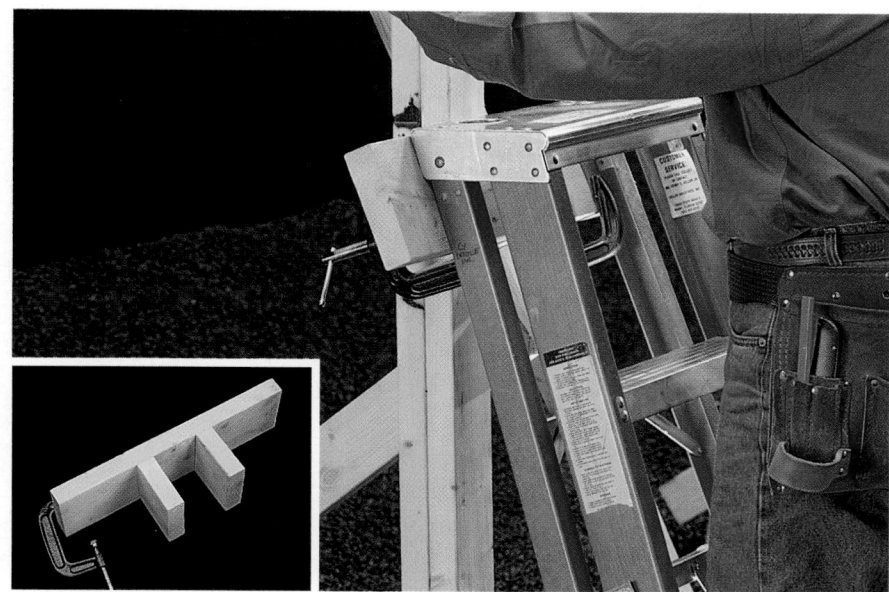

Extension ladders should be leveled and braced. Install sturdy blocking under ladder legs if the ground is uneven or soft, and drive a stake behind each ladder foot to keep it from slipping. Never exceed the weight limit printed on the ladder.

Scaffolding can be rented from rental centers or paint supply stores. When working at heights, scaffolding offers a safer, more stable working surface. Place blocking under the legs of the scaffolding, and level it by screwing the threaded legs in or out.

How to Build a Deck on a Steep Slope

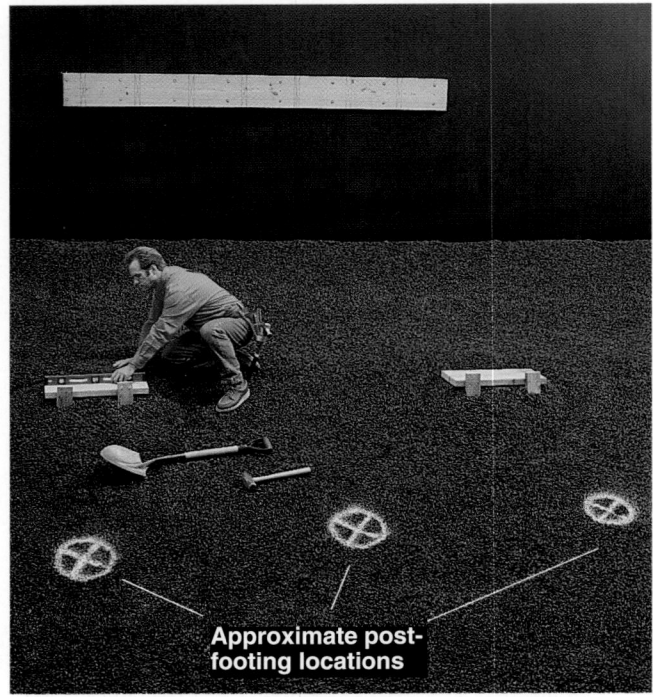

Approximate post-footing locations

1 After installing the ledger, use spray paint or stakes to mark the approximate locations for the post footings, according to your deck plans. Lay two 2 × 12 scraps on the ground to support temporary posts. Level the scraps, and anchor them with stakes. The bases for the temporary posts should be at least 2 ft. away from post-footing locations.

2 Construct two temporary posts by facenailing pairs of long 2 × 4s together. Erect each post by positioning it on the base and attaching a diagonal 2 × 4 brace. Toenail the post to the base.

3 Attach a second diagonal brace to each post, running at right angles to the first brace. Adjust the posts until they are plumb, then secure them in place by driving stakes into the ground and screwing the diagonal braces to the stakes.

4 Mark a cutoff line on each post by holding a long, straight 2 × 4 against the bottom of the ledger and the face of the post, then marking the post along the bottom edge of the 2 × 4. Cut off the posts at this height, using a reciprocating saw.

5 Construct a temporary support beam at least 2 ft. longer than the width of your deck by facenailing a pair of 2 × 4s together. Center the beam on top of the posts, and toenail it in place.

6 Build the outer frame of your deck according to your construction plans, and attach joist hangers to the inside of the frame, spaced 16" on center. With several helpers, lift the frame onto the temporary supports and carefully move it into position against the ledger. NOTE: On very large or high decks, you may need to build the frame piece by piece on top of the temporary supports.

(continued next page)

How to Build a Deck on a Steep Slope (continued)

7 Endnail the side joists to the ends of the ledger, then reinforce the joint by installing angle brackets in the inside corners of the frame.

8 Check to make sure the frame is square by measuring the diagonals. If the measurements are not the same, adjust the frame on the temporary beam until it is square. Also check the frame to make sure it is level; if necessary, shim between the temporary beam and the side joists to level the frame. Toenail the frame to the temporary beam.

9 Use a plumb bob suspended from the deck frame to stake the exact locations for post footings on the ground. NOTE: Make sure the footing stakes correspond to the exact center of the posts, as indicated by your deck plans.

10 Dig and pour footings for each post. While the concrete is still wet, insert J-bolts for post anchors, using a plumb bob to ensure that the bolts are at the exact center of the post locations. Let the concrete dry completely before continuing.

11 Check once more to make sure the deck frame is square and level, and adjust if necessary. Attach post anchors to the footings, then measure from the anchors to the bottom edge of the deck beam to determine the length for each post. NOTE: If your deck uses a cantilever design, make sure to allow for the height of the beam when cutting the posts.

12 Cut posts and attach them to the beam and footing with post-beam caps and post anchors (page 137). Brace the posts by attaching 2 × 4 boards diagonally from the bottom of the post to the inside surface of the deck frame (page 156). Remove the temporary supports, then complete the project using standard deck-building techniques.

Joists on a cantilevered deck can be easily marked for angled cuts by snapping a chalk line between two points on adjacent sides of the deck corner. Marking and cutting joists in this fashion is easier than measuring and cutting the joists individually. To help hold the joists in place while marking, tack a brace across the ends. Mark joist locations on the brace for reference.

Working with Angles

Decks with geometric shapes and angled sides have much more visual interest than basic square or rectangular decks. Most homes and yards are configured with predictable 90° angles and straight sides, so an angled deck offers a pleasing visual surprise.

Contrary to popular belief, elaborate angled decks are relatively easy to plan and build, if you follow the lead of professional designers. As professionals know, most polygon-shaped decks are nothing more than basic square or rectangular shapes with one or more corners removed. An octagonal island deck, for example, is simply a square with all four corners omitted.

Seen in this light, complicated multilevel decks with many sides become easier to visualize and design.

For visual balance and ease of construction, use 45° angles when designing an angled, geometric deck. In this way, the joinery requires only common cutting angles (90°, 45°, or 22½°), and you can use skewed 45° joist hangers, readily available at home centers. You can, of course, build a deck using irregular angles, but computing the cutting angles on such a deck is much more difficult, and you may need to special-order joist hangers and other hardware.

Design Options for Angled Decks

Cantilever design is the easiest and least expensive to build, since it requires the fewest posts. But the length of the angled side is limited by code regulations that restrict the amount of joist overhang. And since the joists rest on top of the beam, cantilever designs are not suited for a deck with a very low profile. On cantilever designs, the joists along the angled side are beveled at 45° at the ends and are attached to the rim joist by endnailing. See page 169.

Corner-post design is a good choice for large decks with long angled sides. It also works well for low-profile decks, since the joists are mounted to the inside faces of the beams. Many builders use a single beveled post to support the angled corners on this type of deck, but our method calls for two posts and footings at each of these corners, making the design easier to construct and more versatile. On a corner-post deck, the joists on the angled side are square-cut, and are attached to the beam with skewed 45° joist hangers. See page 170.

Multilevel design features an upper platform built using the corner-post method (above), but adds a lower platform (see pages 146 to 147). The lower level is supported by a second angled beam, created by sandwiching timbers around the same posts that support the upper platform. On the lower platform, the joists rest on top of the beam and are beveled on the back ends so they are flush with the edge of the beam. See page 173.

Design & Construction Tips for Angled Decks

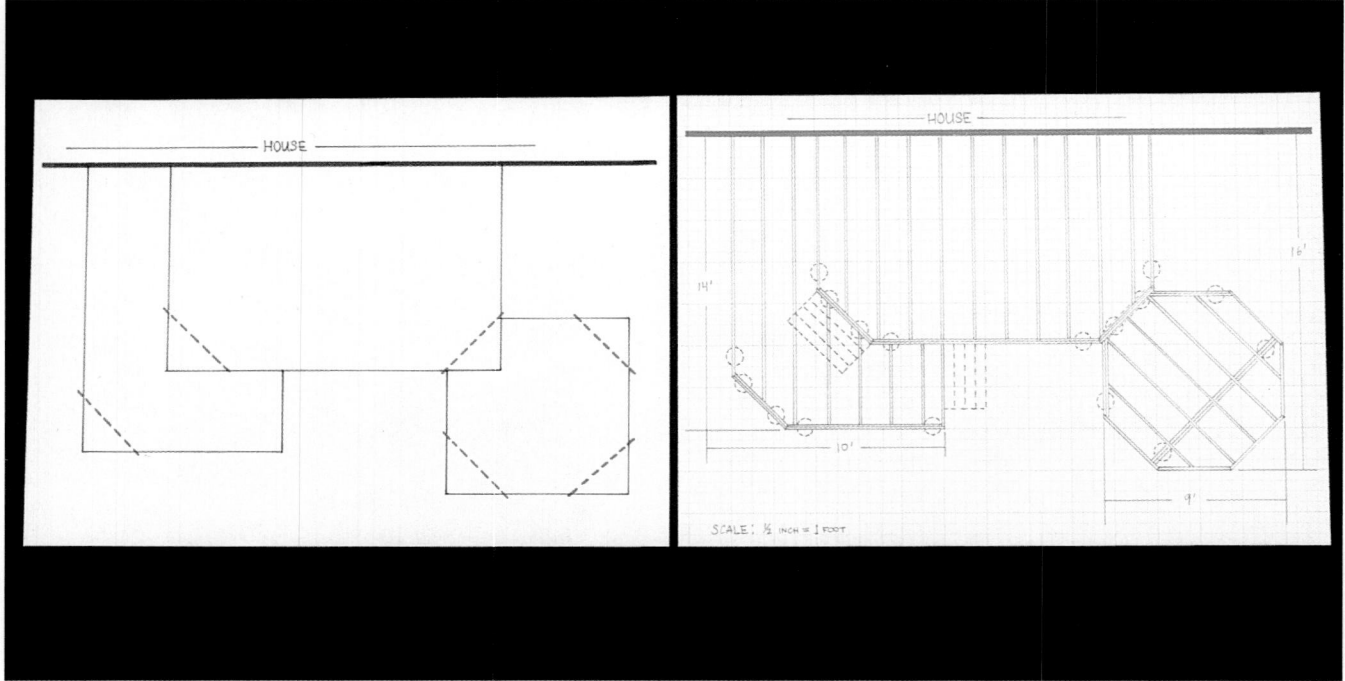

Draw squares and rectangles to create the basic deck platforms, then form angles by eliminating one or more corners. Using this method, you can design an almost infinite variety of single- and multilevel geometric decks. To ensure 45° angles, make sure the sides of the removed corners are the same length.

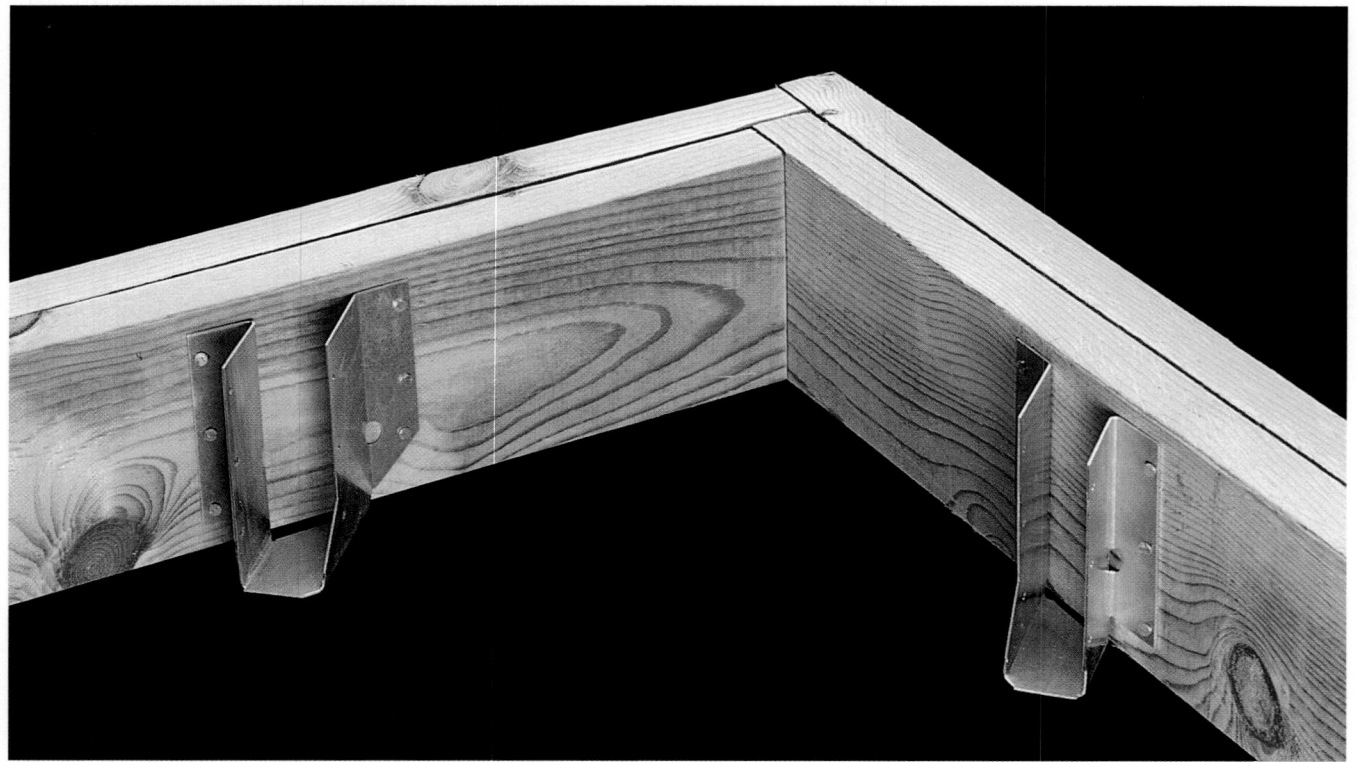

Use skewed 45° joist hangers to install joists when the beams are not parallel to the ledger. When mounted with skewed hangers, joists can be square-cut at the ends. Skewed 45° joist hangers are available at building centers in both left- and right-hand skews. However, if your deck joists angle away from the beam at angles other than 45°, you will need to special order skewed joist hangers to fit your situation.

How to Build an Angled Deck Using the Cantilever Design

1 Lay out and begin construction, using standard deck-building techniques. After installing the joists, mark cutting lines on the angled side by snapping a chalk line across the tops of the joists. Make sure the chalk line is angled 45° to the edge of the deck.

2 At the outside joists, use a speed square to change the 45° chalk line to a line angled at 22½° in the opposite direction. When joined to a rim joist that is also cut to 22½°, the corner will form the correct angle.

3 Use a combination square to extend the angle marks down the faces of the joists. Bevel-cut the deck joists with a circular saw, using a clamped board as a guide for the saw foot. Interior joists should be beveled to 45°; outside joists, to 22½°.

4 Cut and install the rim joists. At the angled corners, bevel-cut the ends of the rim joists at 22½°. Endnail the rim joists in place, and reinforce the inside corners with adjustable angle brackets attached with joist-hanger nails (page 173). Finish the deck, using standard deck-building techniques.

How to Build an Angled Deck Using the Corner-post Design

1 Use boards to create a rectangular template of the deck. To ensure that the template is square, use the 3-4-5 triangle method: From the corner directly below the ledger, measure 3 ft. along the foundation, and mark a point. Measure out along the template board 4 ft., and mark a second point. Measure diagonally between the two points. This measurement should be 5 ft.; if not, adjust the template to square it.

2 Indicate each angled edge by positioning a board diagonally across the corner of the template. To ensure that the angles measure 45°, make sure the perpendicular legs of the triangle have exactly the same measurement. Nail the boards together where they overlap.

3 Mark locations for post footings with stakes or spray paint. At each 45° corner, mark locations for two posts, positioned about 1 ft. on each side of the corner. Temporarily move the board template, then dig and pour concrete footings.

4 While the concrete is still wet, reposition the template and check to make sure it is square to the ledger. Use a nail to scratch a reference line across the concrete next to the template boards, then insert J-bolts in the wet concrete. Let the concrete dry completely.

5 Attach metal post anchors to the J-bolts, centering them on the reference lines scratched in the concrete. The front and back edges of the anchors should be parallel to the reference line.

6 Measure and cut beam timbers to size. On ends that will form angled corners, use a speed square to mark 22½° angles on the tops of the timbers, then use a combination square to extend cutting lines down the face of the boards. Use a circular saw set for a 22½° bevel to cut off the timbers, then join them together with 16d nails.

7 Set posts into the post anchors, then use a mason's string and line level to mark cutoff lines on the posts at a point level with the bottom of the ledger. Cut off the posts, using a reciprocating saw. Attach post-beam caps to the posts, then set the beams into place. Secure beam corners together with adjustable angle brackets attached to the inside of each corner with joist-hanger nails (page 173).

(continued next page)

How to Build an Angled Deck Using the Corner-post Design (continued)

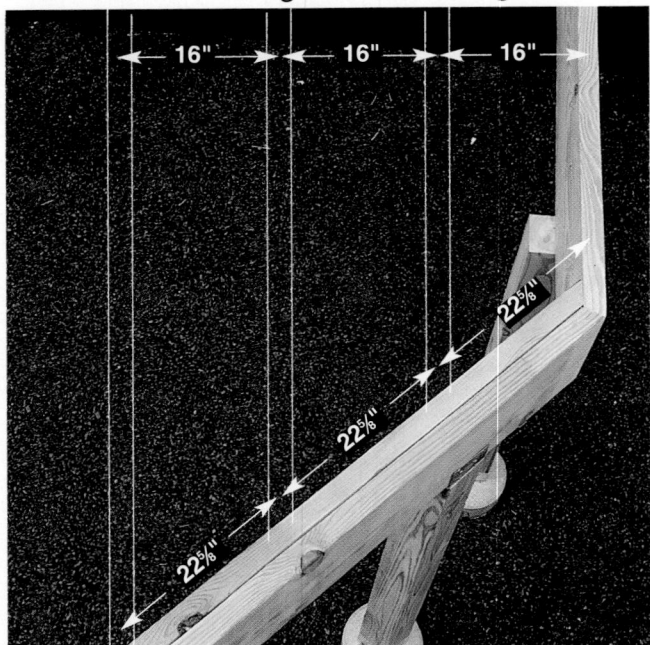

8 Measure and mark joist locations on the ledger and beams. If your joists are spaced 16" on center along the ledger, they will be spaced 22⅝" apart measured along the angled beam. If they are spaced 24" on center at the ledger, the joists will be spaced 33⁵⁄₁₆" apart along the angled beam.

9 Attach joist hangers at the layout marks on the ledger and beam. Use skewed 45° joist hangers on the angled beam.

10 Cut and install joists, securing them with joist-hanger nails. Joists installed in skewed 45° joist hangers can be square-cut; they need not be beveled to match the angle of the beam. Complete the deck, using standard deck-building techniques.

Corner-post Variation: Adding a Second Platform

1 After installing the beam and joists for the top deck platform, mark the posts to indicate where the beam for the lower platform will be attached. Remember that the joists for the lower deck platform will rest on top of the beam (page 143). To help measure for beam length, clamp scrap pieces of 2 × 4 to the front and back faces of the posts over the layout marks. At corners, the ends of the 2 × 4s should touch.

2 Determine the length for each beam timber by measuring from the point where the 2 × 4 blocks touch. Remember that this measurement represents the short side of the bevel-cut timbers.

3 Lay out and cut beam timbers to length. At angled ends, cut the timbers with a 22½° bevel (page 171). Position and attach the beams to the posts, using 3" lag screws and joist ties. Reinforce angled corners with adjustable angle brackets attached with joist-hanger nails (photo, step 4). Install the remaining posts for the lower platform.

4 Measure and cut joists for the lower platform, attaching them to the beam by toenailing with 16d nails. Where joists rest on the angled beam, position the joists so they overhang the beam, then scribe cutting lines along the back edge of the beam. Bevel-cut the joists to this angle. Cut and install rim joists, then complete the deck, using standard deck-building techniques.

Creating Curves

By their nature, curved shapes lend a feeling of tranquility to a landscape. A deck with curved sides tends to encourage quiet relaxation. A curved deck can also provide an effective visual transition between the sharp architectural angles of the house and the more sweeping natural lines of the surrounding landscape.

Curved decks nearly always use a cantilevered design (page 44), in which the curved portion of the deck overhangs a beam that is set back from the edge of the deck. This set-back distance generally should be no more than one-third of the total length of the deck joists, but longer cantilevers are possible if you use a combination of thicker joists, closer joist spacing, and stronger wood species, such as southern yellow pine.

Accurate planning is essential when building a curved deck. Building inspectors carefully scrutinize plans for cantilevered decks, so you will need precisely drawn construction plans and a complete materials list when you apply for a building permit. Detailed plans will also help you define and visualize how you will use the deck, and they can help you save money by determining exact lengths for joists and decking boards.

If your curved deck will be high enough to require a railing, we recommend a design that incorporates a circular curve rather than an elliptical or irregular curve. Adding a curved railing (pages 198 to 201) is much easier if the deck curve is based on a circular shape.

A curved deck is created by cutting joists to match the curved profile, then attaching a curved rim joist, which can be shaped in one of two ways (page opposite). Braces attached to the tops of the joists hold them in place as the rim joist is installed.

Design Options for Curved Decks

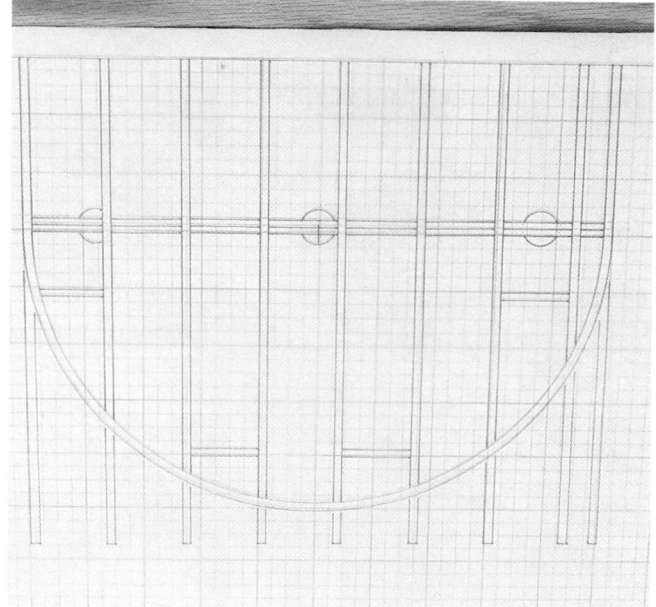

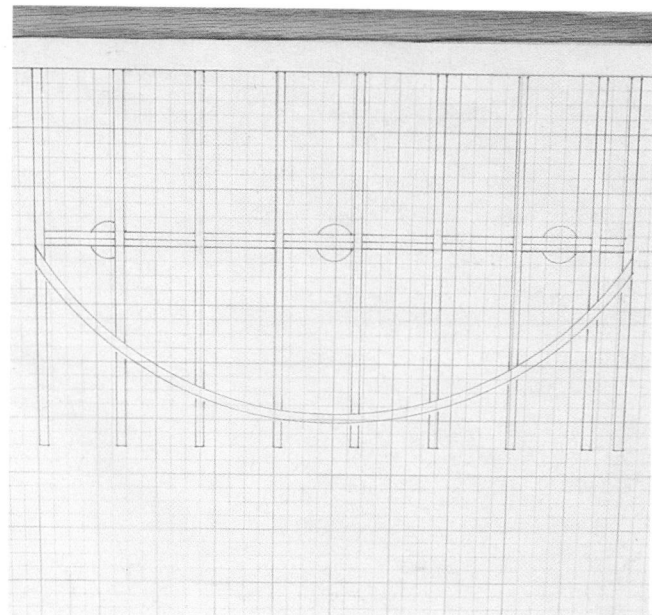

Circular designs are the best choice for curved decks that require railings. However, circular curves require a fairly long cantilever, a limitation that may limit the overall size of your deck. Circular decks are laid out using simple geometry and a long compass tool, called a *trammel,* which you can make yourself. See page 176.

Irregular or elliptical curves should be used only on relatively low decks, since railings are quite difficult to construct for this kind of curve. These designs also work well for large decks, since the amount of overhang on the cantilever is relatively short compared to that for a circular curve. See page 176.

Construction Options

Kerfed rim joist is formed by making a series of thin vertical cuts (kerfs) across the inside face of the board, making it flexible enough to wrap around the curve. A kerfed rim joist made from 2"-thick dimension lumber is sufficiently strong, but if you are kerfing a 1"-thick redwood or cedar fascia board, it should be backed with a laminated rim joist (photo, right). See page 178.

Laminated rim joist is made by bending several layers of flexible ¼" or ⅜"-thick exterior-grade plywood around the curve, joining each layer to the preceding layer with glue and screws. A laminated rim joist can stand alone, or it can provide backing for a more decorative fascia, such as a kerfed redwood or cedar board. See page 179.

How to Lay Out a Curved Deck

1 Install posts and beam for a cantilevered deck. Cut joists slightly longer than their final length, and attach them to the ledger and the beam. Add cross-blocking between the two outside joists to ensure that they remain plumb.

2 Mark the joist spacing on a 1 × 4 brace, and tack it across the tops of the joists at the point where the deck curve will begin. Measure the distance between the inside edges of the outer joists at each end of the beam, then divide this measurement in half to determine the radius of the circular curve. Mark the 1 × 4 brace to indicate the midpoint of the curve.

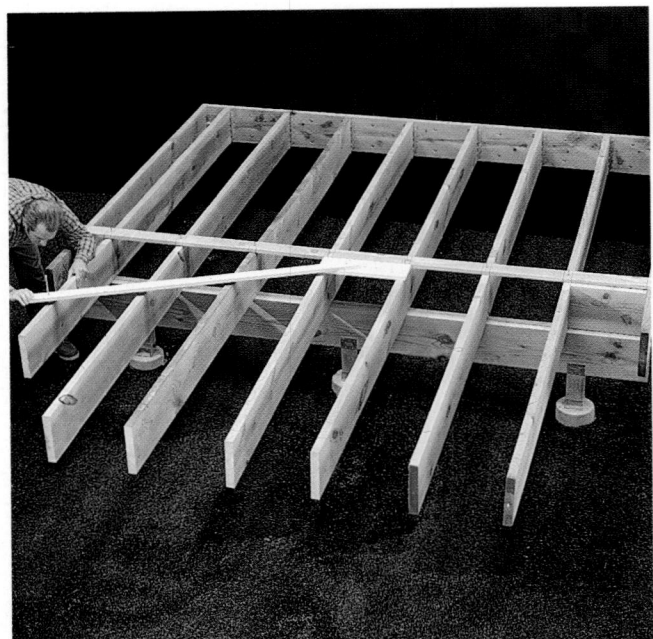

3 Build a trammel by anchoring one end of a long, straight 1 × 2 to the centerpoint of the curve, using a nail. (If the centerpoint lies between joists, attach a 1 × 4 brace across the joists to provide an anchor.) Measure out along the arm of the trammel a distance equal to the curve radius, and drill a hole. Insert a pencil in the hole, and pivot the trammel around the centerpoint, marking the joists for angled cuts.

VARIATION: For elliptical or irregular curves, temporarily nail vertical anchor boards to the outside joists at the start of the curve. Position a long strip of flexible material, such as hardboard or paneling, inside the anchor boards, then push the strip to create the desired bow. Drive nails into the joists to hold it in position, then scribe cutting lines on the tops of the joists.

4 Use a speed square or protractor to determine the bevel angles you will use to cut the joists. Position the square so the top is aligned with the layout mark on the joist, then find the degree measurement by following the edge of the joist down from the pivot point and reading where it intersects the degree scale on the square.

5 Use a combination square to extend the cutting lines down the front and back faces of the joists. At the outside joists where the curve begins, mark square cutting lines at the point where the circular curve touches the inside edge of the joists.

6 Cut off each joist with a circular saw set to the proper bevel. Clamp a straightedge to the joist to provide a guide for the foot of the saw. On the outside joists where the curve begins, make 90° cuts.

7 Where the bevel angle is beyond the range of your circular saw, use a reciprocating saw to cut off the joists.

How to Construct a Kerfed Rim Joist for a Curved Deck

1 Mark the inside face of the rim joist lumber with a series of parallel lines, 1" apart. Using a circular saw or radial-arm saw set to a blade depth equal to ¾ of the rim joist thickness (1⅛", for 2"-thick lumber), make crosscut kerfs at each line. Soak the rim joist in water for about 2 hours to make it easier to bend.

2 Install a cross block between the first two joists on each side of the curve, positioned so half the block is covered by the square-cut outside joist (inset). While it is still damp, attach the rim joist by butting it against the end joist and attaching it to the cross block with 3" deck screws. Bend the rim joist so it is flush against the ends of the joists, and attach with two or three 3" deck screws driven at each joist.

3 Where butt joints are necessary, mark and cut the rim joist so the joint will fall at the center of a joist. To avoid chipping, cut off the rim joist at one of the saw kerfs.

4 Complete the installation by butting the end of the rim joist against the outside joist and attaching it to the cross block. Use bar clamps to hold the rim joist in position as you screw it to the blocking. NOTE: If the rim joist flattens near the sides of the deck, install additional cross-blocking, cut to the contour of the curve, to hold the rim joist in proper position.

How to Construct a Curved Rim Joist with Laminated Plywood

Blocking

1 Install blocking between the first two joists on each side of the deck (step 2, previous page). Cut four strips of ¼"-thick exterior plywood the same width as the joists. Butt the first strip against the outside joist and attach it to the blocking with 1½" deck screws. Bend the strip around the joists and attach with deck screws. If necessary, install additional blocking to keep the plywood in the proper curve. If butt joints are necessary, make sure they fall at the center of joists.

2 Attach the remaining strips of plywood one at a time, attaching them to previous layers with 1" deck screws and exterior wood glue. Make sure butt joints are staggered so they do not overlap previous joints. For the last layer, use a finish strip of ⅜" cedar plywood. Where the finish strip butts against the outside joists, bevel-cut the ends at 10° to ensure a tight fit.

How to Install Decking on a Curved Deck

1 Install decking for the square portion of the deck, then test-fit decking boards on the curved portion. If necessary, you can make minor adjustments in the spacing to avoid cutting very narrow decking boards at the end of the curve. When satisfied with the layout, scribe cutting lines on the underside of the decking boards, following the edge of the rim joist.

2 Remove the scribed decking boards, and cut along the cutting lines with a jig saw. Install the decking boards with deck screws, and smooth the cut edges of the decking boards with a belt sander, if necessary.

Framing for Insets

If your planned deck site has a tree, boulder, or other large obstacle, you may be better off building around it rather than removing it. Although framing around a landscape feature makes construction more difficult, the benefits usually make the effort worthwhile. A deck with an attractive tree set into it, for example, is much more appealing than a stark, exposed deck built on a site that has been leveled by a bulldozer.

The same methods used to frame around a pre-existing obstacle also can be used to create a decorative or functional inset feature, such as a planter box, child's sandbox, or brick barbecue. On a larger scale, the same framing techniques can be used to enclose a hot tub or above-ground pool.

A framed opening can also provide access to a utility fixture, such as a water faucet, electrical outlet, or central air-conditioning compressor. Covering a framed opening with a removable hatch (page 183) preserves the smooth, finished look of your deck.

Large insets that interrupt joists can compromise the strength of your deck. For this reason, inset openings require modified framing to ensure adequate strength. Double joists on either side of the opening bear the weight of double headers, which in turn support the interrupted joists. Always consult your building inspector for specifics when constructing a deck with a large inset.

Inset framing makes it possible to save mature trees when building a deck. Keeping trees and other landscape features intact helps preserve the value and appearance of your property.

Applications for Framed Insets

Trees inset into a deck should have plenty of room around them to allow for growth and wind sway. In this deck, the planter boxes have been positioned around the inset opening to lend a more natural appearance.

Fire pits can be inset into decks, if you are careful to use fireproof masonry materials and follow local code guidelines. This redwood deck has been framed around a brick fire pit that rests on a concrete slab.

Built-in planters can be inset so they are flush with the deck, or they can be built with raised timber sides for more visual impact (above). The same technique can be used to inset a sandbox in a deck.

Hot tubs are often built into a deck. In some situations, the hot tub is supported by the deck structure and is partially enclosed by a secondary platform (pages 184 to 187). Or, the hot tub can be fully inset into the deck, supported by a concrete pad on the ground.

How to Frame for an Inset

1 Modify your deck plan, if necessary, to provide the proper support for the interrupted joists in the inset opening. If the inset will interrupt one or two joists, frame both sides of the opening with double joists. If the opening is larger, you may need to install additional beams and posts around the opening to provide adequate support. Consult your building inspector for specific requirements for your situation.

2 Rough-frame the opening by using double joist hangers to install double joists on each side of the inset, and double headers between these joists. Install the interrupted joists between the double headers and the rim joist and ledger.

3 Where needed, cut and install angled nailing blocks between the joists and headers to provide additional support for the decking boards. When trimmed, decking boards may overhang support members by as much as 4" around an inset opening.

4 Lay the decking boards so the ends overhang the rough opening. Make a cardboard template to draw a cutting line on the deck boards. (When framing for a tree, leave at least 1 ft. on all sides to provide space for growth.) Cut the decking boards along the marked line, using a jig saw.

Framing Variations

Inset box shown cutaway for clarity.

Inset box can be used as a planter for flowers or herbs. Build the box from ¾"-thick exterior-grade plywood, and attach it to the framing members with deck screws. A deep box can be supported by landscape timbers. Line the inside of the box with layers of building paper, then drill ½"-wide holes in the bottom of the box to provide drainage. To keep soil from washing out through drainage holes, line the box with landscape fabric.

Access hatch made from decking can hide a utility feature, such as a water faucet or air-conditioner compressor. Install cleats along the inside of the framed opening to support the hatch. Construct the hatch from decking boards mounted on a 2 × 4 frame. Finger holes drilled in the hatch make removal easier.

Hot Tub Variation

Hot tub inset completely into a deck requires a concrete pad to support the weight. The surface decking is flush with the lip of the tub, but does not bear any of the tub's weight. For this reason, the deck height must be carefully planned when laying out the posts, beams, and joists.

Framing for a Hot Tub

Building a hot tub into a deck is usually done in one of two ways. If you design your deck at exactly the right height, you can create a full inset by resting the hot tub on a concrete pad and building the deck around it (page 181).

But on a low-profile deck, or a tall deck, the most practical solution is to mount the hot tub on the surface of the deck and build a secondary platform around it, creating a partial inset. As shown on the following pages, the structural design of the deck must be modified to ensure that it can support the added weight of a hot tub filled with water. Make sure your deck plans are approved by the building inspector before you begin work.

Installing a hot tub usually requires the installation of new plumbing and electrical lines. When planning the installation, make sure to consider the location of plumbing pipes, electrical cables, switches, and access panels. For convenience, arrange to have the rough-in work for these utilities done before you install the decking boards.

How to Frame for a Hot Tub

1 Plan posts and beams to support the maximum anticipated load, including the weight of the hot tub filled with water. In most cases, this means altering your deck plan to include extra beams and posts directly under the hot tub.

2 Lay out and install the ledger, footings, posts, and support beams, according to your deck plans. Lay out joist locations on the ledger and beams, and install the joists, following local code requirements. Many building codes require joists spaced no more than 12" on center if the deck will support a hot tub. If your hot tub requires new plumbing or electrical lines, have the preliminary rough-in work done before continuing with deck construction.

3 Install the decking boards, then snap chalk lines to outline the position of the hot tub and the raised platform that will enclose the hot tub.

4 Lay out and cut 2 × 4 sole plates and top plates for the stud walls on the raised platform.

5 Mark stud locations on the top and bottom plates. Studs should be positioned every 16" (measured on center), and at the ends of each plate.

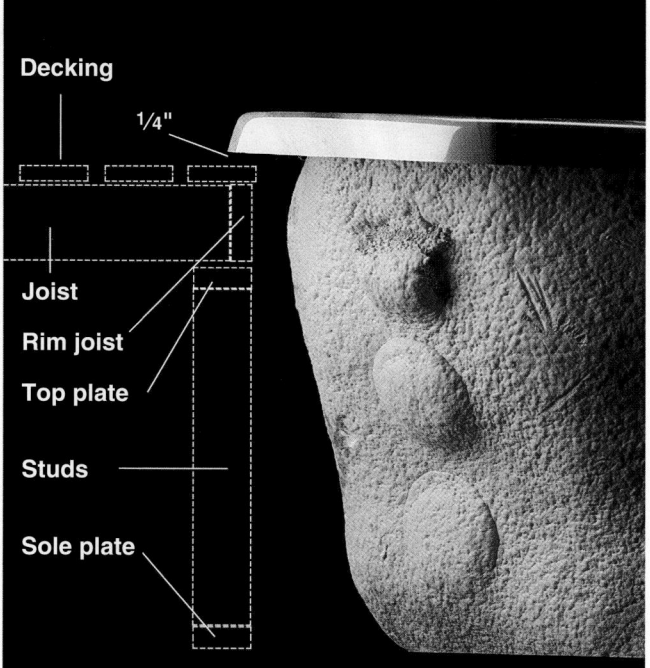

6 Measure the height of the hot tub to determine the required height of the studs in the platform walls. Remember to include the thickness of both wall plates, the joists that will rest on the walls, and the decking material on the platform. The surface of the finished platform should be ¼" below the lip of the hot tub.

(continued next page)

7 Construct the stud walls by screwing the plates to the studs. Position the walls upright on the deck over the outline marks, and anchor them to the deck with 2½" deck screws.

8 At corners, join the studs together with 3" deck screws. Check the walls for plumb, and brace them in position.

9 Toenail a 2 × 6 rim joist along the back edge of the platform, then cut and install 2 × 6 joists across the top of the stud walls at 16" intervals, toenailing them to the top plates. The ends of the joists should be set back 1½" from the edges of the top plates to allow for the rim joist.

Blocking

10 Cut 2 × 6 rim joists to length, and endnail them to the joists with 16d nails. At angled wall segments, cut diagonal blocking and attach it between the rim joist and adjoining joists with deck screws.

11 Cut decking boards, and attach them to the platform joists with 2½" deck screws. If your hot tub requires cutouts for plumbing or electrical lines, do this work now.

12 Set the hot tub in place, then build 2 × 2 stud walls around the exposed sides of the tub. Measure, cut, and install siding materials on the exposed walls.

13 Build platform steps (page 141) to provide access to the platform, using siding materials to box in the risers. Where required by code, install railings around the elevated platform (pages 188 to 193).

Railings are required for safety on most decks, but they also contribute to the overall visual appeal. Curved railings like the one shown here are usually built with the vertical baluster style. See pages 198 to 201.

Building Railings

Railings are the crowning touch for a deck project. Required by code for any deck more than 30" high, railings serve a practical function by making your deck safe. But railings also serve an ornamental function, by helping to create the style and mood of a deck.

There are numerous designs used for deck railings, but most are variations of the styles you will learn how to build on the following pages. (See pages 108 to 115 for another common variation.) The key to successful railing construction is to have detailed plans. When drawing up railing plans, exercise the same care used when creating your deck plans.

Railing construction is governed by specific code requirements. See pages 40 to 41 for basic code guidelines, and consult your local building inspector when designing a deck railing.

Railing Options

Vertical baluster railing is a popular style because it complements most house styles. To improve the strength and appearance of the railing, the advanced variation shown here uses a "false mortise" design. The 2 × 2 balusters are mounted on 2 × 2 horizontal rails that slide into mortises notched into the posts. See page 192.

Horizontal railing visually complements modern ranch-style houses with predominantly horizontal lines. For improved strength and a more attractive appearance, the style shown here features 1 × 4 rails set on edge into dadoes cut in the faces of the posts. A cap rail running over all posts and top rails helps unify and strengthen the railing. See page 193.

Wall-style railing is framed with short 2 × 4 stud walls attached flush with the edges of the deck. The stud walls and rim joists are then covered with siding materials, usually chosen to match the siding on the house. A wall-style railing creates a more private space and visually draws the deck into the home, providing a unified appearance. See pages 194 to 195.

Stairway railings are required for any stairway with more than two steps. They are usually designed to match the style used on the deck railing. See pages 196 to 197.

(continued next page)

Railing Design Variations

Unique railing patterns give your deck a custom-designed look. The railing shown here was built with 2 × 2s joined with lap joints. You can use any pattern you choose; however, the design must comply with code requirements. To ensure the safety of children, railings must be constructed so a sphere 4" in diameter cannot fit through any portion of the railing.

Painted railings create an elegant contrast to the natural wood colors found in the decking boards and stairway treads. When painted to match or complement house trim, painted railings help establish consistency of style.

Cables threaded through deck posts create a modern-looking, unobtrusive railing that does not hinder your view. Turnbuckles installed near the edge of the deck can be adjusted to keep the cables taut.

Wall-style railing with horizontal top rails provides a secure barrier for a deck high above the ground, but does not completely obstruct the view.

Railing Construction Tips

Railing posts can be surface-mounted to the edges of rim joists (left), but to improve strength and preserve the smooth lines of the deck, posts can be mounted inside the deck frame (right). Attach the posts with lag screws driven through the deck framing, then cut and endnail extra blocking between joists to reinforce the posts and to provide a nailing surface for attaching decking boards. To ensure sturdiness, posts should be spaced no more than 5 ft. apart.

Specialty railing hardware and wood products make construction easier and can be used to create a railing with a more customized appearance. Common specialty products include rail brackets (A), post caps (B), milled balusters (C), prenotched posts (D), and grippable stairway rails (E).

How to Build a Vertical Baluster Railing

1 Cut 4 × 4 railing posts to size (at least 36", plus the height of the deck rim joists). Lay out and mark partial dadoes 1½" wide and 2½" long where the horizontal 2 × 2 rails will fit. Use a circular saw set to ½" blade depth to make a series of cuts from the edge of the post to the end of layout marks, then use a chisel to clean out the dadoes and square them off. On corner posts, cut dadoes on adjoining sides of the post.

2 Attach the posts inside the rim joists (page 191). To find the length for the rails, measure between the bases of the posts, then add 1" for the ½" dadoes on each post. Measure and cut all balusters. Install the surface boards before continuing with railing construction.

3 Assemble the rails and balusters on a flat surface. Position the balusters at regular intervals (no more than 4" apart), and secure them by driving 2½" deck screws through the rails. A spacing block cut to match the desired gap can make this work easier.

4 Slide the assembled railings into the post dadoes, and toenail them in position with galvanized casing nails. Cut plugs to fit the exposed dadoes, and glue them in place. The resulting joint should resemble a mortise-and-tenon.

5 Measure and cut the 2 × 6 cap rails, then secure them by driving 2" deck screws up through the top rail. At corners, miter-cut the cap rails to form miter joints.

How to Build a Horizontal Railing

1 Cut all 4 × 4 posts to length, then clamp them together to lay out 3½"-wide × ¾"-deep dadoes for the horizontal rails. Cut the dadoes by making a series of parallel cuts, about ¼" apart, between the layout marks. For corner posts, cut dadoes on adjacent faces of the post.

2 Knock out the waste wood between the layout marks, using a hammer, then use a chisel to smooth the bottom of each dado. Attach the posts inside the rim joists (page 191). Install decking before continuing with railing construction.

3 Determine the length of 1 × 4 rails by measuring between the bases of the posts. Cut rails to length, then nail them in place using 8d splitless cedar siding nails. At corners, bevel-cut the ends of the rails to form miter joints. If the rails butt together, the joint should fall at the center of a post.

Cleat

4 Measure and cut 2 × 2 cleats and attach them between the posts, flush with the top rail, using galvanized casing nails. Then, measure and cut cap rails, and position and attach them by driving 2" deck screws up through the cleats. At corners, miter-cut the ends of the cap rails.

How to Build a Wall-style Railing

1 Cut posts to length, then mark the bottoms of the posts for 1½"-deep notches that will allow the posts to fit flush with the outside edges of the rim joists. Make the cross-grain cut first, then set the circular saw to maximum blade depth and make rip cuts from the end of the post to the first cut. Remove the waste wood, and use a chisel, if necessary, to square off the shoulder of the notch. NOTE: A wall-style railing generally requires posts only at the open ends.

2 Attach the posts inside the rim joists with 2½" lag screws, then add blocking between joists to reinforce the posts (page 191). Install decking before continuing with railing construction.

3 Build a 2 × 4 stud wall to match the planned height of your railing. Space studs 16" on center, and attach them by driving deck screws through the top plate and sole plate.

4 Position the stud wall on the deck, flush with the edges of the rim joists, then anchor it by driving 3" deck screws down through the sole plate. At corners, screw the end studs of adjoining walls together. At open ends, screw the end studs to posts.

5 At corners, attach 2 × 4 nailers flush with the inside and outside edges of the top plate and sole plate to provide a nailing surface for attaching trim boards and siding materials.

6 On inside corners, attach a 2 × 2 trim strip, using 10d splitless cedar siding nails. Siding materials will be butted against this trim strip.

7 On outside corners, attach 1 × 4 trim boards on both sides, so one board overlaps the end grain of the other. The trim boards should extend down over the rim joist. Also attach trim boards around posts.

8 Cut and position cap rails on the top rail, then secure them with 2" deck screws driven up through the rail. Railing caps should be mitered at the corners.

9 Attach siding materials to the inside and outside faces of the wall, using splitless cedar siding nails. Snap level chalk lines for reference, and try to match the reveal used on your house siding; the first course should overhang the rim joist slightly. Where joints are necessary, stagger them from course to course so they do not fall on the same studs.

Building Stair Railings

For safety and convenience, any stairway that has more than two risers or is more than 30" above the ground, should have a railing. The stair railing is generally designed to match the look of the main deck railing.

The dado techniques used to attach deck rails to posts (page 193) are difficult to accomplish with the angled rails on a stairway. Instead, stairway rails can be attached with L-brackets or by toenailing them into the posts.

The sequence shown here demonstrates how to build a horizontal stair railing. A vertical baluster stair railing is built in much the same way, except that it has only two rails, with a series of angle-cut balusters attached between them.

Grippable handrails are required for stairways with more than two risers. The handrail should be shaped so the grippable portion is between 1¼" and 2" in diameter, and should be angled into posts at the ends. The top of the handrail should be 34" to 38" above the stair treads, measured from the nose of a step.

How to Build a Horizontal Stair Railing

1 Use a combination square to mark the face of the top stairway post, where the railings will fit. For most horizontal stairway designs, the top stairway rail should start level with the second deck rail. Mark the other stairway posts at the same level.

2 Position a rail board against the faces of the posts, with the bottom edge against the stringer, then scribe angled cutting lines across the rail along the inside edges of the posts. Cut the rail at these lines, then cut the remaining rails to match.

3 Secure the rails to the posts with galvanized metal L-brackets attached to the inside of the rails.

4 Measure and cut a 2 × 2 cleat, and attach it flush with the top inside edge of the top rail, using 2" deck screws. Anchor the cleat to the posts by toe-nailing with galvanized casing nails.

5 Measure and cut the cap rail to fit over the top rail and cleat. At the bottom of the railing, cut the post at an angle and attach the cap rail so it overhangs the post slightly. Secure the cap rail by driving 2" deck screws up through the cleat.

6 Measure and cut a grippable handrail, attaching it to the posts with mounting brackets. Miter-cut the ends, and create a return back to the post by cutting another mitered section of handrail and nailing it in place between the handrail and post (page opposite).

Building Curved Railings

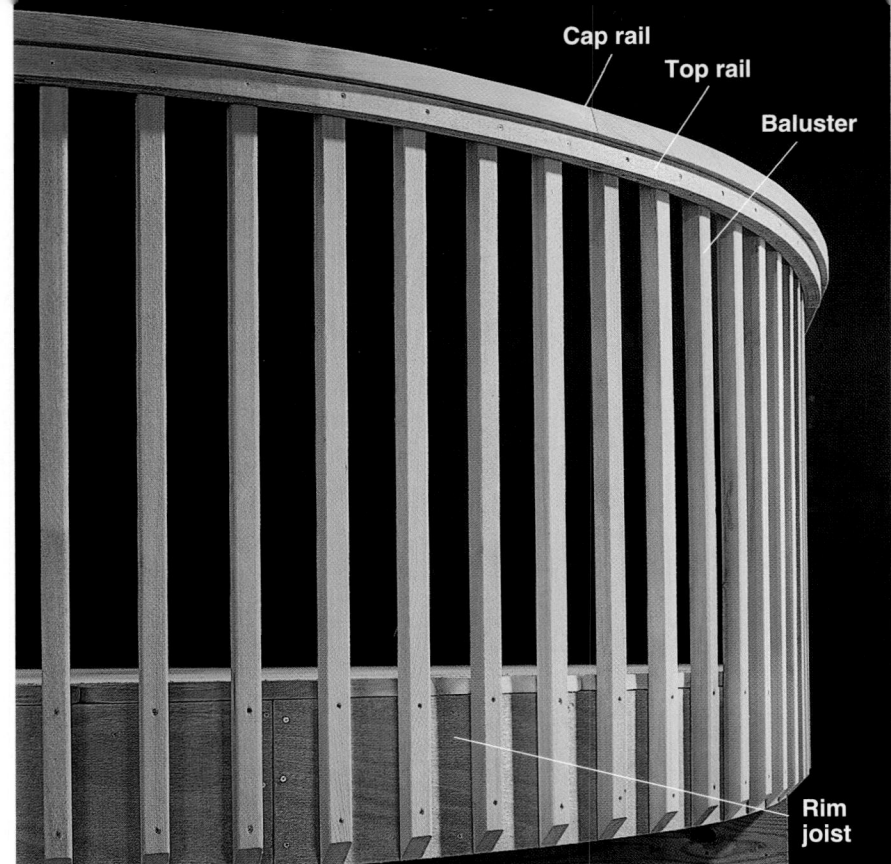

Laying out and constructing a curved railing requires a basic understanding of geometry and the ability to make detailed drawings using a compass, protractor, and a special measuring tool called a *scale ruler*.

The method for constructing a curved cap rail shown on the following pages works only for symmetrical, circular curves—quarter circles, half circles, or full circles. If your deck has irregular or elliptical curves, creating a cap rail is very difficult. For these curves, it is best to limit the railing design to include only balusters and a laminated top rail.

Components of a curved railing include: vertical balusters attached to the curved rim joist, a top rail built from laminated layers of plywood, and a curved cap rail. The cap rail is constructed by laying out mitered sections of 2 × 12 lumber, marking a curved shape, and cutting it out with a jig saw.

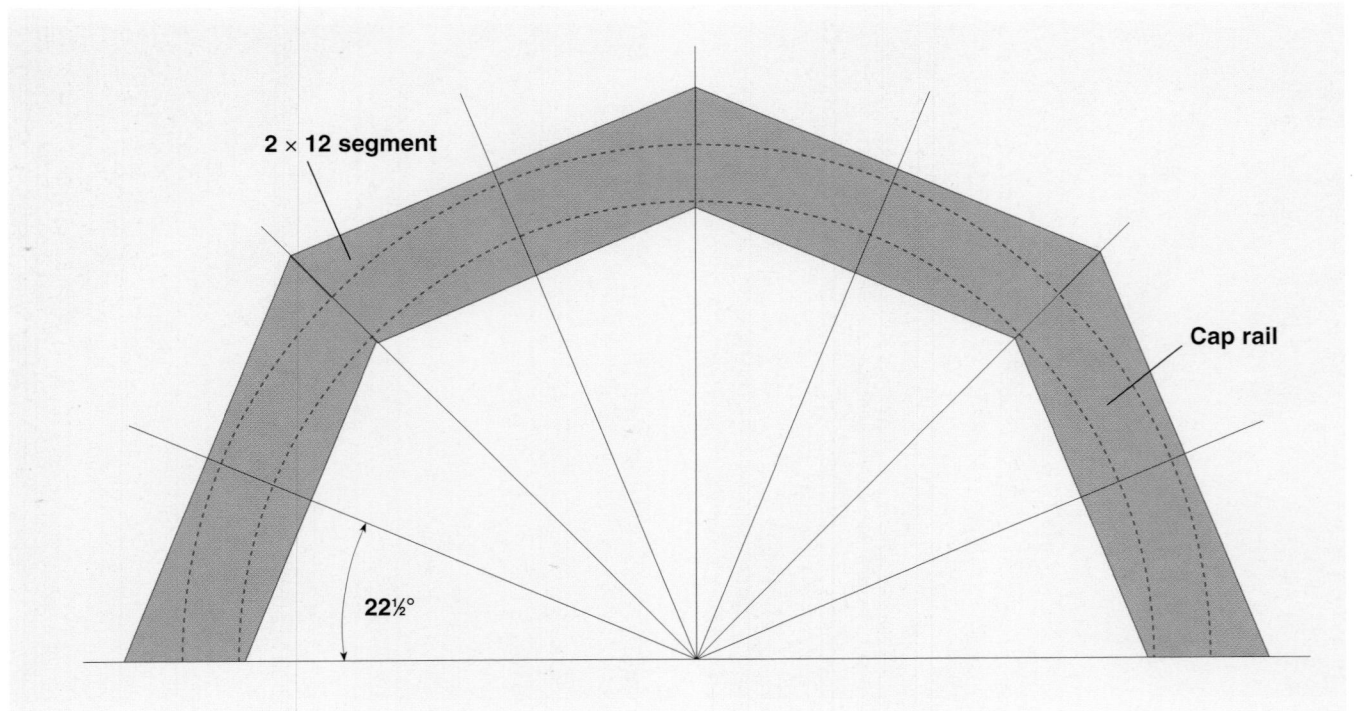

Curved cap rail is created from mitered segments of 2 × 12 lumber. After positioning the 2 × 12 segments end to end, the shape of the 6"-wide cap rail is outlined on the pieces. For a semicircle with a radius of up to 7 ft., four 2 × 12 segments will be needed, with ends mitered at 22½°. For a semicircle with a larger radius, you will need eight segments, with ends mitered at 11¼°.

How to Build a Curved Railing

1 To create a curved top rail, use exterior glue to laminate four 1½"-wide strips of ⅜"-thick cedar plywood together, using the curved rim joist of the deck as a bending form. First, cover the rim joist with kraft paper for protection. Then, begin wrapping strips of plywood around the rim joist. Clamp each strip in position, starting at one end of the curve. The strips should differ in length to ensure that butt joints will be staggered from layer to layer.

2 Continue working your way around the rim joist, toward the other end. Make sure to apply clamps on both sides of the butt joints where plywood strips meet. Cut the last strips slightly overlong, then trim the laminated rail to the correct length after the glue has set. For extra strength, drive 1" deck screws through the rail at 12" intervals after all strips are glued together. Unclamp the rail, and sand the top and bottom edges smooth.

3 Install prenotched 4 × 4 posts (page 191) at the square corners of the deck. Then, cut 2 × 2 balusters to length, beveling the bottom ends at 45°. Attach the balusters to the rim joist with 2½" deck screws, using a spacer to maintain even intervals. Clamp the curved top rail to the tops of the balusters and posts, then attach it with deck screws.

4 After the top rail and balusters are in place, attach 2 × 2 top rails to the balusters in the straight sections of the deck. The ends of the straight top rails should be flush against the ends of the curved top rail. Now, measure the distance between the inside faces of the balusters at each end of the curve. Divide this distance in half to find the required radius for the curved cap rail.

(continued next page)

5 Using a scale of 1" equals 1 ft., make a diagram of the deck. (A scale ruler makes this job easier.) First, draw the arc of the deck with a compass, using the radius measurement found in step 4. Divide the curved portion of the deck into an even number of equal sections by using a protractor to draw radius lines from the center of the curve. For a semicircular curve, it is usually sufficient to draw eight radius lines, angled at 22½° to one another. (For a deck with a radius of more than 7 ft., you may need to divide the semicircle into 16 portions, with radius lines angled at 11¼°.)

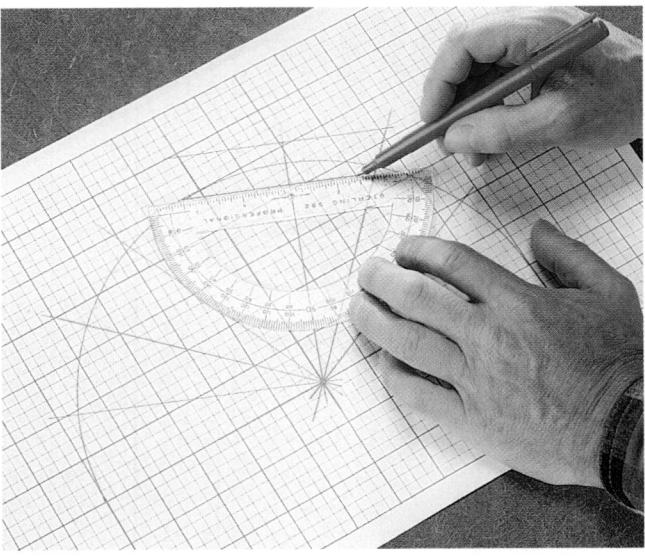

6 From the point where one of the radius lines intersects the curved outline of the deck, use the scale ruler to mark points 5½" above and 5½" below the intersection. From these points, use a protractor to draw perpendicular lines to the adjoining radius lines. The polygon outlined by the perpendicular lines and the adjoining radius lines represents the shape and size for all of the 2 × 12 segments that will be used to construct the cap rail.

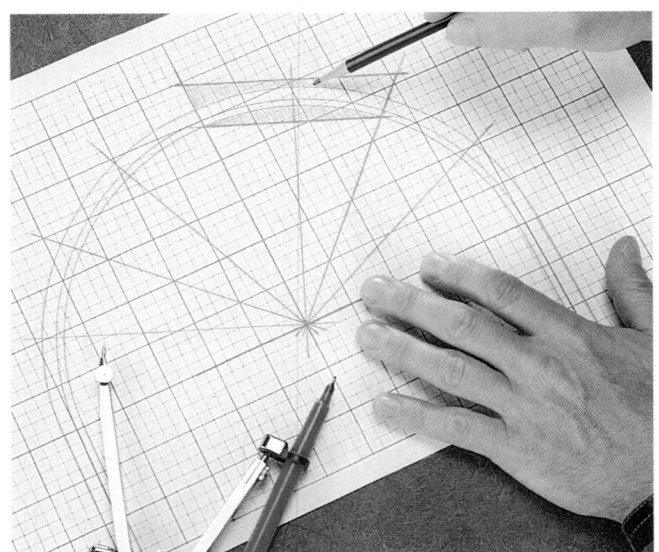

7 Draw a pair of parallel arcs 5½" apart, representing the curved cap railing, inside the outline for the 2 × 12 segments. Shade the portion of the drawing that lies between the straight parallel lines and the two adjacent radius lines. This area represents the shape and size for each of the angled 2 × 12 segments. Measure the angle of the miter at the ends of the board; in this example, the segments are mitered at 22½°.

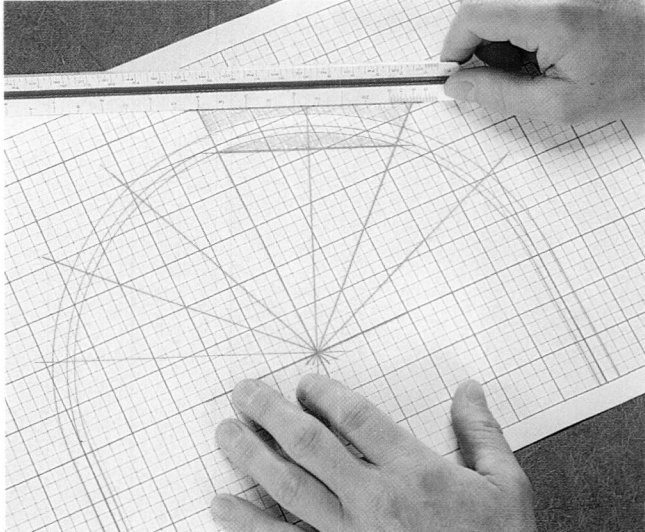

8 Measure the length of the long edge; this number is the overall length for each of the 2 × 12 segments you will be cutting. Using this highlighted area, determine how many segments you will need to complete the curve. For a semicircular curve with radius up to 7 ft., four segments are required, with ends mitered at 22½°. For curves with a larger radius, you will need eight segments, with ends mitered at 11¼°.

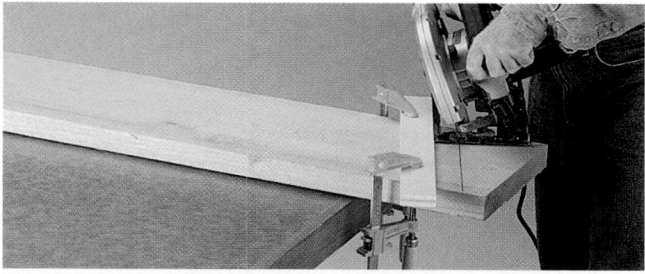

9 Measure and mark 2 × 12 lumber for the cap rail segments, with ends angled inward at 22½° from perpendicular. Set the blade on your circular saw or tablesaw to a 15° bevel, then make compound miter cuts along the marked lines. When cut to compound miters, the segments will form overlapping *scarf* joints that are less likely to reveal gaps between the boards.

10 Arrange the cap rail segments over the curved deck railing, and adjust the pieces, if necessary, so they are centered over the top rail. When you are satisfied with the layout, temporarily attach the segments in place by driving 2" deck screws up through the curved top rail. Measure and install the 2 × 6 cap railing for the straight portion of the railing.

11 Temporarily nail or clamp a long sturdy board between the railings at the start of the curve. Build a long compass, called a *trammel*, by nailing one end of a long 1 × 2 to a 1 ft.-long piece of 1 × 4. Measure from the nail out along the arm of the trammel, and drill holes at the desired radius measurements; for our application, there will be two holes, 5½" apart, representing the width of the finished cap rail. Attach the 1 × 4 base of the trammel to the temporary board so the nail point is at the centerpoint of the deck rail curve, then insert a pencil through one of the holes in the trammel arm. Pivot the arm of the trammel around the cap rail, scribing a cutting line. Move the pencil to the other hole, and scribe a second line.

12 Remove the trammel, and unscrew the cap rail segments. Use a jig saw to cut along the scribed lines, then reposition the curved cap rail pieces over the top rail. Secure the cap rail by applying exterior adhesive to the joints and driving 2½" deck screws up through the top rail. Remove saw marks by belt sanding.

Understanding & Working with Plans

An alternative to developing and drawing your own deck plans is to use an existing plan and drawings. You save the significant amount of time it takes to create quality plan drawings and you can be reasonably certain that the plans cover all necessary details. The only drawback is in finding a plan that meets your needs and fits the requirements of your house.

The eight deck plans on the following pages cover the most popular and versatile styles. At least one of them probably will provide you with the basic plan you need. There also is information to help you make any minor modifications to a plan to make it fit exactly right (see pages 290 to 295).

There also are plans for four common deck furnishings: a bench, box planter, railing planter and arbor. These are designed to complement any of the decks and provide you with options to help make these deck plans match your needs, both functionally and aesthetically.

These step-by-step plans should provide you with everything you need to know to build the deck or furnishing presented, including lumber lists and detailed drawings. If you aren't certain how to accomplish a particular step, review the required building techniques shown in previous sections of this book.

When working with a plan, become familiar with common symbols and conventions before beginning the project. As you prepare to cut lumber, take the time to confirm the exact measurements of all the cuts.

Though a step-by-step plan provides much of the information needed to build a great deck, it is still up to you to evaluate the labor and costs involved. Deck costs vary widely depending on size and materials.

The plans in this book should conform with the building code in your area, but you still need to get approval from your local building inspector.

Before setting an appointment with a building inspector, make a photocopy of your plan. Write down any relevant details about your house, the immediate area around the deck, the grade of the site where the deck will stand and any changes you plan on making to the materials list.

High Rectangular Deck

Simplicity, security and convenience are the hallmarks of this elevated deck.

This simple rectangular deck provides a secure, convenient outdoor living space. The absence of a stairway prevents children from wandering away or unexpected visitors from wandering in. It also makes the deck easier to build.

Imagine how handy it will be to have this additional living area only a step away from your dining room or living room, with no more need to walk downstairs for outdoor entertaining, dining or relaxing.

And if you'd like to add a stairway, just refer to the helpful instructions in the final chapter of this book.

Cutaway View

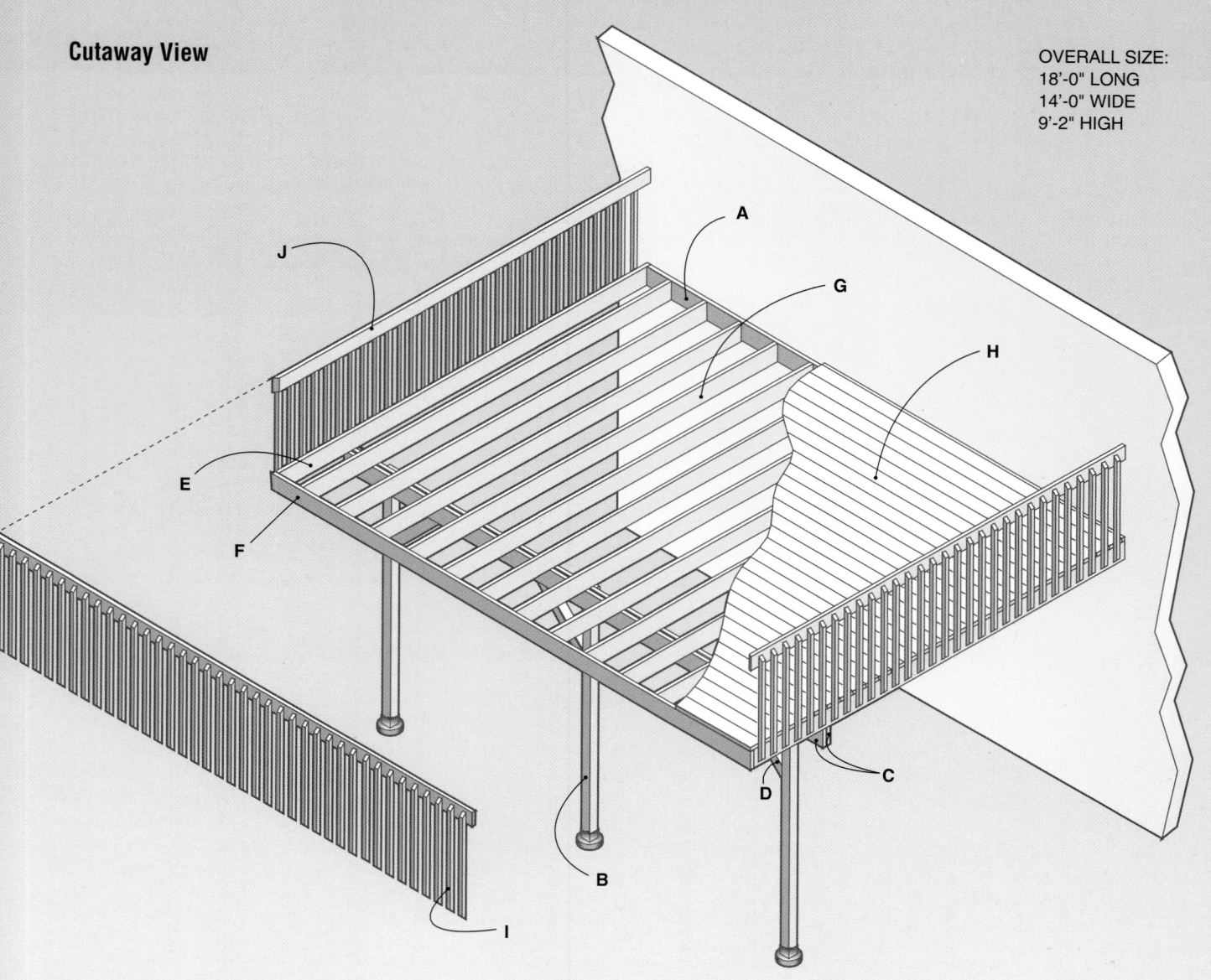

Lumber List			
Qty.	**Size**	**Material**	**Part**
2	2 × 12" × 20'	Trtd. lumber	Beam boards (C)
2	2 × 10" × 18'	Trtd. lumber	Ledger (A), Rim joist (F)
15	2 × 10" × 14'	Trtd. lumber	Joists (G), End joists (E)
3	6 × 6" × 10'	Trtd. lumber	Deck posts (B)
2	4 × 4" × 8'	Trtd. lumber	Braces (D)

Lumber List			
Qty.	**Size**	**Material**	**Part**
32	2 × 6" × 18'	Cedar	Decking (H), Top rail (J)
2	2 × 6" × 16'	Cedar	Top rail (J)
50	2 × 2" × 8'	Cedar	Balusters (I)

Supplies: 12"-diameter footing forms (3); J-bolts (3); 6 × 6" metal post anchors (3); 2 × 10" joist hangers (26); galvanized deck screws (3", 2½" and 1¼"); joist hanger nails; ⅜ × 4" lag screws and washers (28); ¼ × 5" lag screws and washers (16); ⁵⁄₁₆ × 7" carriage bolts, washers, and nuts (6); 16d galvanized nails; metal flashing (18 ft.); silicone caulk (3 tubes); concrete as required.

Framing Plan

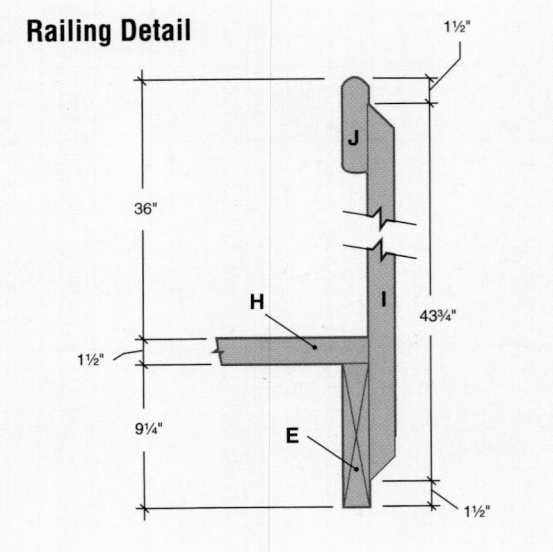
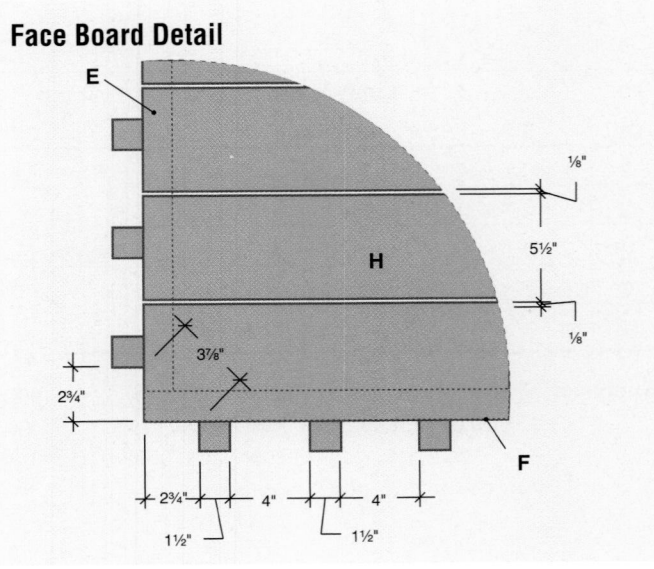

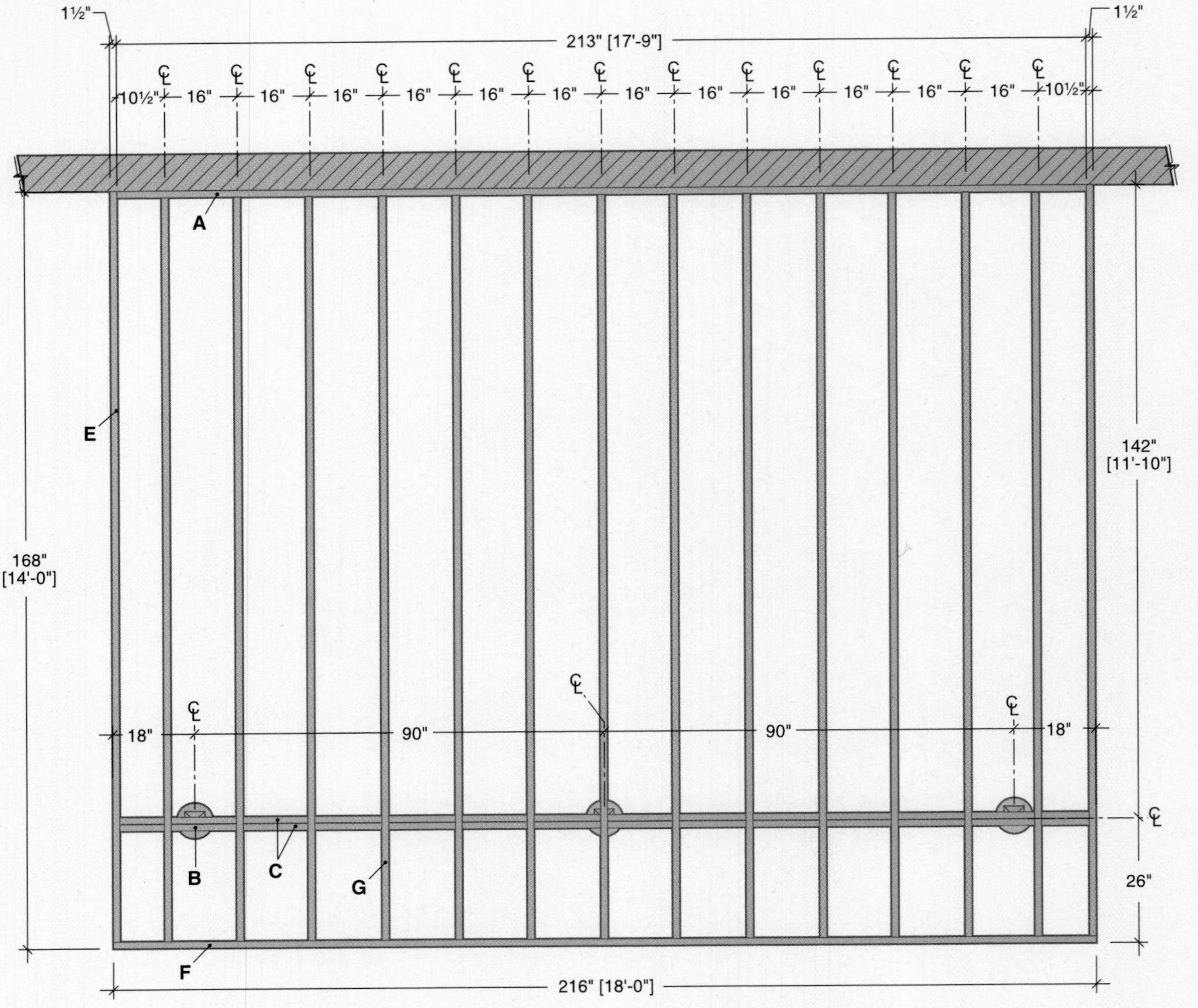

Railing Detail

Face Board Detail

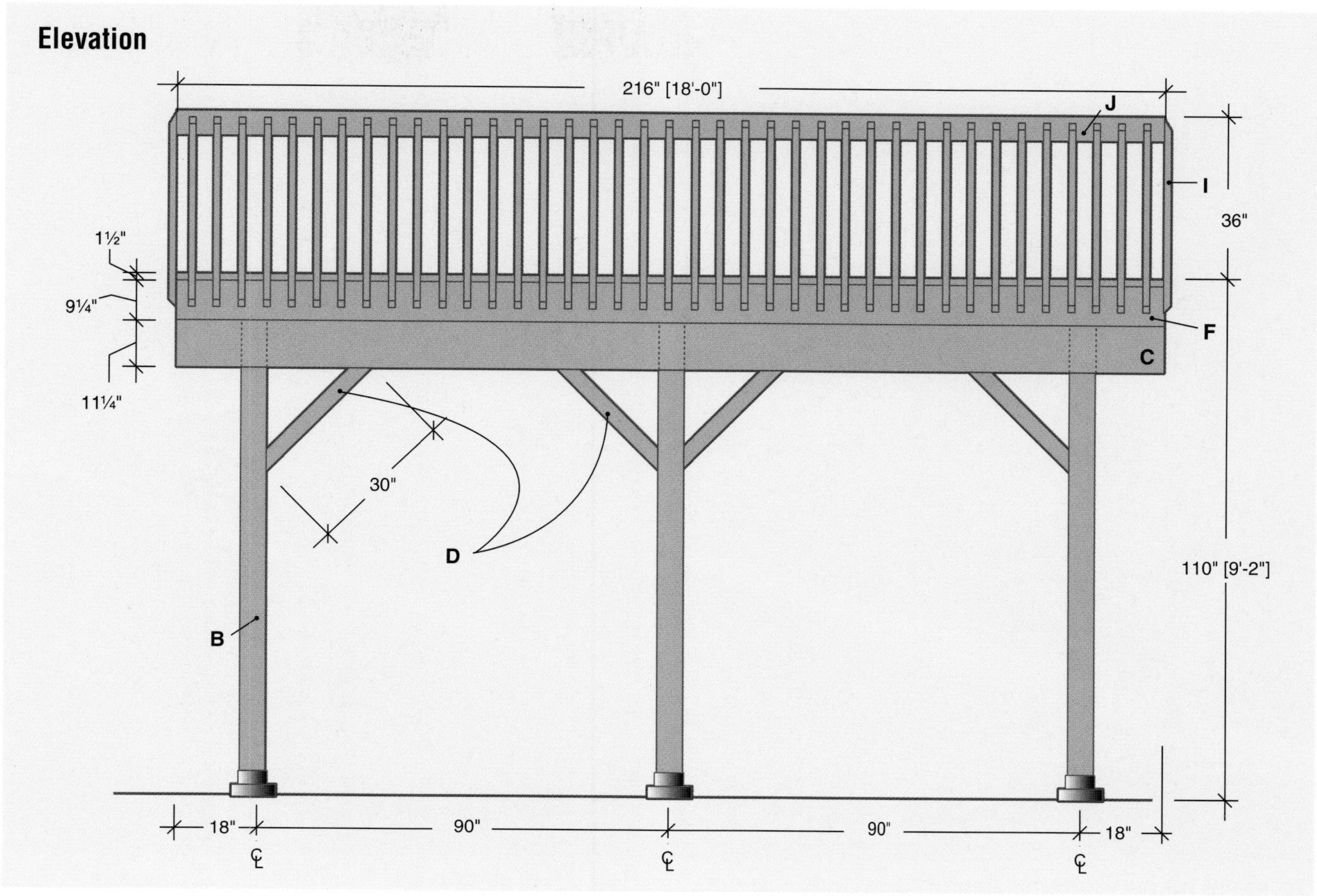

Elevation

216" [18'-0"]

J

I

36"

F

C

1½"

9¼"

11¼"

30"

D

B

110" [9'-2"]

18" 90" 90" 18"

Directions: High Rectangular Deck

Attach the Ledger

1 Draw a level outline on the siding to show where the ledger and the end joists will fit against the house. Install the ledger so that the surface of the decking boards will be 1" below the indoor floor level **(photo A).** This height difference prevents rainwater or melted snow from seeping into the house.

2 Cut out the siding along the outline with a circular saw. To avoid cutting the sheathing that lies underneath the siding, set the blade depth to the same thickness as the siding. Finish the cutout with a chisel, holding the beveled side in to ensure a straight cut.

3 Cut galvanized flashing to

The ledger is anchored through the sheathing to the rim joist of the house with ⅜ × 4" lag screws. Metal flashing protects against water seepage.

To make measurements easier, drop a plumb bob from the ledger to ground level and use the 3-4-5 triangle method to check for square.

Use a template made from 2 × 4s to locate the post footings on the ground, then mark the footings with stakes.

the length of the cutout, using metal snips. Slide the flashing up under the siding at the top of the cutout.

4 Measure and cut the ledger (A) from pressure-treated lumber. Center the ledger end to end in the cutout, with space at each end for the end joist.

5 Brace the ledger into position under the flashing. Tack the ledger into place with galvanized nails.

6 Drill pairs of ¼" pilot holes at 16" intervals through the ledger and into the house header joist. Counterbore each pilot hole ½", using a 1" spade bit. Attach the ledger with 4" lag screws and washers, using a ratchet wrench.

7 Apply silicone caulk between the siding and flashing. Also seal the lag screw heads and the cracks at the ends of the ledger..

Pour the Footings

1 To establish a reference point for locating the footings, drop a plumb bob from the ends of the ledger down to the ground.

2 Position a straight 14 ft.-long 2 × 4 perpendicular to the house at the point where the plumb bob meets the ground. NOTE: If you are building on a steep slope or uneven ground, the mason's string method of locating footing positions will work better (see *Locating Post Footings,* pages 64-69).

3 Check for square, using the 3-4-5 triangle method.

From the 2 × 4, measure 3 ft. along the wall and make a mark. Next, measure 4 ft. out from the house and make a mark on the 2 × 4. The diagonal line between the marks will measure 5 ft. *(photo B)* when the board is accurately square to the house. Adjust the board as needed, using stakes to hold it in place.

4 Extend another reference board from the house at the other end of the ledger, following the same procedure.

5 Measure out along both boards, and mark the centerline of the footings (see *Framing Plan*, page 206).

6 Lay a straight 2 × 4 between the centerline marks, and drive stakes to mark the footing locations *(photo C).*

Insert the footing form into the hole, leaving 2" above the ground. Level the top, and pack soil around the form to hold it in place.

Insert a J-bolt into wet concrete at the center of the footing.

7 Remove the boards and dig the post footings, using a clamshell digger or power auger. Pour 2" to 3" of loose gravel into each hole for drainage. NOTE: When measuring the footing size and depth, make sure you comply with local building codes, which may require flaring the base to 18".

8 Cut the footing forms to length, using a reciprocating saw or handsaw, and insert them into the footing holes, leaving 2" above ground level *(photo D)*. Pack soil around the forms for support, and fill the forms with concrete, tamping with a long stick or rod to eliminate any air gaps.

9 Screed the tops flush with a straight 2 × 4. Insert a J-bolt into the center of each footing *(photo E)* and set with ¾" to 1" of thread exposed. Clean the bolt threads before the concrete sets.

Set the Posts

1 Lay a long, straight 2 × 4 flat across the footings, parallel to the house. With one edge tight against the J-bolts, draw a reference line across the top of each footing to help orient the post anchors.

2 Place a metal post anchor on each footing, centering it over the J-bolt and squaring it with the reference line. Attach the post anchors by threading a nut over each bolt and tightening with a ratchet wrench.

3 The tops of the posts (B) will eventually be level with the bottom edge of the ledger, but initially cut the posts several inches longer to allow for final trimming. Position the posts in the anchors and tack into place with one nail each.

4 With a level as a guide, use braces and stakes to ensure that the posts are plumb *(photo F)*.

5 Determine the height of the beam by using a chalk line and a line level. Extend the chalk line out from the bottom edge of the ledger, make sure that the line is level, and snap a mark across the face of a post. Use the line and level to transfer the mark to the remaining posts.

Plumb each post with a level, then use braces and stakes to hold in place until the beam and joists are installed.

Fasten the beam to the posts with carriage bolts fitted with a washer and nut. Tighten with a ratchet wrench.

Notch the Posts

1 Remove the posts from the post anchors and cut to the finished height.

2 Measure and mark a 3" × 11¼" notch at the top of each post, on the outside face. Use a framing square to trace lines on all sides. Rough-cut the notches with a circular saw, then finish with a reciprocating saw or handsaw.

3 Reattach the posts to the post anchors, with the notch-side facing away from the deck.

Install the Beam

1 Cut the beam boards (C) to length, adding several inches to each end for final trimming after the deck frame is squared up.

2 Join the beam boards together with 2½" galvanized deck screws. Mark the post locations on the top edges and sides, using a combination square as a guide.

3 Lift the beam, one end at a time, into the notches with the crown up. Align and clamp the beam to the posts. NOTE: Installing boards of this size and length, at this height, requires care. You should have at least two helpers.

4 Counterbore two ½"-deep holes using a 1" spade bit, then drill ⁵⁄₁₆" pilot holes through the beam and post.

5 Thread a carriage bolt into each pilot hole. Add a washer and nut to the counterbore-side of each bolt and tighten with a ratchet wrench **(photo G).** Seal both ends of the bolts with silicone caulk.

6 Cut the tops of the posts flush with the top edge of the beam, using a reciprocating saw or handsaw.

Install the Frame

1 Measure and cut the end joists (E) to length, using a circular saw.

2 Attach the end joists to the ends of the ledger with 16d galvanized nails.

3 Measure and cut the rim joist (F) to length with a circular saw. Fasten to the ends of end joists with 16d nails.

4 Square up the frame by measuring corner to corner and adjusting until the measurements are equal. When the frame is square, toenail the end joists in place on top of the beam.

5 Trim the ends of the beam flush with the faces of the end joists, using a reciprocating saw or a handsaw.

Install the Braces

1 Cut the braces (D) to length (see *Elevation*, page 207) with a circular saw or power miter saw. Miter both ends at 45°.

2 Install the braces by positioning them against the beam boards and against the posts. Make sure the outside faces of the braces are flush with the outside faces of the beam and the posts. Temporarily fasten with deck screws.

3 Secure the braces to the posts with 5" lag screws. Drill two ¼" pilot holes through the upper end of each brace into the beam. Counterbore to a ½"-depth using a 1" spade bit, and drive lag screws with a ratchet wrench. Repeat for the lower end of the braces into the posts.

Install the Joists

1 Measure and mark the joist locations (see *Framing Plan*, page 206) on the ledger, rim joist and beam. Draw the outline of each joist on the ledger and rim joist, using a combination square.

2 Install a joist hanger at each joist location. Attach one flange of the hanger to one side of the outline, using joist nails. Use a spacer cut from scrap 2 × 8 lumber to achieve the correct spread for each hanger, then fasten the remaining

side flange with joist nails. Remove the spacer and repeat the same procedure for the remaining joist hangers.

3 Measure, mark and cut lumber for joists (G), using a circular saw. Place joists in hangers with crown side up and attach with joist hanger nails *(photo H)*. Align joists with the outlines on the top of the beam, and toenail in place.

Lay the Decking

1 Measure, mark and cut the decking boards (H) to

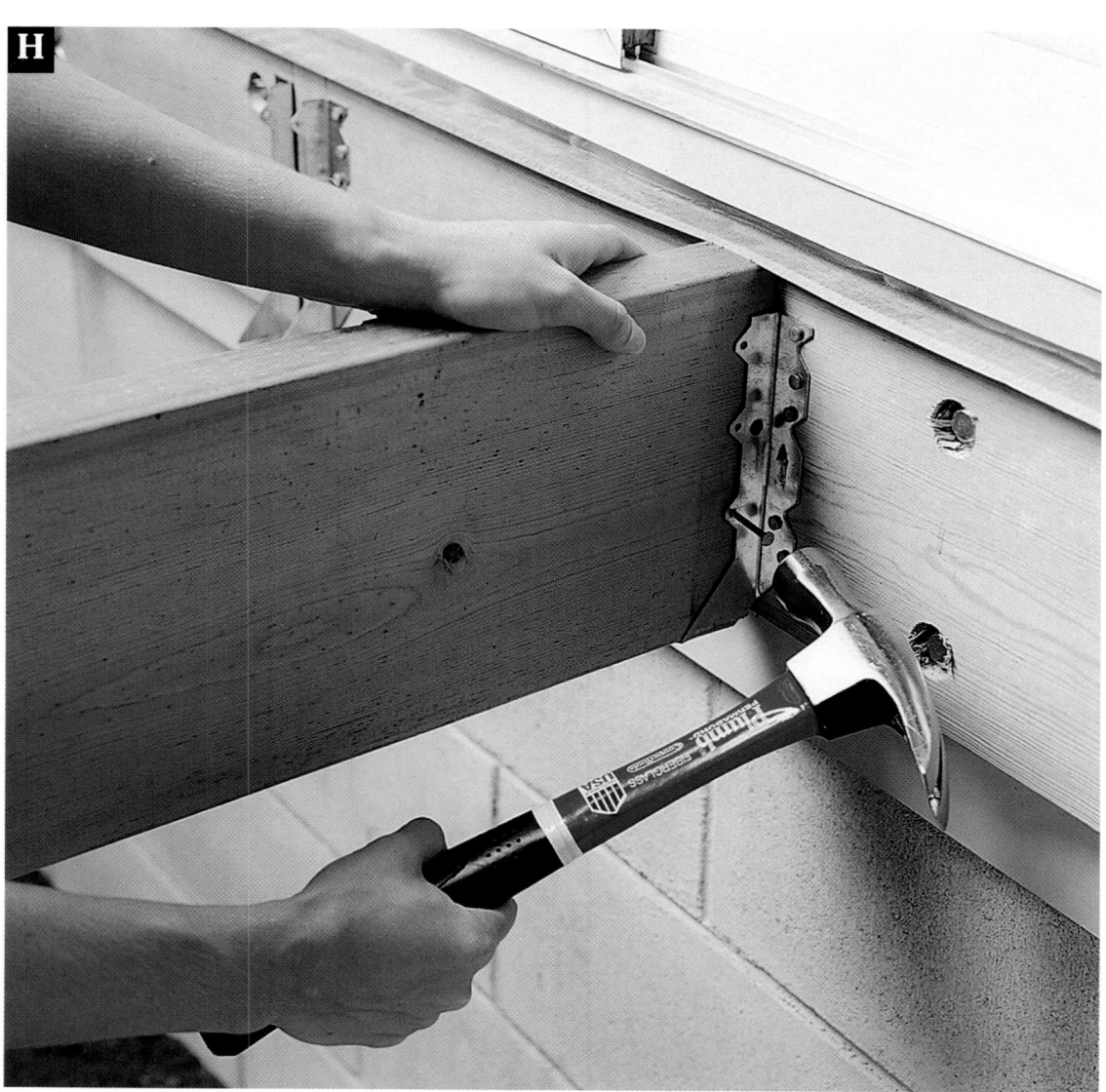

Fasten the joists in the joist hangers with 10d joist hanger nails. Drive nails into both sides of each joist.

Snap a chalk line flush with the outside edge of the deck, and cut off overhanging deck boards with a circular saw.

After cutting balusters to length, gang them up and drill ⅛" pilot holes through the top and bottom.

length as needed.

2 Position the first row of decking flush against the house, and attach by driving a pair of galvanized deck screws into each joist.

3 Position the remaining decking boards, leaving a ⅛" gap between boards to provide for drainage, and attach to each joist with deck screws.

4 Every few rows of decking, measure from the edge of the decking to the outside edge of the deck. If the measurement can be divided evenly by 5⅝", the last board will fit flush with the outside edge of the deck as intended. If the measurement shows that the last

board will not fit flush, adjust the spacing as you install the remaining rows of boards.

5 If your decking overhangs the end joists, snap a chalk line to mark the outside edge of the deck and cut flush with a circular saw set to a 1½" depth *(photo I).* If needed, finish the cut with a jig saw or handsaw where a circular saw can't reach.

Build the Railing

1 Measure, mark and cut the balusters (I) to length, with 45° miters at both ends.
2 Gang the balusters together and drill two ⅛" pilot holes at both ends *(photo J).*

3 Clamp a 1½" guide strip flush with the bottom edge of the deck platform to establish the baluster height (see *Railing Detail*, page 206).
4 To ensure that the balusters are installed at equal intervals, create a spacing jig, less than 4" wide, from two pieces of scrap material.
5 Attach the corner balusters first (see *Face Board Detail*, page 206), using a level to ensure that they are plumb. Then use the spacing jig for positioning, and attach the remaining balusters to the deck platform with 3" deck screws *(photo K).*
6 Measure, mark and cut the top rail sections (J) to

Rest the balusters on a 1 × 2 guide strip, and use a spacing jig to position them at equal intervals. Attach them with 3" deck screws.

length. Round over three edges (see *Railing Detail*, page 206) using a router with a ½" round-over bit. Cut 45° miters on the ends that meet at the corners.

7 Hold or clamp the top rail in position, and attach with 2½" deck screws driven through the balusters.

8 If you need to make straight joints in the top rail, cut the ends of the adjoining boards at 45°. Drill angled ⅛" pilot holes and join with deck screws *(photo L)*.

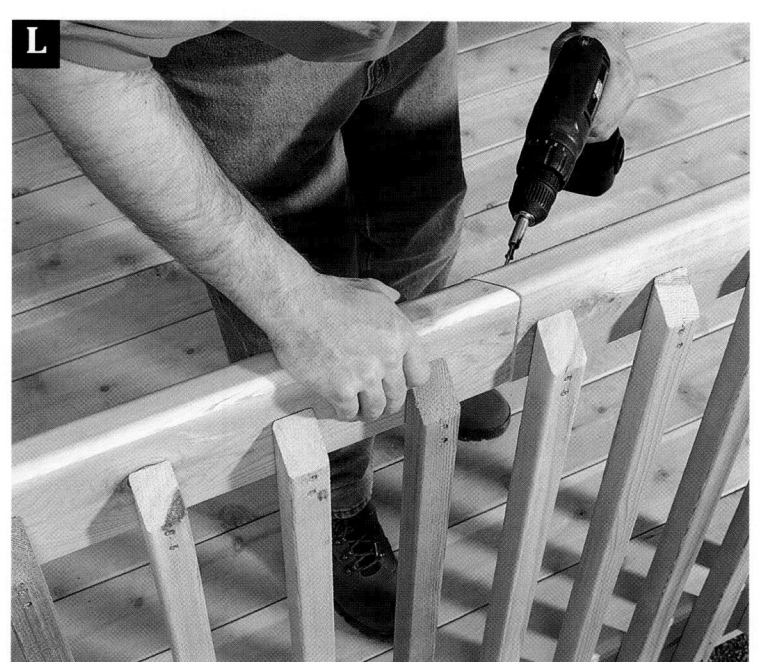

To make a joint in the top rail, cut the ends at 45° and drill a pair of pilot holes. Then fasten the ends together with deck screws.

Rectangular Deck

Extend your living space and increase your home's value.

Here's a deck that's classic in its simplicity. Moderately sized and easy to build, this rectangular deck won't cost you an arm and a leg—in either time or money. The framing and decking plans are quite straightforward, and you can likely build the entire deck in just two or three weekends, even with limited carpentry and building experience. Within just a few weeks time, you can transform your yard into a congenial gathering place for cooking, entertaining and just plain relaxing; a place where you, your family and your friends can enjoy the fresh air in convenience and comfort.

Cutaway View

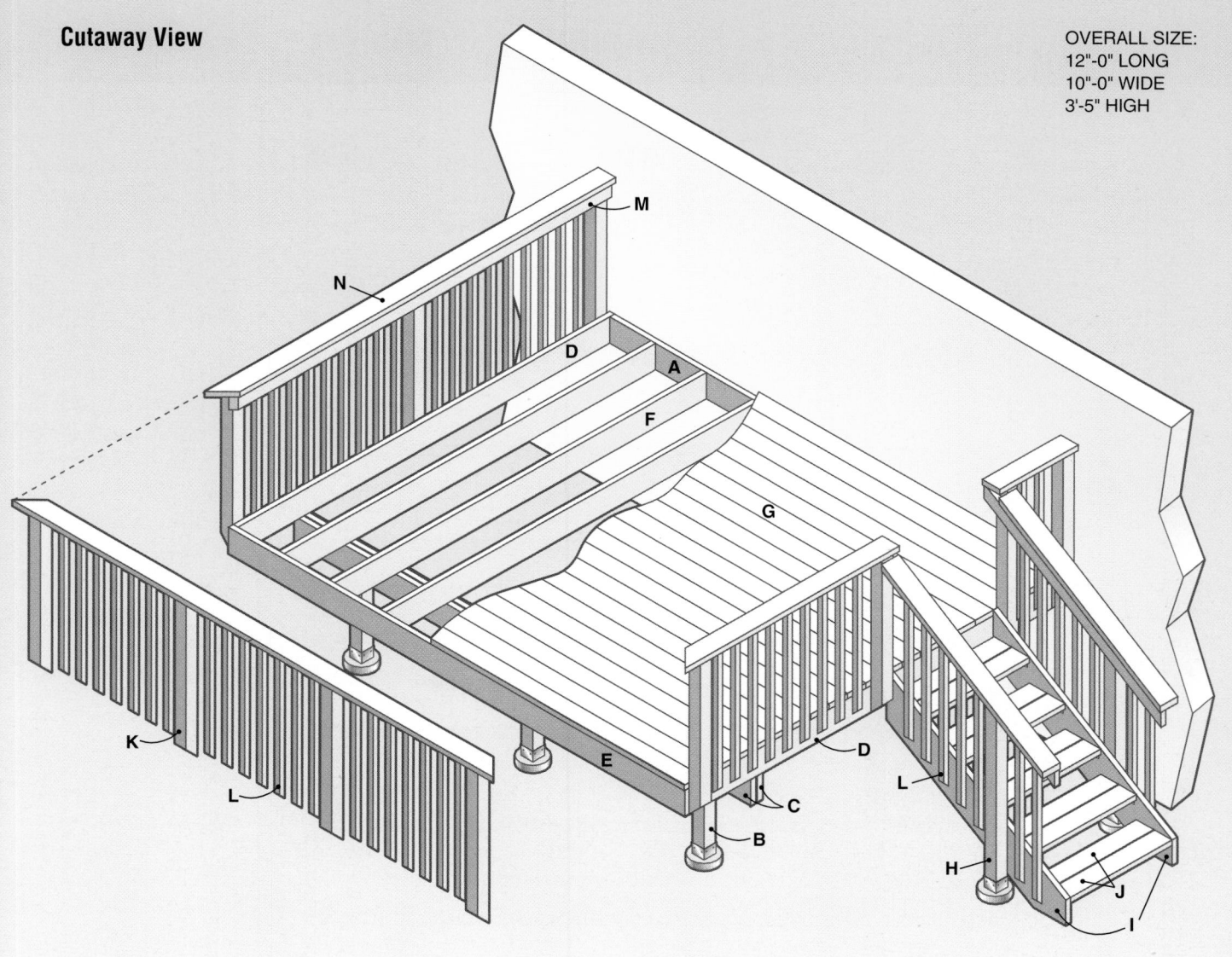

Lumber List			
Qty.	Size	Material	Part
4	2 × 8" × 12'	Trtd. lumber	Ledger (A), Beam bds (C), Rim joist (E)
1	4 × 4" × 8'	Trtd. lumber	Deck posts (B)
10	2 × 8" × 10'	Trtd. lumber	End joists (D), Joists (F)
25	2 × 6" × 12'	Cedar	Decking (G), Rail cap (N)
7	4 × 4" × 8'	Cedar	Stair posts (H), Rail post (K)

Lumber List			
Qty.	Size	Material	Part
2	2 × 12" × 8'	Cedar	Stringers (I)
5	2 × 6" × 6'	Cedar	Treads (J)
32	2 × 2" × 8'	Cedar	Balusters (L)
2	2 × 4" × 12'	Cedar	Top rail (M)
2	2 × 4" × 10'	Cedar	Top rail (M)

Supplies: 8"-diameter footing forms (5); J-bolts (5); 4 × 4" metal post anchors (5); 4 × 4" metal post-beam caps (3); 2 × 8" joist hangers (16); 1½ × 6" angle brackets (6); 1½ × 10" angle brackets (10); 3" galvanized deck screws;16d galvanized nails; 2½" galvanized deck screws; 2½" galvanized screws; ⅜ × 4" lag screws and washers (20); ⅜ × 5" lag screws and washers (22); ¼ × 1¼" lag screws and washers (80); flashing (12 ft.); exterior silicone caulk (3 tubes); concrete as needed.

Framing Plan

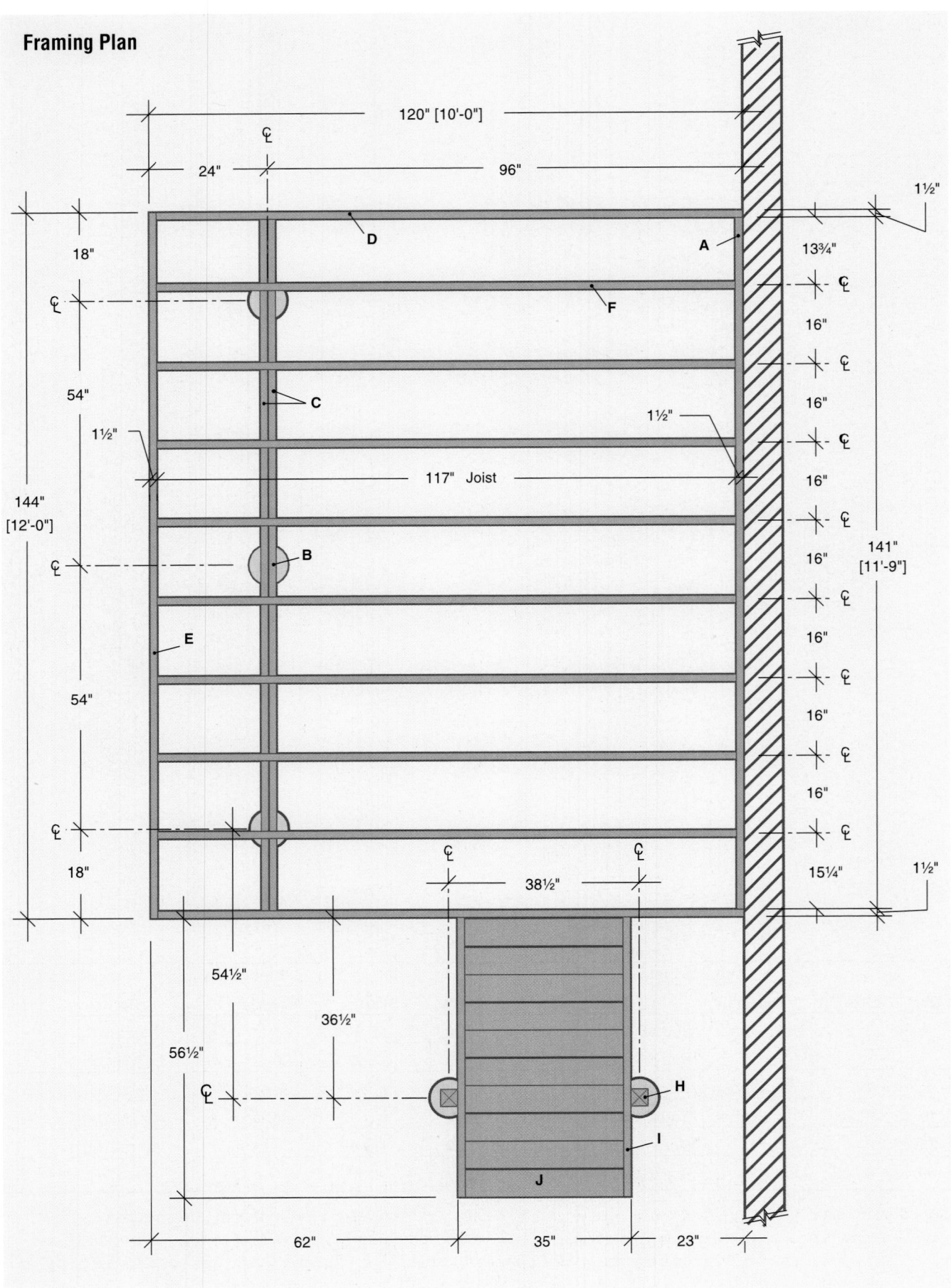

Elevation

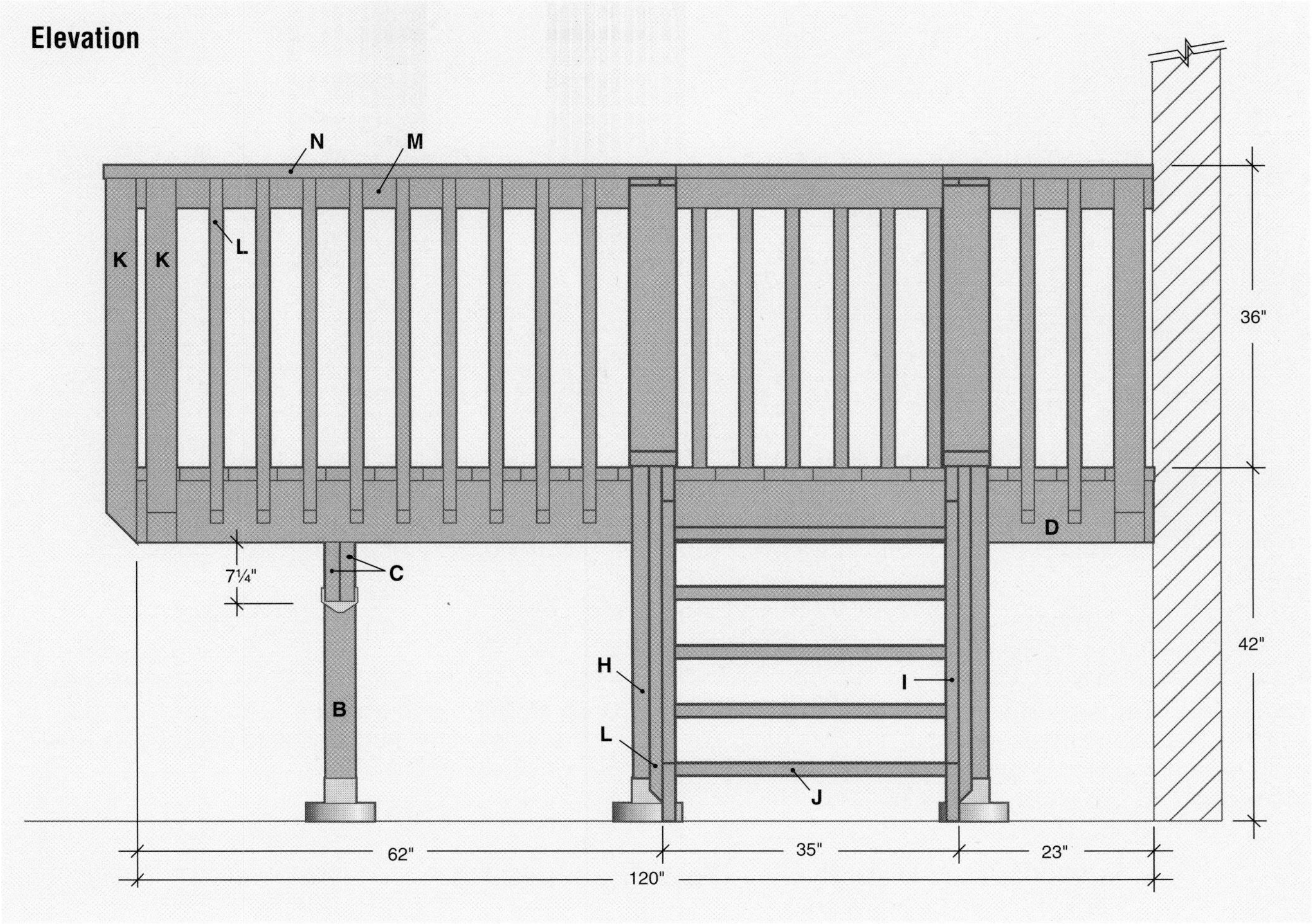

N
M
K K
L
36"
42"
D
7¼"
C
B
H
I
L
J
62"
35"
23"
120"

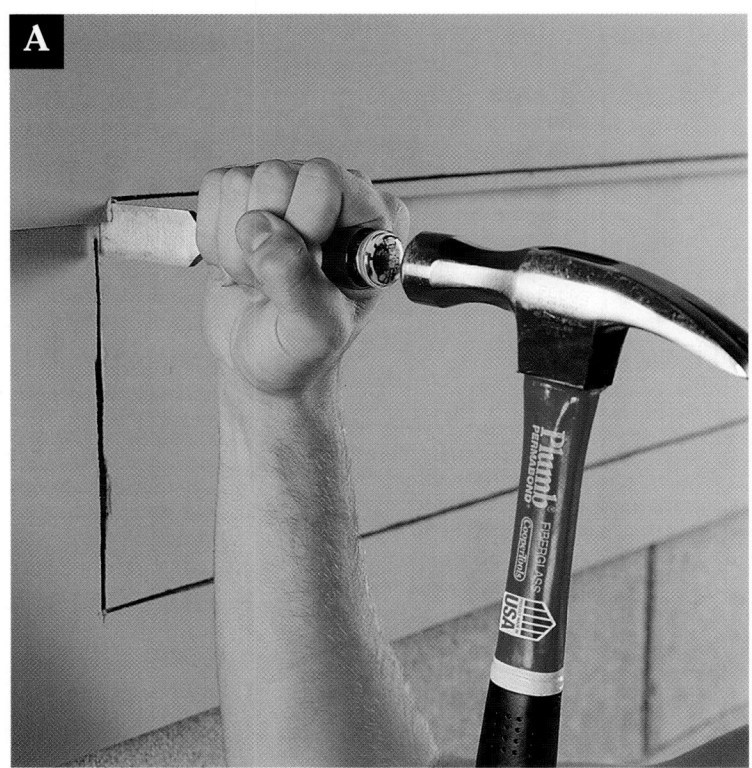

A

After outlining the position of the ledger and cutting the siding with a circular saw, use a chisel to finish the corners of the cutout.

Directions: Rectangular Deck

Attach the Ledger

1 Draw a level outline on the siding to show where the ledger and the end joists will fit against the house. Install the ledger so that the surface of the decking boards will be 1" below the indoor floor level. This height difference prevents rainwater or melted snow from seeping into the house.

2 Cut out the siding along the outline with a circular saw. To prevent the blade from cutting the sheathing that lies underneath the siding, set the blade depth to the same thickness as the siding. Finish the cutout with a chisel *(photo A),* holding the beveled side in to ensure a straight cut.

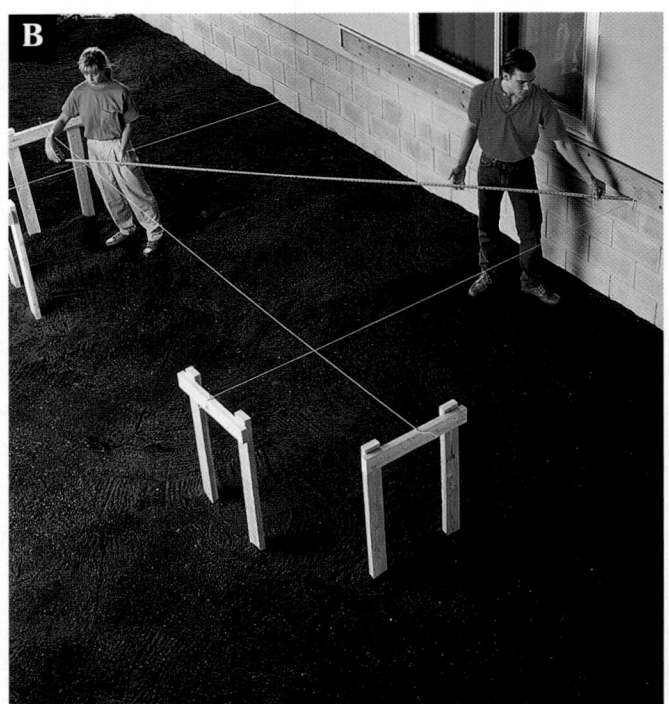

Check the strings for square, by measuring from corner to corner. If the measurements are not equal, adjust the strings on the batterboards. When the diagonal measurements are equal, the outline is square.

Drop a plumb bob from the centerpoint of each footing to transfer the location to the ground. Mark the footing locations with stakes.

3 Cut galvanized flashing to the length of the cutout, using metal snips. Slide the flashing up under the siding at the top of the cutout.

4 Measure and cut the ledger (A) from pressure-treated lumber. Center the ledger end to end in the cutout, with space at each end for the end joist.

5 Brace the ledger in position under the flashing. Tack the ledger into place with galvanized deck screws.

6 Drill pairs of ¼" pilot holes at 16" intervals through the ledger and into the house header joist. Counterbore each pilot hole ½", using a 1" spade bit. Attach the ledger to the wall with ⅜ × 4" lag screws and washers, using a ratchet wrench.

7 Apply a thick bead of silicone caulk between siding and flashing. Also seal the lag screw heads and the cracks at the ends of the ledger.

Pour the Footings

1 Referring to the measurements shown in the *Framing Plan,* page 216, mark the centerlines of the two outer footings on the ledger and drive nails at these locations.

2 Set up temporary batterboards and stretch a mason's string out from the ledger at each location. Make sure the strings are perpendicular to the ledger, and measure along the strings to find the centerpoints of the posts.

3 Set up additional batterboards and stretch another string parallel to the ledger across the post centerpoints.

4 Check the mason's strings for square **(photo B),** by measuring diagonally from corner to corner and adjusting the strings so that the measurements are equal.

5 Measure along the cross string and mark the center

post location with a piece of tape.

6 Use a plumb bob to transfer the footing centerpoints to the ground, and drive a stake to mark each point **(photo C).**

7 Remove the mason's strings and dig the post footings, using a clamshell digger or power auger. Pour 2" to 3" of loose gravel into each hole for drainage. NOTE: When measuring the footing size and depth, make sure you comply with your local building code, which may require flaring the base.

8 Cut the footing forms to length, using a reciprocating saw or handsaw, and insert them into the footing holes, leaving 2" above ground level. Pack soil around the forms for support, and fill the forms with concrete, tamping with a long stick or rod to eliminate any air pockets.

9 Screed the tops flush

D

After the posts have been set in place and braced plumb, use a straight 2 × 4 and a level to mark the top of the beam on each post.

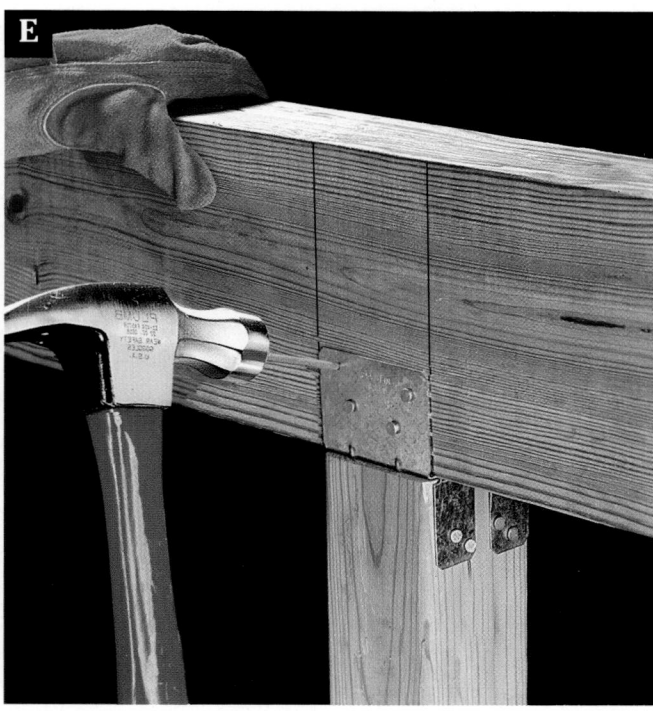

E

With the beam in place, align the reference marks with the post-beam caps, drill pilot holes, and fasten using 10d joist hanger nails.

with a straight 2 × 4. Insert a J-bolt into each footing, set so ¾" to 1" of thread is exposed. Retie the mason's strings and position the J-bolts at the exact center of the posts, using a plumb bob as a guide. Clean the bolt threads before concrete sets.

Set the Posts

1 Lay a long, straight 2 × 4 flat across the footings, parallel to the ledger. With one edge tight against the J-bolts, draw a reference line across each footing.
2 Place a metal post anchor on each footing, centering it over the J-bolt and squaring it with the reference line. Attach the post anchors by threading a nut over each bolt and tightening with a ratchet wrench.
3 Cut the posts to length, adding approximately 6" for final trimming. Place the posts in the anchors and tack into place with one nail.

4 With a level as a guide, use braces and stakes to plumb the posts. Finish nailing the posts to the anchors.
5 Determine the height of the beam by extending a straight 2 × 4 from the bottom edge of the ledger across the face of a post. Level the 2 × 4, and draw a line on the post **(photo D).**
6 From that line, measure 7¼" down the post and mark the bottom of the beam. Using a level, transfer this line to the remaining posts.
7 Use a combination square to extend the level line completely around each post. Cut the posts to this finished height, using a reciprocating saw or hand saw.

Install the Beam

1 Cut the beam boards (C) several inches longer than necessary, to allow for final trimming.
2 Join the beam boards

together with 2½" galvanized deck screws. Mark the post locations on the top edges and sides, using a combination square as a guide.
3 Attach the post-beam caps to the tops of the posts. Position the caps on the post tops, and attach using 10d joist hanger nails.
4 Lift the beam into the post-beam caps, with the crown up. Align the post reference lines on the beam with the post-beam caps. NOTE: You should have at least two helpers when installing boards of this size and length, at this height.
5 Fasten the post-beam caps to the beam on both sides using 10d joist hanger nails **(photo E).**

Install the Frame

1 Measure and cut the end joists to length using a circular saw.

Cut the rim joist to length, and attach to the ends of end joists with 16d galvanized nails.

2 Attach end joists to the ends of the ledger with 10d common nails.

3 Measure and cut the rim joist (E) to length with a circular saw. Fasten to end joists with 16d galvanized nails *(photo F).*

4 Square up the frame by measuring corner to corner and adjusting until measurements are equal. Toenail the end joists in place on top of the beam, and trim the beam to length.

5 Reinforce each inside corner of the frame with an angle bracket fastened with 10d joist hanger nails.

Install the Joists

1 Mark the outlines of the inner joists (F) on the ledger, beam and rim joist (see *Framing Plan,* page 216) using a tape measure and a combination square.

2 Attach joist hangers to the ledger and rim joist with 10d joist hanger nails, using a scrap 2 × 8 as a spacer to achieve the correct spread for each hanger.

3 Measure, mark and cut lumber for inner joists, using a circular saw. Place the joists in the hangers with crown side up *(photo G),* and attach at both ends with 10d joist hanger nails. Be sure to use all the holes in the hangers.

4 Align the joists with the marks on top of the beam, and toenail in place.

Lay the Decking

1 Cut the first decking board (G) to length, position it against the house, and attach by driving a pair of 2½" galvanized deck screws into each joist.

2 Position the remaining decking boards with the ends overhanging the end joists. Leave a ⅛" gap between boards to provide for drainage, and attach the boards to each joist with a pair of deck screws.

3 Every few rows of decking, measure from the edge of the decking to the outside edge of the deck. If the measurement can be divided evenly by 5⅝, the last board will fit flush with the outside edge of the deck as intended. If the measurement shows that the last board will not fit flush, adjust the spacing as you install the remaining rows of boards.

4 If your decking overhangs the end joists, snap a chalk line to mark the outside edge of the deck and cut flush with a circular saw. If needed, finish the cut with a jig saw or handsaw where a circular saw can't reach.

Build the Stairway

1 Refer to the *Framing Plan,* page 216, for the position of the stairway footings.

2 Locate the footings by extending a 2 × 4 from the deck, dropping a plumb bob *(photo H),* and marking the centerpoints with stakes.

3 Dig post holes with a clamshell digger or an

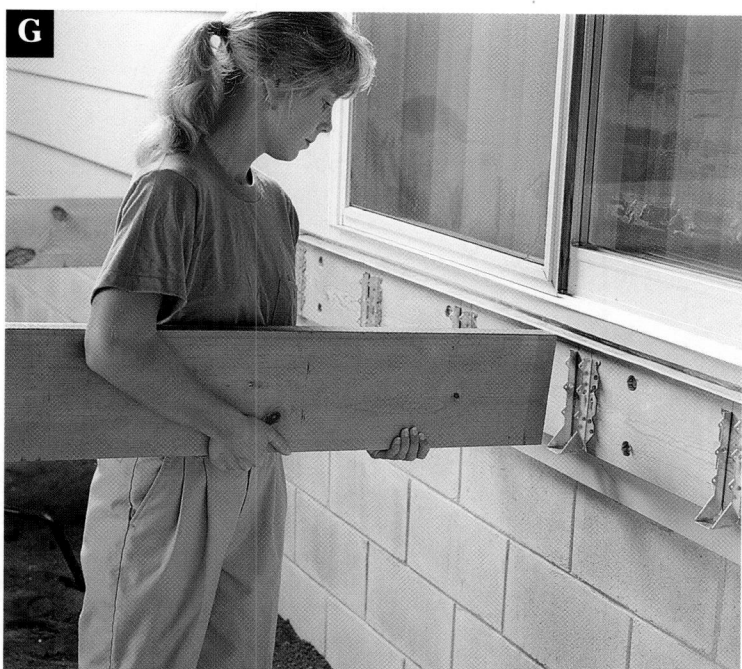

Install joists in hangers with crown side up.

auger, and pour the stairway footings using the same method as for the deck footings.

4 Attach metal post anchors to the footings, and install posts (H), leaving them long for final trimming.

5 Cut the stair stringers (I) to length and use a framing square to mark the rise and run for each step (see *Stairway Detail,* page 222). Draw the tread outline on each run. Cut the angles at the end of the stringers with a circular saw. (For more information on building stairways, see pages 102-107.)

6 Position a 1½ × 10" angle bracket flush with the bottom of each tread line. Attach the brackets with 1¼" lag screws.

7 Fasten angle brackets to the upper ends of the stringers, using 1¼" lag screws; keep the brackets flush with cut ends on stringers. Position the top ends of the stringers on the side of the deck, making sure the top point of the stringer and the surface of

the deck are flush.

8 Attach the stringers by driving 10d joist hanger nails through the angle brackets into the end joist, and by drilling ¼" pilot holes from inside the rim joist into the stringers and fastening with ⅜ × 4" lag screws.

9 To connect the stringers to the stair posts, drill two ¼" pilot holes **(photo I)** and counterbore the pilot holes ½" deep with a 1" spade bit. Use a ratchet wrench to fasten the stringers to the posts with 4" lag screws and washers.

10 Measure the length of the stair treads (J) and cut two 2 × 6 boards for each tread. For each tread, position the front board on the angle bracket so the front edge is flush with the tread outline on the stringers. Attach the tread to the brackets with ¼ × 1¼" lag screws.

11 Place the rear 2 × 6 on each tread bracket, keeping a ⅛" space between the boards. Attach with 1¼" lag screws.

12 Attach the treads for the lowest step by driving deck

screws through the stringers.

Install the Railing

1 Cut posts (K) and balusters (L) to length (see *Railing Detail,* page 223) with a power miter saw or circular saw. Cut the top ends square, and the bottom ends at a 45° angle.

2 Mark and drill two ¼" pilot holes at the bottom end of each post. Holes should be spaced 4" apart and counterbored ½", with a 1" spade bit.

3 Drill two ⅛" pilot holes, 4" apart, near the bottom of each baluster. At the top of each baluster, drill a pair of ⅛" pilot holes spaced 1½" apart.

4 Using a combination square, mark the locations of the posts on the outside of the deck. NOTE: Position corner posts so there is no more than 4" clearance between them.

5 Clamp each post in place. Keep the beveled end flush

To locate the stairway footings, refer to the measurements in the Framing Plan, and extend a straight 2 × 4 perpendicularly from the deck. Use a plumb bob to transfer centerpoints to the ground.

Stairway Detail

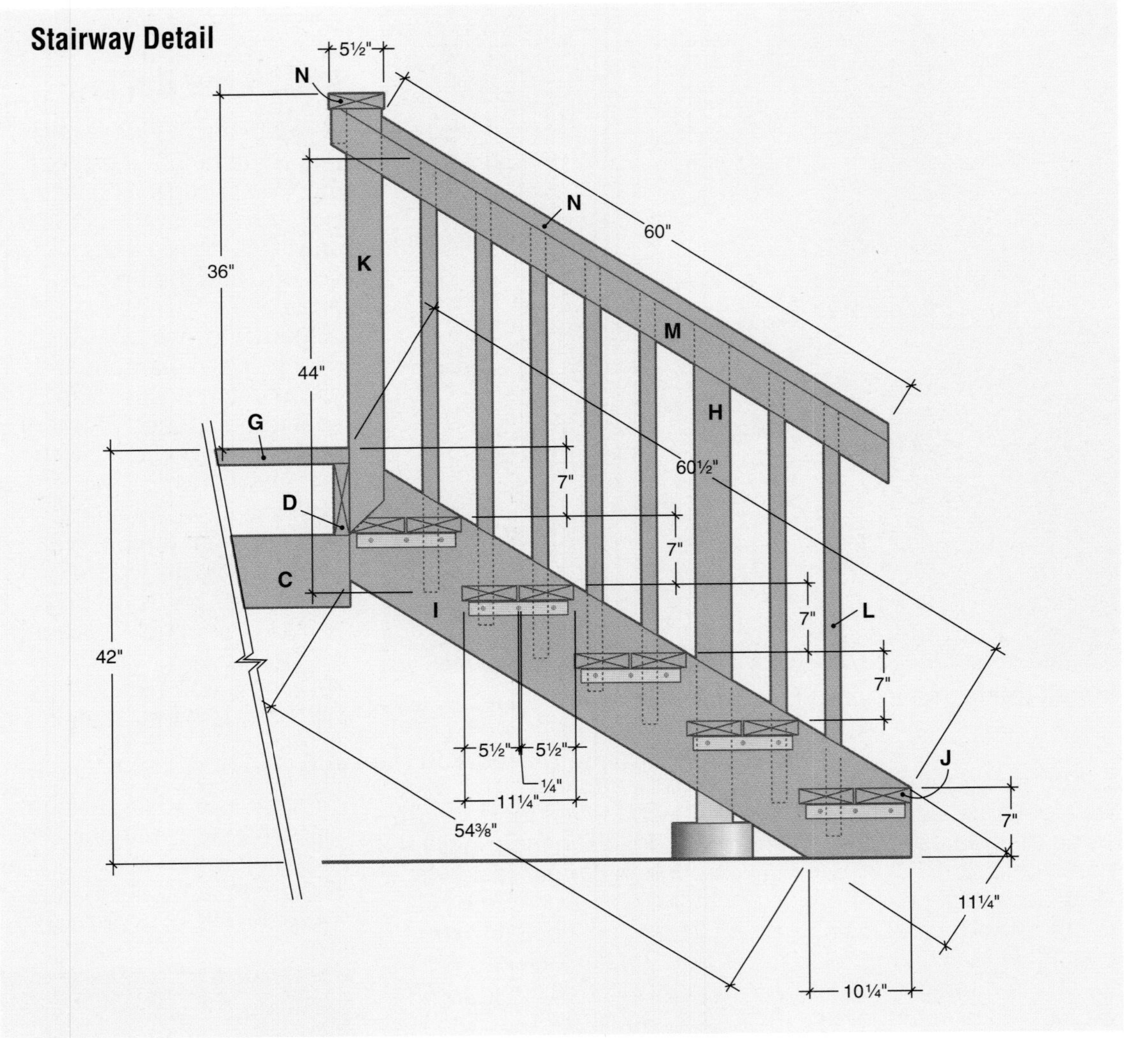

Stairway Detail

5½"

N

N 60"

36"

K

44"

M

H

G 60½"

D 7"

C 7"

42" I

7"

L

7"

5½" 5½"

¼"

J

11¼" 7"

54⅜"

11¼"

10¼"

After attaching the stringers to the deck, fasten them to the posts. Drill and counterbore two pilot holes through the stringers into the posts, and attach with lag screws.

with the bottom of the deck, and make sure the post is plumb. Use an awl to mark pilot hole locations on the side of the deck. Remove posts and drill ¼" pilot holes at marks. Attach the railing posts to the side of the deck with ⅜ × 5" lag screws and washers.

6 Cut top rails (M) to length, with 45° miters on the ends that meet at the corners. Attach to posts with 2½" deck screws, keeping the top edge of the rail flush with the top of the posts. Join rails by cutting 45° bevels at ends.

7 Temporarily attach stairway top rails **(photo J)** with 3" galvanized screws. Mark the outline of the deck

Railing Detail

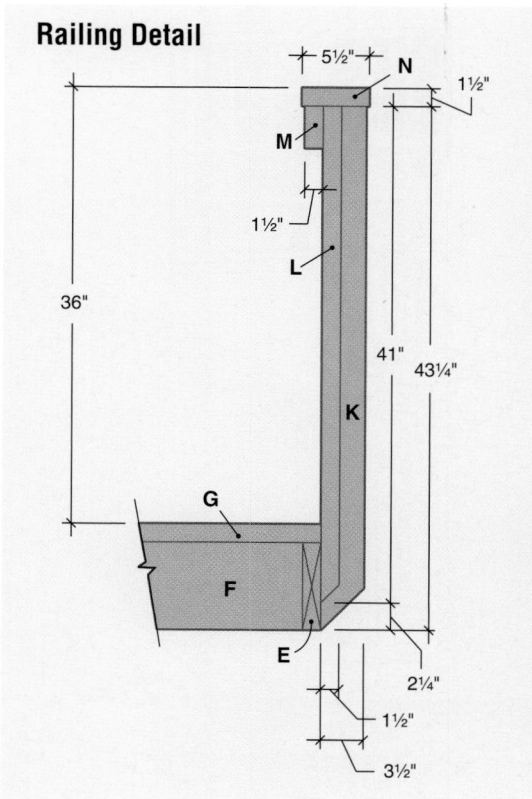

Position the stairway top rail in place against the posts. Attach temporarily and mark for cutting to size.

railing post and top rail on the back side of the stairway top rail. Mark the position of the top rail on the stairway post. Use a level to mark a plumb cutoff line at the lower end of the rail. Remove the rail.

8 Cut the stairway post to finished height along the diagonal mark, and cut the stairway rail along outlines. Reposition the stairway rail and attach with deck screws.

9 Attach the balusters between the railing posts at equal intervals of 4" or less. Use deck screws, and keep the top ends of balusters flush with the top rail. On the stairway, position the balusters against the stringer and top rail, and check for plumb. Draw a diagonal cut line at top of baluster and trim to final height with a power miter saw.

10 Confirm measurements, and cut rail cap sections (N) to length. Position sections so that the inside edge overhangs the inside edge of the rail by ¼". Attach cap to rail with deck screws. At corners, miter the ends 45° and attach caps to posts *(photo K)*.

11 Cut the cap for stairway rail to length. Mark angle of deck railing post on side of cap and bevel-cut the ends of the cap. Attach cap to top rail and post with deck screws. NOTE: Local building codes may require a grippable handrail for any stairway over four treads. Check with your building inspector.

Position the rail cap over the posts and balusters. Make sure mitered corners are tight, and attach with deck screws.

Inside Corner Deck

A distinctive pattern gives this deck visual appeal.

With the help of a diamond decking pattern, this inside corner deck provides a focal point for recreational activities and social gatherings. At the same time, the corner location can offer intimacy, privacy, shade and a shield from the wind.

The design calls for double joists and blocking for extra strength and stability where decking boards butt together. Joists are spaced 12" on center to support diagonal decking.

It takes a little more time to cut the decking boards and match the miter cuts, but the results are spectacular and well worth the effort.

224

Cutaway View

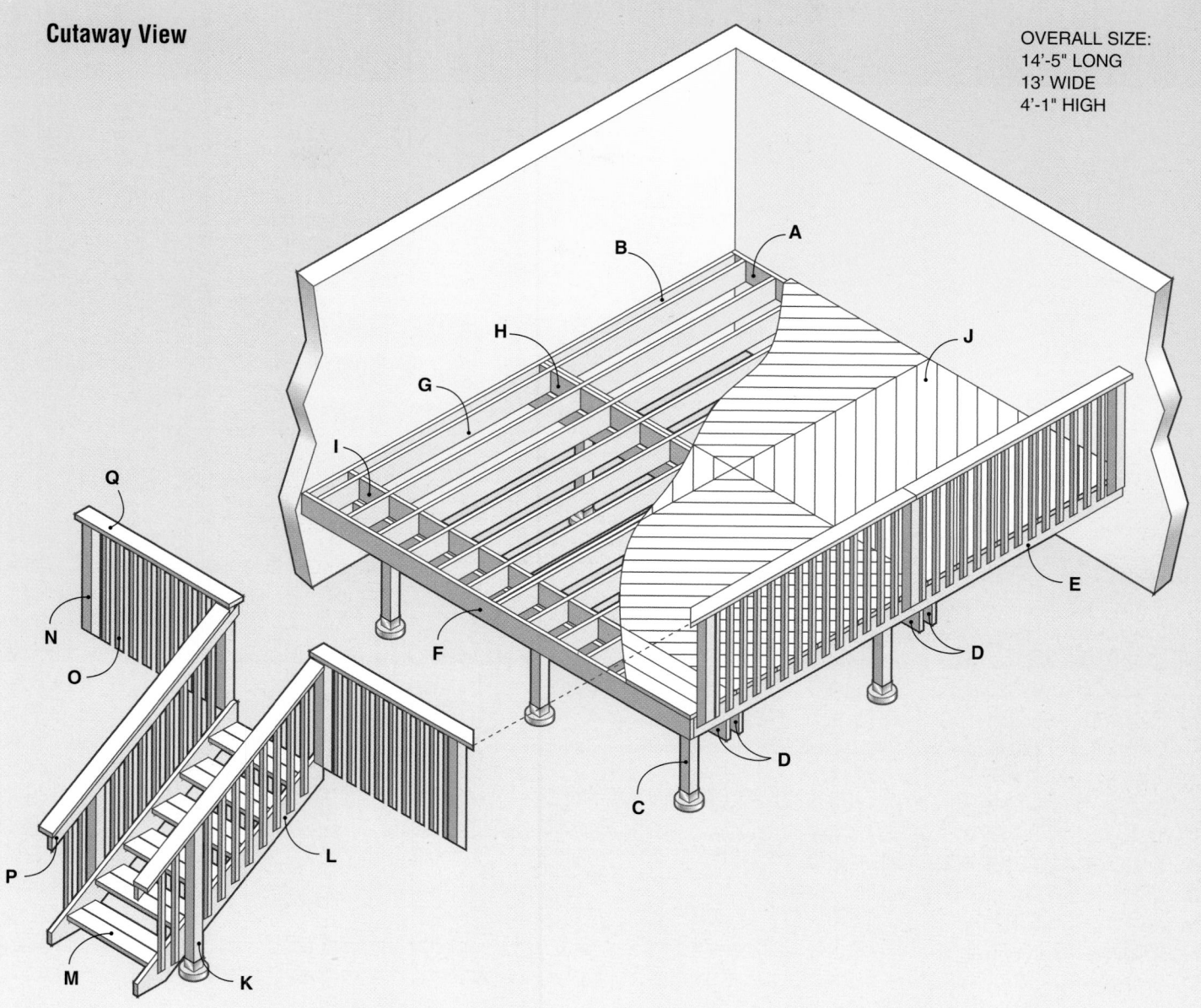

Lumber List			
Qty.	Size	Material	Part
6	2 × 8" × 14'	Trtd. lumber	Short ledger (A), Long ledger (B), Beam boards (D)
14	2 × 8" × 16'	Trtd. lumber	Joists (G), Single blocking (I)
3	2 × 8" × 8'	Trtd. lumber	Double blocking (H)
3	4 × 4" × 8'	Trtd. lumber	Deck posts (C)
1	2 × 8" × 16'	Cedar	End joist (E)
1	2 × 8" × 14'	Cedar	Rim joist (F)

Lumber List			
Qty.	Size	Material	Part
42	2 × 6" × 8'	Cedar	Decking (J), Railing caps (Q)
16	2 × 6" × 14'	Cedar	Decking (J)
1	4 × 4" × 10'	Cedar	Stair posts (K)
6	2 × 6" × 8'	Cedar	Treads (M)
4	4 × 4" × 8'	Cedar	Railing posts (N)
2	2 × 10" × 8'	Cedar	Stringers (L)
33	2 × 2" × 8'	Cedar	Balusters (O)
6	2 × 4" × 8'	Cedar	Top rails (P)

Supplies: 8"-diameter footing forms (8); J-bolts (8); 4 × 4" metal post anchors (8); 2 × 8" single joist hangers (50); 2 × 8" double joist hangers (30); 1½ × 10" angle brackets (12); 3" galvanized deck screws; 2½" galvanized deck screws; 16d galvanized nails; joist hanger nails; ⅜ × 4" lag screws and washers (78); ¼ × 1¼" lag screws (96); ½ × 7" carriage bolts, washers, and nuts (12); exterior silicone caulk (6 tubes); concrete as needed.

225

Framing Plan

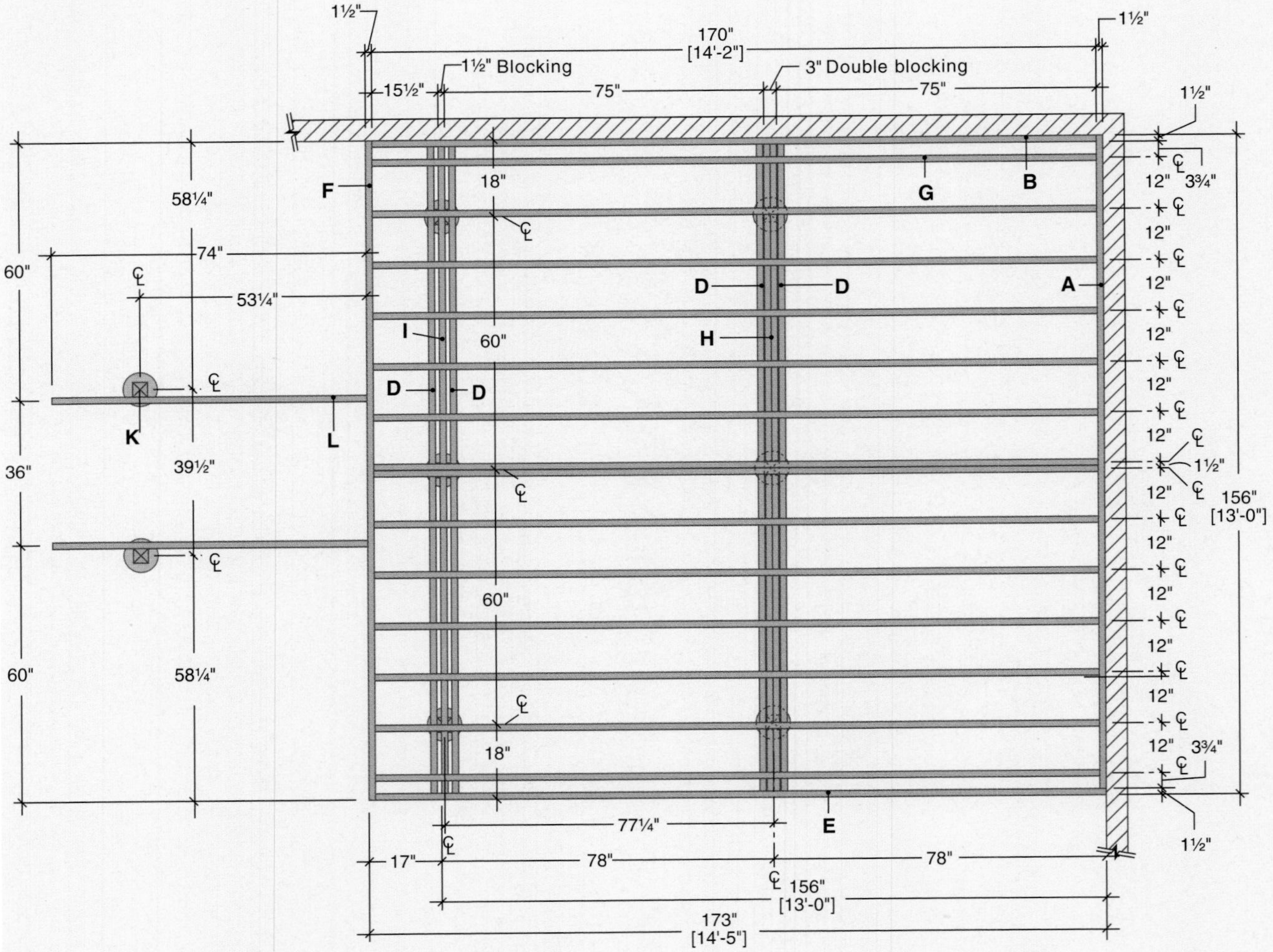

1½"
170" [14'-2"]
1½" Blocking
3" Double blocking
15½"
75"
75"
1½"
58¼"
60"
74"
53¼"
39½"
36"
60"
58¼"
18"
60"
60"
18"
77¼"
17"
78"
78"
156" [13'-0"]
173" [14'-5"]
12" 3¾"
12"
12"
12"
12"
12"
12" 1½"
12"
12"
12"
12"
12"
12" 3¾"
156" [13'-0"]
1½"

A B D E F G H I K L

Elevation

Q P N O
36"
1½"
7¼"
49"
F D D E J
7¼"
P L K C C
17¾"
77¼"
78"
173" [14'-5"]

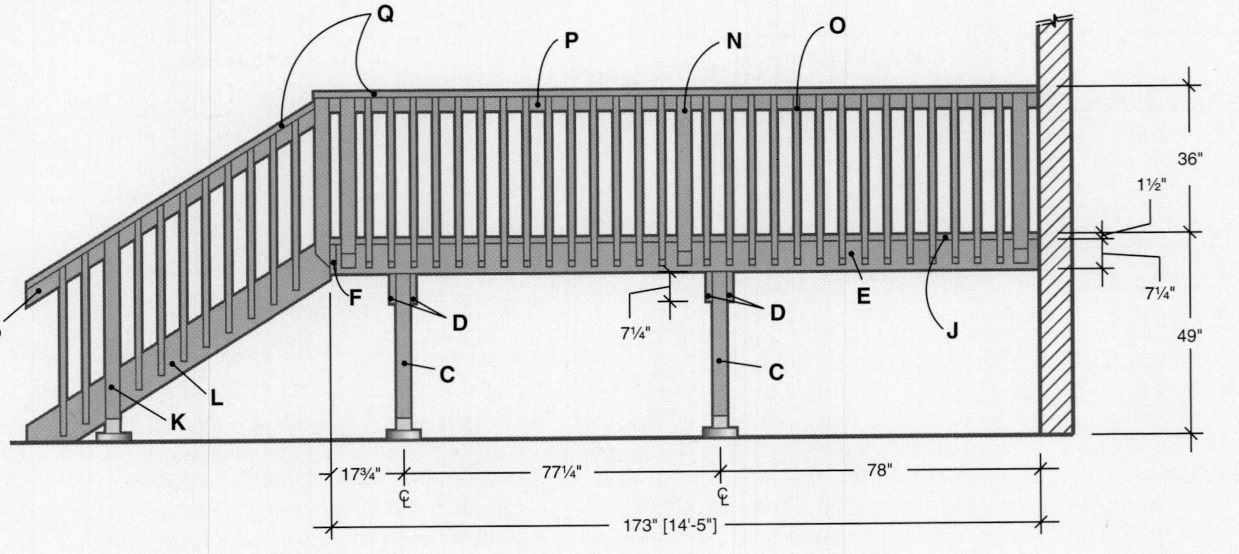

Railing Detail

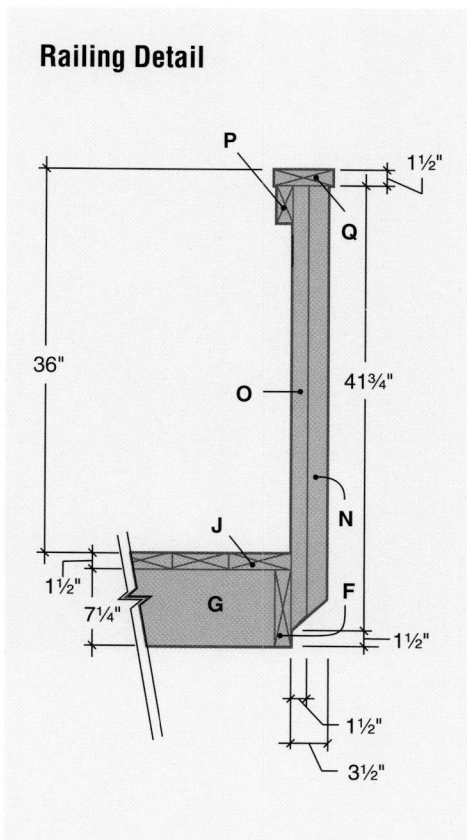

Stairway Detail

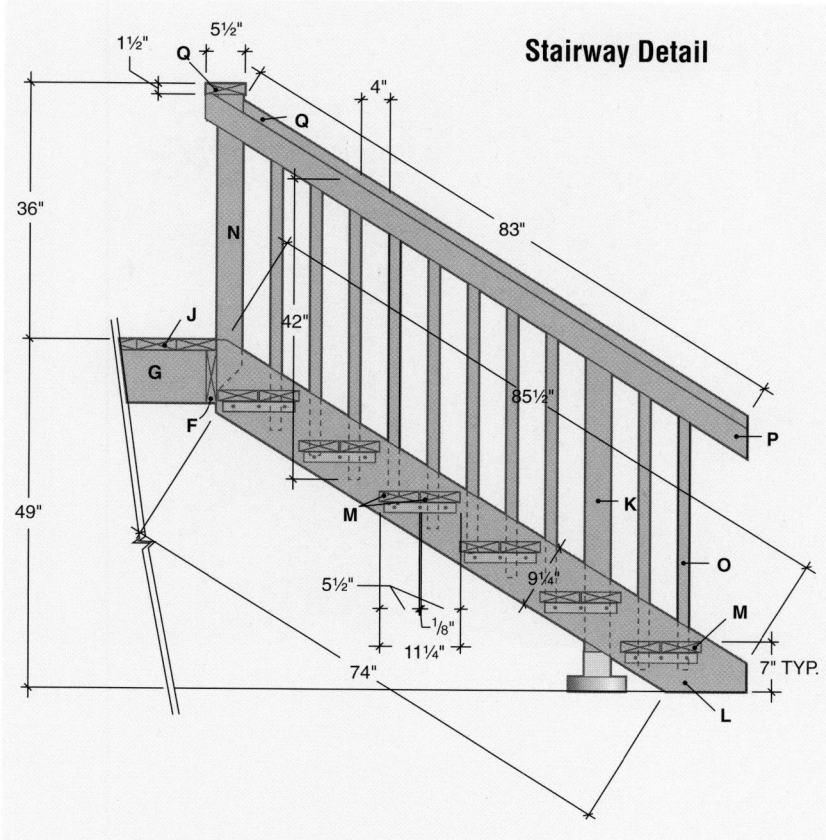

Directions: Inside Corner Deck

Attach the Ledgers

The inside angle of the house should form a right angle. If there is a slight deviation, use shims behind the ledger to create a 90° angle in the corner.

1 To show where the ledgers will be attached to the house, draw outlines on the wall, using a level as a guide. To locate the top of the ledger outline, measure down from the indoor floor surface 1" plus the thickness of the decking boards. This height difference prevents rain and melting snow from seeping into the house.

2 Measure and cut the ledgers to length. They will be shorter than the outline on the wall to allow for the width of the rim joist and end joist.

Once pilot holes have been drilled and the ledger has been positioned and braced against the wall, use a ratchet wrench to attach the ledger with lag screws and washers.

B

To locate the centerpoints of the footings on the ground, drop a plumb bob from the intersections of the mason's strings. Then, drive a stake into the ground to mark each centerpoint.

C

Post anchors keep the post above the footing to discourage rot. The post rests on a metal pedestal that fits over a J-bolt mounted in the footing.

3 Drill pairs of ¼" pilot holes through the ledgers at 16" intervals. Counterbore the pilot holes ½" with a 1" spade bit.

4 Brace the short ledger (A) in place, and insert a nail or an awl through the pilot holes to mark the hole locations on the wall.

5 Repeat the process to mark the hole locations for the long ledger (B).

6 Remove the ledgers and drill pilot holes into the stucco with a ⅜" masonry bit. Then, use a ¼" bit to extend each pilot hole through the sheathing and into the header joist.

7 Position and brace the ledgers against the walls. Use a ratchet wrench to attach the ledgers to the walls with ⅜ × 4" lag screws and washers *(photo A)*. Seal the screw heads and all cracks between the wall and ledger with silicone caulk.

Pour the Deck Footings

To locate the footings, stretch mason's strings between the ledgers and 2 × 4 supports, known as *batterboards.*

1 Referring to the measurements shown in the *Framing Plan,* page 226, mark the centerlines of the footings on the ledgers and drive a nail into the ledger at each location.

2 Set up temporary batterboards and stretch a mason's string out from the ledger at each location. Make sure the strings are perpendicular to the ledger.

3 Check the mason's strings for square, using the 3-4-5 triangle method. From the point where each string meets the ledger, measure 3' along the ledger and make a mark. Next, measure 4' out along the string and mark with tape. The distance between the points on the ledger and the string should be 5'. If it's not,

adjust the string position on the batterboard accordingly.

4 Drop a plumb bob to transfer the footing center-points to the ground, and drive a stake to mark each point *(photo B).* Remove the strings.

5 Dig the post footings, using a clamshell digger or power auger. Pour 2" to 3" of loose gravel into each hole for drainage. NOTE: Make sure the footing size and depth comply with your local building code, which may require flaring the base to 12".

6 Cut the footing forms to length, using a reciprocating saw or handsaw, and insert them into the footing holes so that they extend 2" above grade. Pack soil around the forms for support, and fill the forms with concrete, tamping with a long stick or rod to eliminate any air pockets.

7 Screed the tops of the footings flush, using a 2 × 4. Insert a J-bolt into the wet concrete of each footing, and set it, with ¾" to 1" of thread exposed. Retie the mason's strings and position each J-bolt at the exact center of the post location, using the plumb bob as a guide. Clean the bolt threads before the concrete sets.

Set the Posts

1 Lay a long, straight 2 × 4 flat across each row of footings, parallel to the short ledger. With one edge tight against the J-bolts, draw a reference line across the top of each footing.

2 Center a metal post anchor over the J-bolt on each footing, and square it with the reference line. Attach the post anchors by threading a nut over each bolt and tightening with a ratchet wrench.

3 Cut the posts, leaving an

extra 6" for final trimming. Place each post in an anchor *(photo C)* and tack it in place with one nail.

4 With a level as a guide, use braces and stakes to ensure that each post is plumb. Finish nailing the posts to the anchors.

5 Determine the height of the inside beam by extending a straight 2 × 4 from the bottom edge of the long ledger across the row of posts. Level the 2 × 4, and draw a line on the posts. Use the same method to determine the height of the outer beam.

Install the Beams

1 Cut the beam boards (D), leaving an extra few inches for final trimming.

2 Position one beam board, crown up, against the row of

posts. Tack the board in place with deck screws *(photo D).*

3 Attach the remaining beam boards to the posts in the same way.

4 Drill two ½" holes through the boards and posts at each joint and counterbore the pilot holes ½" with a 1" spade bit. Secure the beam boards to the posts with carriage bolts, using a ratchet wrench.

5 Cut the tops of the posts flush with the tops of the beams, using a reciprocating saw or handsaw.

Install the Joists

A double joist at the center of the deck provides extra support for the ends of the decking boards.

1 Measure, mark and cut the end joist (E) and the rim joist (F), using a circular saw.

2 Attach the end joist to the short ledger and the rim joist to the long ledger, using 16d galvanized nails.

3 Nail the rim joist to the end joist *(photo E).*

4 Toenail the end joist to the tops of the beams, and cut the ends of the beams flush with the end joist.

5 Measure, mark and install the double center joist at the precise center of the deck, with double joist hangers.

6 Measure both ways from the double joist, and mark the centerpoints of the remaining joists at 12" intervals. Using a combination square, mark the outlines of the joists on the ledger, beams and rim joist.

7 Nail the joist hangers to the short ledger and rim joist, using a scrap 2 × 8 as a spacer to achieve the correct spread for each hanger.

8 Cut the joists (G) to

Position the beam against the posts, and attach it temporarily with deck screws.

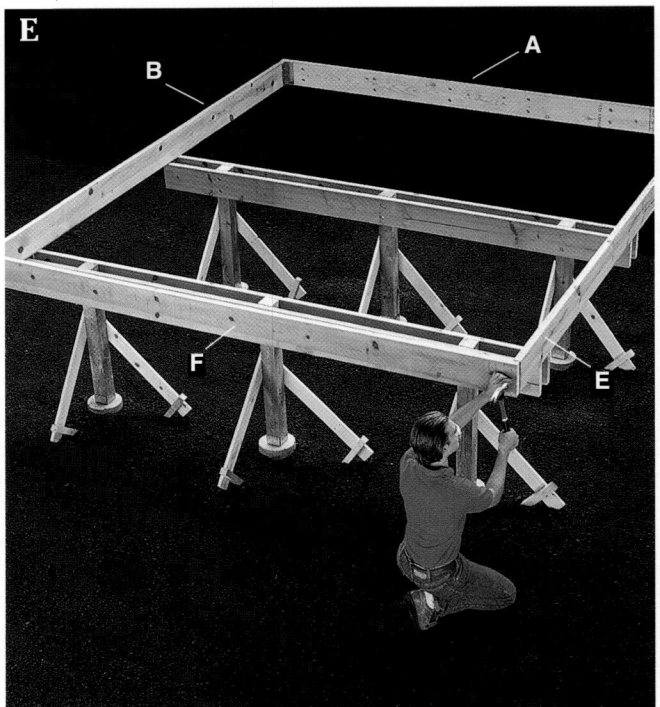

Drive 16d galvanized nails through the rim joist and into the end joist.

Working from a plywood platform, install double blocking to support the ends of the deck boards. Attach the blocking by alternating end nailing with using joist hangers.

length. Insert the joists into the hangers with the crown up, and attach them with joist hanger nails. Align the joists with the marks on the beams and toenail them in place.

Install the Blocking

The ends of the decking boards in the diamond pattern are supported by a row of double blocking at the center of the pattern and a row of single blocking at the edge of the pattern.

1 To locate the rows of blocking, measure from the inside corner of the house along the long ledger (see *Framing Plan*, page 226). Drive one screw or nail at 78", and another at 156". Make corresponding marks across from the ledger on the end joist.

2 Snap chalk lines across the joists, between the ledger and the end joist.

The line at 78" is the center-line of the double blocking. The line at 156" is the outer edge of the single blocking. Don't be concerned if the blocking is not directly over the beams.

3 Cut double blocking pieces from 2 × 8s nailed together with 16d galvanized nails.

4 Install the blocking by alternating end nailing using galvanized joist hangers *(photo F)*.

Lay the Decking

Except for the three rows of straight decking at the top of the stairway, the decking is laid in a diamond pattern.

1 Begin at the center of the diamond pattern, where the double joist and the double blocking intersect. Cut four identical triangles, as large as possible, from 2 × 6" cedar stock.

2 Drill ⅛" pilot holes in the ends, position the pieces as

shown and attach with 3" deck screws.

3 To install the remaining courses, measure, cut, drill, and attach the first three boards in each course. Then, measure the actual length of the last board *(photo G)* to achieve the best fit. For best results, install the decking course by course. Maintain a ⅛" gap between courses.

4 Once the diamond decking pattern is complete, cut and install the three remaining deck boards.

Build the Stairs

1 For the position of the stairway footings, refer to the *Framing Plan* on page 226. Locate the footings by extending a 2 × 4 from the deck, perpendicular to the rim joist, dropping a plumb bob, and marking the centerpoints on the ground with stakes.

G

To achieve the best fit, measure the actual length of the last deck board in each course before cutting.

ground with stakes.

2 Dig postholes with a clamshell digger or an auger, and pour footings using the same method as for the deck footings. Insert J-bolts, leaving ¾" to 1" of thread exposed. Allow the concrete to set. Attach metal post anchors.

3 Cut the stairway posts (K) to length, adding approximately 6" for final trimming. Place the posts in the anchors.

4 Use a level to ensure that the posts are plumb, and attach the posts to the anchors with 16d galvanized nails.

5 Cut the stringers (L) to length and use a framing square to mark the rise and run for each step (see *Stairway Detail*, page 227). Draw the tread outline on each run. Cut the angles at the ends of the stringers with a circular saw. (For a more detailed description of stairway construction, see *Changing*

Stairway Height, pages 294 to 295.)

6 Position an angle bracket flush with the bottom of each tread outline. Drill ⅛" pilot holes in the stringers, and attach the angle brackets with 1¼" lag screws.

7 The treads (M) fit between the stringers, and the stringers fit between the stairway posts. Measure and cut the treads (M) to length, 3" shorter than the distance between the stairway posts.

8 Assemble the stairway upside down on sawhorses. Mark and drill ⅛" pilot holes at the ends of the treads. Position each front tread with its front edge flush to the tread outline, and attach to the angle brackets with ¼ × 1¼" lag screws.

9 Attach the rear treads in similar fashion **(photo H),** leaving a ⅛" gap between treads.

10 Position the stairway in place against the edge of the

deck, making sure the top of the stringer is flush with the surface of the deck. From underneath the deck, drill ¼" pilot holes through the rim joist into the stringers. Attach the stringers to the rim joist with 4" lag screws, using a ratchet wrench **(photo I).**

11 To fasten the stairway to the stair posts, drill two ¼" pilot holes through each stringer into a post. Counterbore the pilot holes ½" deep with a 1" spade bit, and use a ratchet wrench to drive 4" lag screws with washers. Seal the screw heads with silicone caulk.

Install the Deck Railing

1 Cut the railing posts (N) and balusters (O) to length (see *Railing Detail*, page 227) with a power miter saw or circular saw. Cut the tops square and the bottoms at 45° angles.

2 Drill two ¼" pilot holes at the bottom end of each railing post, positioned so the lag screws will attach to the rim joist. Counterbore the holes ½" deep with a 1" spade bit.

3 Drill two ⅛" pilot holes near the bottom of each baluster, spaced 4" apart. At the top of each baluster, drill a pair of ⅛" pilot holes spaced 1½" apart.

Tip

When laying decking, install boards that have a flat grain with the bark side down. Flat-grain boards tend to cup to the bark side and, if installed bark-side-up, often trap water on the deck.

Drill pilot holes and then attach the treads to the stringers, using 1¼" lag screws and angle brackets.

Fasten the stair to the deck with a ratchet wrench, using 4" lag screws.

4 With the help of a combination square, draw the outlines of the railing posts around the perimeter of the deck. The posts at the corner must be spaced so there is less than 4" between them.

5 Hold each railing post in its position, with the end 1½" above the bottom edge of the deck platform (see *Railing Detail*, page 227). Make sure the post is plumb, and insert an awl through the counter-bored holes to mark pilot hole locations on the deck.

6 Set the post aside and drill ¼" pilot holes at the marks. Attach the railing posts to the deck with ⅜ × 4" lag screws and washers. Seal the screw heads with silicone caulk.

7 Cut the top rails (P) to length with the ends mitered at 45° where they meet in the corner. Attach them to the railing posts with 3" deck screws, keeping the edges of the rails flush with the tops of the posts.

8 To position the balusters, measure the total distance between two railing posts, and mark the centerpoint on the top rail. The two railing sections on the long side of this deck will have a baluster at the centerpoint; the two railing sections on the stairway side will have a space at the centerpoint. NOTE: If the dimensions of your deck vary from the plan, calculate whether you will have a baluster or a space at the center of each section.

9 Cut a spacer slightly less than 4" wide. Start at the center of each railing section, and position either a baluster or a space over the line. Measure out from the center both ways, marking the outlines of the balusters on the top rail. The end spaces may be narrow, but they will be symmetrical.

10 To install the balusters, begin next to a railing post and make sure the first baluster is plumb. Install the remaining balusters, holding each one tight against the spacer and flush with the top rail. Attach the balusters with 2½" deck screws.

11 Cut the deck railing cap (Q) to length, with the ends mitered at 45° where they meet in the corner. Position the railing cap sections so the inside edge overhangs the inside edge of the top rail by ¼" *(photo J)*. Attach the cap with 3" deck screws.

Install the Stairway Railing

1 Determine the exact size and shape of the stairway top rail. Tack a cedar 2 × 4 across the faces of the stairway post and deck post with 10d galvanized nails. Make sure the angle of the 2 × 4 is parallel with the angle of the stringer below.

J

After the top rail and balusters have been installed, install the railing cap with its inside edge overhanging the inside face of the top rail by ¼".

K

With the stairway top rail cut to size and installed, attach the railing cap with deck screws.

2 On the back side of the 2 × 4, mark the outline of the deck railing post and the end of the deck top rail. On the stairway post, mark a diagonal cutoff line at the top edge of the 2 × 4. At the lower end of the 2 × 4, use a level to mark a plumb cutoff line directly above the end of the stringer.

3 Remove the 2 × 4 and make the cuts.

4 Drill ⅛" pilot holes through the stairway top rail. Place in position and attach with 2½" deck screws.

5 To trim the top ends of the stairway balusters, hold a baluster against the stairway post and draw a diagonal cut line along the top edge of the rail. Trim the baluster. Using this baluster as a template, mark and cut the remaining stairway balusters.

6 Install the stairway balusters with 2½" deck screws, using the same procedure as for the deck balusters.

7 Measure the railing caps for the stairway. Cut the caps to size, with the upper ends beveled to fit against the deck posts, and the lower ends beveled to align with the end of the top rail. Install the caps by drilling ⅛" pilot holes and attaching them with 2½" deck screws *(photo K).*

Island Deck

The perfect place to visit when you need to relax.

An island deck can transform any area of your yard into a virtual oasis. Since it's not attached to your house, you can position your island deck wherever you like—to capitalize on a spectacular view or to catch the cool afternoon breeze in a shady glen.

Accessible and inviting with its three-sided landing, this deck welcomes visitors of all ages. And it can readily serve as a cornerstone for a total landscaping plan; one that will make your entire yard a more comfortable and attractive space for enjoying the great outdoors.

Cutaway View

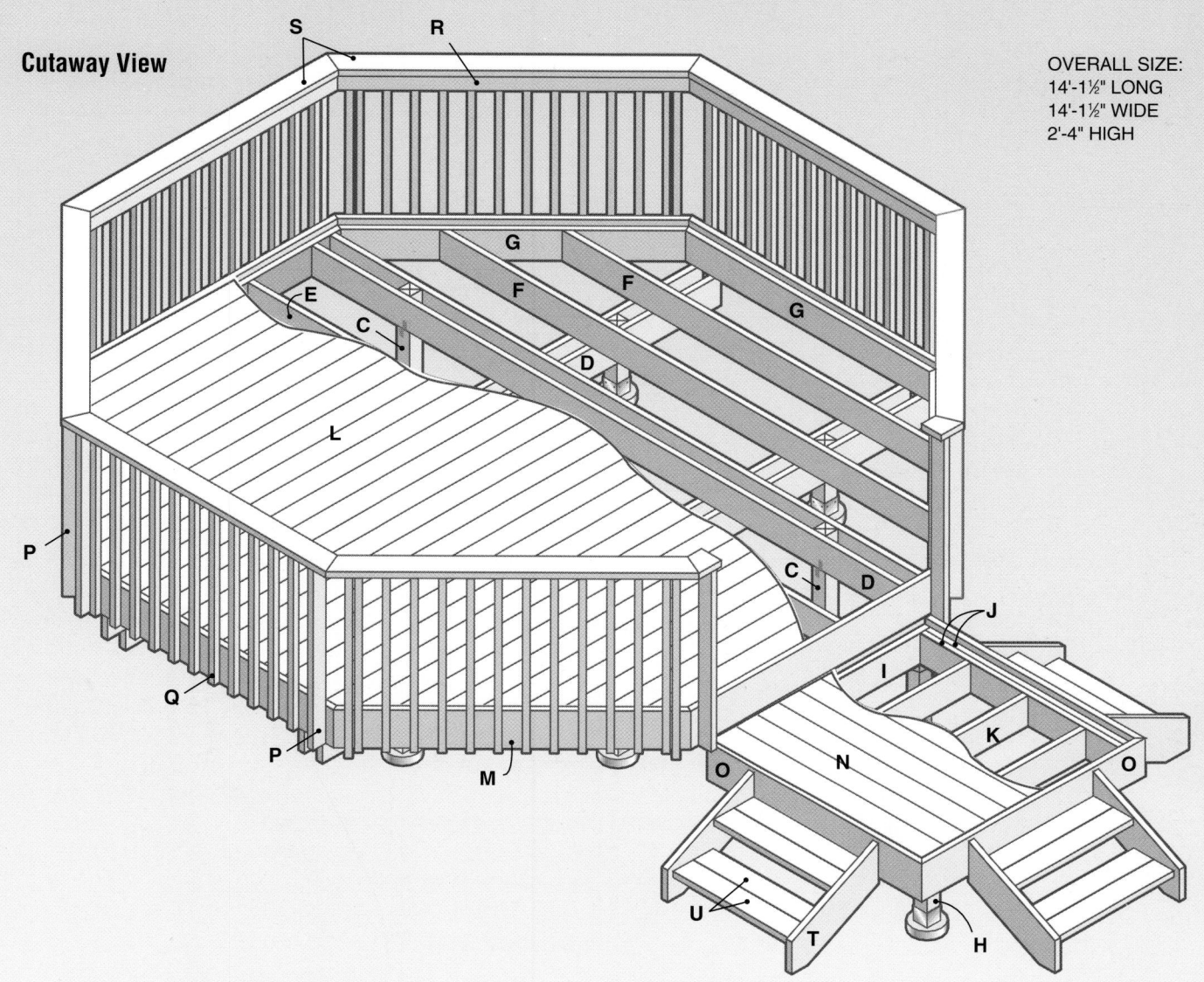

Lumber List					Lumber List			
Qty.	Size	Material	Part		Qty.	Size	Material	Part
4	2 × 4" × 16'	Pine	Site chooser sides (A)		7	2 × 6" × 12'	Cedar	Deck decking (L)
2	2 × 4" × 12'	Pine	Site chooser diagonals (B)		13	2 × 6" × 10'	Cedar	Deck decking (L), Landing decking (N), Treads (U)
2	4 × 4" × 12'	Trtd. lumber	Deck posts (C), Landing posts (H)		4	2 × 6" × 8'	Cedar	Deck decking (L)
10	2 × 8" × 14'	Trtd. lumber	Beam boards (D)		11	2 × 10" × 6'	Cedar	Deck face boards (M), Landing face boards (O)
			Long joists (E)					
2	2 × 8" × 12'	Trtd. lumber	Mitered joists (F)		8	2 × 4" × 8'	Cedar	Railing posts (P)
6	2 × 8" × 10'	Trtd. lumber	Mitered joists (F), Inner rim joists (I), Outer rim joists (J), Landing joists (K)		42	2 × 2" × 8'	Cedar	Balusters (Q)
					7	2 × 4" × 6'	Cedar	Top rail (R)
9	2 × 8" × 6'	Trtd. lumber	Deck rim joists (G), Landing joists (K)		3	2 × 10" × 6'	Cedar	Stringers (T)
25	2 × 6" × 14'	Cedar	Deck decking (L), Railing cap (S)					

Supplies: 8"-diameter footing forms (12); J-bolts (12); 4 × 4" metal post anchors (12); 90° 2 × 8" joist hangers (10); 45° 2 × 8" joist hangers (8); joist ties (16); post-beam caps (4); joist hanger nails; 1½" × 10" angle brackets (12); 3" galvanized deck screws; ¼ × 1¼" galvanized lag screws and washers (96); 16d galvanized box nails; ½ × 7" carriage bolts, washers, and nuts (16); ⅜ × 5" lag screws and washers (32); concrete as required.

Framing Plan

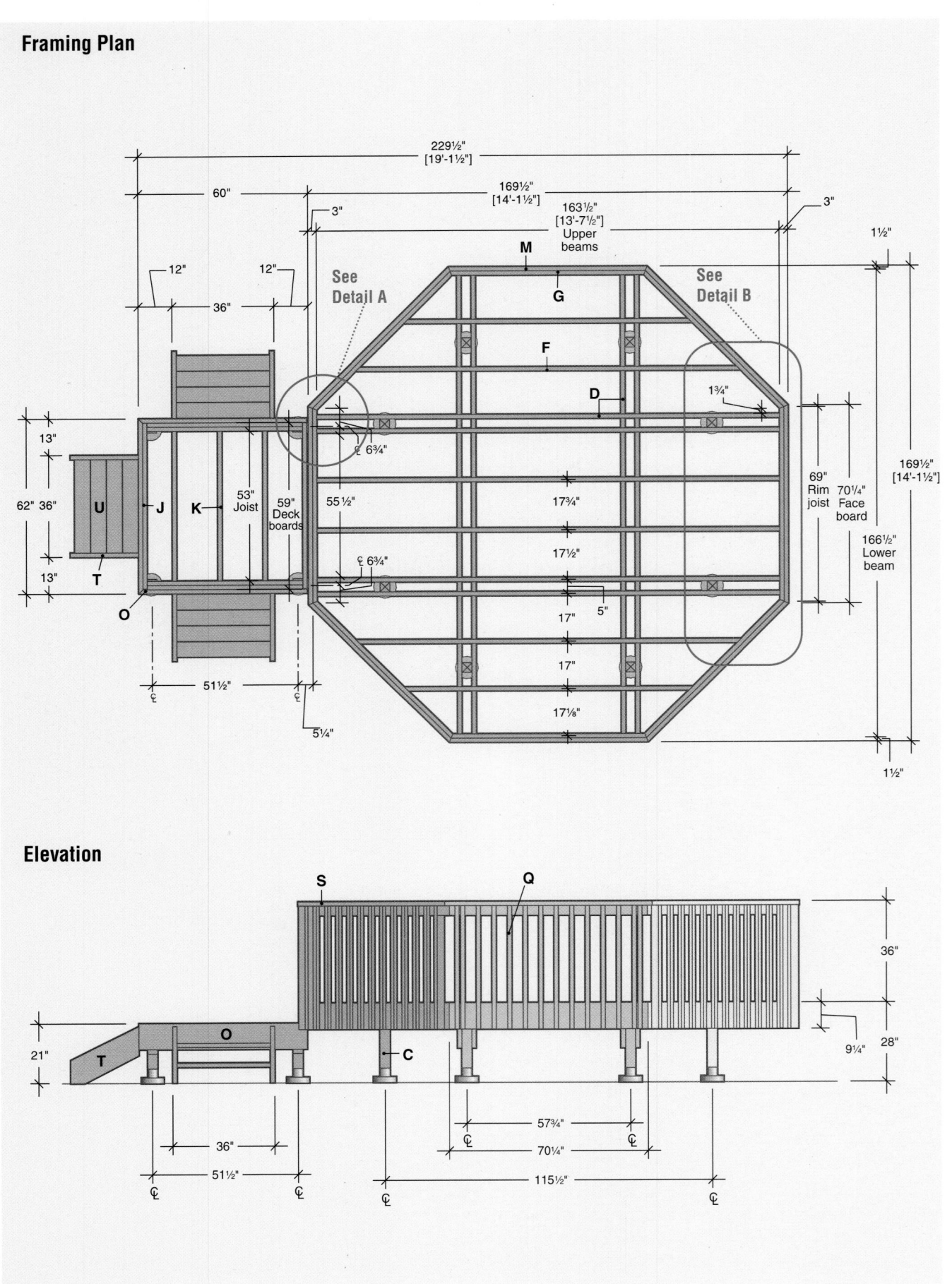

Elevation

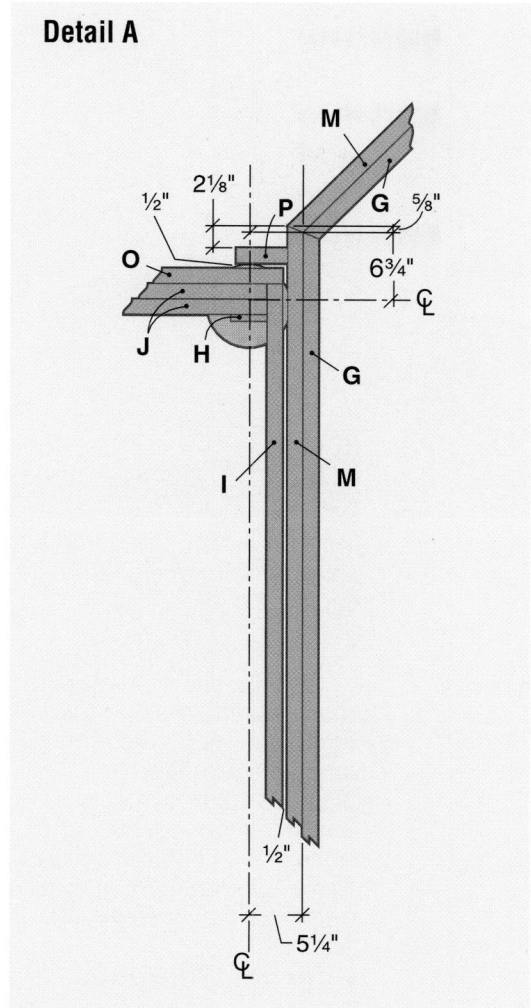

Detail A

2⅛"
½"
M
P
G
⅝"
O
6¾"
C̶L̶
J
H
G
I
M
½"
5¼"
C̶L̶

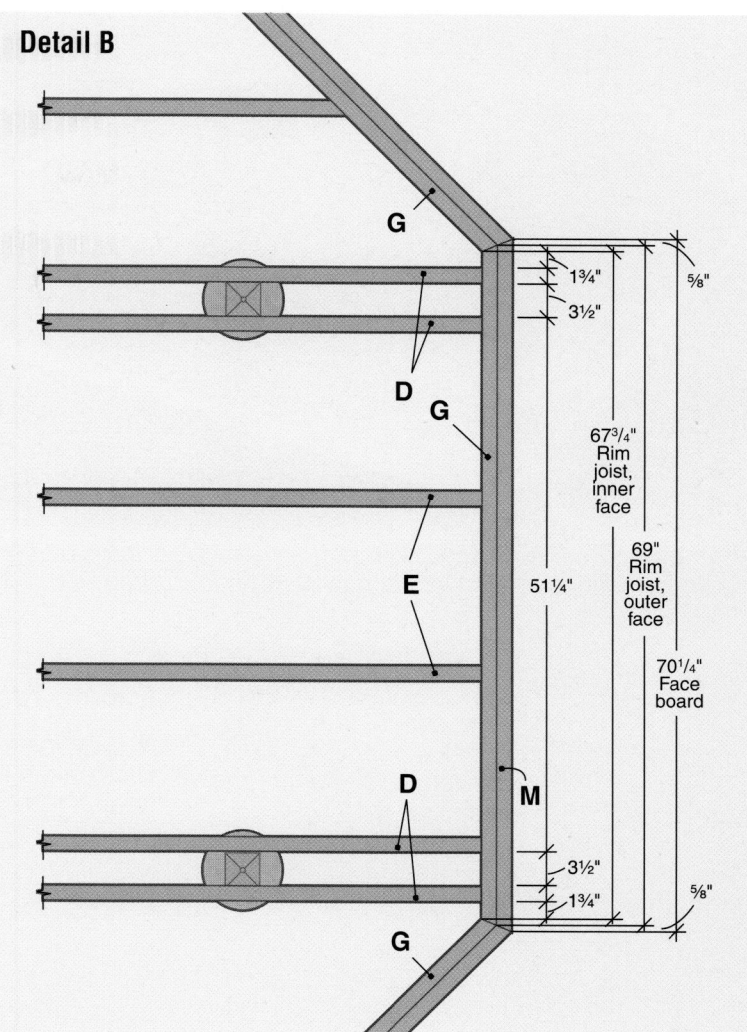

Detail B

G
G
D
1¾"
3½"
⅝"
G
67¾"
Rim joist, inner face
E
51¼"
69"
Rim joist, outer face
70¼"
Face board
D
M
3½"
1¾"
⅝"
G

Use the site chooser to experiment with possible deck locations and to find the site you like best.

Directions: Island Deck

Position the Deck

1 Measure, mark and cut to length the site chooser frame (A) and diagonal braces (B), (see *Site Chooser Detail*, page 238).

2 Fasten the frame together with 3" deck screws, and check for squareness by measuring corner to corner. Adjust the frame so measurements are identical, and attach the diagonal braces with deck screws.

3 With a helper, move the site chooser to select the exact deck location *(photo A).*

4 When you've established

B

C

Locate the deck footings by stretching mason's strings across the site chooser, marking footing locations with tape, and dropping a plumb bob from each mark.

Insert a J-bolt, then drop a plumb bob to check for exact center of the footings.

the deck position, set the site chooser on sawhorses and tack or clamp in place to conveniently find the footing locations.

Locate the Footings

1 Mark the footing centerlines on the frame and stretch mason's string

across the site from mark to mark. Measure along the strings, marking the footing locations with tape.
2 Drop a plumb bob from each marked location, and drive stakes into the ground to mark the centers of the deck footings *(photo B).*

Pour the Footings

1 Remove the mason's strings and dig the footing holes, using a clamshell digger or power auger.
2 Pour 2" to 3" of loose gravel into each hole for drainage. Make sure hole dimensions comply with your local building code, which may require flaring the base to 12".
3 Cut concrete tube forms to length, using a reciprocating saw or handsaw. Insert tubes into holes, leaving 2" of tube above ground level.
4 Pack soil around tubes and fill tubes with concrete. Tamp with a long stick or rod to eliminate air gaps.
5 Screed the concrete flush, using a straight 2 × 4, and insert a J-bolt into each footing, leaving ¾" to 1" of the thread exposed. Retie

Site Chooser Detail

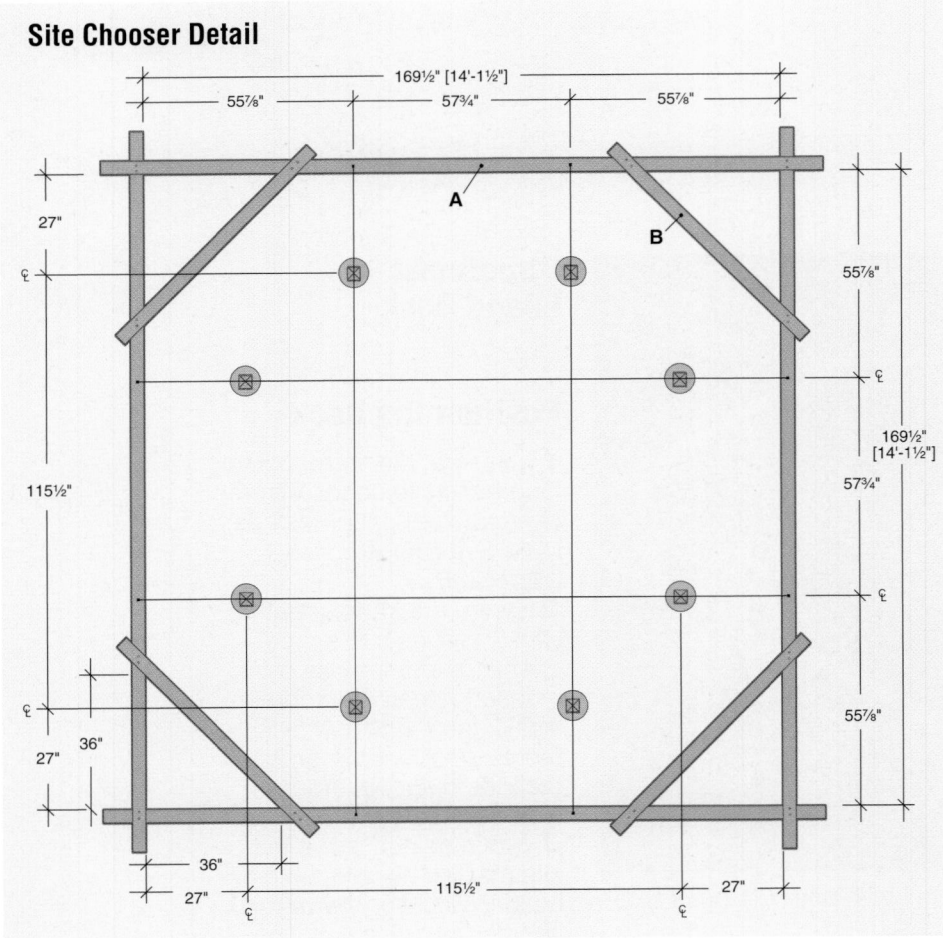

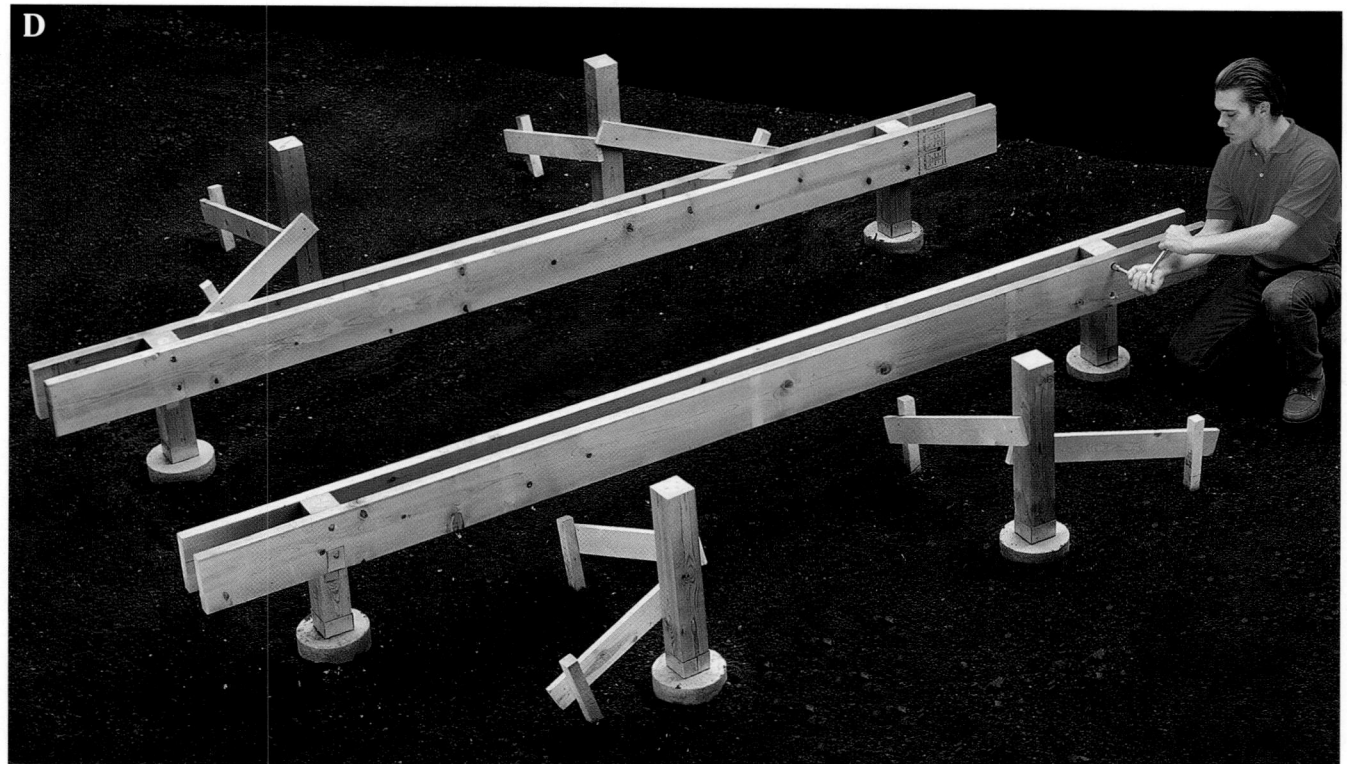

After trimming the lower posts to length, permanently attach the deck beams to the posts with carriage bolts, using a ratchet wrench. The upper deck beams will be perpendicular to, and rest on top of, the lower deck beams.

the mason's strings and position the J-bolt at the center of the footing, using a plumb bob as a guide *(photo C).*
6 Clean bolt threads before concrete sets.

Set the Deck Posts

1 Lay a straight 2 × 4 flat across each pair of footings, with one edge tight against the J-bolts. Draw a line across the top of each footing to help orient the post anchors.
2 Place a metal post anchor on each footing, centering it over the J-bolt and squaring it with the reference line. Thread a nut over each J-bolt and tighten the post anchors in place.
3 Cut the deck posts (C), several inches long to allow for final trimming. Set the posts in the anchors, brace the taller posts plumb, and nail the posts in place.
4 Establish the height of the

taller posts by measuring up 26½" from ground level and marking one post. Using a mason's string and a line level, transfer this mark to the remaining tall posts.
5 To establish the height of the lower beam posts, measure down 7¼" from the first line and transfer a level mark to the four lower posts.

Install the Deck Beams

This deck uses two sets of beams. The lower beams are three inches longer than the upper beams, because the rim joists rest on them. The lower beams support the upper beams and the deck platform.

1 Measure, mark and cut the four lower beam boards (D) to length.
2 Mark the post locations on the tops and sides of the lower beams, using a combination square as a guide.

3 Position the lower beams crown-side-up on their posts. Make sure they are level, and fasten them with deck screws.
4 Trim the tops of the posts flush with a reciprocating saw or a handsaw.
5 Drill two ½" holes through the beams at each post. Securely attach the lower beams with joist ties, carriage bolts and washers, using a ratchet wrench *(photo D).*
6 Measure, mark and, cut the upper beams (D) to length. Mark post locations and attach, following the same steps as for the lower beams.

Install the Rim Joists

1 Cut four of the eight rim joists (G) to length (see *Detail B*, page 237), using a circular saw. Make 22½° miter cuts on the ends.
2 Attach one rim joist to each end of the upper

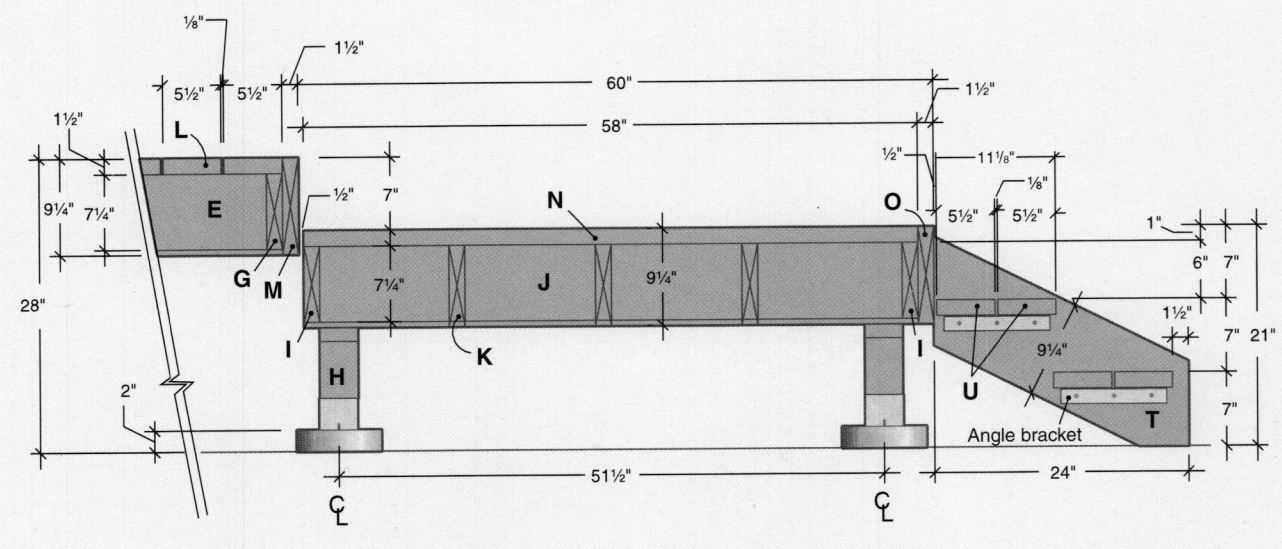

beams (see *Detail B*, page 237) by nailing through the rim joist into the beams with box nails. Toenail the remaining two rim joists to the tops of the lower beams.

3 Verify the measurements of the remaining rim joists, cut to length, miter the ends at 22½°, and install. At the corners, drill pairs of ⅛" pilot holes and fasten the adjacent rim joists to each other with deck screws.

Pour Landing Footings and Install Posts

1 Locate the landing footings by stretching a mason's string out from the rim joist to a batterboard, according to the measurements on the *Framing Plan*, page 236, and *Detail A*, page 237. Make sure the strings are perpendicular to the rim joist and are parallel with each other.

2 Mark the footing locations with tape. Use a plumb bob and stakes to transfer the locations to the ground *(photo E).*

3 Remove the mason's strings and dig holes for the footings, using a clamshell digger or power auger. Pour 2" to 3" of loose gravel into each hole for drainage, making sure hole dimensions comply with your local building code.

4 Use a reciprocating saw or handsaw to cut concrete tube forms to length. Insert tubes into holes. Leave 2" of tube above ground level, pack soil around tubes, and fill tubes with concrete. Tamp the concrete to eliminate air gaps.

5 Screed the tops flush and insert a J-bolt into each footing, leaving ¾" to 1" of the thread exposed. Retie the mason's strings and position the J-bolt at the centerpoint of the footing, using a plumb bob. Clean bolt threads before concrete sets.

6 Install post anchors, cut the landing posts to length (see *Detail*, above), and at-

tach the posts to the post anchors.

Install Landing Beams and Rim Joists

1 Attach post-beam caps to the tops of the landing posts.

2 Verify size, mark, and cut the beam boards (J) and rim joists (I) to length, using a circular saw (see *Framing Plan*, page 236).

3 Hold one pair of beam boards together, then measure and mark the post-beam cap locations on the tops and sides of the boards, using a combination square. Repeat for the second pair of boards.

4 Place beams, crown side up, into the post-beam caps and align. Drill pilot holes and fasten the caps to the beams with deck screws.

5 Position the rim joists flush with the side and top of the beams (see *Detail A*, page 237), drill ⅛" pilot holes

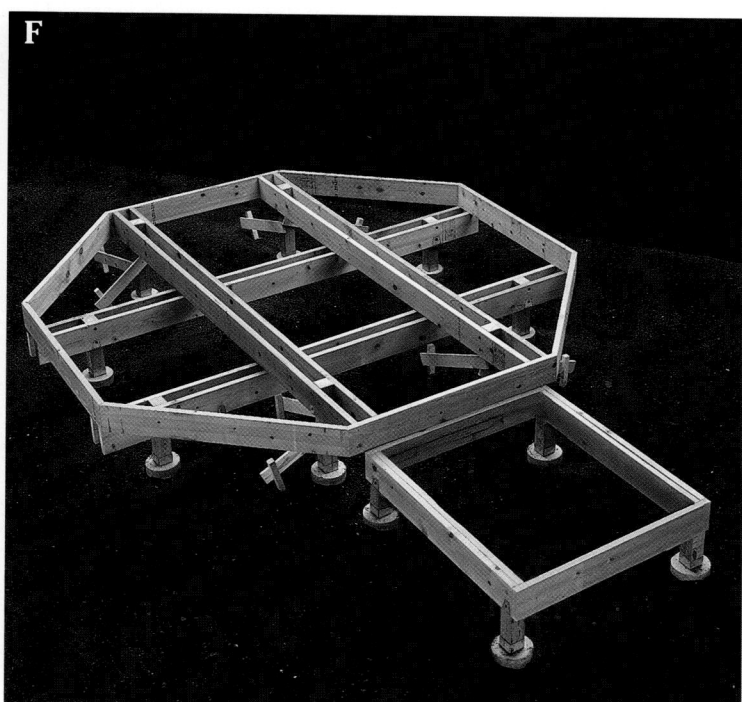

Locate the landing footings with mason's string and a plumb bob.

Measure, mark, and cut the landing beams. Attach them to the landing posts, using post-beam caps.

through the rim joists, and fasten with deck screws *(photo F).*

Install Deck and Landing Joists

For the deck, the inner joists are installed with joist hangers and toe-nailed to the tops of the lower beams. This deck uses 90° joist hangers for the landing and for the two deck joists between the upper beams. For the angled deck joists, we used 45° joist hangers.

1 Using the plan, measure along the deck rim joists and lower beams, marking where joists attach. Draw the outline of each joist on the beams, using a combination square as a guide.
2 Measure, mark, and cut lumber for long joists (E) and mitered joists (F), using a circular saw. Mark the ends of the mitered joists with a 22½° angle, using a speed square, and cut the ends.

Straighten out any bowed decking boards with a pry bar and attach, using decking screws, leaving a ⅛" gap between boards.

Railing Detail

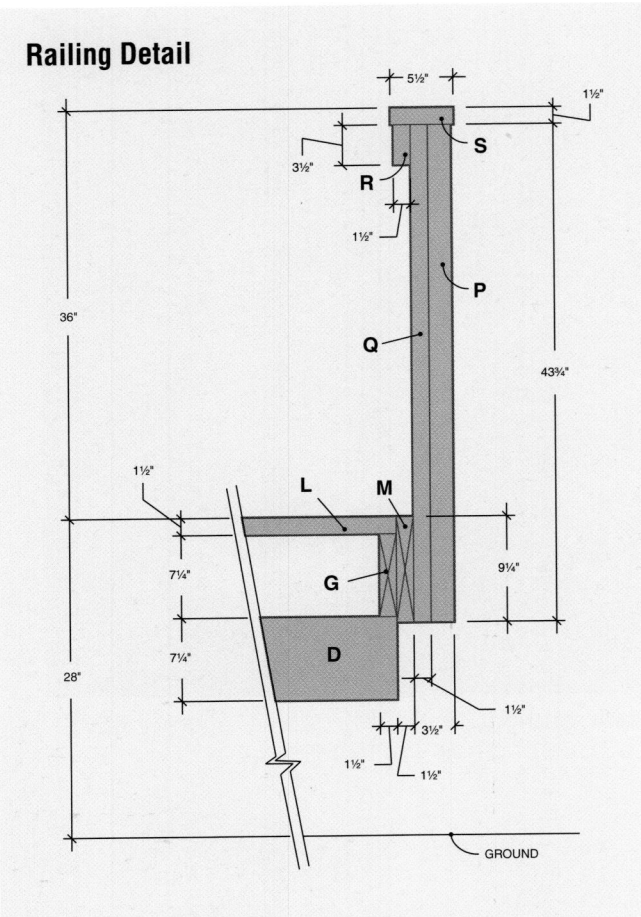

Face Board Detail

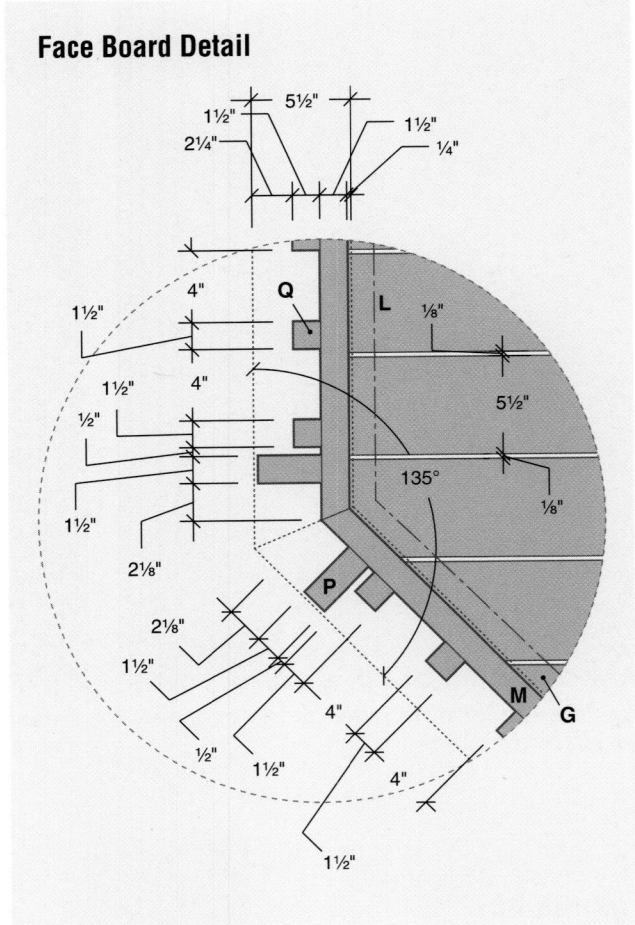

3 Place joists in hangers with crown side up, and attach with nails. Align joists with the outlines on the top edges of the lower beams and toenail in place.
4 Measure and mark locations of landing joists (K) on landing beams. Position joist hangers and attach with nails. Install landing joists and nail in place.

Lay the Deck Decking

1 Measure, cut, and position the first row of decking (L) next to the landing, and attach by driving a pair of deck screws into each joist.
2 Position the remaining decking boards so ends overhang the rim joists, leaving a ⅛" gap between the boards to provide for drainage **(photo G).** Attach boards to each joist with a pair of deck screws.
3 After installing every few rows of decking, measure from the edge of the decking to the far edge of the deck. Adjust the spacing between the remaining boards so the final board can be full width.
4 Snap a chalk line on the decking to mark a line flush with the outside edge of the deck and trim the deck boards with a circular saw.

Install the Face Boards

1 Measure, mark, and cut deck face boards (M). Miter-cut the ends at 22½°. Position face boards flush with decking and attach to rim joists, using deck screws.

2 Verify the measurements, mark, and cut the landing face boards (O) to length. Position top edges flush with decking and attach to landing beams and front rim joist, using deck screws.

Build the Railing

1 Measure, mark, and cut the railing posts (P) to length (see *Railing Detail*, above).
2 At the bottom of each post, counterbore two holes ½" deep, using a spade bit slightly larger than the diameter of the washers.
3 Drill two ¼" pilot holes through the bottom of each post. Position posts (see *Face Board Detail*, above), mark and drill pilot holes in deck, and attach to the face

Drill ⅛" pilot holes, then screw the top rail sections together where they meet at the corners.

After attaching angle brackets, turn stringers upside down and install treads, using 1¼" lag screws.

board and rim joist, using lag screws.

4 Cut each top rail section (R) the same length as the face board below it. Miter the ends of each section at 22½°.

5 Fasten the top rails to the posts with screws.

6 Measure, mark and cut railing balusters (Q) to length.

7 Drill ⅛" pilot holes in the balusters, and attach them to the face boards and the top rails with screws.

8 To strengthen the corners, drill ⅛" pilot holes at an angle and screw the top rail sections together *(photo H).*

9 Verify the measurements for the railing cap sections (S), and cut them to length with 22½° miters where the ends meet. Attach to the posts and top rail with deck screws.

Build the Stairways

1 Measure, mark and cut the stringers (T) to size (see *Landing & Stairway Detail,* page 240).

2 Using a framing square, lay out the top step with a 6" rise (the top of the stringer is installed 1" below the surface of the decking) and 12" run. Extend the rise line to both edges of the stringer, and cut along this line.

3 Lay out the bottom step with a 7" rise and a 12¾" run. At the end of the run, draw a perpendicular line 7" long and make a mark. Draw another perpendicular line to the bottom edge of the stringer and cut to size (see *Landing & Stairway Detail,* page 240).

4 Position the angle brackets

in place and attach to the stringers, using 1¼" lag screws.

5 Measure, mark and cut the treads (U) to length, and attach to the stringers with lag screws through the angle brackets, leaving a ⅛" gap between treads *(photo I).*

6 Install the stairways by propping them in position against the landing and drilling ¼" pilot holes through the rim joists and face boards into the top end of the stringers. Attach with a pair of lag screws at each stringer.

Lay the Landing Decking

After installing the stairways, cut the landing decking (N) to length and attach with deck screws.

Wraparound Deck

Combine multiple seating possibilities with an expansive view.

By wrapping around an outside corner of your house, this versatile deck increases your living space and lets you take advantage of views in several directions. The plan also creates two symmetrical areas for sitting or relaxing, providing space for two distinct activities. Our plan also calls for a front stairway for easy access to your yard or garden. The horizontal rails and notched posts provide striking visual elements that enhance the deck's overall design and add to its intimate nature. By adding a box or rail planter (see *Deck Furnishings*, pages 280 to 283), you can bring your garden right up to the deck.

Cutaway View

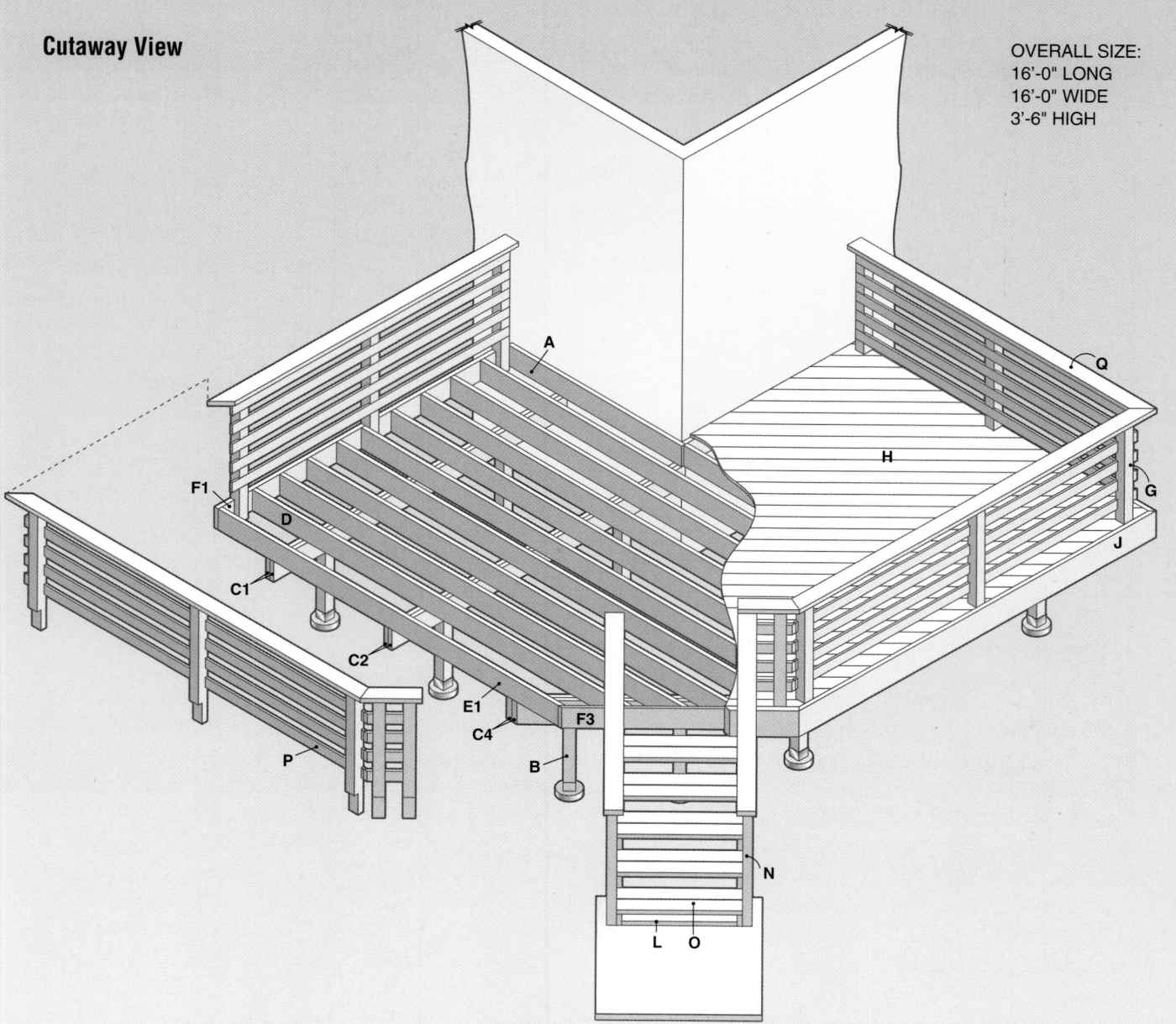

Lumber List			
Qty.	Size	Material	Part
9	2 × 8" × 16'	Trtd. Lumber	Joists (D)
6	2 × 8" × 12'	Trtd. Lumber	Ledgers (A), Beam boards (C), End joist (E), Rim joist (F)
13	2 × 8" × 10'	Trtd. Lumber	Beam boards (C), Joists (D), End joist (E), Rim joists (F), Lower gusset (L)
1	2 × 6" × 4'	Trtd. Lumber	Stairway nailer (I)
1	2 × 4" × 4'	Trtd. Lumber	Upper gusset (L)
3	4 × 4" × 8'	Trtd. Lumber	Deck posts (B)
9	4 × 4" × 8'	Cedar	Deck railing posts (G), Stairway railing posts (N)

Lumber List			
Qty.	Size	Material	Part
28	¾ × 6" × 16'	Cedar	Decking (H)
2	2 × 10" × 12'	Cedar	Face boards (J)
2	2 × 10" × 10'	Cedar	Face boards (J)
1	2 × 10" × 6'	Cedar	Face boards (J)
1	2 × 12" × 12'	Cedar	Stringers (K)
5	2 × 6" × 12'	Cedar	Railing cap (Q)
5	2 × 6" × 8'	Cedar	Treads (O)
10	1 × 4" × 12'	Cedar	Rails (P)
11	1 × 4" × 10'	Cedar	Rails (P)
8	1 × 4" × 6'	Cedar	Rails (P)

Supplies: 8"-diameter footing forms (8); J-bolts (8); 4 × 4" metal post anchors (8); post-beam caps (8); 90° 2 × 8" joist hangers (26); 45° 2 × 8" joist hangers (3); 1½ × 1½" galvanized metal angle brackets (26); joist hanger nails; ⅜ × 4" lag screws and washers (20); ⅜ × 3" lag screws and washers (32); 6 × 30" mending plate (1); silicone caulk (3 tubes); 3" masonry screws; 3" galvanized deck screws; 1½" galvanized deck screws; ⅝" galvanized screws; concrete as required.

Framing Plan

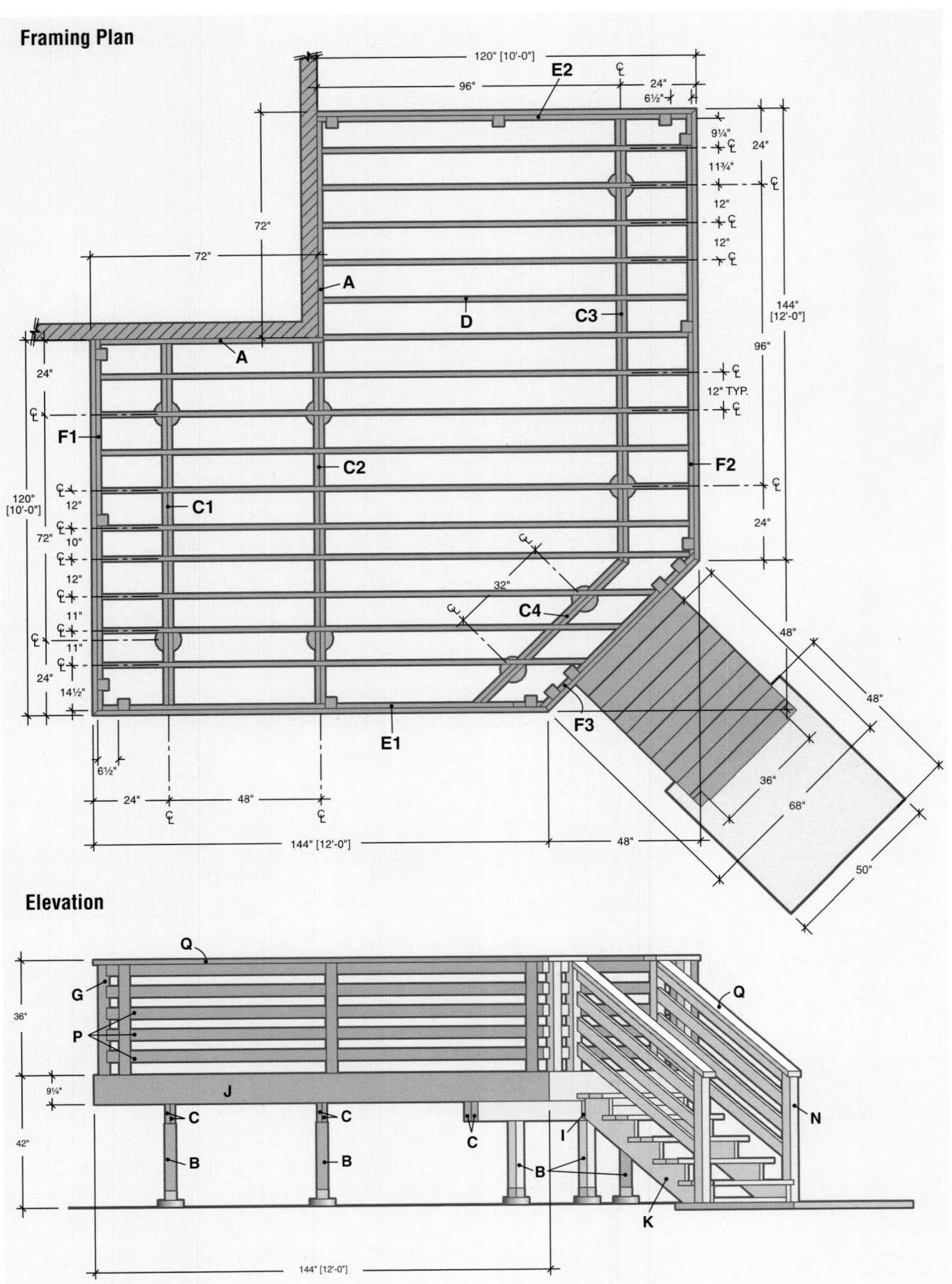

Elevation

Railing Detail

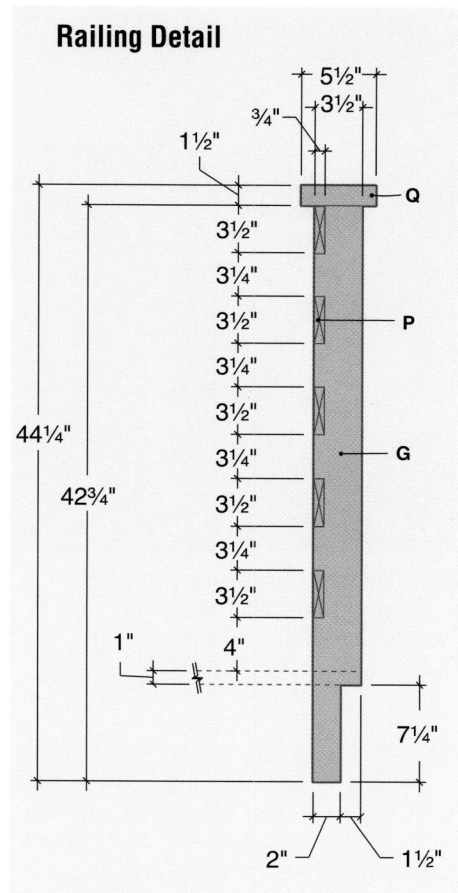

Stairway Detail

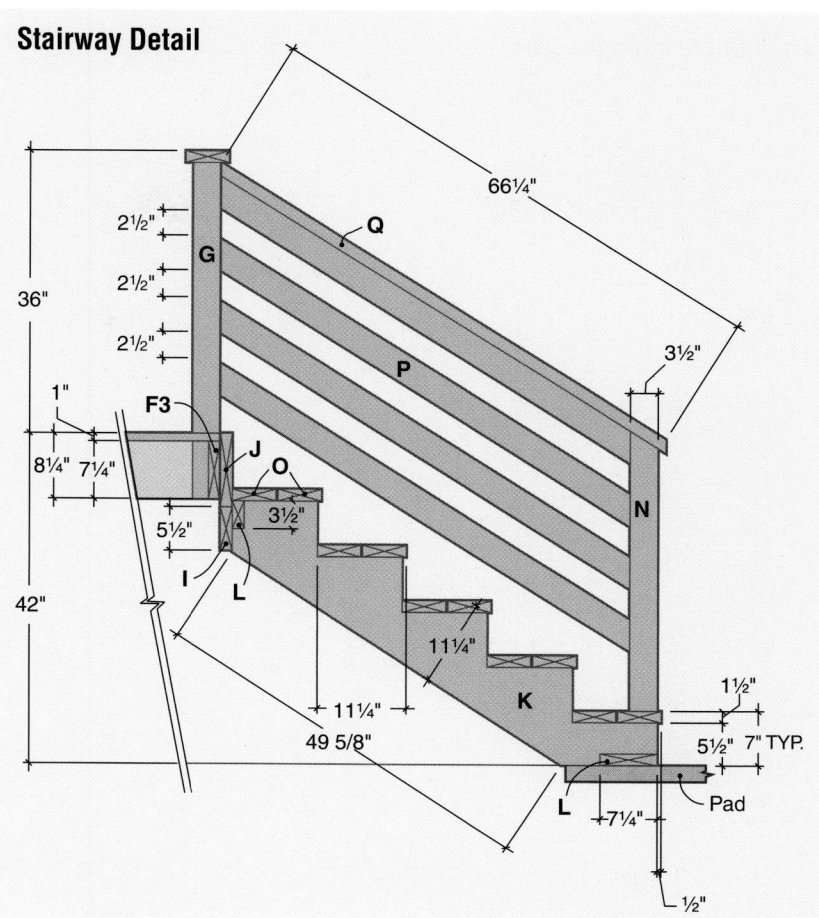

Attach the ledgers to the walls with ⅜ × 4" lag screws and washers, using a ratchet wrench.

Directions: Wraparound Deck

Attach the Ledgers

1 Draw a level outline on the siding to show where the ledgers and the adjacent end joist and rim joist will fit against the house.
2 Position the top edge of the ledgers so that the surface of the decking boards will be 1" below the indoor floor level. This height difference prevents rainwater or melted snow from seeping into the house. Draw the outline long enough to accommodate the thickness of rim joist F-1 and end joist E-2.
3 Cut out the siding along the outline with a circular saw. To keep the blade from cutting the sheathing underneath the siding, set the blade depth to the same

Footing Location Diagram

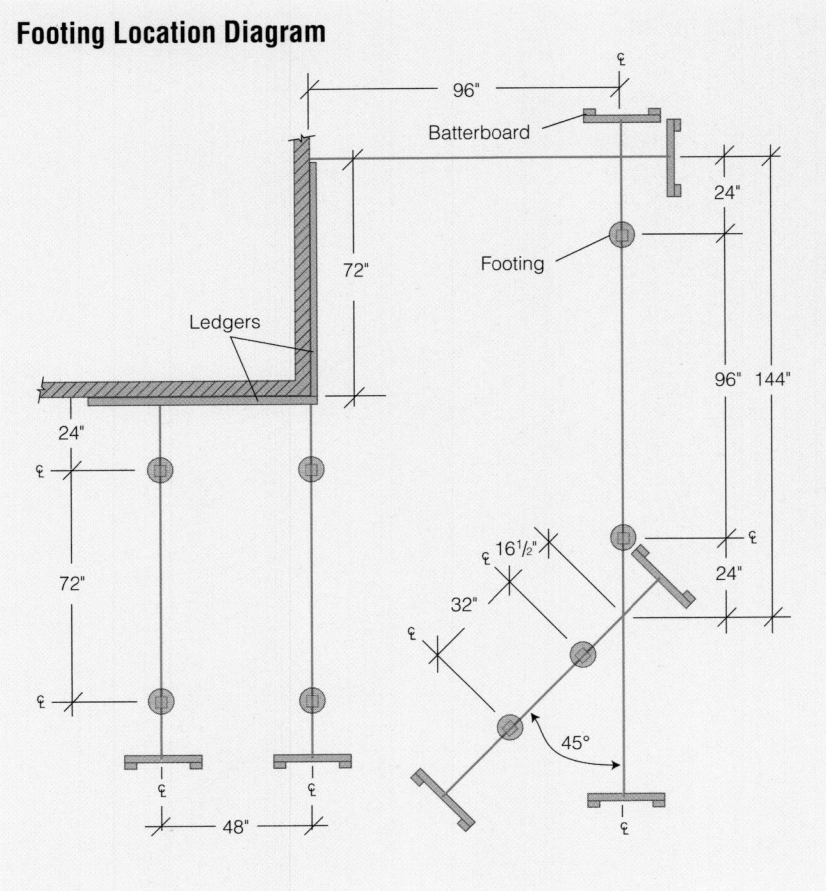

Set the post anchors in place, squaring them with the reference line scribed in the footings.

thickness as the siding. Finish the corners of the cutout with a chisel, holding the beveled side in to ensure a straight cut.

4 Cut galvanized flashing to the length of the cutout, using metal snips, and slide the flashing up under the siding.

5 Measure and cut the ledgers (A) to length from pressure-treated lumber, using a circular saw. Remember, the ledger boards should be shorter than the overall length of the cutouts.

6 Position the ledgers in the cutout, underneath the flashing, and brace them in place. Fasten them temporarily with deck screws.

7 Drill pairs of ¼" pilot holes through the ledger and sheathing and into the house header joist at 2' intervals. Counterbore each

pilot hole ½" deep, using a 1" spade bit. Attach the ledgers to the wall with ⅜ × 4" lag screws and washers, using a ratchet wrench **(photo A).**

8 Apply a thick bead of silicone caulk between the siding and the flashing. Also seal the lag screw heads and any gaps between the wall and the ledger.

Pour the Footings

1 Referring to the *Footing Location Diagram* (above), stretch mason's strings across the site, using 2 × 4 batterboards. Check the mason's strings for square, using the 3-4-5 triangle method. From the point where each string meets the ledger, measure 3' along the ledger and make a mark. Next, mea-

sure 4' out along the mason's string and mark with tape. The distance between the points on the ledger and the string should be 5'. If not, adjust the mason's strings accordingly. Measure along the strings to locate the centerpoints of the footings. Mark the locations with tape.

2 Drop a plumb bob at the tape locations and drive stakes into the ground to mark the centerpoints of the footings.

3 Remove the mason's strings and dig holes for the footings, using a clamshell digger or power auger.

4 Pour 2" to 3" of loose gravel into each hole for drainage. Make certain the hole dimensions comply with your local building code, which may require flaring the footings to 12" at the base.

5 Cut the footing forms to length, using a reciprocating saw or handsaw. Insert the forms into the holes, leaving 2" of each form above grade. Pack soil around the forms.

C

Use a speed square to mark a 22½° miter cut where the ends of beams C-3 and C-4 fit together.

Install the Beams

1 Cut the beams from 2 × 10" lumber, adding several inches to each beam for final trimming. Position the beam boards (C) so the crowns face the same direction, and fasten them together with 10d galvanized nails spaced every 16".

2 Position beams C-1 and C-2 in their post-beam caps and attach them with nails.

3 Mark and cut the angled end of beam C-3 by mitering it at 22½° *(photo C).* Position the beam in the post caps.

4 Make a 22½° miter cut at one end of beam C-4 to form a 45° corner with beam C-3. Leave the other end long for final trimming. Place beam C-4 in the post-beam caps *(photo D).*

5 Fit the beams tightly together, fasten them with 3" deck screws, and attach them to the post caps with 8d nails.

6 Fill the forms with concrete and tamp the concrete with a long stick to eliminate any air pockets. Screed the tops flush with a flat 2 × 4. Insert a J-bolt into each footing, leaving ¾" to 1" of thread exposed.

7 Retie the mason's strings and drop a plumb bob to position each J-bolt at the exact center of the footing. Clean the bolt threads before the concrete sets.

Set the Deck Posts

1 Start by laying a long, straight 2 × 4 flat across each pair of footings. With one edge tight against the J-bolts, draw a reference line across each footing.

2 Place a metal post anchor on each footing, center it over the J-bolt, and square it with the reference line *(photo B).* Thread a nut over each J-bolt and tighten each of the post anchors in place.

3 Cut the posts (C) to their approximate length, adding several inches for final trimming. Place the posts in the anchors and tack them into place with one nail each.

4 With a level as a guide, use braces and stakes to plumb the posts. Once the posts are plumb, finish nailing them to the anchors.

5 To determine the height of the posts, make a mark on the house, 7¼" down from the bottom edge of the ledger. Use a straight 2 × 4 and a level to extend this line across a post. Transfer this line to the remaining posts.

6 Cut the posts off with a reciprocating saw or a handsaw and attach post-beam caps to the tops, using 8d nails.

D

Fit beam C-4 tightly against beam C-3 and attach the two beams to each other with deck screws.

Install the Joists

1 Referring to the *Framing Plan* on page 246, cut rim joist F-1 to final length, and cut end joist E-1 generously long, to allow for final trimming.

2 Fasten one end of rim joist F-1 to the ledger with 16d galvanized nails. Rest end joist E-1 in place on beams C-1 and C-2. Fasten F-1 and E-1 together with deck screws.

3 Use a framing square to finalize the location of E-1 on the beams. Mark the beams and trim them to length. Toenail E-1 in place on the beams.

4 Cut end joist E-2 to length. Install it by nailing it to the end of the ledger, checking for square, and toenailing it to the top of beam C-3. Trim the beam to length.

5 Mark the outlines of the inner joists (D) on the ledger, beams and rim joist F-1 (see *Framing Plan*, page 246), using a tape measure and a combination square.

6 Attach joist hangers to the ledger and rim joist F-1 with 1¼" joist hanger nails, using a scrap 2 × 8 as a spacer to achieve the correct spread for each hanger. NOTE: Spacing between the joists is irregular to accommodate the installation of railing posts.

7 Place the inside joists in the hangers on the ledger and on rim joist F-1, crown up, and attach them with 1¼" joist hanger nails. Be sure to use all the nail holes in the hangers. Toenail the joists to the beams and leave the joists long for final trimming.

8 Mark the final length of the inside joists by making a line across the tops of the joists from the end of end joist E-2. Check for square. Brace the inside joists by tacking a board across

Mark the three remaining inside joists for cutting by snapping a chalk line. Brace and miter-cut the three inside joists.

their edges for stability. Cut them to length with a circular saw.

9 Cut rim joist F-2 long to allow for final trimming, and nail into position with 16d galvanized nails.

10 To mark the remaining joists for trimming at a 45° angle, make a mark 139" from the 90° corner on end joist E-1. Make a second mark 139" from the other 90° corner along rim joist F-2. The distance between these two points should be at least 70". If necessary, move the line back until it measures 70". Regardless of the overall dimensions of your deck, this length will ensure adequate space for mounting the railing posts at the top of the stairway.

11 Mark the last three joists for cutting by snapping a chalk line between the marked points on end joist E-1 and rim joist F-2 **(photo E).** Transfer the cut marks to the faces of the

joists with a combination square, and cut the miters with a circular saw.

12 Measure, cut and attach rim joist F-3 across the angle with deck screws.

Install the Railing Posts

1 Cut the railing posts (G) to size and notch the lower ends to fit around the rim joists (see *Railing Detail*, page 247).

2 Clamp all but two of the posts together to lay out and cut ¾" × 3½" notches, or dadoes, for the horizontal rails. NOTE: The posts at the stairway are not notched for rails.

3 Cut the dadoes by making a series of parallel ¾"-deep cuts within each 3½" space, about ¼" apart, with a circular saw. Knock out the waste wood between the cuts, using a hammer. Then, chisel smooth the bottom of each dado.

4 To locate the railing posts

Drill pilot holes through the posts and into the rim joists, and attach the posts with lag screws. Note the unnotched stairway post.

decking boards so that the ends overhang the deck, leaving a ⅛" gap between the boards to allow for drainage.

3 Where more than one board is required to span the deck, cut the ends at 45° angles and make the joint at the center of a joist.

4 Snap a chalk line flush with the edge of the deck, and cut off the overhanging ends of the deck boards with a circular saw set for a 1½"-deep cut.

Install the Nailer & Face Boards

1 Measure, mark and cut the stairway nailer (I) to size and attach it to the rim joist with a mending plate and deck screws (see *Stairway Detail*, page 247).

2 Measure, mark and cut the face boards (J) to length, making 45° miter cuts at the right angle corners and 22½° miter cuts at the stairway corners. Attach the face boards to the rim and end joists with pairs of deck screws at 2' intervals.

on the diagonal corner, find the centerline of rim joist F-3 and measure 18" in both directions. These points are the inner faces of the railing posts and the outer faces of the stringers. Drill ¼" pilot holes through the railing posts into the rim joist, and secure the posts with lag screws.

5 To position the corner railing posts, measure 3" both ways from the outside corners of rim joist F-3. Predrill the posts, and use a ratchet wrench to attach them to the rim joists with lag screws **(photo F).**

6 Use the *Framing Plan*, page 246, and the *Corner Post Detail*, page 252, to locate the remaining railing posts.

Install the Decking

If possible, buy decking boards that are long enough to span the deck.

1 Measure, mark and cut the decking (H) to size,

making notches to fit around the railing posts. Position the first board above the stairway **(photo G),** and attach it by driving a pair of deck screws into each joist.

2 Position the remaining

Cut the notches for the first decking board and position it above the stairway.

H

Drill ⅛" pilot holes through the treads to prevent splitting. Then, attach the treads to the stringers with deck screws, using a power driver.

I

Clamp the long rails, mark the ends, and transfer the lines across the face of the board with a combination square to ensure a tight-fitting 22½° miter with the short rail.

Corner Post Detail

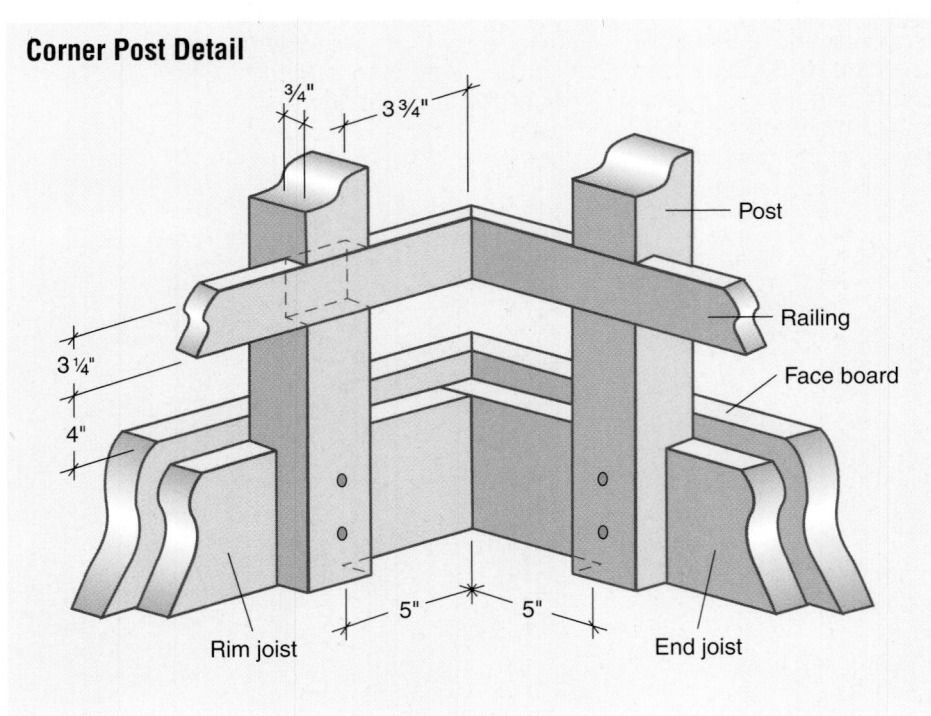

¾"
3 ¾"
Post
Railing
Face board
3 ¼"
4"
5"   5"
Rim joist
End joist

page 246). Level the form at 42" below the finished surface of the deck, to accommodate six 7" stairway rises. Stake the form into place.

4 Fill the form with concrete, screed it flush with a 2 × 4, and let the concrete set overnight.

Build the Stairway

1 Lay out and cut the stringers (K) to size, according to the *Stairway Detail*, page 247. The center stringer is notched at the top and bottom to fit around the gussets. Mark the rises and runs with a framing square. Cut the notches with a circular saw, using a reciprocating saw or handsaw to finish the corners.

2 Measure, mark and cut the gussets (L) to length. Assemble the stairway framework by nailing the gussets in place between the outer

Pour the Concrete Pad

1 Determine the location for the pad. Add 6" in each direction, and excavate the

area approximately 8" deep.

2 Lay and tamp a 4" base of compactable gravel.

3 Build a form from 2 × 6" lumber (see *Framing Plan*,

stringers with 16d nails. Turn the framework upside down and attach the center stringer by nailing through the gussets.

3 Position the framework against the deck, and attach with deck screws driven through the upper gusset into the face board and nailer. Drill pilot holes through the lower gusset into the concrete pad; attach with masonry screws.

4 Cut the stairway railing posts (N) to length. To install the railing posts, clamp them in place against the stringers, drill pilot holes through the stringers into the posts, and attach the posts with ⅜ × 4" lag screws.

5 Measure, mark and cut the treads (O) to length. For the bottom treads, use a piece of railing post scrap to trace a line for the notch. Then, cut the notch with a circular saw. Attach the treads to the stringers with deck screws *(photo H)*.

Use angle brackets to attach the stairway railing pieces and angled rails. To attach the brackets to the rails, use ⅝" galvanized screws.

Build the Railing

1 Measure and cut to length the 10' rails, each with one end mitered at 45°. Install the rails, using 1½" deck screws.

2 Miter one end of the long rails at 45°. Leave the other end long for final trimming.

3 Clamp each long rail in place and use a straight-edge to mark cut lines at the angled corner *(photo I)*. Transfer this line to the face of each rail, using a combination square. Remove the rails and miter-cut the ends for the angled corners at 22½°.

4 Reposition the rails and attach them to the railing posts with 1½" deck screws.

5 Measure, mark and cut the short rails to length with one end mitered at 22½° and the other end cut square.

6 Fasten the ends of the short rails to the railing posts

above the stairway with angle brackets *(photo J)*. Use ⅝" galvanized screws to attach the brackets to the rails and 1½" deck screws to attach them to the posts. Attach them to the notched post as well, using 1½" deck screws.

7 Measure, mark and cut the deck railing cap (Q), and install it with 3" deck screws.

Build the Stairway Railing

1 To mark the stairway posts for trimming, hold the edge of a straight 2 × 4 across the deck post at the top of the stairs and the stairway post below. With the upper end of the 2 × 4 against the underside of the deck railing cap, and the 2 × 4 parallel to the stairway stringer, mark a cut line on the stairway post along the underside of the 2 × 4. Cut the post to length.

2 Repeat the process to mark and cut the other stairway post to length.

3 Measure, mark and cut the stairway railing caps (see *Stairway Detail*, page 247). Place a cedar 2 × 6 on top of the stairway posts, mark the angles for the ends, and cut to length, allowing for a 1" overhang at the end of the stairway.

4 Install the stairway railing caps with 3" deck screws.

5 To cut the stairway rails, hold each one tight against the bottom of the cap and mark the ends. Cut the rails to length so that they fit tight between the posts.

6 To install the rails, mark the positions of the rails on the posts and attach them with angle brackets, using ⅝" screws and 1½" deck screws.

Angled Deck

Give yourself a commanding view from this unique angled deck.

Expand your living space with style. This attractive deck makes creative use of simple geometry to achieve both practicality and pizzazz.

The railing adds interest, with its combination of vertical balusters, horizontal rails and shaped railing posts. And the straight staircase — anchored to a concrete pad for stability — provides direct, convenient access.

Though designed for construction at medium height on level ground, this deck uses heavy-duty posts, beams, joists and footings. By simply lengthening posts and modifying the stairway (see pages 294 to 295) it's readily adaptable for installation at a higher level or on a sloped site.

Cutaway View

OVERALL SIZE:
20'-0" LONG
16'-6¾" WIDE
4'-10" HIGH

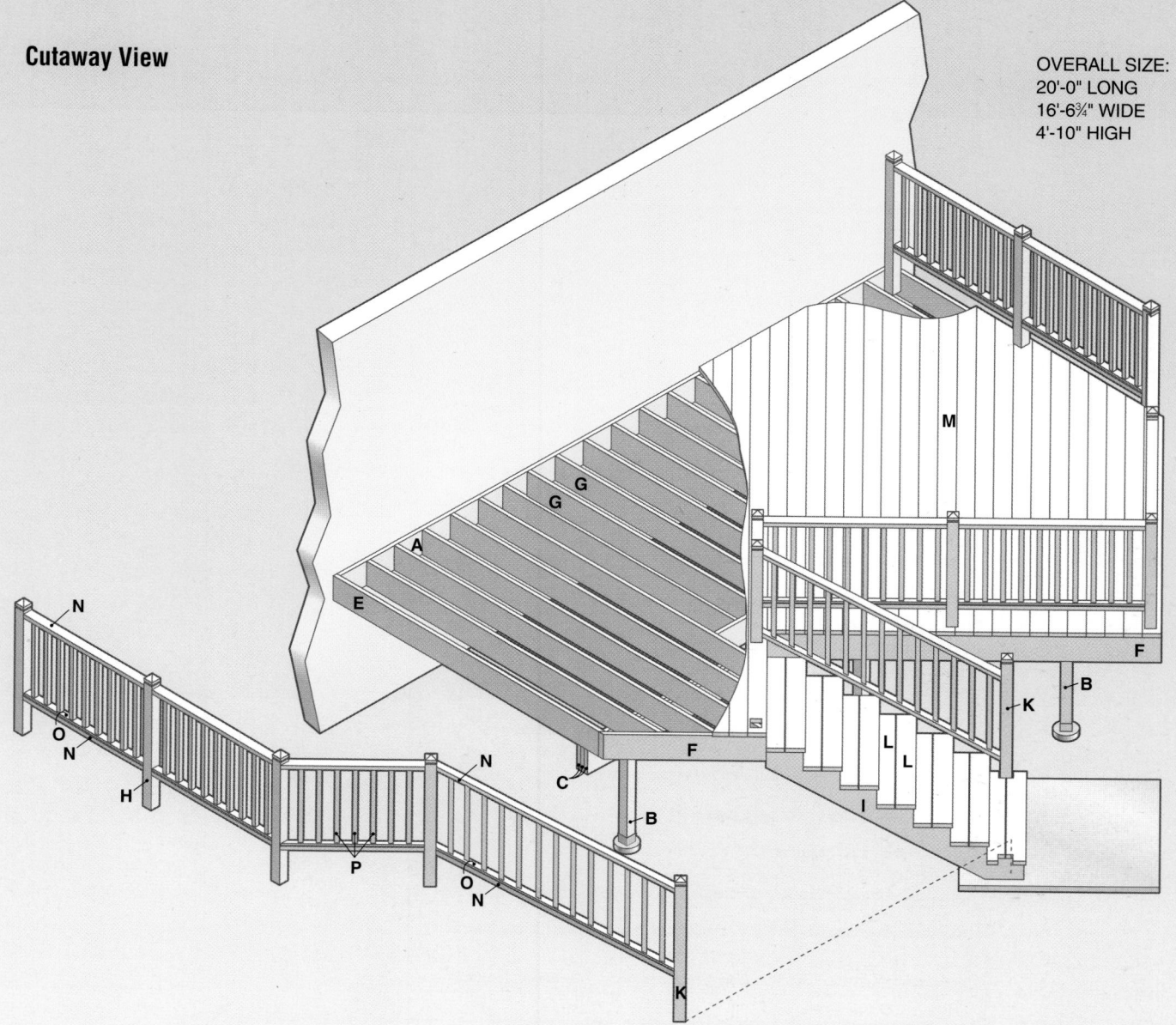

Lumber List			
Qty.	Size	Material	Part
4	2 × 10" × 20'	Trtd. lumber	Ledger (A), Primary beam boards (C)
1	2 × 10" × 18'	Trtd. lumber	Joists (G)
4	2 × 10" × 16'	Trtd. lumber	Joists (G)
5	2 × 10" × 14'	Trtd. lumber	Joists (G)
8	2 × 10" × 12'	Trtd. lumber	Joists (G)
5	2 × 10" × 10'	Trtd. lumber	Joists (G), End joists (E), Rim joists (F)
4	2 × 10" × 8'	Trtd. lumber	Secondary beam boards (D)
2	2 × 10" × 6'	Trtd. lumber	Rim joists (F)
2	6 × 6" × 8'	Trtd. lumber	Deck posts (B)

Lumber List			
Qty.	Size	Material	Part
1	2 × 6" × 8'	Trtd. Lumber	Gussets (J)
6	4 × 4" × 8'	Cedar	Railing posts (H)
4	4 × 4" × 10'	Cedar	Stair railing posts (K)
3	2 × 12" × 8'	Cedar	Stringers (I)
7	2 × 6" × 8'	Cedar	Treads (L)
38	2 × 6" × 16'	Cedar	Decking (M)
8	2 × 4" × 10'	Cedar	Top & bottom rails (N)
2	2 × 4" × 8'	Cedar	Top & bottom rails (N)
11	1 × 3" × 10'	Cedar	Top & bottom inner rails (O)
20	2 × 2" × 10'	Cedar	Balusters (P)

Supplies: 12"-diameter footing forms (4); J-bolts (4); 6 × 6" metal post anchors (4); 90° 2 × 10" joist hangers (22); 45° double 2 × 10" joist hangers (2); 3" galvanized deck screws; 1¾" galvanized deck screws; 3" masonry screws (4); joist hanger nails; 16d galvanized casing nails; ⅜ × 4" lag screws and washers (60); ⅜ × 5" carriage bolts, washers and nuts (22); silicone caulk (3 tubes); concrete as required.

Framing Plan

Post Detail

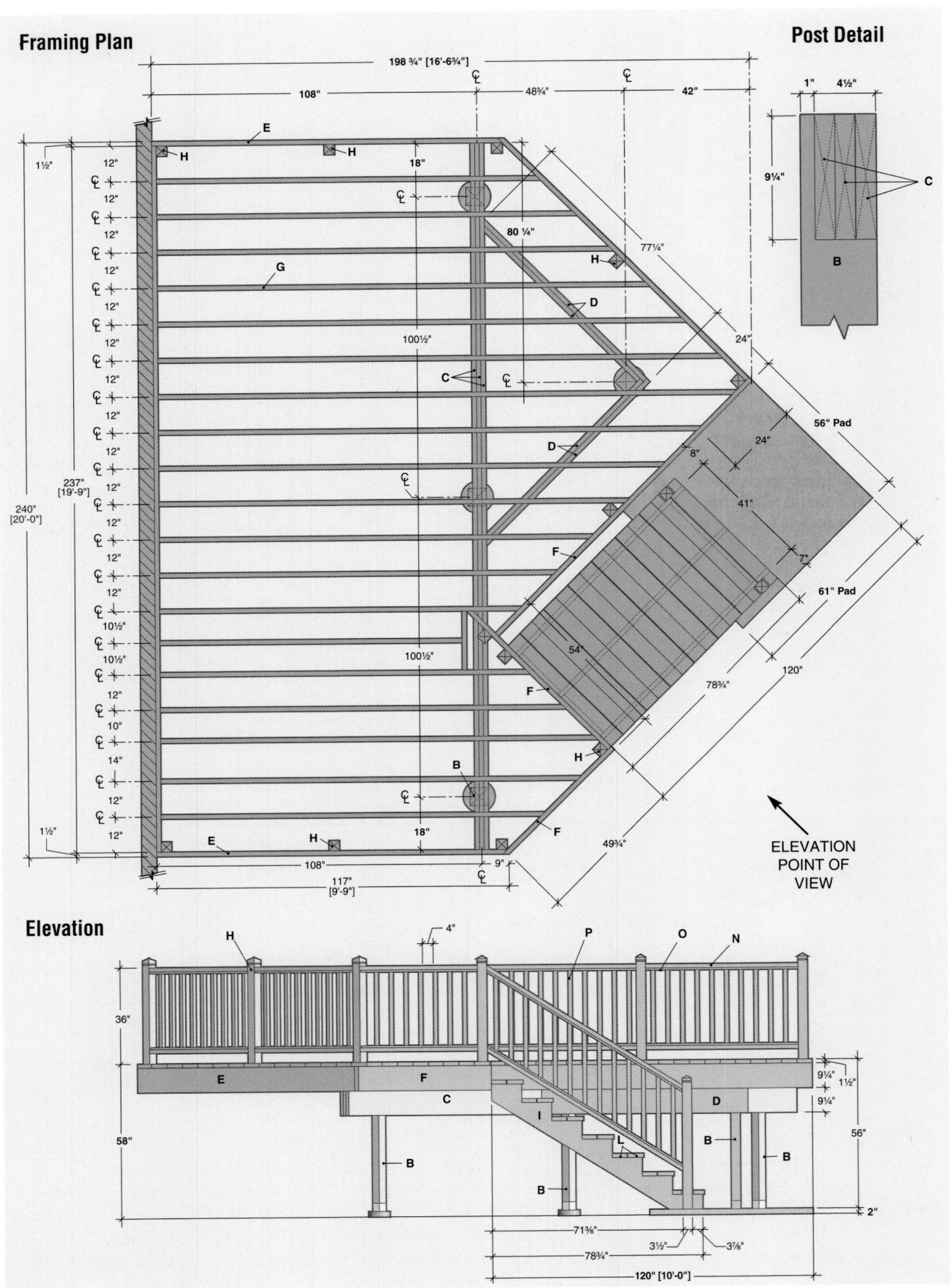

Elevation

Railing Detail

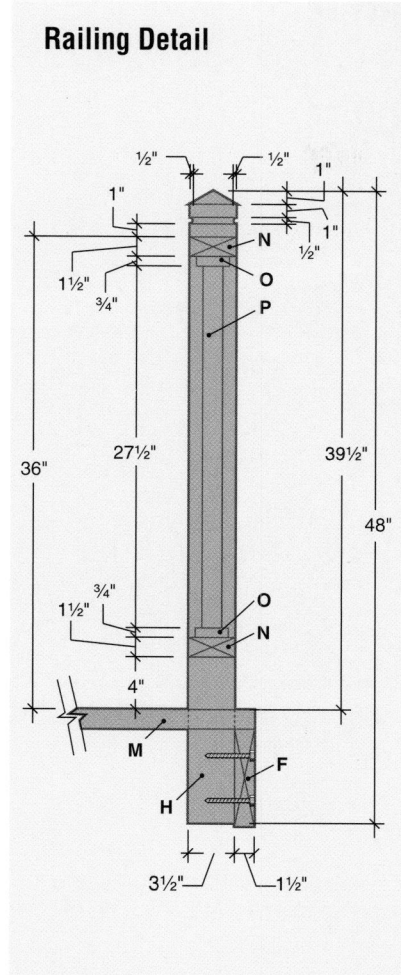

Stairway Detail

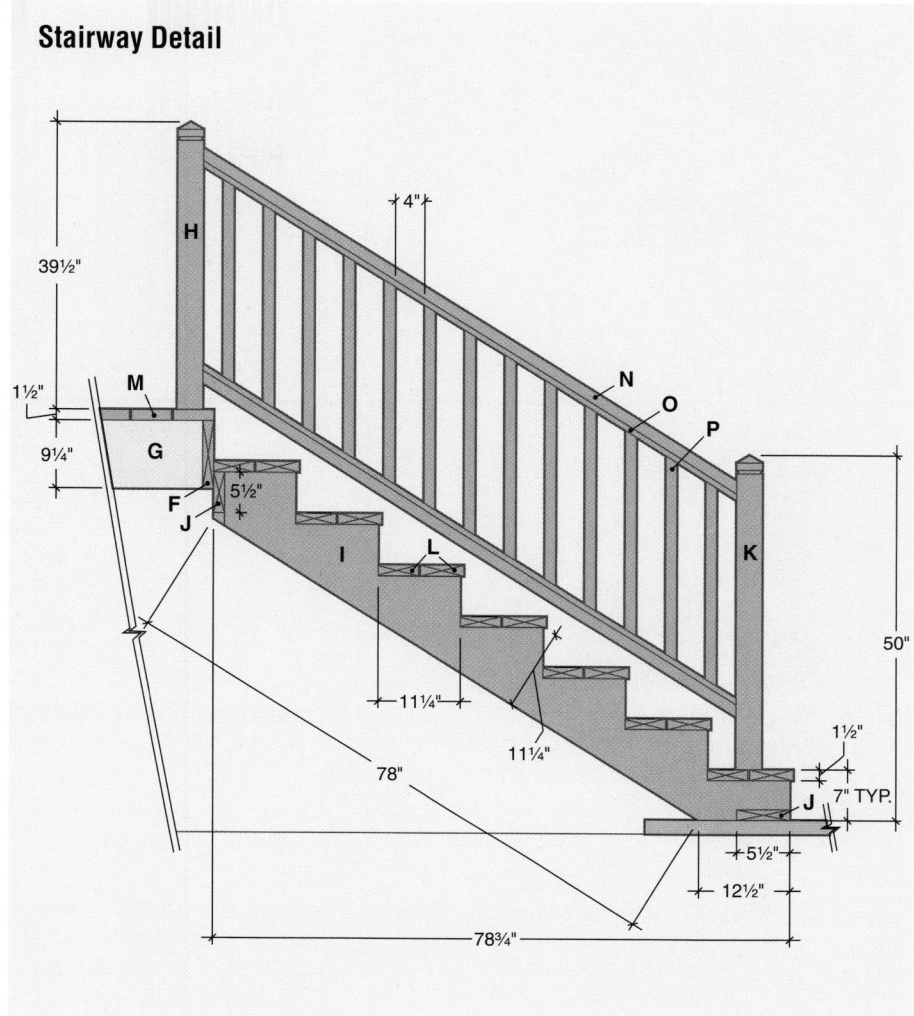

After attaching the ledger, drop a plumb line to a convenient height and stretch mason's strings. Mark footing locations with tape, and use the 3-4-5 triangle method to verify that the strings are square.

Directions: Angled Deck

Attach the Ledger

The ledger anchors the deck and establishes a reference point for building the deck square and level.

1 Draw a level outline on the siding to show where the ledger and the end joists will fit against the house. Install the ledger so that the surface of the decking boards will be 1" below the indoor floor level. This height difference prevents rainwater or melted snow from seeping into the house.

2 Cut out the siding along the outline with a circular saw. To

257

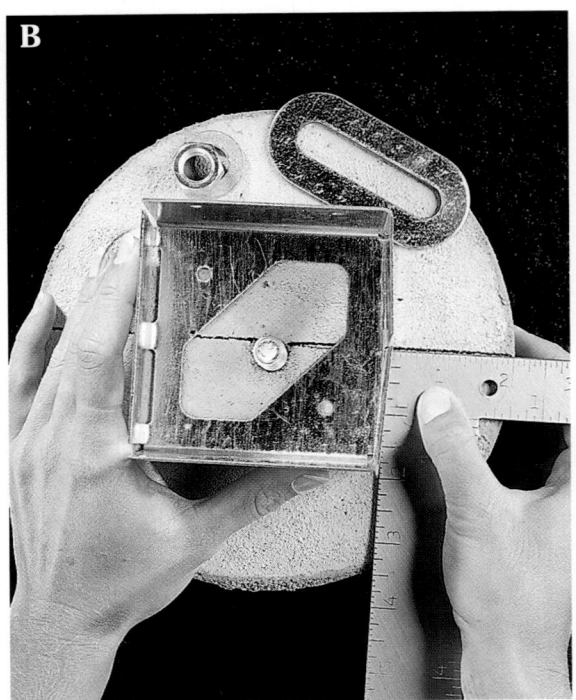

B

Square the post anchors to the reference lines on the top of each footing to ensure that the posts are aligned with each other.

C

Determine the finished post height by leveling a straight 2 × 4 from the bottom edge of the ledger.

prevent the blade from cutting the sheathing that lies underneath the siding, set the blade depth to the same thickness as the siding. Finish the cutout with a chisel, holding the beveled side in to ensure a straight cut.

3 Cut galvanized flashing to the length of the cutout, using metal snips. Slide the flashing up under the siding at the top of the cutout.

4 Measure and cut the ledger (A) from pressure-treated lumber. Center the ledger end to end in the cutout, with space at each end for the end joist.

5 Brace the ledger into position under the flashing. Tack the ledger into place with galvanized nails.

6 Drill pairs of ¼" pilot holes at 16" intervals through the ledger and into the house header joist. Counterbore each

pilot hole ½", using a 1" spade bit. Attach the ledger with lag screws and washers, using a ratchet wrench.

7 Apply a thick bead of silicone caulk between siding and flashing. Also

seal lag screw heads and the cracks at the ends of the ledger.

Pour the Footings

1 To locate the footings,

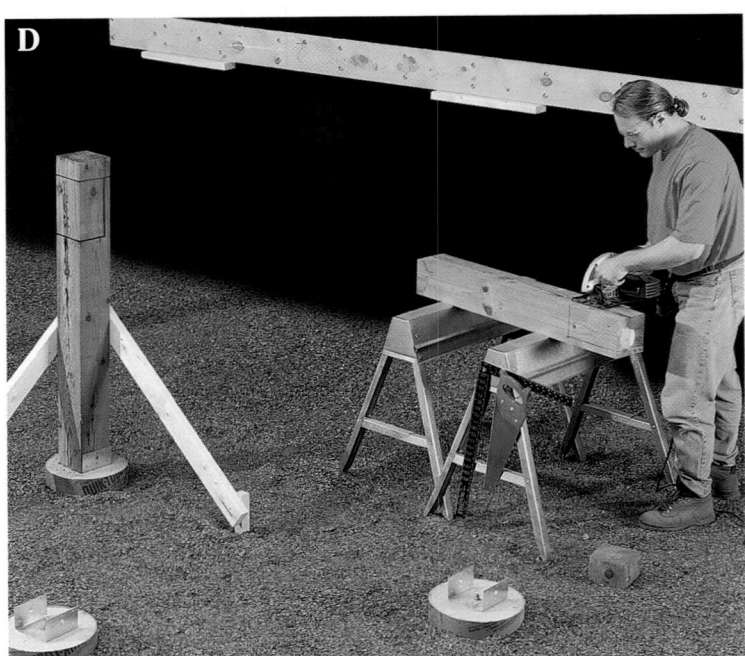

D

After marking the notches for the primary beam, cut out the tops of the posts with a circular saw and a handsaw.

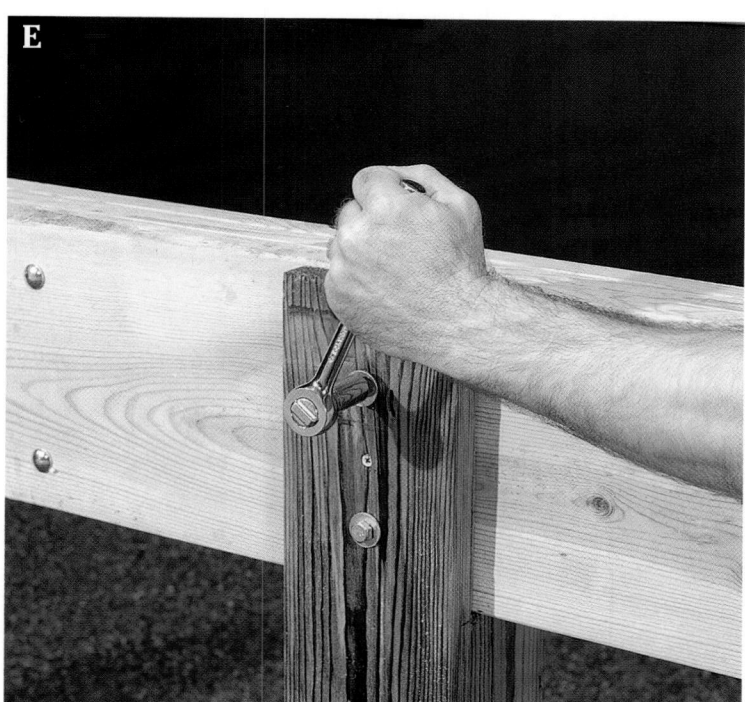

Use a ratchet wrench to tighten the lag screws that secure the primary beam to the notched posts.

drop a plumb bob from the end of the ledger down to a level that's comfortable for making measurements and stretching mason's strings.

2 Measurements for the footing centerpoints are shown on the *Framing Plan*, page 256. Construct, position and install temporary 2 × 4 batterboards.

3 Stretch three strings perpendicular to the house; one at each end of the ledger, and one at the centerline of the footing for the secondary beam, 80¼" from the right end of the ledger.

4 Make sure that the strings are square to the house **(photo A)** by using the 3-4-5 triangle method. Measuring from the point where the string meets the house, make a mark on the house at 3'. Then measure out along the string and make a mark at 4'. When the string is truly perpen-

dicular, the diagonal line connecting the two marked points will measure 5'. Adjust the string on the batterboard as needed.

5 Stretch the fourth string between batterboards, parallel to the house, at the centerline of the primary beam.

6 Measure along the parallel string and use tape to mark the three centerpoints of the footings for the primary beam.

7 To locate the footing for the secondary beam, use tape to mark a point on the middle perpendicular string that is 48¾" out from its intersection with the parallel string.

8 Transfer the locations to the ground by dropping a plumb bob from each tape mark and driving a stake into the ground at each point.

9 Remove the mason's strings and dig holes for the footings, using a clamshell

digger or power auger. Pour 2" to 3" of loose gravel into each hole for drainage. NOTE: When measuring the footing size and depth, make sure you comply with your local building code, which may require flaring the base to 18".

10 Cut the footing forms to length, using a reciprocating saw or handsaw, and insert them into the footing holes, leaving 2" of tube above ground level. Pack soil around the forms for support, and fill with concrete, tamping with a long stick or rod to eliminate any air gaps.

11 Screed the tops flush, using a straight 2 × 4. Insert a J-bolt into the center of each footing, leaving ¾" to 1" of thread exposed. Retie the mason's strings and use the plumb bob to position the J-bolts at the exact center of each footing. Clean the bolt threads before the concrete sets.

Set the Posts

1 To provide a reference line for orienting the post anchors so the posts will be aligned with each other, lay a long, straight 2 × 4 flat across the primary beam footings, parallel to the ledger. With one edge tight against the J-bolts, draw a line across the top of each footing.

2 To mark the post anchor position on the footing for the secondary beam, mark a line across the footing at a 45° angle to the primary beam.

3 Place a metal post anchor on each footing, centering it over the J-bolt and squaring it with the reference line **(photo B).** Thread a nut over each J-bolt and securely tighten the post anchors in place.

After the secondary beam boards have been cut, assembled and attached with deck screws, secure the beam to the post with lag screws.

Cut the 45° angles on the ends of the joists with a circular saw.

4 Estimate the height of each post, and cut the posts slightly long to allow for final trimming. Set the posts in the anchors and tack into place with one nail.

5 With a level as a guide, use braces and stakes to ensure that the posts are plumb.

6 Determine the top of the posts by extending a straight 2 × 4 from the bottom edge of the ledger and marking a line on the posts level with the bottom of the ledger *(photo C)*.

7 Outline a 4½" × 9¼" notch (see *Post Detail*, page 256) at the top of each of the primary-beam posts.

8 Remove the posts from the anchors, cut to finished height, and cut the notches, using a circular saw and handsaw *(photo D)*.

9 Reposition the posts with the notches facing away from the house, brace them plumb and nail them securely to the post anchors.

Install the Beams

We used 20' boards for the primary beam. However, for reasons of cost or availability, you may need to use 10'-long boards. Check with your local building inspector regarding acceptable joining hardware and techniques.

1 Construct the primary beam from 2 × 10" boards. Position the primary beam boards (C) so the crowns face the same direction, and fasten together with 16d galvanized nails. Drill pairs of ⅜" holes through the beam at 24" intervals, and secure with carriage bolts, washers and nuts.

2 Measure, mark and cut the beam to length. Position the beam in the post notches, crown-side-up. Make sure the beam is square to the ledger by measuring the diagonals; adjust the beam position so the diagonal measurements are equal.

3 Drill two ¼" pilot holes through each post into the beam. Fasten with lag screws and washers, using a ratchet wrench *(photo E)*.

4 Measure, mark and cut the post for the secondary beam slightly long to allow for final trimming. Install the post in the post anchor.

5 Locate and mark the points where the secondary beam butts against the primary beam. Run a straight 2 × 4 across the face of the post to the primary beam in both directions. Outline the ends of the secondary beam on the face of the primary beam, and install 45° 2 × 10 double joist hangers at each point.

6 Measure, mark and cut secondary beams boards (D) to length, using a circular saw.

7 Install the boards one at a time, verifying that they are level and attaching them with deck screws.

8 Drill pilot holes through the assembled beam and into the post. Counterbore the holes ½" deep with a 1" spade bit, and secure the secondary beam to the post with lag screws *(photo F).*

9 Fasten the secondary beam to the joist hangers with 10d galvanized nails.

Install the Joists

1 Measure and cut the end joists (E), leaving them several inches long for final trimming. Install by nailing into the ends of the ledger with 16d galvanized nails and toenailing to the top of the primary beam.

2 The joists are not all evenly spaced. Referring to the *Framing Plan*, use a combination square and draw the joist outlines on the face of the ledger and the top of the beams.

3 Install a joist hanger on the ledger at each location. Attach one flange of a hanger to one side of each outline, using joist hanger nails. Use a spacer cut from scrap 2 × 10" lumber to achieve the correct spread for each hanger, then fasten the remaining side flange with joist hanger nails. Remove the spacer and repeat the procedure to install the remaining joist hangers.

4 Measure, mark and cut the joists (G), using a circular saw. Be sure to leave the joists long to accommodate final angled trimming. Place joists in hangers with crown side up and attach with nails. Align joists with the outlines on the top of the beam and toenail in place.

5 Snap chalk lines along the top edges of the joists (see *Framing Plan*, page 256) to mark the perimeter of the deck. All the angles are either 45° or 90°. Allow for the 1½" thickness of the rim joists. Extend the cutoff lines to the faces of the joists, and make the cuts, using a circular saw *(photo G).*

6 Referring to the *Framing*

Pour the concrete into the staircase pad form, and screed flush, using a straight 2 × 4.

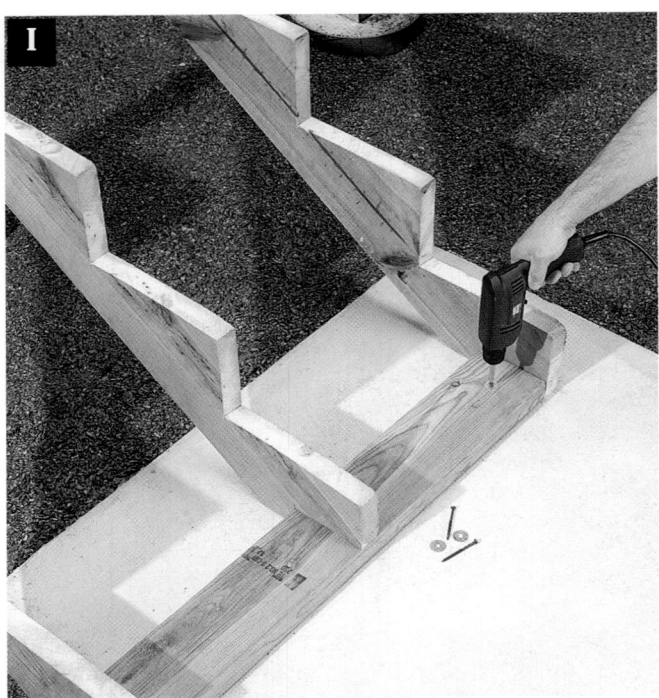

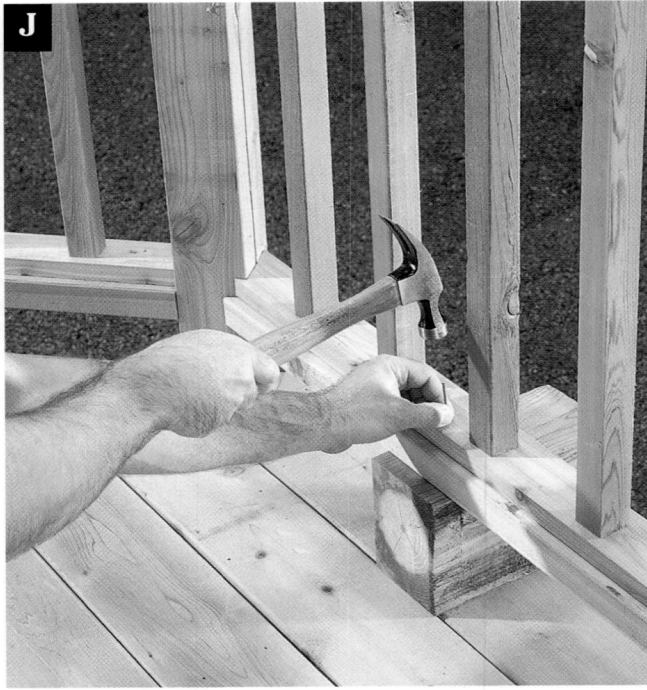

Drill pilot holes through the gusset and into the concrete pad, then attach with masonry screws, using a power drill.

Use a nailing block to support the bottom rail, and attach the baluster assembly with nails. Notice the notch where the rails join the post at a 45° angle.

Plan and confirming the actual dimensions of your deck, measure, mark and cut the rim joists (F) to size and attach them to the joists with deck screws.

Install the Railing Posts

Locate railing posts in the corners of the deck, then center the intermediate posts between them (see *Framing Plan*, page 256).

1 Cut railing posts (H) to length (see *Railing Detail*, page 257). Cut a 60° pyramid on the top of each post, and rout a ½" × ½" groove on all four sides 1" below the pyramid.

2 To install the railing posts, clamp them one at a time into position, and drill ¼" pilot holes through the rim joist into the post. Counterbore the holes ½" using a 1" spade bit, and secure the posts to the rim joists with lag screws.

Pour the Pad

1 Determine the location of the concrete pad. Add 6" in each direction, and excavate approximately 8" deep.
2 Lay and tamp a 4" base of compactible gravel.
3 Build a form from 2 × 6" lumber, and align the inside of the form with the outside rim joists as shown in the *Framing Plan*, page 256. Level the form at 56" below the finished surface of the deck, to accommodate eight 7" stairway rises. Stake the form into place.
4 Fill the form with concrete, screed with a straight 2 × 4 *(photo H),* and let the concrete set up overnight.

Install the Stairway

1 Lay out the stringers (I), according to the *Stairway Detail*, page 257. Notch the center stringer at the top and bottom to fit around the gussets. Mark the rises and

runs with a framing square. Cut the notches with a circular saw, using a reciprocating saw or handsaw to finish the corners.
2 Measure, mark and cut the gussets (J) to length. Assemble the stairway framework by nailing the gussets in place between the outer stringers with 16d nails. Turn the framework upside down and attach the center stringer by nailing through the gussets.
3 Position the stairway framework against the deck rim joist and attach with deck screws driven through the top gusset into the rim joist. Drill pilot holes through the bottom gusset into the concrete pad and attach with masonry screws *(photo I).*
4 Cut the stair railing posts (K) to length. Shape the top ends. Install the posts by clamping them into place against the stringers, drilling pilot holes through the stringers into the posts, and

Drive deck screws up through the top inner rail to attach the top rail to the baluster assembly.

attaching with lag screws and washers.

5 Measure and cut the treads (L) to length, using a circular saw. The bottom treads are notched to fit around the posts.

Install the Decking

If possible, buy decking (M) long enough to span the deck. When joints between deck boards are necessary, center them above joists so the ends of both boards are supported.

1 Position the first deck board along the outer 45° rim joist, and mark the railing post locations. Cut notches for the railing posts, using a circular saw, handsaw and chisel. Attach the board by driving two deck screws into each joist.

2 Cut and attach the remaining deck boards, leaving a ⅛" gap between the boards for drainage.

Install the Railing

The railing for this deck is assembled in sections and then installed. The balusters are first fastened between the inner rails, then the baluster assembly is cut to exact length and attached to the outer rails.

1 Verify the measurements between your railing posts. Measure, mark and cut the top and bottom rails (N) to length.

2 Install the bottom rails by drilling angled ⅛" pilot holes into the posts at the ends, and attaching with deck screws. NOTE: Where the railings meet the posts at a 45° angle, you'll need to notch the ends to fit.

3 Measure, mark and cut the top and bottom inner rails (O), leaving them several inches long for final trimming.

4 Measure, mark and cut the deck balusters (P) to length.

5 Assemble each railing section by positioning the balusters between the top and bottom inner rails, drilling ⅛" pilot holes, and attaching them with deck screws. Trim the section to final length with an equal space at each end.

6 Position the baluster assembly on the bottom rail and nail in place **(photo J)**.

7 Position the top rail above the baluster assembly, drill pilot holes through the top inner rail into the top rail, and attach with deck screws from below.

8 To determine the angle for the ends of the stairway rails and balusters, as well as the length of the inner and outer stairway rails, hold a straight 2 × 4 across one pair of stairway posts. With the top edge of the 2 × 4 crossing each post at the routed groove, mark the angle on the back of the board. NOTE: The angle will be approximately 32°, but you'll get the best fit by marking it from your actual railing posts.

9 Measure, mark and cut the top and bottom rails to length, with the ends angled to fit against the posts. Install the bottom rails.

10 Cut inner rails and balusters to size with mitered ends.

11 Build the stairway railing assemblies using the same procedures as used for the deck railing assemblies, taking care that the space between balusters is 4" or less.

12 Install the stairway railing assemblies by positioning them on the bottom rails and nailing with 6d casing nails.

13 Install the stairway top rails by positioning them above the railing assemblies, drilling pilot holes through the top inner rails and driving deck screws from below **(photo K)**.

Low-Profile Deck

An attractive alternative to a plain patio.

This low-profile deck creates a distinctive focal point for homes with ground-level entries. The composite decking complements the rich tones of the cedar, and the V-pattern directs your view to the centerpoint of the deck. This deck is ideal for flat, level lots or for covering up an old cement patio, and requires no posts, so construction is easier than building a higher deck. Since this deck is less than 24"-high, there's also no requirement for a railing. This deck can hold a BBQ, table, chairs, and our box planter and bench accessories (pages 276 to 289). Our plan also calls for a suspended step that's perfect for areas with snow and frost.

Cutaway View

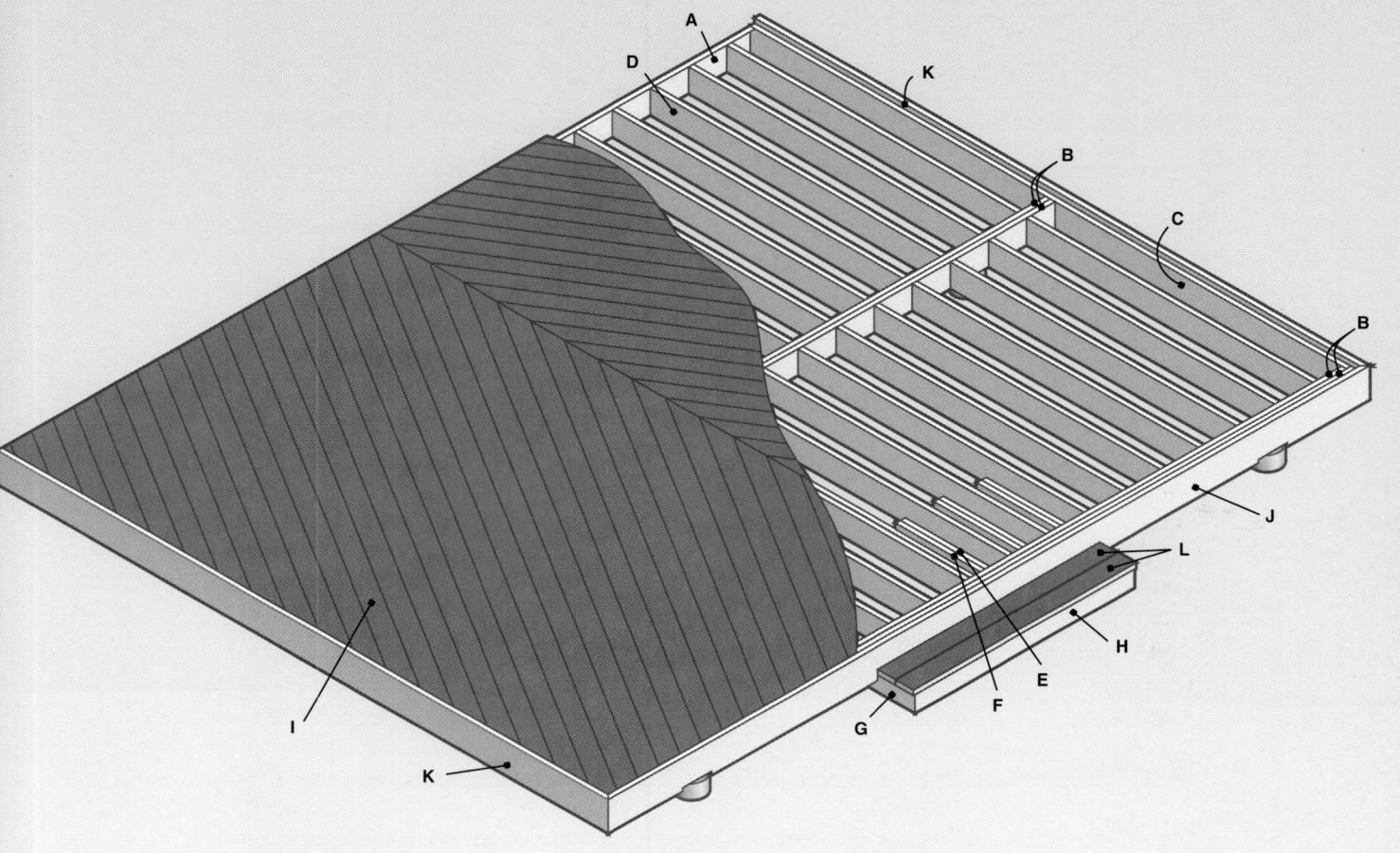

Lumber List			
Qty.	Size	Material	Part
5	2 × 8" × 20'	Trtd. lumber	Ledger (A) & Beam bds (B)
2	2 × 8" × 16'	Trtd. lumber	End joists (C)
40	2 × 8" × 8'	Trtd. lumber	Joists (D)
3	2 × 4" × 8'	Trtd. lumber	Step support spacers (E)
2	2 × 6" × 8'	Trtd. lumber	Interior step supports (F)
1	2 × 6" × 6'	Cedar	End step supports (G)

Lumber List			
Qty.	Size	Material	Part
2	2 × 6" × 6'	Cedar	Step riser (H)
74	2 × 6" × 10'	Composite	Decking (I)
2	2 × 6" × 6'	Composite	Tread (L)
1	2 × 10" × 20'	Cedar	Front face bd (J)
2	2 × 10" × 16'	Cedar	Side face bds (K)

Supplies: 8"-diameter footing forms (6); 3" direct bearing hardware (6); 2 × 8" double joist hangers (4); 2 × 8" joist hangers (72); 2½" composite decking screws; joist hanger nails; 16d galvanized box nails; 12d galvanized casing nails; ⅜ × 4" carriage bolts, washers, and nuts (12); ⅜ × 4" lag screws (22); lead masonry anchors (22); ledger flashing (20 ft.); exterior silicone caulk (3 tubes); concrete as required.

Framing Plan

Elevation and Details

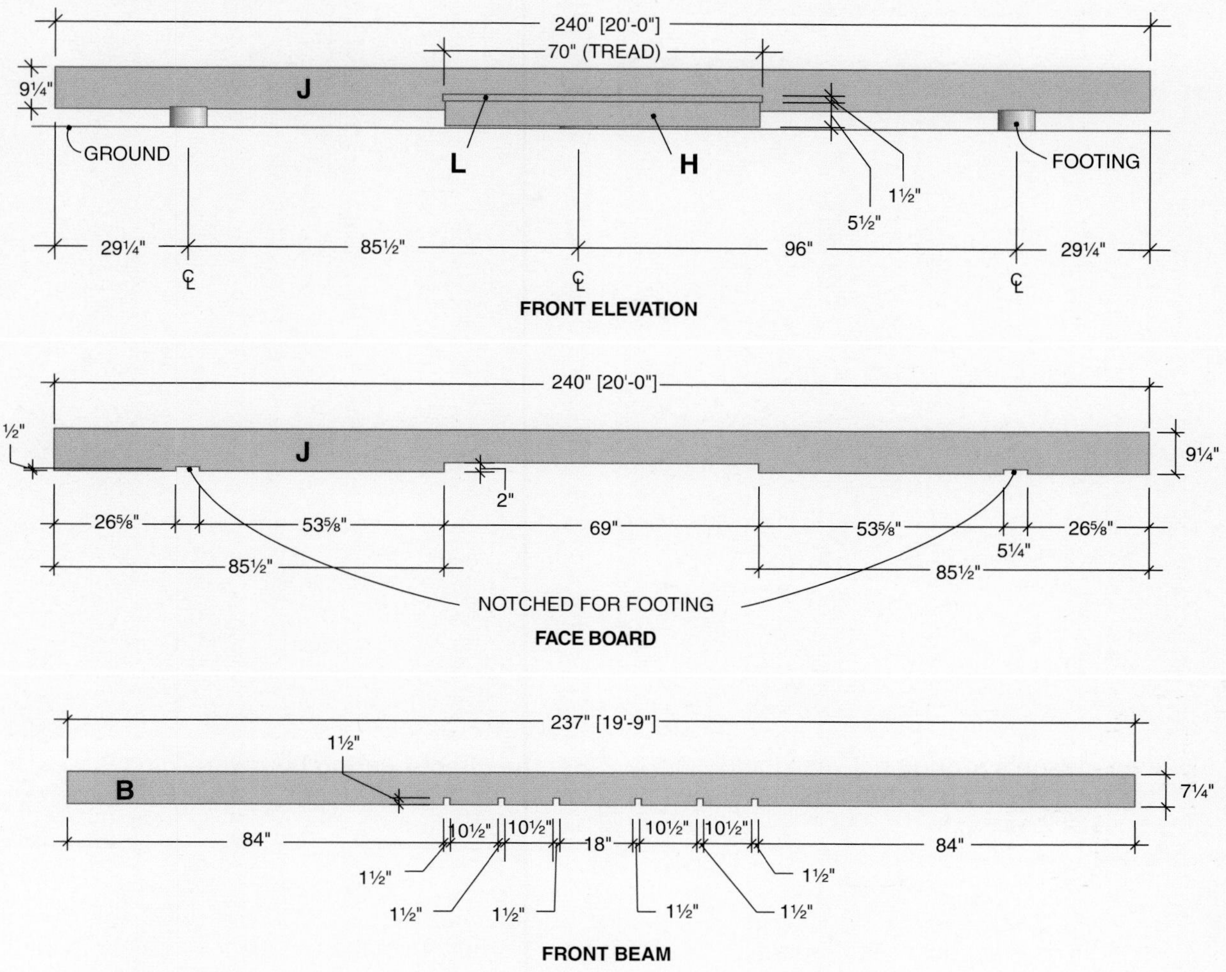

FRONT ELEVATION

240" [20'-0"]
70" (TREAD)
9¼"
J
GROUND
L
H
FOOTING
1½"
5½"
29¼"
85½"
96"
29¼"

FACE BOARD

240" [20'-0"]
½"
J
9¼"
2"
26⅝"
53⅝"
69"
53⅝"
26⅝"
85½"
5¼"
85½"
NOTCHED FOR FOOTING

FRONT BEAM

237" [19'-9"]
1½"
B
7¼"
84"
10½"
10½"
18"
10½"
10½"
84"
1½"
1½"
1½"
1½"
1½"
1½"
1½"

Directions: Low-Profile Deck

Attach the Ledger

1 Measure and cut the ledger (A) to length. Drill pairs of ¼" pilot holes at 2 ft. intervals. Counterbore each hole ½", using a 1" spade bit.

2 Determine ledger location and draw its outline on the wall. Make sure you include a 3" space at each end of the ledger for the end joists and side face boards. Temporarily brace the ledger in position, using 2 × 4s. Make sure the ledger is level and mark the hole locations on the wall with an awl or nail.

Attach the ledger to the masonry wall with lag screws and washers, using a ratchet wrench.

B

Stretch level mason's strings between the bottom of the ledger and temporary batterboards. Level the footing forms against the strings.

C

Set the direct-bearing hardware into the wet concrete, using layout strings to ensure accurate alignment.

3 Remove the ledger and drill anchor holes 3" deep, using a ⅜" masonry bit. Drive lead anchors into the drilled holes, using a rubber mallet, and attach the ledger to the wall with lag screws and washers, using a ratchet wrench **(photo A)**.

4 Seal the screw heads, and the joint between the wall and ledger, with silicone caulk.

Pour the Footings

1 To locate the footings, refer to the measurements in the *Framing Plan* (page 266) and mark the centerline for each pair of footings on the ledger.

2 Construct three temporary 2 × 4 batterboards. Position the batterboards out from the footing marks, approximately 19 ft. from the

ledger. Stretch mason's string from the bottom of the ledger at each mark to the corresponding batterboard, making sure that the strings are level and perpendicular to the ledger.

3 Check for square, using the 3-4-5 triangle method. From the point where each string meets the ledger, measure 3 ft. along the ledger and make a mark. Next, measure 4 ft. out along the string and mark with tape. The distance between the points on the ledger and the string should be 5 ft. If it's not, adjust the string position on the batterboard accordingly.

4 To locate the centers of the six footings, build four more batterboards and stretch two additional mason's strings parallel to the house (refer to the

Framing Plan on page 266 for measurements). Use a plumb bob to transfer the footing centerpoints to the ground, and drive a stake to mark each point.

5 Remove the mason's strings and dig the footings, using a clamshell digger or power auger. Pour 2" to 3" of loose gravel into each footing hole for drainage. NOTE: When measuring the footing size and depth, make sure you comply with your local building code, which may require flaring the base to 12".

6 Cut the footing forms to length, using a reciprocating saw or handsaw, and insert them into the footing holes.

7 Retie the mason's strings, making sure they are level.

8 Level the tops of the forms by setting them flush with the mason's strings

Set the beams in the direct-bearing hardware on the footings. Note the "notch" for the end joist at the end of the outer beam.

Measure, cut and install the joists with joist hangers, verifying the length of each one as you go.

(photo B) and packing soil around them to hold them securely in place.

9 Remove the mason's strings and fill the footing forms with concrete, tamping with a long stick or rod to eliminate any air gaps.

10 Screed the concrete flush, using a straight 2 × 4, then insert direct-bearing hardware into each footing while the concrete is still wet. Reattach the layout strings to ensure that the hardware is aligned correctly *(photo C)*.

Install the Beams

1 Measure, mark, and cut the beam boards (B) to length, using a circular saw. NOTE: Three of the beam boards are the same length as the ledger. The fourth board is 3" longer to accommodate the 1½" end joist on each end.

2 Make each beam by fastening two beam boards together with pairs of box nails driven at 16" intervals. At both ends of the outer beam, the long beam board overhangs 1½", creating a notch for attaching the end joist.

3 Position the beams crown-side-up on the direct-bearing hardware *(photo D)*. Double-check that both beams are correctly aligned with the ledger, and attach to the hardware with carriage bolts.

Install the Joists

1 Measure, mark and cut the end joists (C) to length. The end joists extend from the house to the notch in the end of the outer beam. In our plan the end joists are 189" long, but verify this measurement before cutting. Attach the end joists to the ledger and beams with box nails.

2 Measure, mark and cut double center joists (D). Mark the centerline of the deck on the ledger and beams, install double joist hangers at each mark, and nail the joists in place. Seal the seam between the beam boards in the double joists with silicone caulk to protect against moisture.

3 Locate the remaining joists by measuring along the ledger and beams from the center joists, and marking centerlines at 12" intervals (see *Framing Plan,* page 266). Install a joist hanger at each centerline.

4 Measure, mark and cut the inner joists (D), verifying the actual lengths, and install in joist hangers with joist nails *(photo E)*.

F

Cut 1½" × 1½" notches for the step supports in the outer beam with a reciprocating saw or handsaw. Finish the notches with a hammer and chisel.

G

Lay composite decking boards with a ⅛" to ¼" gap to allow for drainage, and expansion and contraction.

Build the Step

Our plan includes a cantilevered step suspended from the underside of the deck. This step is constructed with 2 × 6 step supports (F, G) attached to the lower portions of the deck joists. Notches in the bottom edge of the outer beam (see *Detail*, page 267) allow the supports to run through. A long notch in the front face board (see *Detail*, page 267) accommodates all the step supports. Spacers (E) offset the step supports from the joists to avoid the joist hangers.

1 Measure, mark and cut the step support spacers (E). Set the spacers back approximately 1" from the front beam, and attach to the deck joists with deck screws (see *Step Detail*, page 271).

2 Cut 1½" × 1½" notches in the bottom edge of the front beam, adjacent to the step support spacers. Use a reciprocating saw or handsaw to make the vertical cuts, and finish each notch with a chisel and hammer *(photo F)*.

3 Measure, mark and cut the step supports (F) and end step supports (G) to length. Make a 45° miter cut at the front of the end step supports where they meet the step riser. Attach the step supports to the spacers with deck screws. The interior step supports extend 11¼" beyond the beam, while the end step supports extend 12¾" to allow for the miter joints at the riser.

4 Measure, mark, and cut the step riser (H) to length, with 45° mitered ends. Attach the riser to the step supports with casing nails.

Lay the Decking

1 To create reference lines, mark a point in the center of the front of the deck. Measure equal distances along the double center joist, and along the outer beam, then snap a chalk line between these points. As you progress with rows of decking, periodically measure between the ends of the decking boards and the reference line to help you maintain a consistent angle.

2 Begin laying the composite decking at the front center of the deck. Cut one end of the first decking board at a 45° angle and leave the other end slightly long. Position it above the step, aligning the 45° cut with the centerline of the double joist, and fasten with 2½" composite screws.

3 Cut and attach the next deck board in similar fashion, leaving a ⅛" space between the boards.

4 Cut and attach the remaining deck boards *(photo G),* periodically checking the angle of the decking against the reference lines and making any necessary adjustments.

5 After installing the decking, trim the excess that overhangs the deck ends. For boards 16 ft. or smaller, leave a gap at the deck ends and at any butt joints— ¹⁄₁₆" for every 20°F difference between the temperature at the time of installation and the expected high for the year—as composite decking will expand and contract. Set the blade depth on your circular saw at slightly more than 1½", and trim the decking to size.

Install the Face Boards

1 Measure, mark, and cut the front face board (J) to size (see *Detail*, page 267), and notch it to fit around the step supports. Cut 45° miters on both ends.

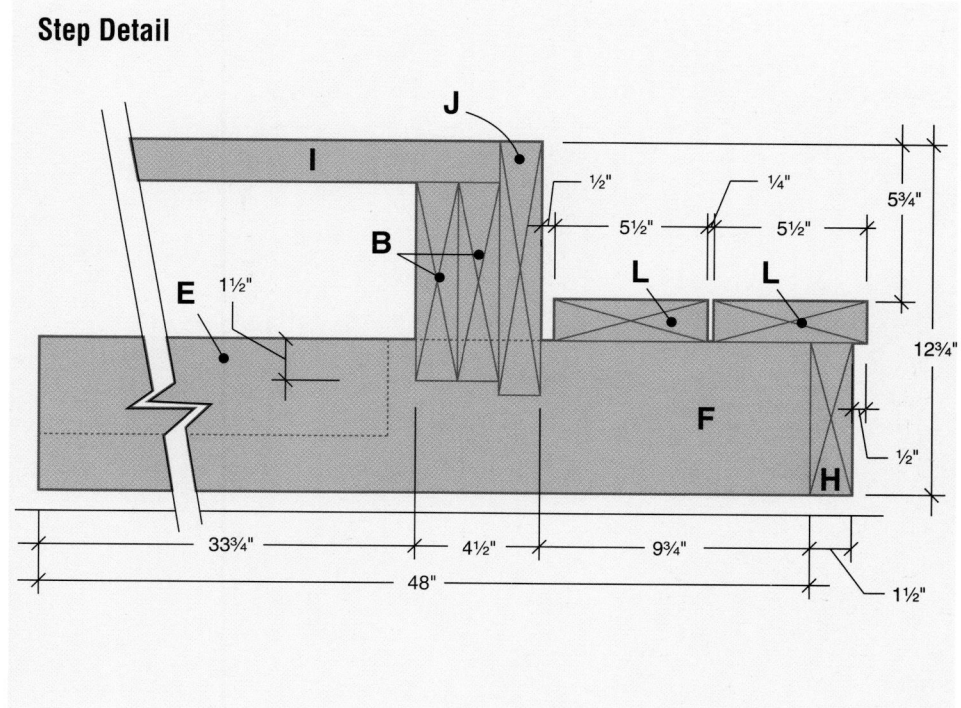

Step Detail

2 Temporarily clamp the face board in place and mark for notching around the footings. Also mark the points where the carriage bolts in the direct-bearing hardware contact the back of the board.

3 Remove the board, cut the footing notches, and chisel out the back of the board to accommodate the carriage bolts. Attach the face board with casing nails.

4 Measure, mark, and cut the side face boards (K) to length, making 45° miter cuts at the front ends. Attach the face boards to the end joists with deck screws.

Install the Step Treads

Complete the suspended step by cutting the composite treads (L) to length and attaching them to the step supports, using 2½"composite screws. Leave a ½" gap at the front face board, and a ¼" gap between the treads *(photo H).*

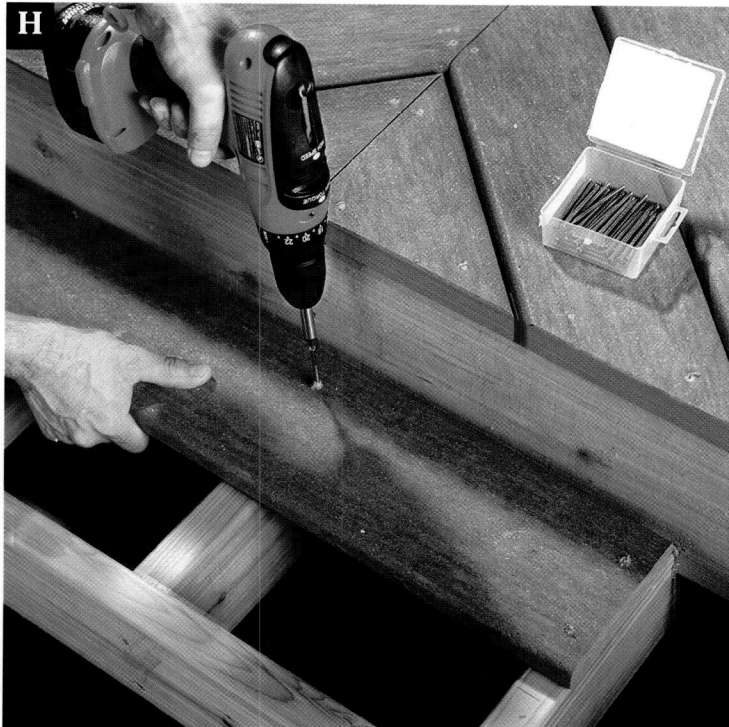

Cut the composite step treads to length and attach with composite screws, leaving a ½" gap between the first tread and the face board.

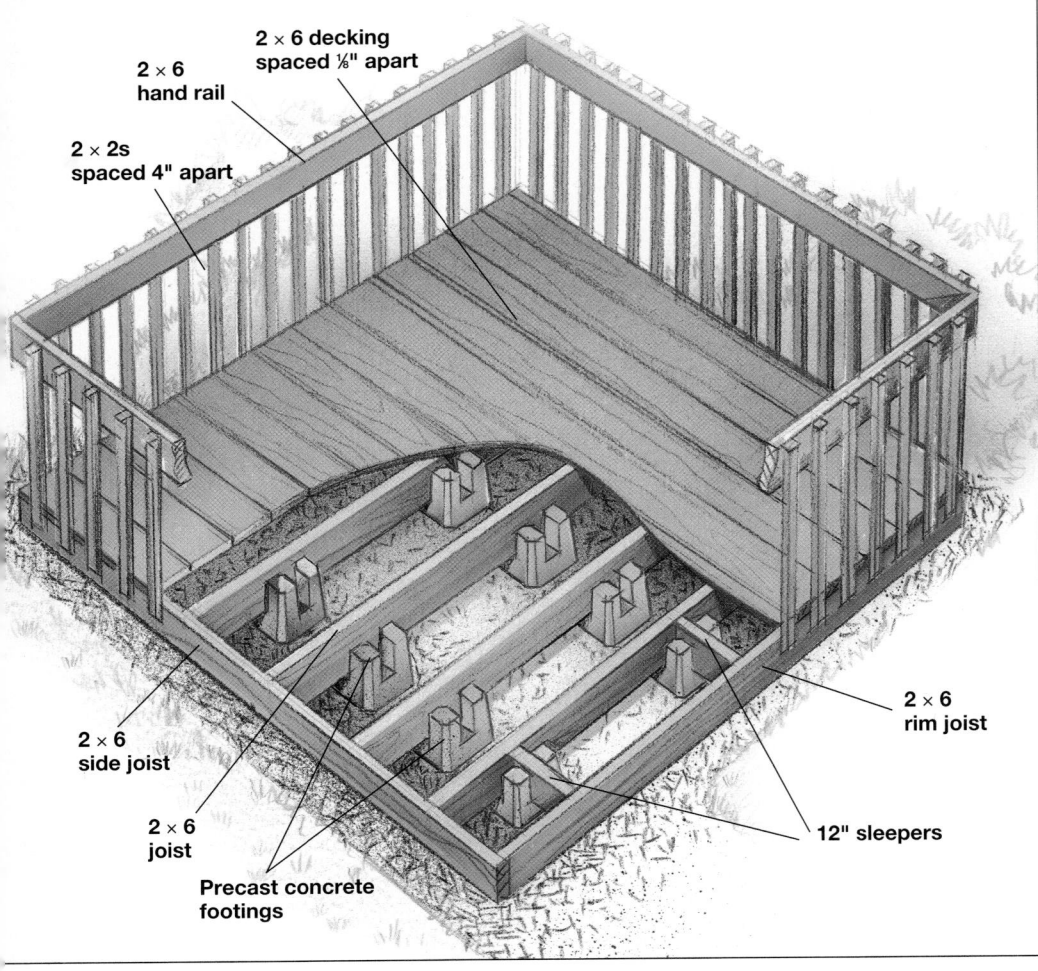

2 × 6 decking spaced ⅛" apart

2 × 6 hand rail

2 × 2s spaced 4" apart

2 × 6 side joist

2 × 6 joist

Precast concrete footings

2 × 6 rim joist

12" sleepers

Platform Deck

A freestanding platform deck is a low-maintenance option for creating an outdoor floor. Because it can be constructed virtually anywhere, in almost any size, a platform deck works in nearly any landscape. The wood can be left natural, stained or painted to blend with your house and other landscape elements.

You'll be able to build this deck over a single weekend. It uses lumber in standard lengths, so you won't need to do a lot of cutting. In addition, this deck uses precast concrete footings, rather than poured footings. These precast footings are available at home improvement centers and lumberyards.

This 12 × 12-ft. deck rests on a 10 × 10-ft. base formed by 18 concrete footings arranged in three rows of six footings each. Joists are secured in slots in the tops of the footings, simplifying the building process.

Directions: Platform Deck

Install & Level the Footings

1 Measure a 10 × 10-ft. area for the deck foundation, and mark the corners with stakes.
2 Position a footing at each corner, then measure from corner to corner, from the center of each footing.

Adjust until the diagonal measurements are equal, which means the footings are square.
3 Place a 2 × 6 across the corner footings for the back row, setting it in the center slots. Check this joist with a level, then add or remove soil beneath footings as necessary to level it.
4 Center a footing between these corner footings. Use a level to recheck the joist, then add or remove soil beneath the center footing, if necessary **(photo A).** Remove the joist.
5 Repeat the process described in #3, #4 and #5 to set and level the footings for the front row.
6 Position the remaining 12 footings at equal intervals, aligned in three rows. Position a 2 × 6 from the front row of footings to the back, and adjust soil as necessary to bring the interior footings into alignment with the front and back rows.

Install the Joists

1 Seal the ends of each 2 × 6 with wood sealer/protectant and let them dry completely.
2 Center a 12-ft. joist across each row of footings. Using a level, check the joists once again and carefully adjust the footings if necessary **(photo B).**

Add the Side Joists & Rim Joists

1 Line up a 2 × 6 flush against the ends of the joists along the left side of the deck, with the ends extending equally past the front and back joists.
2 Attach the side joist by driving a pair of deck screws into each joist.
3 Repeat this process to install the right side joist.
4 At the front of the deck, position a 2 × 6 rim joist flush

between the ends of the side joists, forming a butt joint on each end.

5 Attach the rim joist to the side joists by driving a pair of deck screws through the faces of the side joists, into the ends of the rim joist *(photo C).*

6 Repeat #4 and #5 to install the other rim joist.

Position the Sleepers

1 Measure and cut six 2 × 6 sleepers to fit between the front and back joists and the rim joists. Seal the cut ends with wood sealer/protectant and let them dry completely.

2 Position one sleeper in each row of footings, between the first joist and the rim joist *(photo D).* Attach each sleeper by driving a pair of galvanized deck screws through each of the joists and into the sleeper.

Square Up the Frame

1 Once the framing is complete, measure the diagonals from corner to corner. Compare the measurements to see if they are equal *(photo E).*

2 Adjust the framing as necessary by pushing it into alignment. Have someone help you hold one side of the framework while you push against the other.

Framing Plan

12 ft. × 12 ft. decking

12 ft. 2"

10 ft.

> ### CONSTRUCTION MATERIALS
>
> - *Precast concrete footings (18)*
> - *12-ft. 2 × 6s (38)*
> - *2 lbs. galvanized 3" deck screws*

A

Position the corner footings and the center footing for the back joist. Remove or add soil beneath the footings to level them.

B

Position the remaining footings and insert the joists. Check to make sure the framework is level, and adjust as needed.

Install the front and back rim joists between the ends of the side joists, securing them with pairs of deck screws.

Position the sleepers in the slots of the footings, then attach them to both joists with pairs of deck screws.

Lay the Decking

1 Seal the 2 × 6 decking boards with wood sealer/protectant and let them dry. Seal all exposed framing members as well.

2 Lay a 2 × 6 over the surface of the deck, perpendicular to the joists and flush with the rim joist. Secure this board with deck screws.

3 Repeat # 2 to install the rest of the decking *(photo F).* Use a framing square to set a ⅛" space between boards. Rip cut the last decking board if needed.

After the framing is completed, measure the diagonals and adjust the frame until it's square.

Install the decking by driving a pair of screws into each joist. Use a framing square to leave a ⅛" space between boards.

Variation: Adding a Railing

Although this platform deck rests low to the ground, you may want to add a hand rail around two or three sides of the deck, especially if the deck will be used by young children or an elderly person. For each side of the deck to which you're adding railings, you'll need 25 2 × 2s, 42" long.

Prepare the Balusters

1 Place the 2 × 2s flush together, adjust them so the ends are even, and draw a pair of straight lines, 3" apart, across each board, 1½" above the beveled end. Repeat the process and draw a single line 2¾" from the top of the other end. Using the lines as guides, drill pilot holes into the 2 × 2s *(photo A)*.
2 Apply wood sealer/protectant to the ends of the 2 × 2s.

Attach the Balusters

1 Position a 2 × 2 flush with the bottom of the joist, then clamp it in place to use as a placement guide.
2 Position the corner 2 × 2s against the side joists, beveled end down, 4" in from the corner. Check for plumb, then drive deck screws through the pilot holes.
3 Attach the remaining 2 × 2s for each side, spacing them 4" apart *(photo B)*.

Attach the Hand Railing

1 Hold a 12-ft. 2 × 6 that forms the top of the railing in place, behind the installed 2 × 2s.
2 Attach the 2 × 2s to the 2 × 6 top rails by driving deck screws through the pilot holes *(photo C)*.
3 Connect the top rails at the corners, using pairs of deck screws.
4 Finish the railing by applying a coat of wood sealer, according to the manufacturer's directions.

CONSTRUCTION MATERIALS

- *12-ft. 2 × 6s (3)*
- *42" 2 × 2s (75, one end beveled)*
- *2½" galvanized deck screws*

Gang together the 2 × 2s, then drill a pair of pilot holes into the beveled ends, and a single pilot hole in the opposite end.

Attach the 2 × 2s to the side joists, leaving a 4" gap between them.

Level the 2 × 6 railing behind the 2 × 2s, then attach it by driving screws through the pilot holes.

Deck Furnishings

Elements that add personal style and charm to your deck

Lumber for arbor provided by P & M Cedar Products, Inc.

OVERALL SIZE:
16" HIGH
18" WIDE
48" LONG

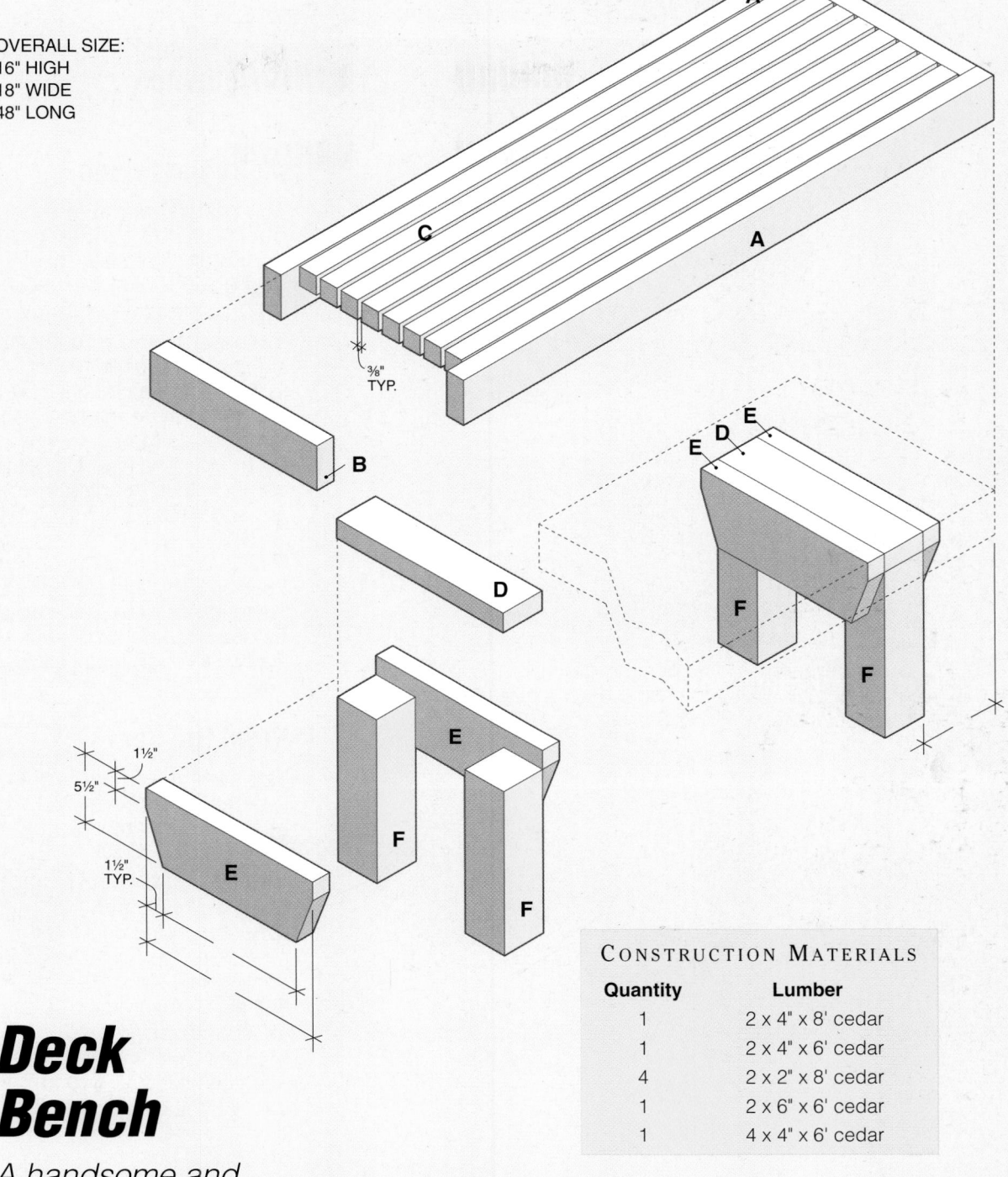

A

C

A

3/8"
TYP.

B

D

E **D** **E**

E **D** **E**

F

F

1½"

5½"

E

1½"
TYP.

E

F

F

Deck Bench

A handsome and comfortable bench that's easy to make.

Due to its modular design, this bench can be mixed or matched with planters or other benches. Cedar wood enables this bench to withstand sun, rain, and even snow. This bench will enhance your enjoyment of your deck and its beauty.

CONSTRUCTION MATERIALS

Quantity	Lumber
1	2 x 4" x 8' cedar
1	2 x 4" x 6' cedar
4	2 x 2" x 8' cedar
1	2 x 6" x 6' cedar
1	4 x 4" x 6' cedar

Cutting List				
Key	**Part**	**Dimension**	**Pcs.**	**Material**
A	Sides	1½ x 3½ x 48"	2	Cedar
B	Ends	1½ x 3½ x 15"	2	Cedar
C	Slats	1½ x 1½ x 45"	8	Cedar
D	Stretchers	1½ x 3½ x 15"	2	Cedar
E	Braces	1½ x 5½ x 15"	4	Cedar
F	Legs	3½ x 3½ x 13"	4	Cedar

Supplies: 3" gold-colored deck screws (60), 2½" gold-colored deck screws (16).

Note: Measurements reflect the actual thickness of dimensional lumber.

Use spacers to help you position the slats. Then, holding each slat firmly against the spacers, secure the slats with 3" screws driven through pilot holes.

With the stretchers positioned between the reference lines, attach the stretcher to each slat using 2½" screws.

Directions: Deck Bench

Make the Frame

The butt joints make this bench sturdy and easy to construct. For strength and good looks, we used gold-colored deck screws.

1 Measure, mark and cut the sides (A) and ends (B) to length, using a circular saw.
2 Position the ends between the sides so the edges are flush. Measure from corner to corner. When the diagonals are equal the frame is square.
3 Drill ⅛" pilot holes through the sides and into the ends. Fasten the sides to the ends by driving 3" gold-colored screws through the pilot holes.

Build the Seat

The slats that make up the seat are spaced ⅜" apart to allow rain water to run off.

1 Cut the slats (C) to length using a circular saw.
2 Set the frame on a flat surface and place ⅜" spacers against one side. Place the first slat in the frame against the spacers. Drill ⅛" pilot holes through both ends into the slat. Secure the slat to the ends with 3" deck screws. Repeat this process of positioning and attaching slats until all the slats are in place *(photo A).*
3 Measure, mark and cut the stretchers (D) to length.
4 To mark the stretcher outlines, measure in 5" and 3½" from the inside of each end piece on the back of the slats and make a mark.
5 Position the stretchers between the marks. Drill ⅛" pilot holes through the stretchers into the slats. Attach the stretchers with 2½" screws *(photo B).*

Assemble the Bench

The braces hold the legs in place against the stretchers.

1 Measure, mark and cut the braces (E) to length.

2 To shape the ends of each brace, mark the angle by measuring down 1½" from the top edge and 1½" along the bottom edge. Draw a line between the two end points and cut along that line *(photo C)*. Repeat this step at the other end of the brace.

3 On each brace, measure down ¾" from the top edge and draw a reference line across the stretcher for the screw positions. Drill ⅛" pilot holes along the reference line. Position a brace on each side of the stretchers and fasten it with 3" screws driven through the braces and into the stretchers.

4 Measure, mark and cut the legs (F) to length, using a circular saw. If needed, finish any cuts with a handsaw.

5 Position each leg between the braces and against the sides of the bench frame. Drill pilot holes through each brace and attach the leg to the braces by driving 3" screws through the braces and into the leg. Repeat the process for each leg until all legs are installed *(photo D)*.

Apply the Finishing Touches

1 Sand all surfaces with 150-grit sandpaper. Be sure to sand edges thoroughly to remove all splinters and rough edges.

2 Because cedar is naturally resistant to decay, it will age to a natural gray. To preserve its reddish color, you can apply a clear sealer as we did. Cedar is also suitable for painting.

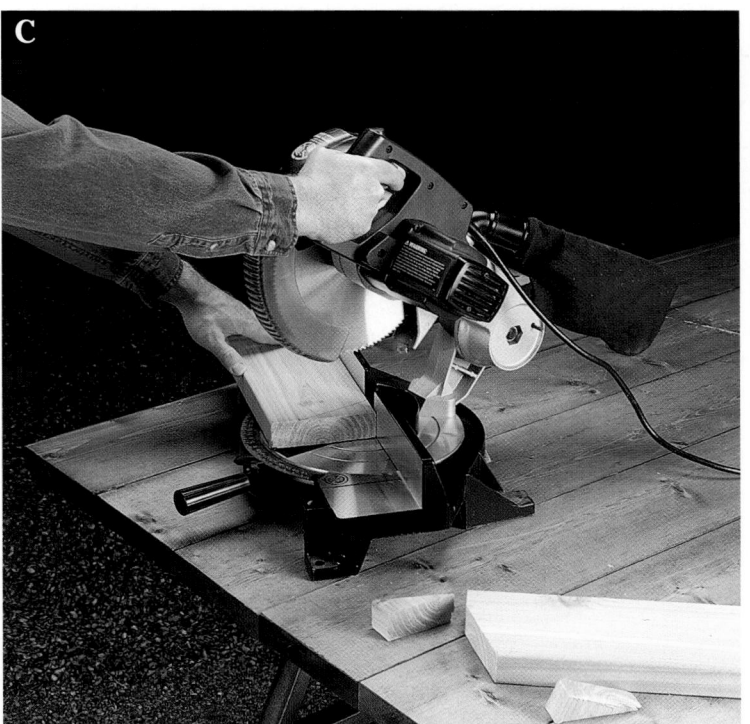

Measure and mark the angles on the braces, then cut the angles using a circular saw or a power miter saw.

Position each leg between the braces and against the sides. Fasten the legs to the braces with 3" screws.

OVERALL SIZE:
24½" HIGH
18¾" WIDE
18¾" LONG

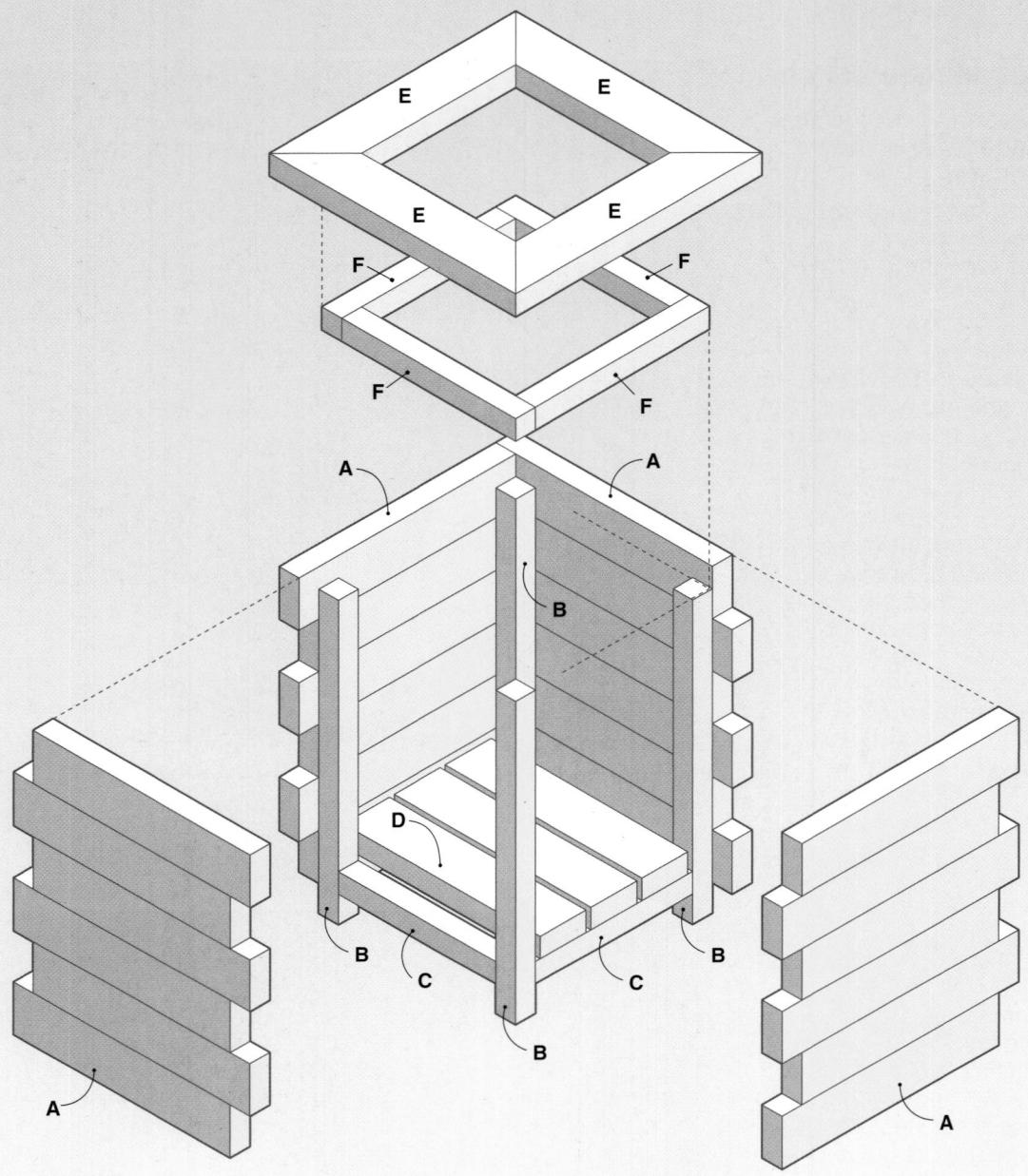

Box Planter

The versatile design of this planter offers a variety of uses.

This planter is large enough to hold a potted shrub, mixed flowers or even a miniature herb garden.

The "tiered" construction process makes it both easy to build and sturdy enough for years of use.

CONSTRUCTION MATERIALS

Quantity	Lumber
8	2 × 4" × 6' cedar
3	2 × 2" × 6' cedar

Cutting List

Key	Part	Dimension	Pcs.	Material
A	Side	1½ × 3½ × 16½"	24	Cedar
B	Stringer	1½ × 1½ × 21½"	4	Cedar
C	Bottom cleat	1½ × 1½ × 12"	4	Cedar
D	Bottom	1½ × 3½ × 14¾"	3	Cedar
E	Frame	1½ × 3½ × 18¾"	4	Cedar
F	Top cleat	1½ × 1½ × 13¼"	4	Cedar

Supplies: 2½" gold-colored deck screws (120), 10d casing nails (10).

Note: Measurements reflect the actual thickness of dimensional lumber.

Place spacers into the corners of the first tier, stand the stringers on end, and attach, using deck screws.

Drill pilot holes through the bottom cleats, and attach with deck screws.

Directions: Box Planter

This planter is assembled upside down. The rows of side pieces, or tiers, are constructed independently, then stacked on top of each other and fastened together from the inside through the stringers.

1 Measure, mark and cut the side pieces (A) to length from 2 × 4" cedar stock.

2 Drill a pair of ⅛" pilot holes through each side piece, about ¾" from one end.

3 Form each of the six tiers by screwing four side pieces together with deck screws driven through the pilot holes.

4 Measure, mark and cut the stringers (B) to length.

5 Lay the first tier on a flat worksurface, then position a stringer upright in one corner using a scrap of 2 × 2" lumber as a spacer to raise the stringer off the worksurface.

6 Drill ⅛" pilot holes and attach the stringer to the tier with 2½" deck screws.

Attach the other three stringers in the same fashion **(photo A)**.

7 Add the remaining tiers one at a time, positioning each tier so the butt joints are offset with those of the previous tier. Drill ⅛" pilot holes and attach each tier to the stringers with deck screws as you go.

8 Measure, mark and cut the bottom cleats (C) to length from 2 × 2" cedar stock.

9 With the planter box still upside down, position a bottom cleat between two stringers, so the edge of the cleat is flush with the edge of the side.

10 Drill angled ⅛" pilot holes, and attach the bottom cleat to the side using deck screws. Attach the remaining bottom cleats in the same fashion **(photo B)**.

11 Measure, mark and cut bottom pieces (D) to length from 2 × 4" cedar stock.

12 Turn the box assembly right-side-up, and set the bottom pieces into the planter so they rest on the cleats and are evenly spaced.

13 Attach the bottom pieces by drilling pilot holes and

driving deck screws through the bottom pieces into the cleats.

14 Measure, mark and cut the frame pieces (E) from 2 × 4" cedar stock, mitering the ends at 45°.

15 Dry-fit the frame pieces together, with the miter joints tight. Join the frame pieces with casing nails.

16 Cut top cleats (F) to size from 2 × 2" cedar stock. Position the cleats on the assembled frame so the edges are flush with the inside edge of the framing pieces. Drill pilot holes through the cleats and attach by driving deck screws through the cleats and into the frame.

17 Position the frame on the planter so the cleats fit tightly inside box. Attach the frame by drilling pilot holes and driving deck screws through the inside face of the top cleats.

18 Soften the corners and edges of the box planter with a rasp, then apply a finish of your choice; our planter is protected with a coat of clear sealant-preservative.

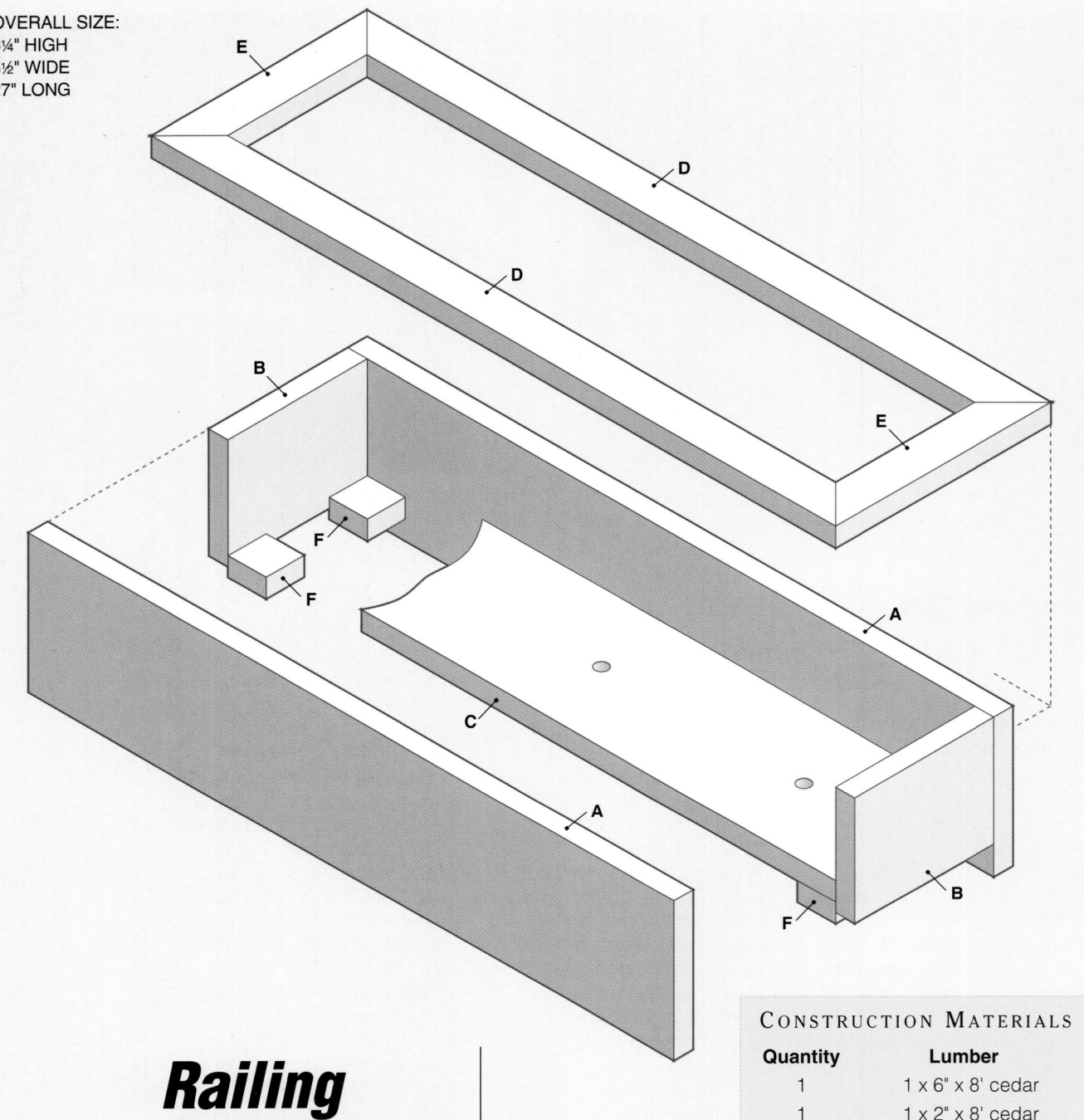

OVERALL SIZE:
6¼" HIGH
8½" WIDE
27" LONG

Railing Planter

Grow flowers or herbs in this sturdy cedar planter.

Though this planter is built with inexpensive ¾" cedar, adding a planter to your deck will add a touch of class. Build a few planters and create an attractive, colorful privacy hedge.

CONSTRUCTION MATERIALS

Quantity	Lumber
1	1 x 6" x 8' cedar
1	1 x 2" x 8' cedar

Cutting List

Key	Part	Dimension	Pcs.	Material
A	Sides	¾ × 5½ × 25½"	2	Cedar
B	Ends	¾ × 4⅜ × 5½"	2	Cedar
C	Bottom	¾ × 5½ × 24"	1	Cedar
D	Frame sides	¾ × 1½ × 27"	2	Cedar
E	Frame ends	¾ × 1½ × 8½"	2	Cedar
F	Feet	¾ × 1½ × 1½"	4	Cedar

Supplies: 6d finishing nails (26), 4d finishing nails (28).

Note: Measurements reflect the actual thickness of dimensional lumber.

Assemble the box by predrilling the sides and attaching them to the ends with 6d finishing nails.

After attaching the feet to the bottom, insert the bottom into the planter box so it is flush with the reference line. Fasten with 6d finishing nails.

Directions: Railing Planter

The railing planter is designed with longer sides to fit over a standard size railing. Feet are installed to keep the planter off the railing and allow water to drain and air to circulate.

1 Measure, mark and cut the sides (A) and ends (B) to size from 1 × 6" cedar stock. NOTE: The grain runs horizontally on the sides and vertically on the ends.

2 Position the ends between the sides with the top edges flush. Drill pilot holes, and fasten with 6d finishing nails *(photo A).* Make sure the end pieces are oriented so the wood grain runs vertically.

3 Measure, mark and cut the bottom (C) to size, using a circular saw.

4 Draw a reference line down the middle of the bottom. Use a ½" spade bit to drill three drainage holes evenly spaced along the line.

5 Measure, mark and cut the feet (F) to size from ¾" cedar. Position the feet flush at the corners of the bottom piece and attach with 4d nails.

6 Draw reference lines on the inside faces of the side pieces, 1½" from the bottom edges.

7 With the box frame on its side, insert the bottom piece into the box, and tap into place until the bottom surface is flush with the reference lines. Drill pilot holes and drive 6d finish nails through the sides and ends to secure the bottom piece in place *(photo B).*

8 Measure, mark and cut the frame sides (D) and frame ends (E) to size from ¾" cedar, mitering the ends at 45°.

9 Position the frame pieces over the top of the planter box so the inside edges are flush with the inside surfaces of the box. Drill pilot holes and attach the frame pieces to the side and end pieces with 4d finishing nails. Lock-nail the miter joints with 4d finishing nails.

10 Recess all nail heads with a nail set, then finish as desired. Cedar will age naturally, but you can also seal it, as we did, with a clear wood preservative to maintain its original color.

Tip

You can prevent rot and extend the life of your planter by adding a plastic insert to hold the soil and plants.

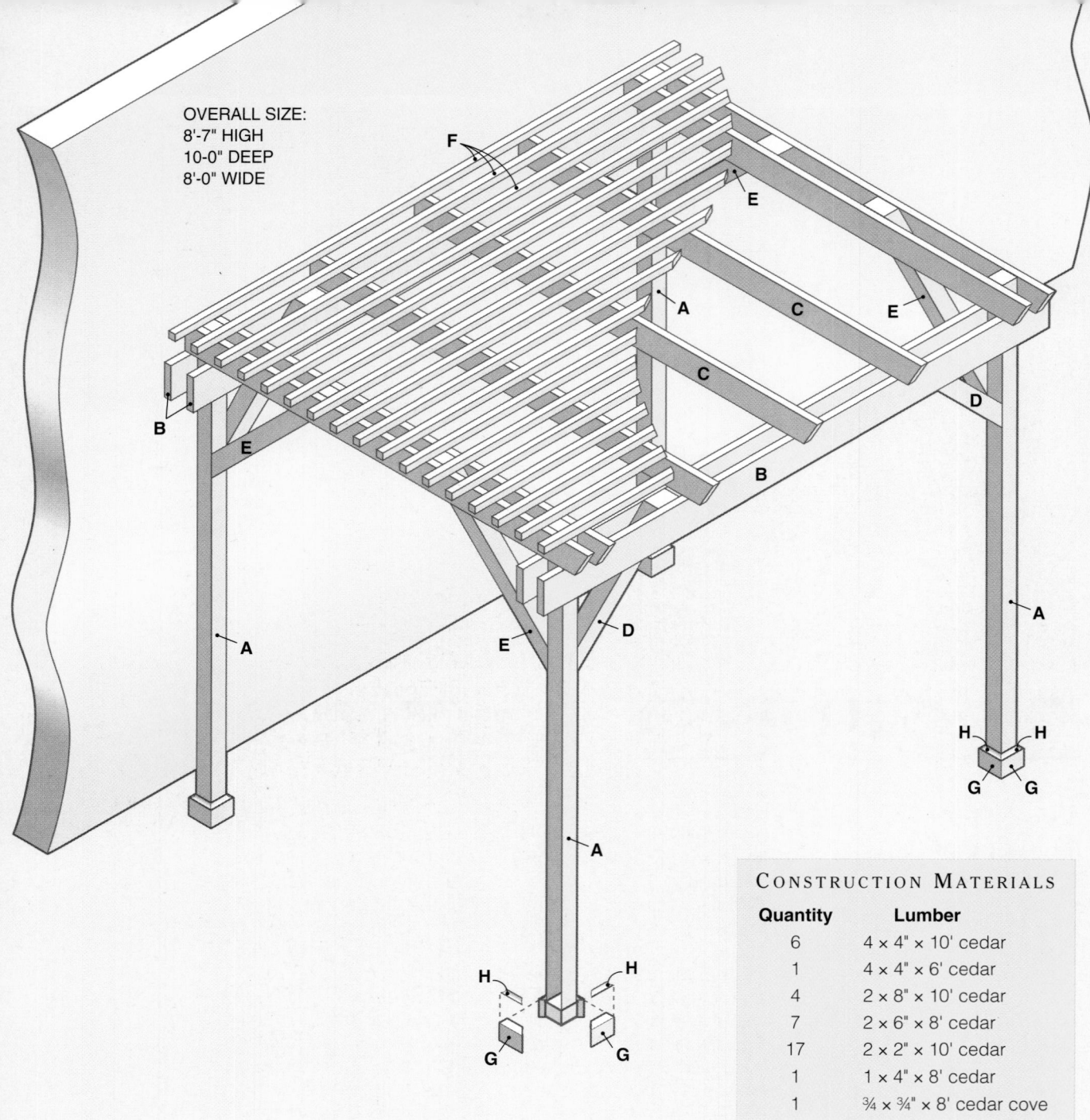

OVERALL SIZE:
8'-7" HIGH
10-0" DEEP
8'-0" WIDE

CONSTRUCTION MATERIALS

Quantity	Lumber
6	4 × 4" × 10' cedar
1	4 × 4" × 6' cedar
4	2 × 8" × 10' cedar
7	2 × 6" × 8' cedar
17	2 × 2" × 10' cedar
1	1 × 4" × 8' cedar
1	¾ × ¾" × 8' cedar cove

Arbor

Create a pleasant outdoor shelter.

Arbors provide a cozy feeling of enclosure without boxing you in. Sit back and enjoy the cool summer breeze in this simple structure, personalized with your wind chimes, bird feeders, banners or vines.

Cutting List				
Key	**Part**	**Dimension**	**Pcs.**	**Material**
A	Corner posts	3½ × 3½ × 101½"	4	Cedar
B	Beam boards	1½ × 7¼ × 120"	4	Cedar
C	Rafters	1½ × 5½ × 96"	7	Cedar
D	End braces	3½ × 3½ × 34¼"	4	Cedar
E	Side braces	3½ × 3½ × 42"	4	Cedar
F	Slats	1½ × 1½ × 120"	17	Cedar
G	Post trim	¾ × 3½ × 5"	16	Cedar
H	Post molding	¾ × ¾ × 5"	16	Cedar

Supplies: ⅜ × 6" lag screws and washers (16); ½ × 7" carriage bolts, washers, and nuts (8); 2½" galvanized deck screws (200); 4 × 4" metal post anchors (4); galvanized metal rafter ties (6); 6d galvanized casing nails (12); 3d finishing nails (8).

A

Fasten the corner posts in the post anchor hardware with 10d joist hanger nails.

B

Use string and a line level and transfer the height of the beams to each corner post. Note temporary bracing on posts.

Directions: Arbor

Even though this arbor is structurally independent and not attached to your house, it's designed to be built next to a wall. If you want to build it away from your house, on a far corner of your deck, simply lengthen the rafters and angle-cut both ends.

Locate the Arbor

When positioning the arbor, make sure the back posts are at least 6" from the house (see *Side Eleva-* *tion*, page 286) to allow room for attaching the back beam boards. The corner posts should rest on joists. If necessary, add blocking between the joists at post locations for added support.

Set the Posts

1 Mark the corner post locations on your deck (see *Elevations*, page 286). Position the post anchor hardware and attach to the decking with deck screws.
2 Measure, mark and cut the corner posts (A) to length. You may wish to cut the posts slightly longer than the final height to allow for leveling the beams and rafters.

3 Cut eight temporary braces, approximately 6' long, with a 45° angle on one end.
4 Set the posts in the post anchors and attach with deck screws *(photo A)*. Use a level to ensure that the posts are plumb, and fasten in position by tacking two temporary braces to the deck and each post. Leave the temporary braces in place until the permanent braces are installed.
5 Mark the height of the beam boards on one corner post, using a combination square. Stretch a string between posts and use a line level to transfer this mark to the other corner posts *(photo B)*.

Front Elevation

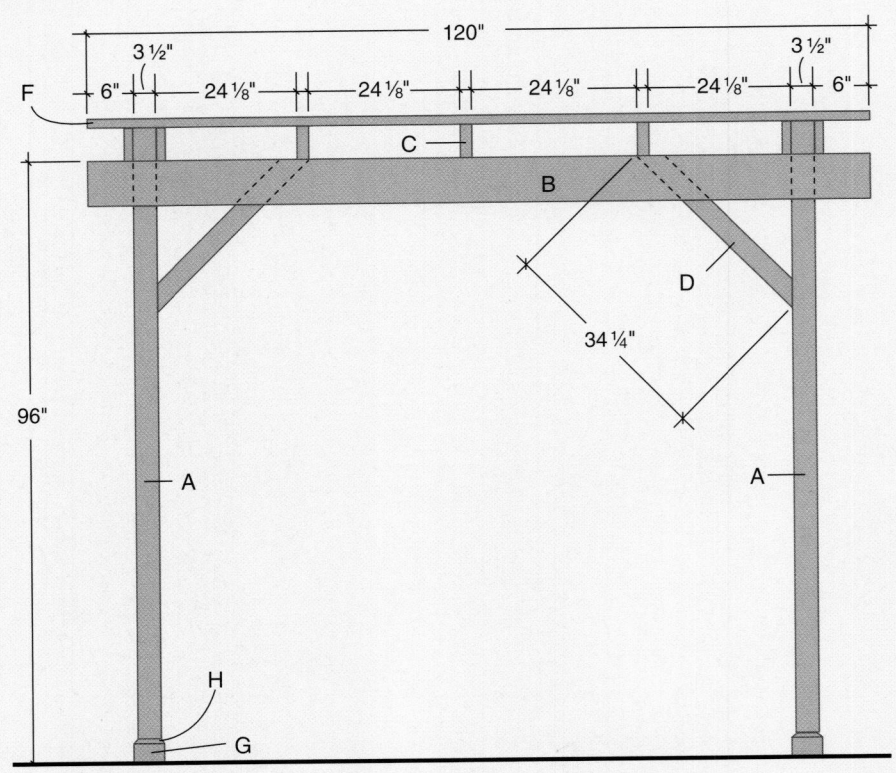

Side Elevation

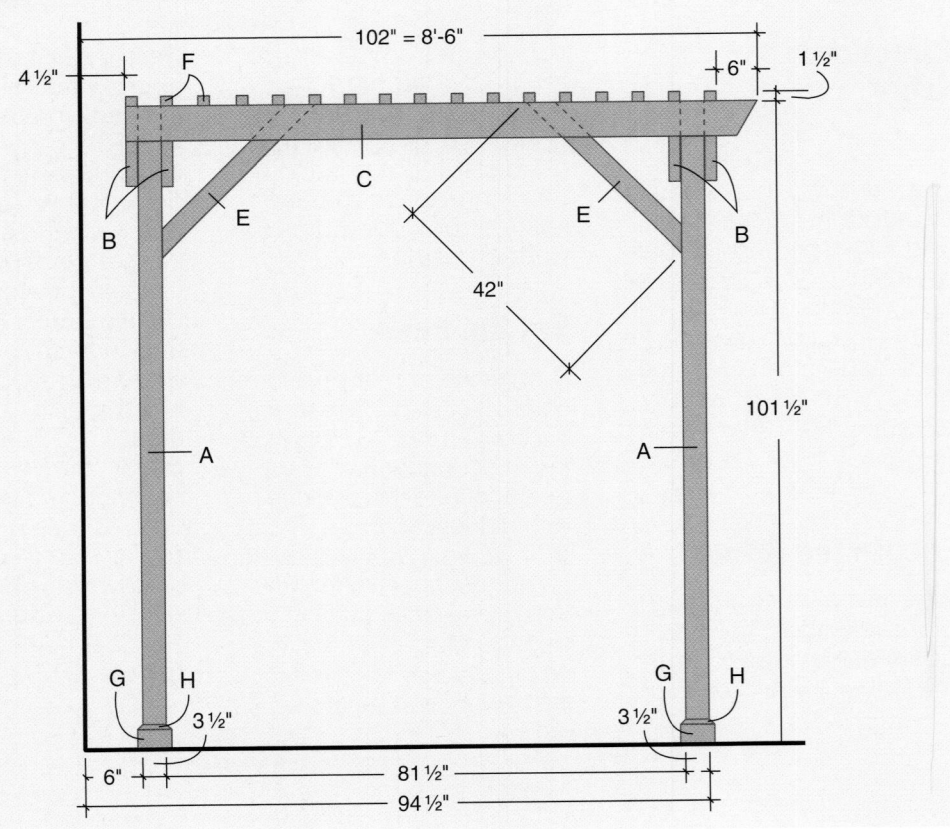

Detail A

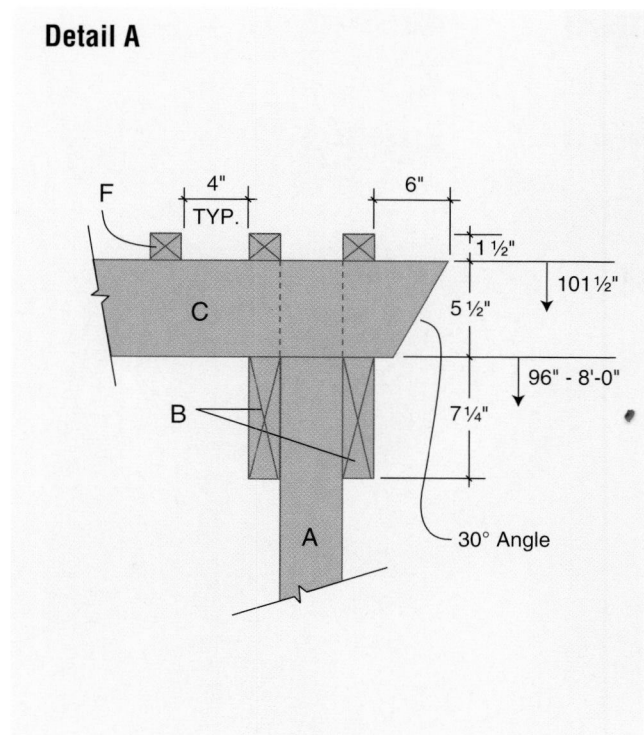

Drill two ½" holes through the beam boards and post for the carriage bolts.

Install the Beams

The beams are installed between the posts, parallel to the house.

1 Measure, mark and cut the beam boards to length (see *Front Elevation*, page 286).

2 Stand the beam boards together on edge, ends flush. Measure and mark the outlines of the rafters on the top edges of the boards, using a combination square as a guide.

3 With a helper, hold each beam in position on the corner posts, and tack in place with deck screws. NOTE: If you're working alone, cut four 12"-long 2 × 4s, to use as temporary supports. Attach these pieces to the sides of the posts at the bottom edge of the beam position. Rest the beam boards on the supports.

4 Mark the carriage bolt locations, and drill ½" holes through the beam boards and corner posts *(photo C)*.

Attach the inner rafters with galvanized rafter ties and deck screws.

Use a circular saw to cut the 45° angles on the end and side braces.

To secure the top of each brace, drill and countersink a ¼" hole, insert a 6" lag screw, and tighten with a ratchet wrench.

5 Secure the beams to the corner posts with carriage bolts, washers and nuts.

Install the Rafters

The rafters are installed perpendicular to the house, and overhang the front beam by 6". The front ends of the rafters are cut at a 30° angle (see *Detail A*, page 287).

1 Measure, mark and cut the rafters (C) to size, using a circular saw (see *Side Elevation*, page 286).
2 Set the rafters in position. Attach the outer rafters to the posts with deck screws. Attach the inner rafters to the beams, using metal rafter ties and 10d joist hanger nails *(photo D)*.
OPTION: If you prefer a less visible method of attaching the inner rafters, toenail them with 16d galvanized nails.

3 Trim the posts to final height if necessary, using a reciprocating saw or a handsaw.

Install the Braces

The braces provide lateral support for the canopy. The end braces fit between the beams and the corner posts; the side braces fit between the rafters and the corner posts.

1 Cut the end braces (D) and the side braces (E) to size (see *Elevations*, page 286). Cut 45° angles on both ends with a circular saw *(photo E)*.
2 Position an end brace between the beam boards, with the lower end tight against the post and the upper end flush with the top of the beam. Tack the brace into place with deck screws.

3 Drill a ¼" pilot hole through the lower end of the brace into the post. Countersink the pilot hole ¼" deep with a 1" spade bit, and attach the brace with a lag screw.
4 To fasten the upper end of the brace to the beam, drill a ¼" pilot hole 5" deep. Countersink the hole ¼" deep with a 1" spade bit. Insert a lag screw and tighten with a ratchet wrench *(photo F)*.
5 Use the same procedure to position and install the remaining braces.

Install the Slats

1 Measure, mark and cut the slats (F) to length.
2 Attach the back slat directly above the back beam board. Attach the remaining slats at 4" intervals, fastening them with deck screws *(photo G)*.

G

Position slats at 4" intervals with a 6" overhang and attach by driving 2½" deck screws through the slats and into the rafters.

Add the Finishing Touches

1 Measure, mark and cut the post trim (G) and post molding (H) to length, with the ends mitered at 45°.

2 Fit and attach the trim to the posts with 6d galvanized casing nails *(photo H).* You may need to chisel out the back side of the trim to accommodate the post anchor screws.

3 Fit the molding and attach it tight to the posts with 3d finishing nails.

4 Though cedar is naturally resistant to decay and doesn't require an applied finish, you may want to use a coat of clear sealant-preservative for added protection and to preserve the original color of the wood.

H

Attach the post trim and molding with 16d galvanized nails.

Photo courtesy of P&M Cedar Products, Inc.

Modifying a Deck Design

Modifying a plan lets you adapt your deck to unique situations.

Although the seven deck designs presented in this book offer a wide selection of styles and placements, it's possible that you'll want to modify a plan to fit the size or shape of your yard or just to suit your tastes. When you modify a design, you need to think about safety and structural integrity, the two most important features of your deck. This chapter will walk you through the most common modifications, showing you how to figure lumber dimensions so that your deck will be safe and durable.

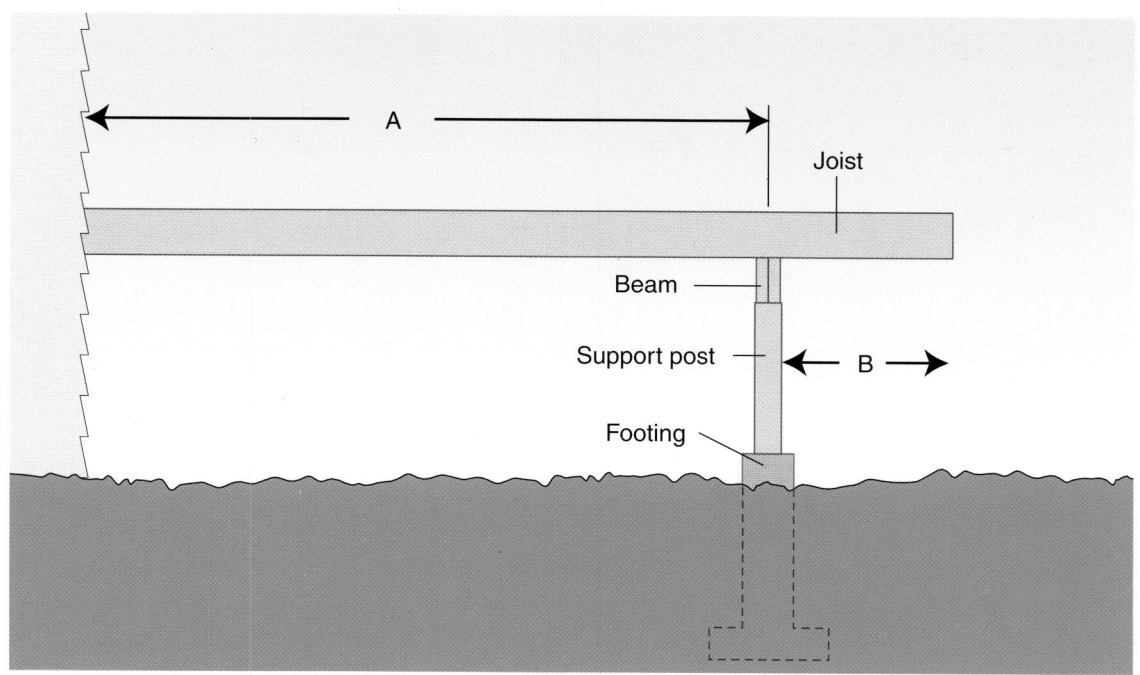

The length of the cantilever (B) must be taken into account when figuring beam and footing sizes. The cantilever should not be more than 2' unless special supports are added. A building inspector can advise you of the code restrictions in your area.

The Parts of a Deck

The major structural parts of a deck are the *ledger, footings, posts, beams, joists, decking* and *stringers*. Once you're familiar with these parts, you can make sensible decisions about where extra support may be required and what kinds of modifications you can include without weakening your deck. (Remember to consult your local building inspector before modifying a deck design.)

In addition to a deck's structural members, decking boards are always a prominent feature. Your deck will probably also include *railings, balusters, risers, fascia boards* and a variety of less prominent parts.

Figuring Span Limits

To alter a design safely, you need to know the distance that a given board can travel between supports — known as the span limit. The larger the lumber, the greater the span limit. In addition, some species of wood are stronger than others and have a greater span limit. Of the structural members, only the ledger is immune from span limits, since it is attached directly to the house with lag screws.

For any cantilevered deck plan, including those shown in this book, refer to the *Determining Lumber Size* information on pages 42 to 45, to find minimum sizes for your deck's joists and beam. Use the post spacing and the length of the joists, A + B (A), to select acceptable joist and beam sizes from the chart.

If you lengthen a deck and add a second beam, use the post spacing and the distance from the inside beam to the rim joist to find joist and beam sizes. Remember, joists must be no more than 16" (OC) for decking boards that run perpendicular to the joists; 12" (OC) if the decking boards are installed diagonally.

Estimating Concrete

When mixing or ordering concrete for footings or a pad, you'll need a rough estimate of the concrete required. Mixes usually include estimated concrete needs for projects, as well as the yield per bag in cubic feet. Concrete companies measure per cubic yard.

When pouring 4' footings that are 12" in diameter, expect to use about 3¼ cu. ft. of concrete per footing, or about half that much for footings 8" in diameter. If local code calls for flared bottoms, you will need to increase your estimate.

For a 4"-deep pad at the base of the stairs, figure ⅓ cu. ft. of concrete per sq. ft. of pad surface. A 4' × 5' pad would require 6.6 cu. ft. of concrete, or about ¼ cu. yd. (2 to 3 wheelbarrow loads).

Changing the Height of Your Deck

The plans in this book assume you are building on level ground and that the deck plan you choose is optimally suited to your home and yard. Of course, not all building sites are level and no yard is exactly like another. Your home may have a nonstandard doorway height or an uneven landscape. Or, you may simply choose to alter the height of the deck in the plan to suit your tastes.

When you change the height of the deck, you need to move the ledger, change the length of the posts and reevaluate post and footing sizes. You'll need to consider the need

for railings, a step or stairs and post-to-beam braces. You may want to reconsider your joist placement (suspended from the side of the beam or resting on top). Finally, you may need to change either the length or the layout of the stairway, or both. You may even need to add a stairway or a landing that wasn't in the original design.

Increasing Deck Height

Raising a deck's height obviously means that the ledger will be higher and the posts will be longer. The posts may also need to be larger in thickness. If your deck is higher than 6', use 6 × 6 posts in place of 4 × 4 posts. Your inspector will probably also recommend enlarging the footings from 8" to 12" in diameter.

If you add posts to a ground-

level deck and the height exceeds 30", you will need to add railings and stairs. Stairways with more than three risers require grippable railings as well. If your deck is over 12' high, braces are usually required for stability.

If you're adapting a ground-level design to an elevated installation, you'll probably want to extend the joists over the top of the beam to create a cantilever instead of hanging them with joist hangers on the beam's face.

Changes to the stairway design are covered on pages 294 to 295.

Decreasing Deck Height

Decreasing the height of a deck obviously means that the ledger will be installed lower and the posts will be shorter. And it's possible that your lumber needs may decrease significantly. If the deck height is less than 30", you can safely eliminate the deck railings, and cross bracing won't be necessary.

Consult the section on stairways and landings for issues to consider when decreasing the deck height.

Adapting to Ground Level

When you adapt a deck design to a ground-level installation, you eliminate several construction steps and simplify others. You won't need railings, posts, stairways or landings — though you may need a single step if there's a slight rise. In place of posts, install direct-bearing hardware in the concrete footings while they are still wet. Once they are dry, fasten the beam directly to the hardware. The classic

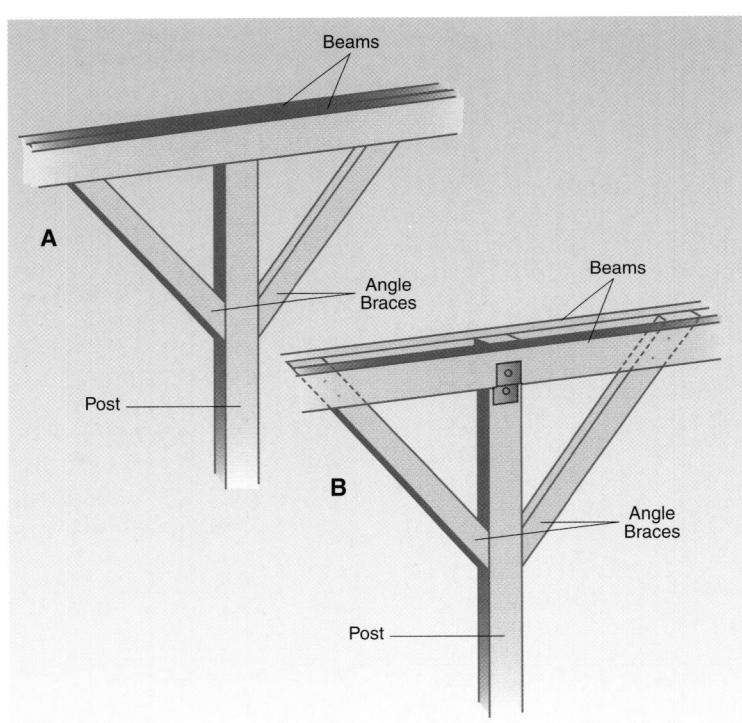

To reinforce an elevated deck built with a solid beam (A), install a Y-brace by attaching beveled 2 × 4s with lag screws to the sides of the post and the bottom of the beam. On a deck with a sandwich beam (B), use carriage bolts and slightly longer braces that can be mounted in between the two beam timbers.

cantilever design — with the beam set back from the ends of the joists — is seldom used.

If you're building your deck very close to the ground, you may need to attach the ledger to the foundation wall rather than to the house's rim joist. To attach the ledger securely, drill pilot holes through the ledger and use the pilot holes to drill 3"-deep guide holes into the wall with a ⅝" masonry bit. Sink masonry sleeves into the wall. Then, position the ledger and attach it with lag screws driven through the ledger and into the masonry sleeves.

For a step leading to a ground-level deck, build a suspended step (pages 270 to 271).

Set direct-bearing hardware into footings while they are still wet. Use mason's strings to check the alignment.

Changing Deck Size

You may want to change the size of your deck to match the dimensions of building walls, to avoid windows or to work around other natural obstacles.

Increasing Deck Size

There are two ways to enlarge a deck. You can "widen" your deck by lengthening the joists and extend them out farther from the ledger. Or, you can add to the "length" of the deck by lengthening the ledger and increasing the number of joists.

If you're widening your deck, you'll want to know how far you can extend the joists beyond the beam. The cantilevered end of the joists (illustration, page 291) should typically extend no more than 2' past the beam,

unless the deck contains special supports.

If you want to extend your deck farther than this, you can move the beam out farther from the ledger and enlarge the size of the joists to allow for an increased span. To determine the proper joist and post sizes, use the *Determining Lumber* size information on pages 42 to 45.

Another way to provide support for an extended deck is to install a second, outer beam 2' or less from the deck's edge.

Lengthening the deck is usually a simpler alteration. It requires that you increase the length of the ledger and the beams, and that you add more joists.

Of course, when enlarging a deck you'll need to adjust

the amount of decking and railing materials accordingly.

Decreasing Deck Size

It's a good deal easier to decrease the size of your deck than to increase it. When you decrease the size there are usually fewer code issues to address. Since the overall load will be less, you don't have to worry about structural issues.

One strategy for making your deck smaller is to shorten the ledger and beam and reduce the number of joists. The alternative is to reduce the width of the deck by moving the beam closer to the house and reducing the length of the joists. Your local lumberyard or home center can help you adjust the amount of decking and railing materials you will need.

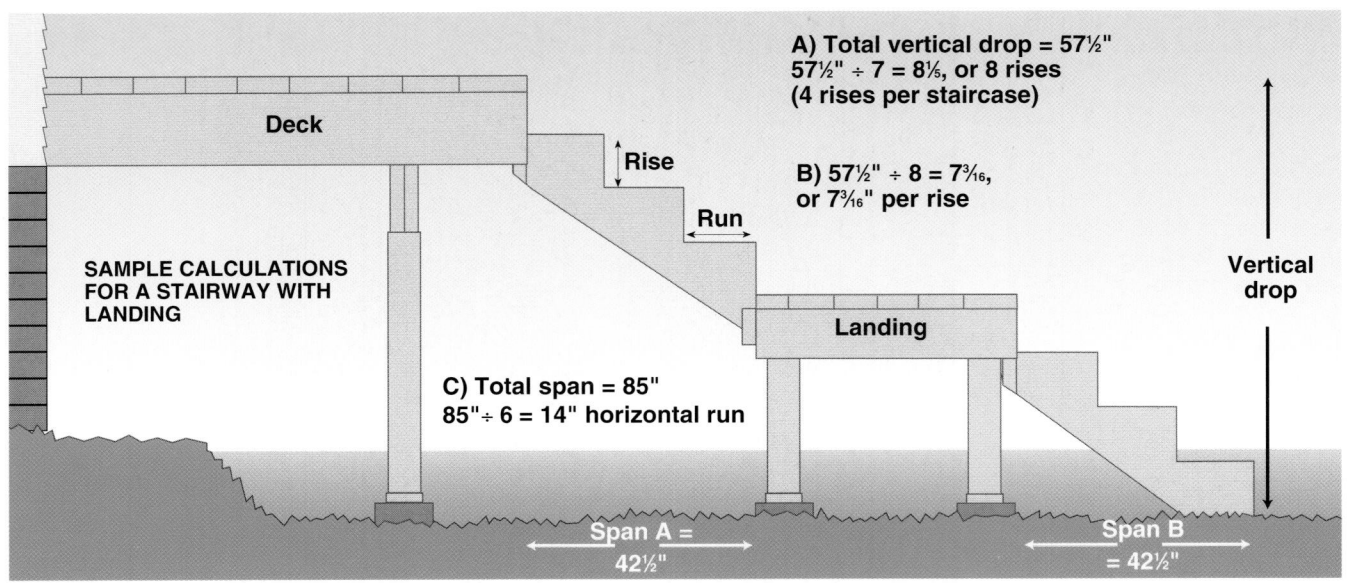

A) Total vertical drop = 57½"
57½" ÷ 7 = 8⅙, or 8 rises
(4 rises per staircase)

**B) 57½" ÷ 8 = 7³⁄₁₆,
or 7³⁄₁₆" per rise**

C) Total span = 85"
85" ÷ 6 = 14" horizontal run

Deck

Rise

Run

SAMPLE CALCULATIONS
FOR A STAIRWAY WITH
LANDING

Landing

Vertical
drop

Span A =
42½"

Span B
= 42½"

Changing Stairway Height

If you change the height or design of a deck, you may need to change the stairway layout as well. Elevating a deck, for example, may require that you construct a stairway that has two staircases joined by a landing (illustration, above). And even relatively small changes in a design may require that you alter the vertical rise and horizontal run of each step.

Vertical drop and horizontal span are the key variables when designing or changing a stairway. Vertical drop is the distance from the deck surface to the ground. The span is the horizontal distance from the deck's edge to the stairway's starting point on the ground. It is determined by whatever starting point you select. Once you know these variables, you can calculate the rise and run. Just remember this general rule: the span should be 40–60% greater than the vertical

drop. For example, the span of a stairway with an 8' vertical drop should be between 11' 3" and 12' 10".

Stairway Basics

For safety and comfort, the components of a stairway must be built according to clearly prescribed guidelines. The rise, the vertical dimension of each step, must be between 6½" and 8". The run, the horizontal depth of each step, must be at least 9". The number of runs in a staircase is always one less than the number of rises. The combined sum of the step rise and run should be 18–20".

Steps that meet these guidelines are the most comfortable to use. Variation between the largest and smallest rise or run should be no more than ⅜".

Stair width must be at least 36", enabling two people to pass one another comfortably on the stairway.

Stringer spacing depends on the width of the stairs and the thickness of the treads, but should never

exceed 36". A center stringer is recommended for any staircase with more than three steps. Very wide stairs may require more than one center stringer.

Finding the Horizontal Span & Vertical Drop

To determine the stairway's vertical drop, extend a straight, level 2 × 4 from the deck to a spot directly over the stairway's starting point on the ground. Measure the distance to the ground; this is the total vertical drop. NOTE: If the starting point is more than 10' from the deck, use a mason's string and line level to establish a reference point from which to measure.

The horizontal span is found by measuring the distance from the edge of the deck to the point directly over the starting point for the stairway. Remember that the span should be 40–60% greater than the vertical drop. If it's not, you'll need to adjust the starting point for the stairway until the ratio fits this range.

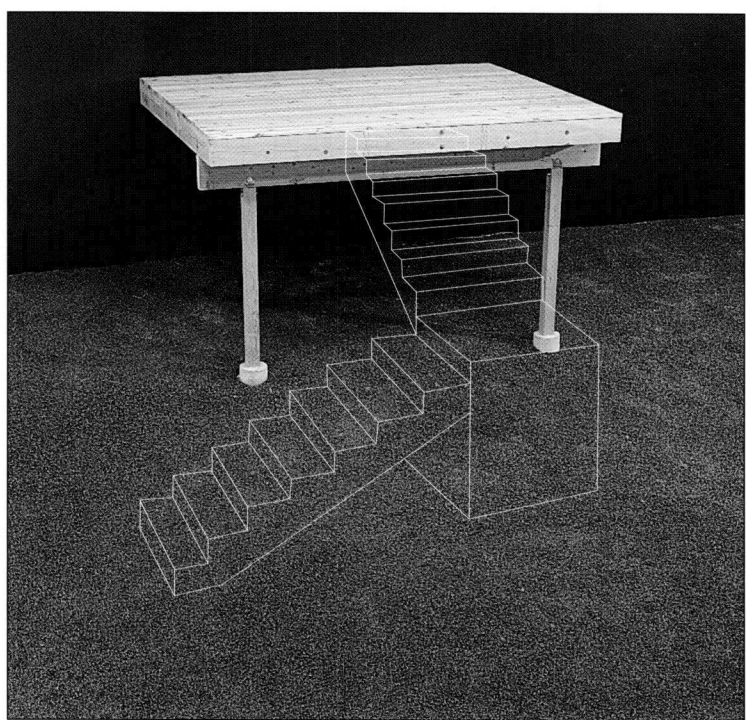

Visualize a stairway design that will fit your needs. Most stairways with landings are built with upper and lower staircases of equal length, although this is not required.

Footings & pads

Footings and pads serve slightly different purposes, although they are at times interchangeable. A footing is typically poured into a form in the ground, reaching down several feet in regions where the ground freezes, and rising 2" or more above the ground to keep posts or stringers away from moisture.

If you want a concrete landing at the base of the stairs, pour a pad, typically 4–6" thick. Ask your inspector whether footings are required beneath the pad to withstand harsh winter weather.

Lengthening or Shortening the Stairway

If you are altering the height of your deck, or if your building site is uneven, it's likely that you will need to lengthen or shorten your stairway.

Bear in mind that if the vertical drop is more than 12'—for example, if you are building a second-floor deck—a landing is required. In most cases it's best to construct the stairway so the upper and lower staircases are of equal length.

If you've decreased the deck height, you can shorten the stairway and bring the starting point closer to the deck.

To determine the number of step rises, divide the vertical drop by 7, rounding off fractions. Next, determine the exact height for each step rise by dividing the vertical drop by the number of rises.

Find the horizontal run for each step by dividing the span by the number of runs. If your stairway contains a landing, add the span for each of the staircases together, then divide this number by the number of runs. Remember that the number of runs in a staircase is always one less than the number of rises.

Once you have the exact rise and run for each step, it's an easy matter to use a framing square to lay out the steps on stringers.

Building on a Steep Slope

The deck plans in this book assume you're building on level ground. But what if your yard is on a hillside?

Building a deck on a steep slope is more complicated than building on level ground because of the physical demands of raising the deck frame, and because of the challenge of taking precise measurements before locating footings and cutting posts. The best approach involves modifying standard deck-building sequences.

The general idea when building on a steep slope is to start by building the outside frame and propping it on the ledger using a set of temporary posts, and only then determine the permanent locations for posts and footings. By modifying the conventional deck-building sequence you avoid the risk of digging and pouring footings only to find, after setting up the deck frame, that the footings are slightly off center.

Appendix

Converting Measurements

To Convert:	To:	Multiply by:
Inches	Millimeters	25.4
Inches	Centimeters	2.54
Feet	Meters	0.305
Yards	Meters	0.914
Square inches	Square centimeters	6.45
Square feet	Square meters	0.093
Square yards	Square meters	0.836
Cubic inches	Cubic centimeters	16.4
Cubic feet	Cubic meters	0.0283
Cubic yards	Cubic meters	0.765
Ounces	Milliliters	30.0
Pints (U.S.)	Liters	0.473 (Imp. 0.568)
Quarts (U.S.)	Liters	0.946 (Imp. 1.136)
Gallons (U.S.)	Liters	3.785 (Imp. 4.546)
Ounces	Grams	28.4
Pounds	Kilograms	0.454

To Convert:	To:	Multiply by:
Millimeters	Inches	0.039
Centimeters	Inches	0.394
Meters	Feet	3.28
Meters	Yards	1.09
Square centimeters	Square inches	0.155
Square meters	Square feet	10.8
Square meters	Square yards	1.2
Cubic centimeters	Cubic inches	0.061
Cubic meters	Cubic feet	35.3
Cubic meters	Cubic yards	1.31
Milliliters	Ounces	.033
Liters	Pints (U.S.)	2.114 (Imp. 1.76)
Liters	Quarts (U.S.)	1.057 (Imp. 0.88)
Liters	Gallons (U.S.)	0.264 (Imp. 0.22)
Grams	Ounces	0.035
Kilograms	Pounds	2.2

Drill Bit Guide

Twist Bit	Carbide-tipped Masonry	Glass & Tile	Spade Bit	Adjustable Counterbore	Hole Saw

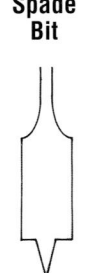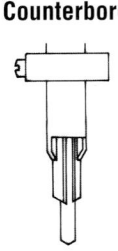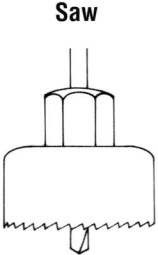

Counterbore, Shank & Pilot Hole Diameters

Screw Size	Counterbore Diameter for Screw Head	Clearance Hole for Screw Shank	Pilot Hole Diameter Hard Wood	Soft Wood
#1	9/64	5/64	3/64	1/32
#2	1/4	3/32	3/64	1/32
#3	1/4	7/64	1/16	3/64
#4	1/4	1/8	1/16	3/64
#5	1/4	1/8	5/64	1/16
#6	5/16	9/64	3/32	5/64
#7	5/16	5/32	3/32	5/64
#8	3/8	11/64	1/8	3/32
#9	3/8	11/64	1/8	3/32
#10	3/8	3/16	1/8	7/64
#11	1/2	3/16	5/32	9/64
#12	1/2	7/32	9/64	1/8

Resources

Photography Contributors

Archadeck
800-722-4668
www.archadeck.com

California Redwood Association
888-225-7339
www.calredwood.org

Eon Outdoor Systems Inc.
877-433-9133
www.eonoutdoor.com

Lindal Cedar Homes, Inc.
800-426-0536
www.lindal.com

Master Mark Plastics/
Rhino Composite Decking
 and Railing Systems
800-535-4838
www.rhino.com

Milt Charno and Associates Inc.
414-475-1965
Wauwatosa,WI

Pultronex Corporation /E.Z.Deck
800-990-3099
www.ezdeck.com

Timbertech
800-307-7780
www.timbertech.com

Materials Contributors

DEKBRANDS, Inc.
(Dek-Block Piers)
(612) 331-4755
800-664-2705

Pultronex Corporation /E.Z.Deck
800-990-3099
www.ezdeck.com

Glossary

Baluster — a vertical railing member.

Batterboards — temporary stake structures used for positioning layout strings.

Beam — the main horizontal support for the deck, usually made from a pair of 2 × 8s or 2 × 10s attached to the deck posts.

Blocking — short pieces of lumber cut from joist material and fastened between joists for reinforcement.

Cap — the topmost horizontal railing member.

Cantilever — a common construction method (employed in some of the deck plans in this book) that involves extending the joists beyond the beam. The maximum overhang is specified in the Building Code.

Corner-post design — a construction method that incorporates posts at the outside edges of the deck, so the joists do not overhang the beam.

Decking — the floor boards of a deck (also known as deck boards).

End joists — the joists that are at each end of a series of parallel joists.

Face board — attractive wood, usually redwood or cedar, used to cover the rim joists and end joists.

Footing — a concrete pier that extends below the frost line and that bears the weight of the deck and any inset structures or furnishings.

Horizontal span — the horizontal distance a stairway covers.

Inset — an area of a deck that has been cut out to accommodate landscape features such as trees or to provide access to fixtures.

Joist — dimensional lumber, set on edge, that supports decking. Joists on attached decks hang between the ledger and rim joist.

Joist hanger — metal connecting pieces used to attach joists at right angles to ledger or header joists so that top edges are flush.

Ledger — a board, equal in size to the joists, that anchors the deck to the house and supports one end of the joists.

Open step — a step composed of treads mounted between stair stringers without any risers.

Post — a vertical member that supports a deck, stairway or railing.

Post anchors — metal hardware for attaching deck posts to footings and raising the bottom of the post to keep it away from water. The end grain itself can be protected with sealer as added protection from rot.

Rim joist — a board fastened to the end of the joists, typically at the opposite end from the ledger. Rim joists attach to both ends of a free-standing deck.

Rise — the height of a step.

Riser — a board attached to the front of a step between treads.

Run — the length of a step.

Sandwich beam — a beam design that incorporates a pair of beam timbers attached to either side of the post with carriage bolts.

Span limit — the distance a board can safely cross between supports.

Stair cleat — supports for treads that are attached to stair stringers.

Stair stringer — an inclined member that supports a stairway's treads. A stair stringer may be solid, with treads attached to cleats mounted on the inside face, or cut out, with treads resting on top of the cutouts.

Tread — the horizontal face of each step in a stairway, often composed of two 2 × 6" boards

Vertical drop — the vertical distance from the deck surface to the ground.

Index

Creative Publishing international, Inc.
offers a variety of how-to books.
For information write or visit our website:
   Creative Publishing international, Inc.
   Subscriber Books
   18705 Lake Drive East
   Chanhassen, MN 55317

www.creativepub.com

More Outstanding Praise for **WHERE ARE MY KEYS?®**
Memory Lady **Judy Marcus'** popular workshop and book:

". . . A popular and much needed presentation . . . Thank you for your energetic and uplifting seminar . . ."

> **Fran Hankin, Director, Program Services,**
> **Alzheimer's Association**

"Highest turn-out for any of our seminars and presentations . . . I watched the way the 285 people in the audience participated. It was 90 minutes of learning with a touch of humor throughout the program . . . you had a large audience in your control with such ease . . ."

> **Doug C. Johnson, Elgin Township Supervisor**

"Judy is a warm and gifted teacher with a rich imagination . . . who shows us how to creatively remember — and retrieve — the details that keep us present, awake and alert in our lives."

> **Carol Stone, Ph.D, Awareness Based Psychotherapist. Attendee,**
> **Alzheimer's Association WHERE ARE MY KEYS?® Seminar**

"Thanks for a great presentation at our support group leaders conference. It was just the right recipe of helpful hints, interactive exercises and fun . . ."

> **Susan Reese, MA, RN, LCSW, Director American Parkinson Disease**
> **Association Information & Referral Center**

"Judy's Memory Workshop was interesting and entertaining . . . ! "

> **Erin Molloy, Chicago Living Pavilion Coordinator,**
> **TASTE OF CHICAGO**

"I was never good with names before. Now, after playing along with the LOVE Memory Method, I'm great with names"

> **Al Rose, Aspen, Colorado**

WHERE ARE MY KEYS?® listed as a book that helps inspire and guide!
Chicago Tribune

"Your seminar on remembering with LOVE was wonderful! I now use your system daily and have found it truly easy to remember. I would highly recommend your seminar to others."
Caren Luke, The HallTree Manager, Muscatine, IA

"As a writer, my mission is to try to make sense of an increasingly complex and fast-paced world. Judy Marcus' LOVE memory training method is an appealing, simple and often whimsical way to clear away clutter and keep a sharp mind."
Brad Herzog, author of Small World and States of Mind

". . . participants experienced their power to actually use the tools Judy Marcus gave them to retain and recall at will."
Judi Geake, Director,
The Women's Exchange, Winnetka, Illinois

"Judy Marcus taught me how to use her simple and creative aids in order to consciously remember a client's goals. Get ready to step into her easy ways to never forget. It's fun too!"
Nilda Carlo, Feng Shui Consultant

"Your methods are superb and of great value for business as well as personal purposes."
Mayer Stiebel, President, Samax Industries, Inc.

"Effervescent Judy passionately and dramatically shared her LOVE memory tool, and techniques for creating a stress-free functional memory environment — all applicable to completing daily tasks, to remembering names, and to mastering new learning experiences."
Judy Falk, Past President,
Highland Park Hadassah

"A lively and inviting collection of mnemonic devices, enhanced by strategies for supporting good brain and memory functioning. The concepts are easy to grasp and apply in a user-friendly method."

Rana Matteson, PhD, Former Instructor of Memory Development and Disorders, Northwestern University, Evanston, Illinois

"I loved having you on the air with us as a guest speaker. Come visit anytime!"

Anne Maxfield, The Steve Cochran Show, WGN Radio, Chicago, IL

"Upbeat . . . enjoyable . . . The easy-to-understand LOVE method Ms. Marcus teaches, along with the concepts of overstatement and visualization, made the training fun and valuable. It is my pleasure to recommend this training to any individual or group of any age seeking to improve, retain or regain memory function."

Joyce H. Davidoff, Project Coordinator, Ageless Health Initiative, Rio Grande Area Agency on Aging, El Paso, Texas

"As a pro-active measure to keep my good memory strong for the rest of my life, I attended Judy's program. Her tips and memory games are awesome. I now incorporate those tools into many aspects of my day, and I remember more details on a variety of levels. I'm also having fun in the process!"

Evey Horwich, Trade Show and Exposition Manager

"Judy Marcus' workshop based on her book **WHERE ARE MY KEYS?®** . . . was well received by all who participated. Judy has some wonderful concepts that all of us can use to recover our innate memory skills and to keep them from dissipating. She presents the workshop with humor and enthusiasm and I recommend her to all people everywhere. These are skills that we all can develop to keep our memories at the levels that they presently are, and improve them as well! And, most importantly, THEY WORK!!!"

Rev. Dean G. Van Wie, Minister, Unity Church, Moline, IL

"Judy's LOVE™ methods truly work for me. I LOVE having her for my mom in lots of ways . . . including using the fun, practical memory tools she taught to create my own strong memory aids.
— Thanks, Mother, I can do it myself!"

Felicia Marcus, Graduate Student,
Naropa University, Boulder, CO.

"Judy's materials are always fresh, insightful, and inspiring. People love her and her memory workshops. She's an awesome delight!"

Teri Hartman, Program Coordinator,
Parker Adult School

"This is a simple to read . . . easy to learn . . . and effective memory method."

Joyce Lerner, Graphic Designer

"My most frequent memory problem was I'd go to another area of the house to get something that I needed for the task at hand. Upon arriving, I had already forgotten what I came for. I'd have to go back to see what I was doing so that I'd know again what I needed. Now I take time to take a longer "**LOOK**" at the task and "**VISUALIZE**" the object I need. When I get there I can quickly find the needed object or ingredient. With the LOVE method there's no more not remembering what I went into another room to get."

Sarah Blumen, Chicago, IL

"This was one of the best programs we have ever had. Judy was awesome and we all had many laughs. I think we could all identify with not only losing our keys but walking into rooms and forgetting what we entered the room for, etc. Judy gave us a simple formula to remember — and it works!"

Betsy Skibinski
Women In Careers

WHERE ARE MY KEYS?®

Memory Training You'll Absolutely LOVE™
by
Judy Marcus , M.A.T., Memory Lady

The Love™ Method in Four Fun and Easy Steps
Plus other powerful strategies to improve your memory now,
keep your brain sharp for the rest of your life

Judy Marcus, Master Teacher · Memory Lady
Judy@memorylady.com
www.memorylady.com

Table of Contents

I.
LOVE TO REMEMBER
BRAIN TRAINING MADE FUN AND EASY

II.
PUT YOUR BEST FOOT FORWARD
BRAIN-FRIENDLY LIFESTYLE CHOICES

Dear Readers:

The outlook for brain longevity keeps getting better! Studies confirm what we can't help but notice for ourselves if we're lucky enough to be around energetic seniors with sharp minds: yes, our brains can continue to work for us throughout our lifetime, especially with training.

Wouldn't you LOVE to tap into this "fountain of mental youth"? The strategies set out in WHERE ARE MY KEYS?® take a fun approach to the very serious business of keeping your brain young.

So much of our forgetfulness is caused by thinking of one thing while attending to another. "I'm doing too much" has truly become a national epidemic. In this second edition, I have added a chapter on Over-Multi-Tasking so you can take an even closer look at how to focus on what you choose to remember.

Life's more fun when you can trust your brain to remember, upon demand. So please do give yourself the gift of brain assurance. I invite you to jump on the brain wagon and join the thousands of people of all ages who have fun as they remember with LOVE™. You'll be glad you did!

Judy Marcus,
Memory Lady

This book is dedicated to my parents Florence and Sam,
and to my sisters-in-heart Leila and Barbara.
Their inspirations accompany me always.

Introduction

From coast-to-coast, when people hear that I teach **WHERE ARE MY KEYS?®**, a "how to remember better" workshop, the overwhelming response is, "Sign me up!"

When they hear of my book, they immediately say, "I need one!" And they're glad they did . . .

People yearn for the control we once had over our memory.

Just look at our national lifestyle and it's easy to understand the growing "words on the tip-of-the-tongue" paralysis and the scatterbrain syndrome. We are a nation of high-functioning multi-taskers. Our minds are overburdened by data overload, information bombardment, and the chaos of world events — in addition to the challenges of everyday living.

It's frustrating, embarrassing and scary to not be able to recall upon demand. And with the longevity revolution granting us bonus decades, the 76 million plus boomers, are not the only generation demanding quality of life — quality that is useless if the brain fails us.

Even twenty and thirty year olds complain about trouble remembering as they struggle to name the book they finished only yesterday. And they worry about misplaced keys.

Modern, over-busy America lives in fear of evaporating brain cells.

WHERE ARE MY KEYS?® offers positive action and success! In friendly, easy-to-understand terms, **WHERE ARE MY KEYS?®** will motivate you to jump on the brain-wagon — and join the growing multitudes that have fun learning proactive measures to keep their mind razor-sharp.

A good memory gives people of any age a sense of well-being. Just like people who exercise and eat well look and feel better, people who take active steps to use and improve their memory skills lead more fulfilling lives.

If I sound like a cheerleader for the Memory Squad, well, I am. Here in these pages is a fun approach to the serious task of remaining mentally vital for the rest of your life.

I invite you to have fun as you build a great memory! Play along with The **LOVE** Method. It's an outlandishly memorable strategy in four (4) fun and easy-to-follow steps. **WHERE ARE MY KEYS?®, Memory Training You'll Absolutely LOVE™** is divided into two sections.

The first, LOVE TO REMEMBER, gives you creative, fun and easy-to-use memory techniques, like how not to have to slink away and hide from someone because you can't remember his or her name.

The second, PUT YOUR BEST FOOT FORWARD, is full of those oh-so-important brain-friendly lifestyle choices. Life works better when you free up your mental energy to let your brain perform to its max!

Even people who still have a great memory will benefit from learning the exercises in this book. Think of it as "brain assurance." Use it, so you don't lose it.

Keep your Brain Young — Starting Today — You'll be glad you did!

Memory
invisible glue
linking-together-all
particles of
experience.
— Judy Marcus

I

LOVE™ TO REMEMBER

BRAIN TRAINING MADE FUN AND EASY

ACT LOVE-STRUCK

The LOVE™ Method

This memory strategy truly works. It's fun, it's simple, and at the same time, in the back-burner of your brain, it performs complicated tasks that strengthen your ability to retain and recall upon demand what you want to remember.

It's effective!

· LOVE forces you to pay attention to what you want to remember.

· LOVE creates an unforgettable impact.

· LOVE makes you the gardener who consciously plants the memory in both the right and left hemispheres of your brain.
    · left side: language and logic;
    · right side: visualization and creativity.

· LOVE grows huge memory tabs so that you can access what you want to remember — fast.

LOVE (in Four easy steps)

Each letter in the word **LOVE** is the first letter of the four actions you need to take to plant a memory and keep that memory strong.

1. Look

2. Overstate

3. Visualize

4. Engrave

<u>L</u>OVE

1. **Look.**

Pay attention to what you want to remember.

The "L" in LOVE forces you to focus. If you don't look, you don't see. If you don't listen, you don't hear. If you don't see or hear, how can you possibly expect to recall?

Mission Impossible. I blindfold you and hand you five items. You quickly toss them into a bag. I close the bag before taking your blindfold off. Name the five items.

Easy Solution
Don't wear a blindfold. **Do** peek . . . stare . . . LOOK!

Mission Impossible. I tell you my name but you're so excited that I'm wearing the same outfit as your cousin Matilda that you don't hear the words I'm saying.

Easy Solution
Don't get lost in your own drama.

Do pay attention to what I'm saying . . .
Take a deep breath and . . . LISTEN!

L<u>O</u>VE

2. Overstate.

Make an outrageously big deal out of what you want to remember.

The "O" in LOVE is the circle around the memory that makes it stand out. If everything is the same and kind of blurs together, how can you count on the memory being distinct enough to not vanish the moment your attention shifts.

Don't let images fade into the woodwork: When fifty people are sitting in a crowded room, forty-nine of them wearing white shirts, you'll notice the person in red, especially if she is the only one waiving a black and yellow striped flag. And when you think about that crowd a week later, what do you think you'll remember?

Do be a drama queen or king. Dramatize each person, place or thing that you want to remember into an outrageous image. Make it silly; make it unlikely; make it bizarre. Include the senses: Does it look overgrown? Does it feel clammy? Prickly? Cold? Can you taste salt? Peppermint? Can you hear it ping? Thud? Echo? Is the smell fresh like sweet butter or stinky like last month's fish?

LO<u>V</u>E

3. **V**isualize.

See the overstated, outrageous image in your mind's eye.

The "V" in LO<u>V</u>E trains your mind to use both hemispheres of the brain: the left side, which processes language and logic; and the right side, which processes visualization and creativity.

Don't just think the words.

Do turn your words and ideas into an action film, and use the inside of your forehead as the movie screen. Actually visualize a short movie in your mind's eye.

You know the old adage, "A picture is worth a thousand words". When you apply the LOVE method, you've got the picture <u>and</u> the words!

LOV<u>E</u>

4. Engrave.

Repeat, Review, Rehearse, so you can Recall, upon demand.

The "E" in LOVE keeps the image — the overstated, outrageous visualization — fresh in your mind and easier to find.

Each time you see the image in your mind's eye, it's like coloring the image over and over with a magic marker, making the image lines thicker and darker and easier to see. It's like etching the image with a sharp point. Each time you trace the outline, you're engraving it deeper, thus making it more permanent.

Don't let the image fade away.

Do review the words and images **immediately**. Repeat (aloud or silently to yourself) in ten minutes, then every half hour, then every few hours, then every few days, and then weekly, and then monthly. How often you review depends on the specific memory and how long you need to hold it in your memory bank. Discard the shopping list as soon as you make the purchases. And engrave the phone number weekly, monthly, or as needed.

Engraving a memory in both brain hemispheres is like making an oversized multi-layered tab on a file folder. When you're looking for the file, it's much quicker and easier to find.

<u>LOVE</u>

That's it! Four easy steps! That's all you have to know to be a great LOVER. (At this point, because you **L**ook, **O**verstate, **V**isualize and **E**ngrave, you can rest assured that you'll **R**emember.)

* * * *

You won't forget
when you
make the time
to fall in LOVE with
what you want to remember.

Just take a deep breath, follow the four easy steps to **L-O-V-E**, and you'll rest assured that you can **R-emember**.

* * * *

Now that you know <u>how</u> to LOVE . . . you can apply the LOVE Method to anything and everything you choose to LOVE.

Read on . . .

LOVEr's Lane

Does this scene seem familiar? As you pull into the grocery parking lot, your mind is focused on getting home quickly to eat dinner so you can get to your bridge game. By the time you're at Aisle 6 tossing a box of fiber cereal into your shopping cart, you realize you don't know where your car is parked and your feet begin to ache just thinking of the upcoming search.

What can you do to avoid the frazzle of forgetting? Fall in **LOVE**™ with where you park your car. Here's how:

Look. As soon as you park, look at where your car sits in relation to the entrance to the grocery store. Then look at the nearest sign marker. For example, you may park in an area designated 2-North.
Listen to yourself say it out loud: "Two-North."

Overstate. Create an outrageous image to associate with your parking space. How about an image of two giant north winds with faces blowing directly on your car?

Visualize. Now that you've created this outrageously overstated image, don't just think the words. Actually visualize a short movie in your mind's eye. Watch the two winds with puffy cheeks blow on you as you leave your car. Feel the refreshing cold wind tickling your skin?

Engrave. Feel the two cold north winds blowing at your back as you're in the store pushing your cart through the produce section. Repeat this image every twenty minutes to engrave it in your mind.

When you leave the store, no matter how crowded the parking lot, you'll easily head straight to your car!

<u>Your</u> Turn

Now, take a deep breath and try these four easy **LOVE** steps for yourself.

Can you LOVE where you put your checkbook?

Your glasses?

Your keys?

If, while reading this section, you're surprised to find you cannot remember where you've put those items, take a deep breath, retrace your steps, and once you find the objects, **Fall in LOVE**.

Be a LOVE Machine. (You wouldn't want to remember **everything**. It would crowd your mind. Save the time to fall in LOVE with what you **choose** to remember.)

Here's three more things (objects of my affection) I can LOVE to remember:

1.

2.

3.

NOTES

CREATE LOVE HANDLES
(Pegs that help you hang onto what you want to remember)

AAA, OOH: Acronyms, Acrostics, And Other Handy Helpers

A *mnemonic (pronounced "knee-mon-ick") device — acts as a peg-board, or ladder, or series of handles to help you remember better. Words or ideas you want to recall pop right into your awareness, upon demand, when you treat them with LOVE. That's why I call mnemonic devices "LOVE Handles".

Mnemonic is a Greek word that means "an aid to memory." It's a hard word to pronounce. So, I LOVE, to remember how to say it.

Look: First I break it into phonic sounds.
                * (Knee-mon-icKs).

Overstate: Next, I create an outlandish image.
                I picture a harmonica playing on my knee.

Visualize: I see on the movie screen inside my forehead, a face on my knee, with the lips playing a harmonica, which is hovering at knee height.

Engrave: I rerun the movie from time to time,
                and every time I think of the word "mnemonic."

There are many word and idea clues you can use as reminders. Once you understand how they work, you can make up your own. Here are some of my favorites. Write or email me yours. (You'll find my address at the back of this book.)

Acronyms and Acrostics.

They tell you two things:

1. The first letter and sound of the item you want to remember.

2. How many items you want to track.

Acronym

An acronym is a word where each letter in the word stands for the first letter in another word. Together the words make a list of what you want to remember.

> MADD: <u>M</u>others <u>A</u>gainst <u>D</u>runk <u>D</u>riving
> SCUBA: <u>S</u>elf-<u>C</u>ontained <u>U</u>nderwater <u>B</u>reathing <u>A</u>pparatus
> ROY G. BIV: <u>R</u>ed, <u>O</u>range, <u>Y</u>ellow, <u>G</u>reen, <u>B</u>lue, <u>I</u>ndigo, <u>V</u>iolet
>   (colors of the rainbow)
> HOMES: <u>H</u>uron, <u>O</u>ntario, <u>M</u>ichigan, <u>E</u>rie and <u>S</u>uperior
>   (the five Great Lakes)
> LOVE: <u>L</u>ook, <u>O</u>verstate, <u>V</u>isualize, <u>E</u>ngrave

(the four actions to plant a memory and keep that memory strong)

Acrostic

An acrostic is a group of words that make up a phrase or a sentence. The first letter of each word in the acrostic reminds you of what you want to remember.

> EGBDF: <u>E</u>very <u>G</u>ood <u>B</u>oy <u>D</u>oes <u>F</u>ine
>   And, the current version:
>   <u>E</u>mpty <u>G</u>arbage <u>B</u>efore <u>D</u>ad <u>F</u>lips
>   (in music, Spaces on the G staff)

Other Handy Helpers

There's a memory solution for every kind of confusion.

The words acronym and acrostic do similar functions. Sometimes people get confused as to which is which. Here's how I keep them straight:

Acronym: The <u>nym</u> in acronym reminds me of <u>name</u>. A name is one word, ie LOVE.

Acrostic: The <u>st c</u> in acrostic reminds me of a <u>sentence</u>, ie Every Good Boy Does Fine.

Spelling Reminders: Here's some helpful hints to remember the spelling of words that sound alike but look different.

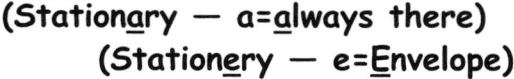

(Stationary — a=<u>a</u>lways there)
(Stationery — e=<u>E</u>nvelope)

Principle —
Something you
stand for

Principal —
He's my pal

Rhyme, Rhythm, LOVEsongs

Words set to poetry and music are easier to remember.

In 1492, Columbus sailed the ocean blue.

Thirty days hath September, April, June and November....

Driving Directions: In Chicago, the Kennedy Expressway veers off into two different directions: Highway 290 and Highway 90/94. Driving west one-half-hour out of my way, and then another half-hour back east to where I started was a big waste of my time. Once was enough for me. To make certain I never repeat that mistake, I've made up a rhythmic poem to keep me on the right road.

"N.O. to 2.9.0.
I'm for 94."

Area Codes: My daughter used to live in Alaska, area code 907. Now she lives in Colorado, area code 970. To keep them straight in our minds, we made up a rhyme:

"9.7.0. — Color-a-do."

Don't forget to send me <u>your</u> favorite LOVE Handles!

www.memorylady.com or judy@memorylady.com

The Fantasy Wardrobe

The Fantasy Wardrobe is a clothesline that becomes a valuable LOVE Handle. The items on this list are the pegs onto which you will attach other items you want to remember.

Read on. This will all become perfectly clear in a few minutes

This Fantasy Wardrobe never goes out of style. Once you LOVE the items on this clothesline, you'll never have to replace any of them. And if you keep LOVEing them, they will always be ready for you to wear.

Wash and Wear. You'll use this Fantasy Wardrobe over and over. **Really get to know this LOVE Handle Clothesline of pegs.** Each handle on this clothesline is a place-holder that allows you to remember all kinds of lists.

Once you no longer need to remember the items you attach, you simply wash them off and your Fantasy Wardrobe is ready to wear when you next need it as a memory device.

Here's your clothesline:

Let's have a little fun as you learn this list.   Play along:

FANTASY WARDROBE
No matter how you're **really** dressed, carry this list of imaginary clothes with you always:

Clothesline
Shoes
Pants
Belt
Shirt
Cufflinks
Collar
Necklace or Neck Tie
Earmuffs
Hat
Gloves

> Clothesline
> Shoes, Pants, Belt, Shirt, Cuff links, Collar, Necklace or Neck tie, Earmuffs, Hat, Gloves

Let's LOVE the clothesline.

Begin LOVEing the shoes.

Look at the word: **Shoes**

Overstate: Shoes. Big. Cumbersome. My feet are swimming in them. Flip, flop, the big red and yellow striped shoes make noise as I wiggle my toes in them. Tap the heels of your red and yellow striped shoes. Stomp the floor. Do your shoes stay on or fall off?

Visualize: Make these shoes come alive. See them in your mind's eye. On the movie screen on the inside of your forehead, run the action of the oversized red and yellow striped floppy shoes.

Engrave: Do it again. Actually wiggle your toes. Shake your sole from side to side. Repeat in your mind's eye, all the action in the LOVE your shoe movie. Run it in your head again, even describe the action aloud as you pound and wiggle your feet in your imaginary shoes.

Got the picture? Good. Let's move on to the next item.

Look: Pants

Overstate: Can you step right into your scratchy mohair pants? Are the legs wide enough, or do you have to take off the big red and yellow striped shoes first?

Visualize: You know the routine. Run the movie in your head. Actually see yourself take off the shoes and step into the scratchy mohair brown pants with the white polka dots. One leg at a time. Yuk. Sure does put goose bumps on your skin.

Engrave: Again. Run the movie in your inner forehead screen.

Got it? Good.

Look: **Belt**

Overstate: As you run the brown belt through the belt loops, the huge buckle gets caught on each loop and you have to tug it through. Oh-oh. The belt is all the way through the loops of the pants and it's just a little short of buckling. Perhaps all you need to do is take a deep breath and suck up your waist another inch and you're there. Ahhhh, the clasp clicked. Just don't bend down to look at your red and yellow striped shoes or the belt might burst.

Visualize: You know the routine. Actually see in your mind's eye the brown belt getting caught on the loops. Run the movie in your inner forehead screen.

Engrave: Again. Run the movie in your inner forehead screen.

Quick review. What are the first three items on your list? Amazing, isn't it, how quickly you can learn, and you haven't even written anything down!

Let's move on to the next item.

Look: Shirt

Overstate: This isn't just any old shirt. This bright purple shirt is the softest, thickest velvet material you ever felt. Problem is, it's too warm and you're sweating. Your underarms are actually growing dark circles in the sleeve pits. If you keep your arms close to your side, it won't show.

Visualize: You know the routine. Actually see in your mind's eye, the dark circles in the sleeve pits of your soft, thick velvet, bright purple shirt. Run the movie in your inner forehead screen.

Engrave. Again. Run the movie in your inner forehead screen.

You're getting good at this routine!

Look: Cuff Links

Overstate: How can these solid rhinestone cuff links fit through a too small slot? Push a lot harder. Harder. Harder. There. The point of your links finally pushed through the hole. Whew! That was a chore.

Visualize: You know the routine. Actually see in your mind's eye, the point of your solid rhinestone cuff links poking and poking and poking and finally pushing through the too small slot of the soft, thick velvet, bright purple shirt. Run the movie in your inner forehead screen.

Engrave: Again. Run the movie in your inner forehead screen.

Now for the collar.

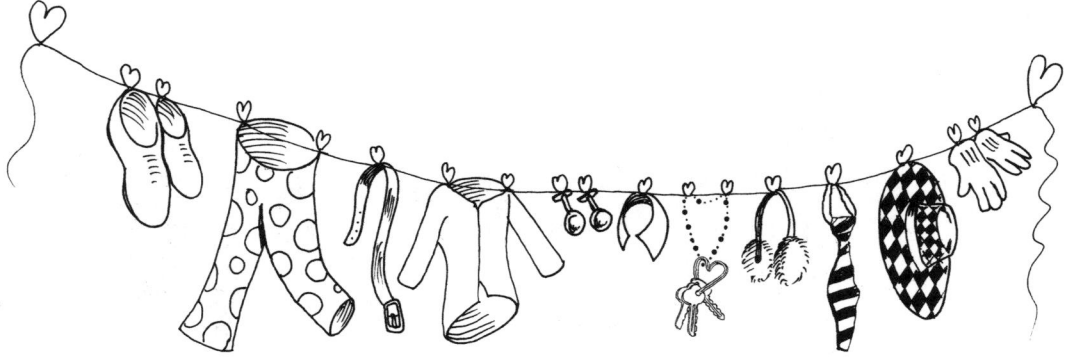

Look: Collar

Overstate: What kind of collar would you choose to go with a purple velvet shirt and cuff links? The bright white stiff starched collar looks great, but it sure is hard to fold down to rest nicely. It keeps popping up and hitting you in the neck. Lay still, you silly collar. Pop! Lay still.

Visualize: You know the routine. Actually see in your mind's eye, the bright white stiff starched collar. Is it laying flat yet?

Engrave: Again. Run the movie in your inner forehead screen.

Gender determines the next item of your Love Handle Clothesline.

Oh-oh!

Gal Look: Necklace

Overstate: Make it a LOVE necklace with a pretty heart and key. What a great method to remember where I put my keys! Will it jingle when I walk? How's the clasp? Easy to put on? It' so pretty!!! I just LOVE my necklace.

Guy Look: Neck tie

Humm...

Overstate: Picture the neck tie clashing with your shirt. How embarrassing to have extra wide stripes on the tie conflicting with circles and squares on the shirt.

Visualize: You know the routine. Actually see in your mind's eye, the necklace, or the extra wide patterned tie. Color it turquoise and red. Run the movie in your inner forehead screen.

Engrave: Again. Run the movie in your inner forehead screen.

Three left to learn. Back to the clothesline.

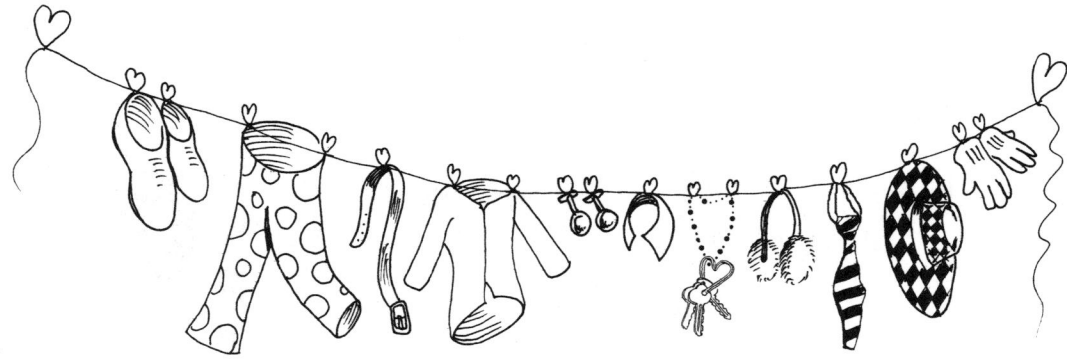

Look: Earmuffs

Overstate: Put on these huge orange plastic earmuffs, one on each ear, linked together by a barbed wire that will keep the earmuffs from sliding down your hair. Isn't this a clever invention? Put them on carefully, or you know what will happen . . . .

Visualize: You know the routine. Actually see in your mind's eye, how carefully you put on the huge orange plastic earmuffs. Don't they go well with your outfit?

Engrave: Again. You might even touch your ears as you run the movie in your inner forehead screen. See yourself in your entire outfit: The red and yellow striped shoes. The brown pants with the white polka dots. The brown belt. The soft purple velvet shirt. The too big solid rhinestone cuff links. The bright white stiffly starched collar that doesn't want to stay down. The heart and key necklace or the widely striped neck tie. The huge orange plastic earmuffs that go well with your outfit.

Great goings! You look so snazzy. Next.

Look: Hat

Overstate: A purple and white checkerboard hat with a bright orange pompom sitting right on the top of your head. What color will you choose for the tie strings?

Visualize: You know the routine. Actually see in your mind's eye, how the purple and white checkerboard hat with the bright orange pompom sits on your head. Is it smack-dab on the top or off to one side?   Feel how well dressed you are as you tie the double knot.

Engrave: See it in your mind's eye. Run the movie in your inner forehead screen.

No outfit is complete without the last item . . .

Look: **Gloves**

Overstate: Gee. These grass green rubber gloves feel like they're glued shut. Rub them in your hands and then, blow into the right glove like it is a balloon. There you go. Now it's ready for your fingers and thumb. Smooth it on and then blow up the left glove. Put it on. Now that's a fit. Ahhh.

Visualize: Again, the routine. Actually see in your mind's eye, how you rub the grass green rubber gloves together in your hands. Feel your cheeks puff up and your diaphragm tighten, as, one at a time, you blow the gloves up like balloons. Actually hear the whoosh of air going into the grass green gloves. Notice how easily each finger works into its appropriate slot.

Engrave: See it in your mind's eye. Run the movie in your inner forehead screen.

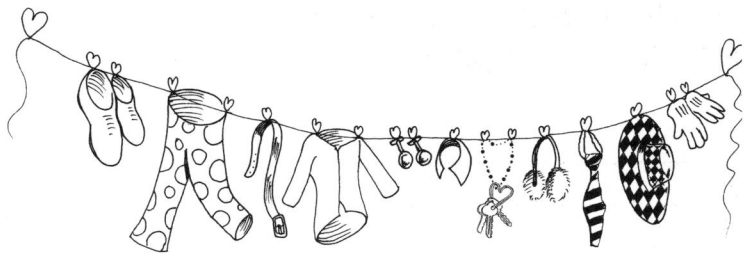

Look at you! You sure are a sight for sore eyes! Don't you just **LOVE** wearing your LOVE-Handle Fantasy Wardrobe?!?!?

Now, are you ready to look in the mind's mirror to check out how well you remember your LOVEly outfit?

Turn over this book and see how many of the LOVE Handles you can name?

Most likely, you remembered them all. If you missed any, that's okay. That just means you didn't love them enough. Take a good Look. Overstate even more. Visualize and then Engrave in your mind's eye. Try it again.

Really get to know this LOVE Handle Clothesline. It's important. Each handle on this clothesline is a placeholder that allows you to remember all kinds of lists.

LOVE-Handle Clothesline:
(fill in the blanks)

1. _____
2. _____
3. _____
4. _____
5. _____
6._____
7. _____
8._____
9. _____
10. _____

As soon as you know all ten of the clothesline handles from the top down, from the bottom up, you're ready for the next phase — MATCHMAKER.

MATCHMAKER. I call this the matchmaker because now we're going to use the Fantasy Wardrobe clothesline LOVE Handles as place-holders to remember a shopping list.

You're going to LOVE this list!

Match and Attach

MATCH AND ATTACH lets you quickly remember any shopping list. It's handy in emergencies when you're without pencil and paper. It's also fun to do, and it certainly keeps your brain sharp.

Now that you've learned the clothesline LOVE Handle, you're ready to make unforgettable matches — with you in charge of how long you remember each item.

Here's a new list we're going to play with. This list is temporary. We're going to LOVE it, and then, when we no longer need it, we're going to allow ourselves to be fickle and leave it.

So — let's go shopping — or should I say matchmaking?

Shopping list:
Eyeglasses
Bread
Oranges
Cookies
Watermelon
Eggs
Spinach
Hamburgers
Cucumbers
Radishes

Let's have some fun as we LOVE our shopping list and, at the same time match and attach it to our Clothesline Fantasy Wardrobe LOVE Handle.

Look: **Eyeglasses**

Link to LOVE Handle: **Shoes**

Overstate: By now, you've got-
ten the hang of how this system
works. You might be ready to pick
an exaggeration of your own. I'm
going to give you suggestions.
Chose whichever seems most memorable to you. Whether you use
your own creation, or go with one
suggested here, the important
thing is you take the time to
actively involve yourself in the process, and that you actually see it in
your mind's eye.

Don't your feet need to see where they're going? Place your eyeglasses on your red and yellow striped shoes. Where are the lenses?
On top of your feet or on the bottom of your soles? Are the ear
stems wrapped around your ankles to keep the eyeglasses on?

Visualize: See in your mind's eye how carefully you attach the eyeglasses to your shoes. Run the movie in your inner forehead of how
much clearer your toes see through the eyeglasses.

Engrave: Repeat the movie.

Look: **Bread**

Link to LOVE Handle: **Pants**

Overstate: Are you slipping each brown polka dotted pants leg into its own bread bag, or are both legs sharing a loaf?

Visualize: See in your mind's eye how the slices of rye bread mingle with the polka dots to create unusual curlicues. Are the crumbs falling into your pants cuffs? Can you hear the crinkle of the bread's plastic wrapper? What holds the bread wrapper on the pants leg? A giant bread wrapper tie, of course.

Engrave: Repeat the movie.

Look: **Oranges**

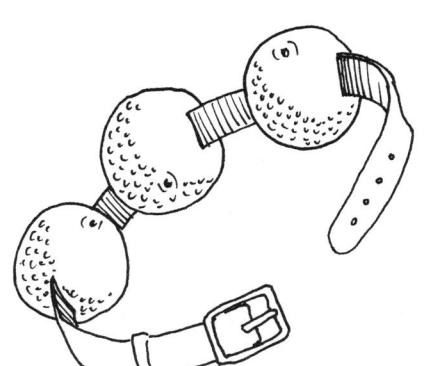

Link to LOVE Handle: **Belt**

Overstate: String a chain of oranges by running your belt through them, and then put them through each belt loophole so they can hold up your pants.

Visualize: See in your mind's eye the actual work of pushing the belt through each round orange, and then focus the movie camera on how much energy you expend in pushing the orange through each belt loophole. Does any orange juice squirt out and run down your pants leg into the bread bag, or fall to the floor, smudging your eyeglasses on your shoes?

Engrave: Again. Replay the scene in your mind's eye.

Look: **Cookies**

Link to LOVE Handle: **Shirt**

Overstate: How are you going to attach the cookies to your purple velvet shirt? Use them as buttons, of course. Sew the chocolate marshmallow cookies with graham cracker bottoms opposite from each button hole. Do you have to enlarge the hole to get the cookie through? Lick the excess chocolate off your fingers so you don't get chocolate from the cookies on the purple velvet shirt.

Visualize: See the scene in your mind's eye.

Engrave: Repeat the scene on the movie screen in the inside of your forehead.

Look: **Watermelon**

Link to LOVE Handle: **Cuff links**

Overstate: Cut two chunks of red watermelon into squares and squish them onto your rhinestone cuff links. Aren't they colorful? What about the black watermelon seeds? Did the cuff links flick out a few? Where did they land?

Visualize: See the scene in your mind's eye.

Engrave: Repeat the scene on the movie screen in the inside of your forehead.

Look: **Eggs**

Link to LOVE Handle: **Collar**

Overstate: Don't the eggs fit perfectly into the ridges of the starchy stiff bright white collar? The white of the eggs blends right into the white of the collar. Except, of course, the yellow seeping onto the collar because one of the yolks cracked. Yuck. What a mess.

Visualize: See the scene in your mind's eye.

Engrave: Repeat the scene on the movie screen in the inside of your forehead.

Look: **Spinach**

Link to LOVE Handle: **Necklace** <u>or</u> **Neck tie** (I guess you can wear both, if you like.)

Overstate: The Necklace and/or Neck tie are on the outside of your clothing, so it will be pretty easy to wrap the green spinach around the neckwear, or even braid it into a spinach badge of honor. If the egg from your collar drips down to the spinach, you have the beginnings of spinach soufflé.

Visualize: See the scene in your mind's eye.

Engrave: Repeat the scene on the movie screen in the inside of your forehead.

Look: Hamburger

Link to LOVE Handle: Earmuffs

Overstate: How perfect to fit the round brown hamburgers right onto the round orange earmuffs. Can you use glue? Perhaps you're better off putting the hamburgers under the barbed wire comb holding the earmuffs onto your hair. Ouch. Handle the earmuffs carefully.

Visualize: See the scene in your mind's eye.

Engrave: Repeat the scene on the movie screen in the inside of your forehead.

Look: Cucumber

Link to LOVE Handle: Hat

Overstate: If you cut the cucumber into circles, you can play checkers on your purple and white checkered hat. Just ignore the orange pompom in the middle of the hat. It won't get in the way. Better yet, use the green cucumber peel as ribbon to stick in the pompom. Is this recycling at its finest?

Visualize: See the scene in your mind's eye.

Engrave: Repeat the scene on the movie screen in the inside of your forehead.

Look: **Radishes**

Link to LOVE Handle: **Gloves**

Overstate: Red radishes in clusters. How about pinning the radish clusters like a corsage to your green grass gloves. Red radishes and green grass gloves. Hmmmm. Wave your hands in circles and you'll look like a Christmas wreath.

Visualize: See the scene in your mind's eye.

Engrave: Repeat the scene on the movie screen in the inside of your forehead.

That's it. You've got a match made in your imagination. And if you repeat the scenes from time to time, running the movie in your mind's eye, you'll remember all the way to the store.

The love handles will tweak a reminder of your shopping list. And when you no longer need to remember the shopping list, you'll just drop it from your awareness.

What you want to remember long term is the **Fantasy Wardrobe Clothesline Love Handle.** How do you keep this memory alive? Just review it daily until you know it well enough to review it weekly, or more often if you need to. It's a handy memory device.

Use it! And you won't lose it!

Wait a minute!

Time Out!

Take a deep breath!

A big chunk of time and space in this book is devoted to the Fantasy Wardrobe. That's because it falls out-of-your-ordinary everyday experiences. It takes a little explaining. And it takes a little time to make it your own. But once you get it — it will make your mental life easier.

I believe the benefits you reap make it well worth any time you invest in making the Fantasy Wardrobe part of your everyday life.

In fact these imaginary clothes might become the most favorite clothes in your wardrobe!

Use the Match and Attach as a practical tool for those times when you're in a crunch and you just have to attach a "mental sticky note" to yourself — somewhere. . . .

Think of Velcro on each piece of clothing. And matching Velcro on each item you're going to Match and Attach.

Try using this amazing LOVE-Handle when something just pops into your mind. It works! All it takes is one time — and you're hooked!

> You know how you go from the kitchen to the bedroom to get something, but can't remember what? The thought completely evaporated . . .
>
> Next time you're standing at the kitchen sink (or wherever) and it pops into your head that you need the scissors in your nightstand drawer — immediately — before you do anything else — mentally stab the scissors on your fantasy shoe (remember, this is only a visualization in your mind's eye, you don't actually stab anything on your real shoe).

Because you make a time-out to listen to what you're thinking . . . because you're making such a huge OVERSTATEMENT about the scissors you need to get . . . because you're visualizing in your mind's eye the scissors stabbing your shoe . . . you'll hold onto that thought/image . . . and you'll be able to recall it upon demand as you get to your bedroom nightstand!

Know Your LOVE Spots
(Location, Location, Location)

The Fantasy Wardrobe is actually a memory device based on a fixed location. Perhaps it will help you to know that this is a recycled and updated version of a memory device used by ancient Greeks.

About 500 BCE, the poet and orator Simonides was at a banquet. He was called outside to speak with some visitors. While standing outside, the building collapsed, crushing — beyond recognition — all those inside.

Those were the days before dental records and DNA testing. However, Simonides was able to identify each of the bodies because he was able to see in his mind's eye the banquet table before the accident, and was thus able to visualize who was sitting where. By "walking his mind" around the table, he named each of the persons by their LOCATION!

You, too, can recreate any list you LOVE.

Even a speech can be remembered this way. Merely break down the parts and visually attach each part to a location. Then, when your mind roams around the location in logical order, you'll have your speech parts as well. Try it — and engrave by practice!

On the following pages you'll find two more location LOVE Handles. Use these fun and creative devices to establish a "fixed location" on which to "match and attach" things you want to remember.

Once you get the hang of it — you'll be creating LOVE Handle locations of your own. I'd love to hear your story — and how it worked for you. Go to **www.MemoryLady.com** or **Judy@memorylady.com**.

Roam Around the LOVE Nest

Here's another LOVE Handle. Create a LOVE nest of any room or series of rooms in your house.

For example:
Take a mental walk around your bedroom. Pick out 10 key places.

<u>Mine</u>:

Doorway

Mirror

Nightstand

Headboard

Bed

Closet

Lamp

Dressing table

Window

Television

<u>Yours</u>:
1.
2.
3.
4.
5.
6.
7.
8.
9.
10.

Learn **your** 10 locations — In the order they appear as you walk around **your** bedroom.

(Groups of ten work well because we're accustomed to counting in decimals and they're easy to keep track of. However, if you need to create a group of 12 — or whatever the number — go ahead.)

Meanwhile, put on the music and get ready to dance . . .

I'm going to pick a dance partner to help me LOVE my 10 LOVE nest locations. <u>Read along to see my pattern, and then create your own fantasy to actually learn your 10 LOVE nest locations.</u>

Location LOVE Story

Ginger Rogers, John Travolta and Michael Jackson appear outside my doorway and hold out their hands to dance. I choose one. (You decide which one, since you're going to visualize along with me.) Taking his or her hand, we waltz, strut or moonwalk into the **Doorway.** I peek at the **Mirror** to see how great we look together. Wow! He lifts me onto the **Nightstand.** We jump onto the **Headboard** and sum- 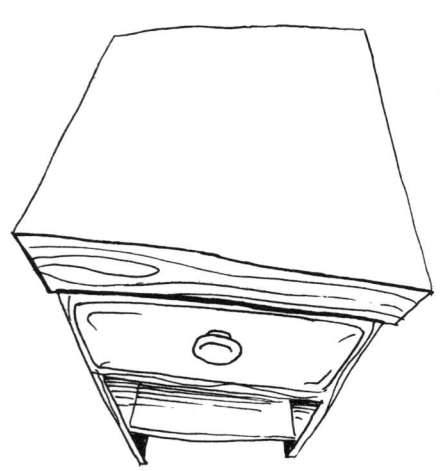 mersault onto the **Bed,** and then, land- ing upright on the floor, we dance halfway into the **Closet** doorway, pause, and abruptly turn back into the room. Twirling past the **Lamp,** it lights up automatically as if to say hurrah! We pause at the **Dressing table** where I apply fresh lipstick and he combs his hair. We then look out the **Window** to wave at all the watching neighbors, and then saunter past the **Television** and guess who's on the screen? It's me and my dance partner. We've been videotaped. Great!

I can even run the tape backwards, starting with the Television. Try it!

I've already **L**ooked at what I want to learn, **O**verstated, and **V**isualized it in my mind's eye. Now I can do the fourth step of **LOVE:** **E**ngrave by replaying the scene in my mind's eye from time to time.

Your Bedroom LOVE handle locations never change. What you Match and Attach can fade away once you no longer need to remember the items.

Your Match and Attach list can be anything you need to remember, i.e.:

- Things to Do
- Items to pack
- People to call

This technique can be applied to any room or area familiar to you. Create as many LOVE handle locations as you wish, and use them to link together as many items as you wish. For example, if you want to remember 20 items, link two LOVE handle locations together, and Use them to Match and Attach the 20 items. Your links are limitless!

<u>Your</u> Turn

Your trouble spots?

_____

_____

_____

_____

Your mnemonic solutions?

_____

_____

_____

_____

Review your Fantasy Wardrobe.

1._____

2._____

3._____

4._____

5._____

6._____

7._____

8._____

9._____

10._____

Match and Attach Your Shopping List

Your Location LOVE Story: Pick your own dance partner to help you LOVE your 10 LOVE nest locations.

1._____

2._____

3._____

4._____

5._____

6._____

7._____

8._____

9._____

10._____

NOTES

FALL IN LOVE WITH
THE PEOPLE YOU MEET

Catch the Name, Attach the Face

Most people are "hit and run" when it comes to names. Do you find your mind wanders as you're being introduced, paying attention to what you need to tell that person, or you're thinking that they look like Aunt Sally who you need to talk to about . . .?

Instead, apply the LOVE™ Method. Here's how you fall in **LOVE** with a new friend:

Meet **Arthur Goldstein.**

Take a deep breath — and smile!

Look and Listen: Look at Arthur's face as you Listen to his name. Say his name out loud: "Arthur Goldstein. Nice to meet you."

(By repeating his name, you make certain that you've heard it correctly. If you haven't heard, ask, "How do you spell your name?" Or say, "I didn't catch that. Tell me again.")

Overstate: Be creative. Arthur, as in King Arthur, head of the roundtable — and Goldstein, as in a large stein of beer made out of gold. (You can say this aloud to Arthur, or just think it to yourself.)

Visualize: Don't just think the words. Actually visualize a short movie in your mind's eye. See Arthur's face, blue eyes, bushy eyebrows, and high cheekbones, peering out of his suit of armor. What's he doing as he sits at the roundtable? Of course, he's drinking from his gold stein!

Engrave: Reflect how strong his muscles must be for him to lift the heavy gold stein while wearing his King Arthur's suit of heavy armor. Repeat this strong visual image every 15 minutes during the party. Then, review the image as you drive home. You might want to write this description on an index card. Review the cards in your file from time-to-time.

Helpful hint: You don't have to recreate the wheel. For every Arthur you meet, imagine this new Arthur's face in a helmet wearing a suit of armor.

Variations on the theme: Goldstein has two components: Gold and Stein. To remember Goldman, picture a man made of gold. For Goldberg, picture a gold ice berg. For Steinberg, picture a stein sitting atop an iceberg. Get the picture?

Now You Try it. Take a deep breath, and follow all the steps to Fall in **LOVE** with . . .

Eleanor Fox.

Quick. Put your hand over the next few paragraphs. Take a few minutes to visualize her name. There's no right or wrong way. Whatever works for you, use it.

If you have an Aunt Eleanor, you might imagine her sitting on Eleanor Fox's shoulders. If not, be creative.

Eleanor isn't as difficult as it first appears. The name just needs a breakdown into recognizable, picturable, parts.

Envision a huge letter "L" with oars sticking through it and this lovely woman who you just met sitting at the top of the "L," rowing the oars. What's chasing her? A fox, of course. Just picture a fox (outrageously exaggerated, of course, like tall as a two story building, swishing its tail). Notice the color of the spots on Eleanor's cheeks as she frantically rows her boat. Is her hair flying in the wind?

Run the movie in your mind's eye. Engrave by repeating the image from time to time.

If Eleanor Fox is someone you're only going to see during the week's resort vacation, you can stop reviewing her name and face once your trip is over.

On the other hand, if you plan to meet Eleanor next year, same time, same place, you might take a photo. Place a caption under her picture describing the outrageous visualization you created and played in your mind's eye. Then, before you reconvene, you merely recall and review the picture and the image. When you see **Eleanor Fox** again, you'll WOW her with how memorable she is — and how well you remembered her name!

F.A.Q.: "But how can I remember everyone's name if I'm introduced to six people at one time?" is one of the most frequent questions I'm asked about introductions. It's akin to "How can I get to play at Carnegie Hall?"

The answer to both questions is: practice. You don't build a muscle the first time you lift a weight, but if you keep lifting the weight, the muscle will appear.

Start with one name, and work your way up. Go off to the side to review, at first each name, then every few names. Before you know it, you will be successfully remembering the people as you work the crowd.

Party Ice-Breakers

Here's a great icebreaker and memory enhancer. While you're in training, tell the next new group of people you meet that you're reading a memory book (ahem: be sure to mention **WHERE ARE MY KEYS?® Memory Training You'll Absolutely LOVE™**). Say you would LOVE to share your new method. Then you can all work together on learning the names and faces, and have fun in the process.

I'd love to hear your story — and how it worked for you. Go to **www.MemoryLady.com** or **Judy@memorylady.com**.

Have Fun at the Movies

Movies are a great time to practice Falling in LOVE.

Pick a character and mentally remember his or her name. **LOVE** that name, just as you would a new friend. When you're confident that you know that name, pick another character to **LOVE**. By building characters, you're also building your name remembering skills.

Have fun. Make it a game.

As you walk out of the movie theatre, talk with the people around you about the plot and the characters. You'll find that you'll remember more details, and you'll have richer, more enjoyable movie discussions with your friends.

Remember to LOVE the name of the movie, as well!

Leo Di Caprio was great as Jack the rogue. At first I thought that he looked too immature to play opposite the sophisti-cated Kate Winslet, but then, I began to understand how his Jack and her Rose could be attracted to each other. They were each trying to flee from the people they were with on the Titanic . . .

<u>Your</u> Turn

Fall In Love With Your Friends.   Be prepared for any occasion.
Start with the names you encounter. Make a list of your friends.
Get familiar with an image for each name. Remember, you don't have
to recreate the wheel. One image per name; if you know two Carols,
think of the same image for both of them. May I suggest an image
of each Carol's face with Xmas carolers standing on her cheeks and
singing. Of course, pick an image that works for you.

1._____   6._____

2._____   7._____

3._____   8._____

4._____   9._____

5._____   10._____

When you've mastered these names, you're ready for more.

Movies and books.
Same drill as above.

Title_____

Key characters_____

Plot_____

_____

_____

_____

Title_____

Key ideas_____

Plot_____

_____

_____

TURN NUMBERS
INTO LOVE WORDS

Whisper Sweet Numbers Into My Ear

My husband the accountant deals with numbers all day long. For him, numbers have meaning, so for him, all he has to do is hear a set of numbers and they stay in his mind.

The rest of us have to be creative when it comes to remembering numbers. Here are some fun approaches to turn numbers into friends. Look these methods over, play with them, and see what works for you. I tend to use them all, depending on the circum-stances. Let me know your preferences, and if these ideas lead to a new strategy for you:

Chunk. It's easier to remember four numbers than nine. A popular strategy is to break numbers into chunks:

Instead of: 123456789   =   Chunk to: 12 345 67 89

Make numbers memorable. Words with meaning are easier to remember than plain numbers. Here are some strategies to give numbers meaning.

Turn numbers into recognizable ideas
98.6 = normal temperature
32 = freezing
12 = dozen
76 = 76 trombones, a song from <u>The Music Man</u>

Read on . . .

Turn numbers into recognizable dates
14 = Valentine's Day
1225 = 12/25 = Christmas
1776 = the year the Declaration of Independence was signed
12741 = 12/7/41 = Pearl Harbor Day
101965 = 10/19/65 = your brother's birthday

Create meaning for numbers with no apparent meaning
Here's where you become creative.

552542577351614365 — This is TOO LONG to remember.

Let's break the 18 digit number into meaningful chunks.
      55-25-4257-735-1614-365

      55 = highway speed limit
      25 = a quarter ($0.25)
      4257 = $42.57
      735 = 7:35 p.m. — time
      1614 = my first address
      365= days in the year

Next, we'll make up a number's LOVE story. Remember to visualize the action, see it in your mind's eye, run every detail on the movie screen on the inside of your forehead:

I was driving down the highway at the speed limit, **55**, I can see it in my mind's eye, when I stopped at a toll booth. The sign blinked on and off: $0.**25**. So, I tossed in a quarter, and, much to my surprise, I got change. Out came a check, made payable to me, for **$42.57**. What? Forty-two dollars and fifty-seven cents? Let me THINK about this. I don't care if everyone's beeping. I'm driving at the speed limit, 55, when I stop at the toll booth. I put in my quarter and out comes a check made payable to me for $42.57.

Wow. I look at my watch. It's **7:35** p.m. I'm early for my next appointment. I have time to drive by my first house, **1614** South Ridgeway. It's been a whole year, **365** days since I've been there. Good, I'll go visit the new tenants. After all, it's only 7:35 and I have time to stop at 1614; its been a year. Think I'll tell them my story. I was driving down the highway . . .

Let's see how well this worked for you. Turn over the page. See the story in your mind's eye. Write down the number.

How many chunks did you recall? Don't give up if you didn't get all six chunks (eighteen digits) this first time. Try again!

As you review the story, see each segment in your mind's eye. If you're stumped by any particular chunk — stop. Take a closer look. Ask yourself: "what is there about this number chunk that will help make it memorable to me?

The key is getting involved. Go ahead. You'll find that actually playing with these number chunks, making them love words, will turn them into friends you can count on to reappear as you need them — upon demand!

Tell Me A LOVE Rhyme

Another way to turn your numbers into meaningful words is to convert the numbers themselves into strong visual images. I like to use words that rhyme with the number, because that makes it easier to recall what is familiar.

0. Nero
1. Sun
2. Chew
3. Tree
4. Roar
5. Hive
6. Sticks
7. Heaven
8. Gate
9. Wine
10. Hen

LOVE these number rhymes. Actually see them in your minds' eye. Nero in his Roman toga, fiddling while Rome burned; the big, round **sun** shining brightly; the huge teeth **chew**ing; the tall bushy **tree**; the lion with a huge **roar** coming out of his wide-open mouth; bees buzzing around a **hive**; brown prickly **sticks** laying on the ground; clouds floating around **heaven**; a big white swinging **gate** with sharp pointed tips; a bottle of your favorite **wine**; a big juicy **hen.**

When you know all your number rhymes, and can automatically think, "wine/nine" or "six/sticks," you're ready for **Match and Attach a Number's LOVEstory.**

Match and Attach: A Number's LOVEstory

For example: Mike Green's phone number is 798-4023.

We'll turn his phone number into: heaven wine gate roar Nero chew tree.

<u>7</u>   <u>9</u>   <u>8</u> - <u>4</u>   <u>0</u>   <u>2</u>   <u>3</u>
heaven wine gate roar Nero chew tree

Now let's make up a **LOVEstory** to better remember our visualization. We're including a visualization for Mike Green so we know it's his phone number. See this in your mind's eye.

Picture Mike Green holding a green microphone. He's sitting on the clouds in **heaven**, and puts down the microphone to open a bottle of red **wine**. He spills the wine as he bumps into a **gate,** getting red wine all over the white gate. On the other side of the gate is a lion **roar**ing loudly while **Nero**, standing next to the lion, is fiddling. At the end of his fiddle bow is a set of teeth trying to **chew** the leaves off a **tree.**

There you have it! A quick translation of 798-4023. Repeat this story from time to time to engrave it in your memory.

You can apply this Match and Attach Number's LOVEstory to any numbers you wish to recall.

Right now, translate your phone number into a LOVEstory:

<u>Your</u> Turn

Translate these numbers into meaningful words:

78103

2118211

17491225010

Turn often-called phone numbers into memorable images:

1._____=_____
2._____=_____
3._____=_____
4._____=_____
5._____=_____

On a separate sheet of paper that you'll want to tear up, write your bank and other pin numbers. Decode them into meaningful words and images.

Possible translations for turning these below numbers into love words:

78013
(Rhymes with):

Heaven's gate opened to let Nero run in holding a tree.
7 8 0 1 3

211876 = 21-18-76
(Chunk/give meaning/make up story):

21 = blackjack
18 = voting age
76 = 76 trombones

I was playing blackjack. I stopped to go vote. 76 trombones played music as I walked out.

16122532 = 16-12/25-32
(Chunk/give meaning/make up story):

At my sweet-sixteen party on Christmas Eve it was freezing.

NOTES

II

PUT YOUR BEST FOOT FORWARD

BRAIN-FRIENDLY LIFESTYLE CHOICES

ORGANIZE: MAKE TIME FOR YOUR LOVE-LIFE

Where Are My Keys?

Does it feel like at least 473 hours each year are wasted searching (usually frantically) for misplaced keys, purses, wallets, theatre tickets . . . ?

Add in the stressful wear and tear on the body, the friends telling you to get your act together, and the awfulness of feeling just plain dumb . . .

If the description fits — here's something you can do about it:

CLEAR AWAY THE CLUTTER. <u>Find</u> A place for everything . . . and . . . <u>Put</u> <u>away</u> everything in its Memory Place.

It's worth carving out time now, to organize the things you do. By getting all the basics into routines, you'll free your mind to fall in LOVE with what you want to remember.

Think of yourself as the CEO (Chief Executive Organizer) of your life. Pretend you are newly hired and you want to see just how well run this company of YOU is run. So, with your Efficiency Expert at your side, let's examine your procedures!

Two's Company, Three's A Crowd
(The fallacy of Over-Multi-Tasking)

Are you feeling scattered? Overwhelmed? Forgetful? Doing more now but enjoying it less?

If your focus is shattered by information bombardment and your daily schedule reads "overload", you may be one of the millions of Americans suffering from OVER-MULTI-TASKING PARALYSIS SYNDROME.

Multi-taskers are people who do too many things at once in the guise of saving time. Sometimes it pays to slow down. Pay attention as you read this section, and see if you can recognize yourself engaging in the perils of multi-tasking gluttony.

Does this sound familiar? You forget to show up for appointments, rummage through pockets for notes scribbled on paper scraps, and are so frazzled that you leave Fido behind in the car as you rush into the vet's office for a check-up. Whoah!

It takes special skill and energy to remember details when you're gasping for breath under a mountain of to-do lists. Sometimes more is better. Other times it's safer and more efficient to tend to one single item at hand.

Stop to think about what kinds of activities you're doubling up.

Doing two or more activities at the same time:

It works to wash the dishes, and at the same time talk on the phone. But, can you really talk to Aunt Susie on the phone and read the newspaper at the same time? Your attention is divided. The result:

conversation becomes dull because she can sense that your mind is wandering. And you have to re-read the newspaper because you can't remember what you just read.

Multi-tasking, in the above example, results in eroding interpersonal relationships, losing reading comprehension, and wasting time by having to repeat a task, to name but a few consequences of divided attention. However, the stakes are raised when you are cutting radishes with a knife while looking at the television screen. Or driving on autopilot while talking on the cellphone . . .

"I am simply doing too much."

Switching back and forth between two or more activities:

Say you're working on one project and get called away to work on another project. When you go back to the first place, your brain has to reconstruct the details of what happened and where it left off. Sometimes you can get right back in the flow. However, the more complicated the activity, the longer it takes the brain to recover. Plus, little details get lost in the shuffle.

The outcome of juggling activities can run the gamut from ok to a point of total inattention and forgetfulness. Since you work faster and smarter without interruptions, the ideal situation is to work on one project at a time until you reach a logical breaking point.

One of my favorite stories is of the Zimbabwe sculptors. They sit before a rock and wait for the rock to tell them what to chip away. They chip away until the rock stops talking to them. Then they move onto the next rock, working again until they hear no more. They juggle back and forth at logical breaks, and wind up with magnificently beautiful pieces of art.

We can all benefit from juggling tasks, as best we can, like the Zimbabwe sculptors.

How do you know when you're suffering from OVER-MULTI-TASKING PARALYSIS SYNDROME?

Many people today believe multi-tasking is not a good thing. Unchecked, it can make us overworked and over-obsessive. Sometimes it stifles our memory, looms as a health hazard, and takes a lot of fun out of life.

Take this quiz and see if you need to put on the multi-tasking brakes.

QUIZ: Do you recognize yourself in these examples?
        (Count 1 point for each YES)

  1 You're holding the refrigerator door open, but you can't remember why.

  2 You thought you filled the gas tank on the way home yesterday, but this morning the gauge is on empty.

  3 Thinking about your upcoming weekend, you drive on automatic pilot. Meanwhile, you turn left to go to your office, when your pounding jaw jolts you back to reality. You really meant to turn right to go to your dentist.

4   Thumbing through a waiting room magazine while your teenagers get their braces tightened, a diaper ad reminds you that you left the baby sleeping in the back seat of the car.

5   You fail to check your palm pilot and miss your 10:30 a.m. haircut.

6   You thought you put your front door key in your pocket when you left the house, but then, why isn't it there now?

7   You're not sure: did you take your antibiotic this morning before you brushed your teeth?

8   You've dialed a phone number, but when a woman says "hello," you're not sure whom it is you're calling.

9   You made up a password, wrote it down, and put it in a safe hiding place somewhere, but where, oh where, oh where?

10 You're talking on the phone to your neighbor. The doorbell rings and your call waiting signals. It's your mother. YOUR ATTENTION IS NOW DIVIDED IN THREE DIRECTIONS. You wonder who's at the front door. You <u>think</u> you put your neighbor on hold. You <u>think</u> you're telling your mother you'll call her back if and when your neighbor finishes her long, boring story. Guess what . . . you clicked back onto the wrong line . . .

11 Your heart is racing, your head is spinning, it's almost time to go to dinner, and you still have three unfinished projects sitting on your to-do list.

12 You're three blocks away from home when the question
   looms: Did I unplug the coffee pot? Mental images of your
   house on fire torture you for the next two blocks. Enough
   suffering! You drive back home to check.

————————

A score of 9-12.
OVERWHELMED. You're definitely doing too many things at once.

Stop. Take a deep breath. Make a list of all the things you're doing.
Prioritize. Then resume, one task at a time, starting with the most
urgent. Be sure to do some form of relaxation or exercise before
starting another task.

At least five minutes a day, just close your eyes and breathe —
preferably with soothing music in the background. (One of my
favorite tapes is Steve Halpern's **Enhancing Creativity**). Here's a
simple and easy method to give your brain a rest and to rejuvenate
your energy:

> Find a quiet place. Sit in an upright position, with your eyes
> closed, feet and hands unfolded. Take a deep breath, filling
> your belly with air. Bring your mind to your feet and slowly
> work your mind up your body, feeling any tension dissolve:
> toes, heels, ankles, calves, knees, thighs, stomach, back, chest,
> shoulders, arms, fingers, neck, and head. Then, work your mind
> back down, from your head, through your neck, shoulders,
> arms, fingers, chest, back, stomach, thighs, knees, calves,
> ankles, heels, toes. Repeat this process as often as you like.

Also, be sure, with your doctors permission, that you're eating lots of
fruits, vegetables and fish and cutting down on the sweet desserts.

A score of 5-8.
BORDERLINE. Drop a few chores/projects, take some deep breaths, and try the above relaxation technique from time to time. Re-assert your intentions to pay attention to what you want to remember, like, be sure the keys are in your hand <u>before</u> you lock your house or car.

A score of 4-7.
DON'T WORRY — YOU'RE HAPPY. Keep up the good work! Everyone forgets once in a while. Just remember to take those deep breaths and sneak in some personal time like an hour of soaking in a bubble bath while reading your favorite novel, or a steam bath along with a pleasant daydream.

A score of 3 or less.
UNDERACTIVE. There's room for growth. Stretch yourself with some exciting and brain-stretching activities. Careful. Add one activity at a time.

Don't Be A Scatterbrain

Have you ever marched from room-to-room throughout your house looking for your wallet? Or checkbook? Or eye glasses?

DO BE ALERT.   Organize your environment. Take a deep breath, and then find a place for everything. And put everything back in its memory place!

A key rack or even a spare cookie jar in your kitchen to hold your keys will eliminate frantic searches.   Remote controls, purses, stamps and mobile phones are among the essentials that need their own homes.

Here's where my husband Steve keeps his things.
He walks in the house, says hello, gives me a kiss, and goes right to the bedroom nightstand to empty his pockets.

Nightstand Memory Place.
- Glasses
- Wristwatch
- Post-its (those wonderful little yellow self- sticking note pads)
- Pen
- Keys
- Wallet
- Handkerchief
- Things-to-do-list

Get Ready the Night Before

Plan ahead. You'll save time and eliminate frazzle.

Whether the next day's activities are filled with work, or play, or any combination thereof, get ready the night before.

Check your calendar.

Choose your clothes and lay them out before you go to sleep, when you're not as rushed as in the early morning.

Pack your "stuff" for the next day's activities.
(When I'm doing three things in one day, without coming home in between — my car becomes my closet!)

Place a yellow sticky note on the doorknob
so you won't forget to take your lunch with you.

Take Control of Your Dates

Know where you're going . . . and when.

Write down every appointment. Free your mind. Be there on time.

DO keep a trustworthy calendar.
List everything in an orderly fashion. Make your entries readable.

DON'T get caught double-booking. It's wise to use one calendar only.
Writing dates in more than one place gets confusing.

> # PALM PILOT SMARTS:
> Keep it Charged ● Uploaded ● In a Safe Place.

<u>AHEM.</u> <u>Good</u> <u>Habit</u>: Remember to look at your calendar or Palm Pilot each night before you go to sleep . . . and again when you awake!

LOVE Potions, and Other Routine Trackers

Eliminate guesswork: Did I or did I not take my vitamins? My pills?

Get into a routine. Find a place for your medicines and put them back in the same place. Take your medicines at the same time each day. What works best for you? After meals? Before you brush your teeth?

Get a pill sorter. There's lots of different style containers you can buy in drugstores that mark off compartments into days or hours to house your pills.

My friends Lynne and Larry — at the beginning of each month — sort their vitamins into separate plastic baggies, one for each day.

I'd love to hear from you. Write and tell me your favorite organizing stories. Go to **www.MemoryLady.com** or **Judy@memorylady.com.**

Lists, Lists, and More Lists

Keep "to do" lists, preferably prioritized.

The mere act of writing it down causes you to concentrate and focus, even if just for a moment. When you see the words on paper, you have a handle on what you've listed so far, can see if you've left anything out, and put the items in some sort of order. Furthermore, once you've made your list, you can relax and know it's on paper so you are free to start thinking about other needs or wants. A bonus is that you get the self-satisfaction and sense of accomplishment of checking off an item when it's completed.

Post-it notes are a staple in our house.
Lists are good for:
1. organizing your needs,
2. as reference check-posts,
3. freeing your mind to attend to other activities,
4. self-satisfaction and sense of accomplishment at checking off an item when it's completed.

The flip side to lists is you still have to challenge your memory to remain on the positive side of the use-it-or-lose it syndrome. Every so often, just for the fun of it, and for brain assurance, choose a mnemonic technique and LOVE a list.

<u>Your</u> Turn

Find a place for everything . . .
Put everything back in its Memory Place:

What You Need to Take for the Next Day
(Ignore my suggestions; take what <u>you</u> want):

Tote Bag A:
1. Brief case_____   6._____
2. Umbrella_____   7._____
3. Finance Book_____   8._____
4. Lunch_____   9._____
5. _____   10._____

Tote Bag B:
1. Running shoes_____   6._____
2. Fanny pack_____   7._____
3. Water bottle_____   8._____
4. Warm-up suit_____   9._____
5. _____   10._____

Tote Bag C:
1. Make-up repair kit_____   6._____
2. Wipe-its_____   7._____
3. Fresh sweater_____   8._____
4. _____   9._____
5. _____   10._____

More . . .

Lists you keep:
(Pens and paper and post-it notes always handy in same places)

1. _____ 6. _____
2. _____ 7. _____
3. _____ 8. _____
4. _____ 9. _____
5. _____ 10. _____

Priority TO-DO List to Avoid Over-Multi-tasking:
(Rethink daily)

1. _____ 6. _____
2. _____ 7. _____
3. _____ 8. _____
4. _____ 9. _____
5. _____ 10. _____

What's your medicine routine? Where do you keep them? What time do you take them? What kind of organizing container do you keep them in? How do you remind yourself to take them?

1. _____ 6. _____
2. _____ 7. _____
3. _____ 8. _____
4. _____ 9. _____
5. _____ 10. _____

Routine items you can find Memory Place homes for:

1. _____ 6. _____
2. _____ 7. _____
3. _____ 8. _____
4. _____ 9. _____
5. _____ 10. _____

NOTES

TUNE-UP YOUR HEART & SOUL: EAT, DRINK AND BE MERRY

Diet Do's and Don'ts*

Good eating habits help your memory work better!

It is widely agreed that anti-oxidant vita-mins found in vitamin A, C, and E and the mineral selenium, are beneficial. They keep free-radicals from causing damage to our bodies and interfering with our brain processes.

In addition, the B-vitamin nutrients, espe-cially B-12, keep our nervous system func-tioning and the messages flowing between the brain cells.

Another memory food "biggie" is essential fatty acids, which transmit nerve impulses as well as help the brain continue to devel-op and function.

Water is yet another necessity. It consti-tutes approximately 70% of our bodies, and is paramount to just about every bodily function.

Here's some food-for-thought eating habits recommended by licensed registered dietitian Karen Raden, MS, RD, LD.

*Always check with your doctor first.

DIET DO's

Eat a balanced diet focusing on such whole grains as brown rice, millet and quinoa, as well as healthy fats and lean proteins.

Include richly colored fruits and vegetables: the deeper the color, the richer the nutrients. Explore. Go on a fruit and veggie safari hunt at your grocery store. Discover new tastes.

Treat yourself to a rainbow of fruits, especially blue- berries, strawberries, oranges, and bananas.

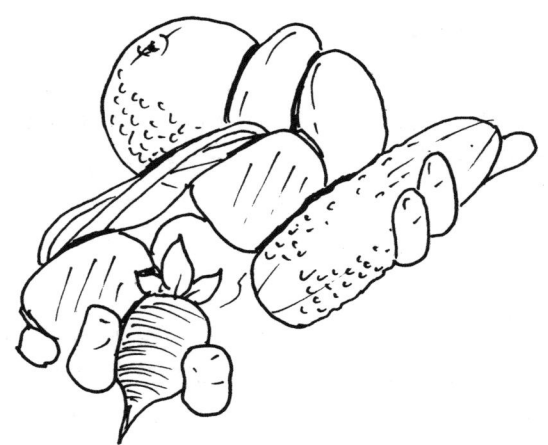

Eat lots of greens: broccoli, spinach, kale, kelp, collard greens, okra, and red chard top the list of memory veggies.

Eat small meals throughout the day: A handful of almonds and a piece of fruit, or a snack of hummus and carrots, will help you avoid the pockets of low blood sugar which interfere with the thinking process. Also, fresh fruit and veggie juices make a quick energy and nutritious pick-me-up. Find yourself a local juice bar or buy yourself a juicer.

Learn to enjoy Water. Drink at least eight glasses of water per day to replenish what you lose through sweat and elimination. In fact, if you're feeling tired or your brain is fuzzy, take a deep breath and drink some water, and that might be enough to revive you.

*Always check with your doctor first.

Choose Good Fats. Your brain needs the Omega 3's and 6's found in such foods as avocado, olive oil, flax seed oil, sesame oil, sardines and salmon. Choose wild fish found in the ocean over their farm-raised counterparts. The wild fish have higher amounts of the oh-so-essential fatty acids.

Consider Supplements. The herb Ginkgo biloba leads the suggested list of "memory aids" that supply oxygen to the brain cells and enhance brain function.

Note: Opinions vary as to how much Ginkgo and other supplements like DHEA and melatonin actually work to increase memory retention. Like all the other diet suggestions, before making any changes, check with your doctor.

*Always check with your doctor first.

DIET DON'Ts

Avoid bad fats: Stay away from high fat items like whole milk, fatty meats, coconut oil and vegetable shortening. They clog the arteries and slow down the thinking process.

Eliminate refined sugar: Avoid foods like donuts, white bread and sugary cereals. They contain refined sugars that don't contain many helpful nutrients, and also slow down your thinking process.

Reduce processed foods: Keep processed foods with a whole laundry list of chemicals to a minimum. They contain preservatives and additives that may not be beneficial to your health. Instead, focus on eating whole foods like fruits, nuts, seeds, and whole grains. You'll have more sustained energy that your brain will appreciate!

We feel so much more energetic when we eat healthy!

*Always check with your doctor first.

Energize with Exercise*

Exercise is good for the brain. Not only will you feel, better . . . exercise will help you think better, think clearer, decrease depression and anxiety, and increase brain function, attention span and learning.

There's an abundance of exercise programs to chose from based upon your endurance and agility, as well as your inclinations. Yoga and Tai Chi are exercises worth looking into for their additional benefits of relaxation and strength building.

Whatever your preference, movement is good for your memory.

Even 15 or 20 minutes of daily walking will:

✓ Oxygenate every cell of your body.
✓ Get your blood flowing
✓ Release endorphins
✓ Reduce blood pressure
✓ Reduce risk of stroke.
✓ Make you feel better
✓ Relax your mind

This is important. Somehow, I'll find at least 15 minutes a day to get some exercise.

Go for it! Exercise. **Give yourself plenty of Brain Power!**

*Always check with your doctor first.

Relax, De-Stress, Revitalize*

Of course, we all have stress in our lives. We're human. It's what we do about it that counts. Our power comes in working to defuse the angst rather than let it tie us into knots or get us down — or keep us from recalling what we want to remember.

Stress strangles. It's as if there's a roadblock at the neck so thoughts cannot connect because oxygen is slowed to a snail's pace on its way through to the brain. Relaxation allows oxygen and other nutrients to flow freely to every part of your body.

Sleep deprivation and depression also get in the way of oxygen flow, and slow down the thinking process.

When you relax, you'll sleep better, think clearer, and speak those words right off the tip-of-your-tongue. (Flip to page 100 for more on tip-of-the-tongue de-strangulation hints.)

WORDS ON THE TIP OF YOUR TONGUE?

Stress relievers come in many sizes and shapes. Choose whatever works best for you. Here's a few suggestions.

Breathe. Take the pause that lets you refresh, re-energize, re-focus.

It's free and you need no outside supplies. Just put a smile on your face, and breathe.

Follow your breath in and out three times. . . .

Watch yourself fill your belly with air as you breathe in through your nose. This actually breaks the cycle of anger and frustration. And, it allows more oxygen to flow smoothly to the brain again.

Yoga. My friend Sandi called to tell me she took her first ever yoga class. She walked in totally stressed over a political candidate she didn't like who got the upper hand over her favorite choice. What a gift yoga was for Sandi. After an hour of deep breathing and stretching, came the best part. The end when she just lay there as the yoga teacher helped everyone relax each and every muscle in their body. Ahhhhh. Peace, contentment, joy. Total release.

Tense? Angry? Frustrated?

For small and medium stress relievers:
- Warm bath
- Massage
- Dance
- Exercise
- Meditate
- Play with a friend
- Journal daily
- Draw, paint, color
- Lose yourself in a book

For heavy-duty stress relievers: any and all the above, plus:
- Vent big time.
- Write it down.
- Act it out.
- Shout it out.
- Throw rocks into the water (make sure no one's within hitting distance).

So bad? Write it on as many sheets of toilet paper as you need. Put it in the toilet. Do your business. Flush. Watch your anger disappear down the drain.

*Always check with your doctor first.

Your Turn

Give your heart and soul a tune-up*.

Changes you'll make to your diet:

1. _____   6._____
2. _____   7._____
3. _____   8._____
4. _____   9._____
5. _____   10._____

Exercise program:

1. _____   6._____
2. _____   7._____
3. _____   8._____
4. _____   9._____
5. _____   10._____

Relaxation (aahhhhh):

1. _____   6._____
2. _____   7._____
3. _____   8._____
4. _____   9._____
5. _____   10._____

Vent and De-stress strategies:

1. _____   6._____
2. _____   7._____
3. _____   8._____
4. _____   9._____
5. _____   10._____

NOTES

PEAK YOUR
MENTAL PERFORMANCE

Use It Or Lose It

This is about as technical as this book gets. We each have billions of brain cells, called neurons. Each neuron, when stimulated, grows threadlike appendages. At one end of the neuron, the appendages are called axons. At the other end of the neuron, the appendages are called dendrites. Axons send signals to other neurons. Dendrites receive the messages. The connections between the brain cells are called synapses. The nutrients that feed the synapse connections are called neurotrophins. Think of the neurotrophins as squirrels that scamper from tree to tree, transmitting messages from branches to roots.

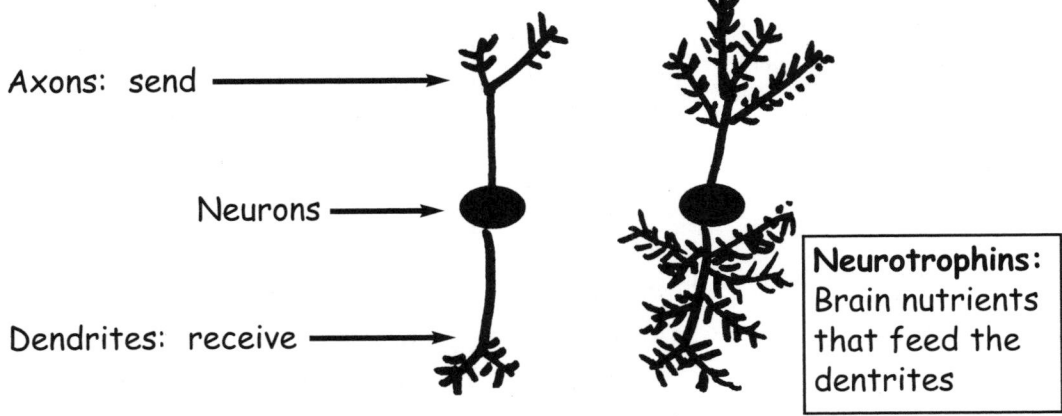

Axons: send

Neurons

Dendrites: receive

Neurotrophins: Brain nutrients that feed the dentrites

Here is a rough illustration of two isolated neurons, each from a different brain. One is much fuller than the other. Notice how the neurons of an Einstein grow many more appendages than the neurons of a person with a much less exerted brain.

At one time, it was thought that an adult brain was set. Like adult bones, it supposedly had all the appendages it would ever get, and would only shrink and atrophy with age. Lucky for us, that thinking turns out to be incorrect.

The great news is the brain is changeable. "So what's so great about that?" you might ask.

There are at least three exciting reasons, in no particular order:

First. <u>Use it and you maintain it.</u> Mental stimulation keeps the neurons and their appendages well oiled, clean and working. Axons and dendrites expand as you stimulate the brain to learn new challenges; its appendages shrink when you don't use the new pathways, or when what you do becomes automatic.

I wonder how Fred's doing? Hmmmm. Why can't I remember his phone number?

A perfect example is a telephone number. If you call your cousin Fred about once a week, his number will stay in your recent memory and will come to you upon demand, without effort. After a while, both your lives get busy and you and Fred start drifting apart.

Now, as you call him every few months or so, his number floats into the gray atmosphere, and you have to consciously work at recalling his number. Then, you don't speak to him for a year. Quite possibly, when you go to call him, his phone number has floated into the outer space of your consciousness. You have to look at your phone book first to refresh your memory. If you start calling Fred more often, the dendrites and axons will again expand; if you stop, they shrink and Fred's phone number will float back into oblivion. Use-it-or-lose-it.

Second. <u>New interests grow new appendages</u>. Think of them as insurance policies. Should the old dendrites and axons get injured, disabled, blocked or dried out, you have other pathways.

For instance, learning a second language is helpful. Not only will it enrich your lifestyle; it could someday save you a lot of anguish. Should something prevent your English language pathways from connecting, you would have additional language pathways already in place. This has made it much easier for some stroke victims to relearn to speak.

Also, the new appendages can compensate for damaged tissue, and can help delay the onset of senility and Alzheimer's disease.

Third. <u>You **can** continue to learn for all of your life.</u> Yes. By using your brain in new and exciting ways, and keeping yourself healthy with good diet, exercise, and stress management, you can keep your brain as strong as possible for as long as possible. Indeed, learning is the mental fountain of youth!

Be smart. **Choose to USE the Brain so you don't LOSE the Brain.** The next section talks about the variety of stimulation the brain needs.

Variety is the spice of life.

When an activity becomes automatic, you stop making decisions and your dendrites start shrinking. The wake-me-up call comes when you're yawing from boredom. It's your brain saying, "FEED ME."

Heed the warning. Take action. Expand your knowledge in what you already like to do, and also find a new project or activity that calls for a different type of mental activity.

I LOVE to FEED my brain!

Think of new mental adventures as brain insurance that makes life more exciting as they stimulate your brain's capacity to strengthen existing pathways and grow new appendages. New appendages can compensate for damaged tissue, and can help delay the onset of senility and Alzheimer's disease.

You don't have to take up rocket science to keep your brain growing. Almost any activity will do. It just has to challenge and stimulate you. It's good to expand your repertoire of activities to include different sets of challenges.

Whatever your choices, just dig in and enjoy!

Jump on the brain-wagon and head straight towards new mental adventures.

Here's three great brain-stretching routes (travel them all):

1. Expand your knowledge in what you already like to do. You don't have to do the proverbial throwing out the baby with the dirty bathwater.

For example, if you're a photo buff, you can keep on taking pictures. Just dig a little deeper into your camera capabilities, or if you haven't yet done so, open your world by buying yourself a digital camera.

Widen your mental lens. Switch subjects. If you're taking photos of flowers, instead try people. Start snapping head shots of every variety of hairstyle you can find. When you tire of the coiffure search, explore another subject. There's no limit to where your imagination can lead you — and think of the fun you'll have and the people you'll meet!

2. Find a new project or activity that calls for a different type of mental stimulation.

<u>Do crossword puzzles and solve jigsaw puzzles.</u> Filling in the cross-word puzzle words allows your brain to scan and retrieve. Figuring out where the puzzle pieces go draws on and strengthens your spatial perception.

<u>Learn a new language.</u> Learning a second language is helpful. Not only will it enrich your lifestyle; it could someday save you a lot of anguish. Should something prevent your English language pathways from connecting, you would have additional language pathways already

in place. This has made it much easier for some stroke victims to
relearn to speak.

<u>Use your less-dominant hand to brush your teeth and comb your hair.</u>
It works to strengthen the other hemisphere of your brain (right
hand/left brain/logic — left hand/right brain — creativity). An
artist in one of my WHERE ARE MY KEYS® memory workshops told
me how her life changed when she broke her dominant right hand.
Being forced to use her left hand to perform almost every task
turned out to be a blessing for her artwork. Six months after her
cast came off, friends started commenting how much more complex
and interesting her new paintings were. She didn't realize until my
class that by using her left hand she had strengthened her
creativity.

Play bridge *Act out poetry * Play a musical instrument * Go square
dancing * Take computer classes * Be adventurous *

Brain power is truly a use-it-or-lose-it phenomenon.

3. Create your own mental adventure hunts and focus drills.

This is a great way to fill in the gaps of waiting time at the doctors
office or while standing in line at the deli counter.

<u>Scan the people in your life, both past and present</u>. Pick categories,
and actually see their faces on the movie screen in the inside of your
forehead, as you name their names.

Review the children in your kindergarten class. If you're up to it,
what about all the children in your children's kindergarten class?

When you remember the people you met at a party last week, you're not only doing your brain homework, you're also keeping these people in the forefront of your memory so you can more quickly remember their names at your next encounter.

The brain doesn't allow you to rest on your laurels for long. When a mental outing becomes routine — switch to a new category.

<u>Visualize a routine you perform regularly.</u> It can be any routine: Getting up in the morning, preparing your breakfast, brushing your teeth . . . Those are three separate routines. Actually see in your mind's eye each step you take.

When you open your eyes after a night's sleep, do you get out of bed right away, or do you stretch your arms and legs first? See yourself flipping off the covers, even see the covers. Notice how far across the bed they flipped. It's amazing how many little details come back to you when you stop to think about them.

<u>Imagine a path that you walk or drive each day.</u> Actually see in your mind's eye the details of the buildings on each street. Where are the stop signs? How many street names can you identify? When this becomes rote, start visualizing another route.

Be smart. Be creative. Choose to USE the brain in new and exciting ways, so you don't LOSE the brain. You'll have fun as you increase those pathways that lead to longer, stronger brain power. Indeed, variety is the mental spice of life!

Whatever your choices, just dig in and enjoy!

Read the Tip-of-Your-Tongue

Does this seem familiar? You're talking to someone you just met at a party, and along comes your best friend and suddenly all you can think of is, "Oh, no! I have to introduce them and I can't remember my own best friend's name. I'm sooooo embarrassed. . . . What will I do?" And your heart sinks while your mind feels erased, like a clean, white, blank sheet of paper.

How about this one? You're about to name the book you just read or the movie you've just seen, and you can see it in your minds eye, and you know that you know it, but the words are stuck on the tip-of-your-tongue.

When it feels like this:

The Boston Strangler has his hands wrapped so tightly around your throat that the oxygen and blood just can't pump past the squeeze, and your brain can't do it's job.

That's how words on the tip-of-your-tongue can make you feel. Strangled. Your thoughts don't connect because oxygen is slowed to a snail's pace on its way through to your brain.

Don't panic.

Do put a smile on your face and breathe.

Yes. Take a quick stress break. Follow your breath.
Watching yourself fill your belly with air and breathe out through
your nose actually breaks the cycle of anger and frustration. And, it
allows more oxygen to flow smoothly to the brain again.

Take the pause that lets you refresh, re-energize, re-focus.
　　　Breathe into your belly.
　　　　　　Breathe out through your nose.

Then, start talking. And keep talking. Talk about the person you
want to introduce. Tell anything you remember. "Hi. I'd like you to
meet my best friend. We went to the ballgame last night. I've
known this guy since I was five . . ." and on and on... "This is Bill
Jones. We just met at the party . . ."

Or, talk about the book or the movie, describing what you do remember. Don't skip a beat. Trust that as you relax while talking around
the word you're looking for, the back burner of your brain is at work.
What you're trying to remember will suddenly pop right off the tip-
of-your-tongue and into your consciousness.

Get Your Head Out of the Clouds Focus Drill

We all have moments, or days, when our head feels foggy or cloudy. Sometimes, a breath of fresh air will clear the cobwebs. When that doesn't work, here are three good drills that will pull you back into focus and help you feel sharp again:

- **Name as many animals as you can in 30 seconds.**
  When this becomes rote, switch categories, ie. cities, colors, etc.

- **Count backwards from 100 by 9's.**

Too easy? Switch to 8's, then 7's, etc.

- **Visualize a routine you perform regularly.**
  See in your mind's eye each little step. Imagine making a peanut butter and jelly sandwich. Actually see yourself opening the refrigerator door . . . reaching in and taking the peanut butter jar off the shelf, carrying it to the counter, placing it down, going back to the refrigerator door, scanning the shelf for the blueberry jelly, etc. Visualize all the steps. Even anticipate the joy of eating! When this becomes rote, start visualizing another routine.

  p.s. Don't forget to see yourself cleaning up before you eat!

The "Yes, I Do Have a Great Memory" Checklist.

❑ I use **The LOVE™ Method** (in four fun and easy-to-do steps) on everything I want to remember.

And, I use my memory support systems:

❑ I have a place for each of my essentials (i.e. keys, wallet, sticky notes) and put everything back in its special "Memory Place."

❑ I plan ahead, i.e. put out my clothes and organize whatever I need for the next day <u>before</u> I go to sleep when I'm not as rushed as in the early morning.

❑ I make and prioritize "to do" lists.

❑ I write down dates and check my calendar.

❑ I add stimulation and variety to my life.

❑ I keep from doing too many activities at one time (over-multi-tasking).

❑ I eat well, especially those all-important green B-vitamin veggies and Omega-3 and -6 fats found in foods such as salmon, avocados, olive oil, flax seed oil, and sardines.**

❑ I exercise on a regular basis.**

❑ I get enough sleep.

❑ I pause often throughout the day to take a deep breath, recharge my entire body, and refocus.

LOVE™ your memory today.
Keep your memory strong throughout your lifetime!

Judy Marcus * Master Teacher * MemoryLady
Judy@memorylady.com   VISIT: www.memorylady.com

(**Check with your doctor before you start any new exercise program or eat new foods.)

<u>Your</u> Turn

LOVE your Memory Training:

Here's brain stretching activities you'll explore because you want to stimulate your dendrites, expand your brain power, and grow memory muscles:

1. _____   6._____
2. _____   7._____
3. _____   8._____
4. _____   9._____
5. _____   10._____

Here's your plan when words get stuck on the tip of your tongue:
Cleaning out the cob-webs focus drill:
Categories to name:

1. _____   6._____
2. _____   7._____
3. _____   8._____
4. _____   9._____
5. _____   10._____

Routines to visualize:

1. _____	6. _____
2. _____	7. _____
3. _____	8. _____
4. _____	9. _____
5. _____	10. _____

Don't forget to check your "Yes, I Do Have a Great Memory" Checklist!

NOTES

Afterward

Dear Readers/LOVErs:

If you've already started using the LOVE Memory Method — then you know how easy it is to learn — how much fun it is to use — and best of all – you know that sense of satisfaction that comes with recalling what you choose to remember — upon demand!

I'd love to hear from you. Please send me the stories of your LOVE Memory Method experiences: the successes, the challenges, funny moments, the creative OVERSTATEMENTS. . . . I'll share as many stories as I can on my website: www.MemoryLady.com. With your permission, I'll use your name.

Just don't forget to keep up the good work! Life's better when you trust your brain to remember.

Have fun as you remember with LOVE.

Judy Marcus

Stories to share? Questions?

Contact me at P.O. Box 432, Highland Park, IL 60035 or email Judy@memorylady.com.

Bibliography

Golden, Daniel. **Building a Better Brain**, pp. 63-70, LIFE, Time Inc. (New York), July, 1994.

Katz, Lawrence C. and Rubin, Manning. **Keep Your Brain Alive**. Workman Publishing Company, Inc. (New York) 1999.

Krill, Allan, http://www.memoes.com, Middleton, A.E. **All About Mnemonics**, Chapter II, The History of Mnemonics and Chapter III, Modern Mnemonical Systems, (London) 1885.

Lapp, Danielle C. **Don't Forget! Easy Exercises for a Better Memory at Any Age**. McGraw-Hill Book Company (New York), 1987.

Lorayne, Harry and Lucas, Jerry. **The Memory Book**. Ballantine Books (New York), 1975.

Schacter, Daniel L. **The Seven Sins of Memory**. Houghton Mifflin Company (Boston), 2001.

Additional Reading

Choquette, Sonia. **True Balance: A Common Sense Guide for Renewing Your Spirit**. Random House (New York), 2000.

Tolle, Eckhart. **The Power of Now**. New World Library (Novato, CA), 1999

Acknowledgements

While it is impossible to trace all the steps that led me to this point in my Memory Lady career, here are some of the more obvious people to whom I am forever grateful for their help along the way.

First and foremost, I acknowledge my husband Steve and two children Jerry and Felicia who support me with wisdom, laughter, and affection. They are the solid bottom line in the Maslow hierarchy of my life, the foundation that frees all else to bubble and spring forth.

For helping me realize the dream come true of turning my workshop into a book, I am forever appreciative of and beholden to:

Jerry Marcus who held my heart and walked me through a writer's block that imprisoned my creative flow; Felicia Marcus who shared her insightful wisdom as she joined me in hours of joyful discussion on the how-to and importance of focus and attention; Ruth Berger and Nilda Carlo, my writing buddies, editorial and marketing advisors and sounding boards, along with Holly Hayes, Mim Neal, Steve Marcus and Jerry Marcus for editorial opinions; and Joyce Lerner and Mark Superczynski of Graphic Solutions for their "a picture is worth 1,000 words" illustrations.

Reuben Weisz, M.D., neurologist, for assuring me that the technical information I translated into easy to understand terms in the "Use-It-Or-Lose-It" and "Variety Is the Spice of Life" sections of this book are nicely simplified and appropriate.

Karen Raden, M.S., R.D., L.D., licensed registered dietitian and nutritional counselor, for her brain-friendly nutrition advice.

Rana Matteson, PhD, former instructor of Memory Development and Disorders, for adding her eagle eye approval.

Before the book, first came my workshop. My Table Talk Ladies of the Verbal Quilting Bee gave me reason to research so many interesting discussion topics. It is for them I first developed a hands-on memory training session. Arlene Block, Helen Baron-Sorosky, Bernice Deitch, Burt Feltman, Marion Katz, Gladys Klemptner, Sylvia Levey, Dorothy Pogoff, Ida Ryback, and Esther Simon, were there at the beginning. Many others came in and out over the years, adding their energy, enthusiasm, and bright insights. Most of the originals, and the relative newcomers Faye Israel, Rosh Kagan, Phyllis Raave and Alice Tuler, still gather to lunch and discuss a variety of topics. All are inspirations to me and dear to my heart.

Good luck happens when preparation meets opportunity. Rabbi Jonathan Magidovitch and Judy Bederman led me to Alice Nasatir who hired me to teach my dear Ladies in the first place.

Sheila Marks expanded my Memory Workshop by bringing me to the Southlake Campus Adult Education Program. It grew from there. Teri Hartman and her marketing group at Parker Adult Evening School renamed my workshop the catchy title, **WHERE ARE MY KEYS?®**. Then there's Judi Geake of The Women's Exchange; Erin Molloy of Taste of Chicago; Flora Alderman of The Perlstein Resort & Conference Center; Rabbi Zalman Schachter-Shalomi, Eve Ilsen and Lori Miller of the Spiritual Eldering Institute; and Joyce Davidoff of the Rio Grande Area Agency on Aging, Ageless Health Initiative, to name a few of those who helped me take my work to larger audiences.

For my website which reflects the flavor of my book and workshop, I am so pleased to thank Gregg Zissman for his amazing website graphics design and development.

My second edition production gurus include Bob Garcia who smoothed the text production, Jim Rooke who smoothed the printing process; Paul Smith for his eye-catching cover; and networking pros Lillian Duoforce and Rob Lubow who put me on their respective trails.

Last, but not least, I am grateful to my memory students, people of all ages. Your eagerness to keep your mind growing and vital is contagious. And that makes this world, for all of us, a better place to be.

ABOUT THE AUTHOR

Judy Marcus, author of **WHERE ARE MY KEYS?**® **Memory Training You'll Absolutely LOVE**™, teaches people of all ages how to remember better.

While researching memory tips for a discussion group she leads, Judy recognized memory training as the key to mental vitality. She was hooked. In 1995, she took memory on as a client, and dug in to study the centuries old memory techniques used by the ancient and modern memory gurus. Combining her teaching and public relations expertise, Judy infused her own insights and techniques into the proven strategies and created her own fun and easy-to-learn lessons.

Judy developed the **LOVE**™ acronym as part of **WHERE ARE MY KEYS?**®, a workshop she teaches nationwide to people of all ages. It is a fun way to build a great memory.

A lecturer, workshop leader, and vital living cheerleader, Judy is thrilled to teach tools that keep your memory alive and growing.

For over fifteen years, Judy headed JBM Communications, a public relations firm where she researched, developed and implemented positive campaigns for corporations and individuals. She holds a Bachelor of Arts in English and a Master's Degree in the Art of Teaching. The Memory Lady and her husband Steve live in Highland Park, IL.

Judy welcomes your memory stories. To schedule a workshop, speaking engagement, or share your stories, visit her website, **www.memorylady.com**, or send her an email at **Judy@memorylady.com**.

JUDY MARCUS' MEMORY WORKSHOP

"... A popular and much needed presentation ... Thank you for your energetic and uplifting seminar ..."

Fran Hankin, Director, Program Services, Alzheimer's Association

"Highest turn-out for any of our seminars and presentations ... I watched the way the 285 people in the audience participated. It was 90 minutes of learning with a touch of humor throughout the program ... you had a large audience in your control with such ease ..."

Doug C. Johnson, Elgin Township Supervisor

"Judy's materials are always fresh, insightful, and inspiring. People love her and her memory workshops. She's an awesome delight!"

Teri Hartman, Program Coordinator, Parker Adult School

Judy Marcus, Memory Lady, is available for workshops, special events, and keynote speeches.

For more information, visit www.MemoryLady.com

BOOK ORDER FORM

YES! I want to order _____ more copies today.

www.MemoryLady.com

WHERE ARE MY KEYS?®

Memory Training You'll Absolutely LOVE™
by Judy Marcus
2nd Edition
ISBN 0-9746439-1-2 • ISBN 978-0-9746439-1-5

WHERE ARE MY KEYS?®

Mail to: Front Porch Connections, P.O. Box 432, Highland Park, IL 60035
E-Mail Judy@MemoryLady.com

Name_____ Phone_____

Address_____ E-mail_____

City_____ State_____Zip_____

Please send me _____ copies @$20.00 per book plus $3.50 shipping and handling.
Enclosed is my check for $_____.
Or charge my account:

_____ Expiration Date:_____
Credit Card # (MC/Visa only)

Signature of Cardholder_____